INTRODUCING ACCOUNTING

FOR AS

IAN HARRISON

Hodder Arnold

A MEMBER OF THE HODDER HEADLINE GROUP

Orders: please contact Bookpoint Ltd, 130 Milton Park, Abingdon, Oxon OX14 4SB. Telephone: (44) 01235 827720. Fax: (44) 01235 400454. Lines are open from 9.00 – 6.00, Monday to Saturday, with a 24 hour message answering service. You can also order through our website: www.hoddereducation.com.

British Library Cataloguing in Publication Data
A catalogue record for this title is available from the British Library

ISBN-10: 0 340 87305 1
ISBN-13: 978 0 340 87305 2

First Published 2004
Impression number 10 9 8 7 6 5 4
Year   2008 2007 2006

Hodder Headline's policy is to use papers that are natural, renewable and recyclable products and made from wood grown in sustainable forests. The logging and manufacturing processes are expected to conform to the environmental regulations of the country of origin.

Artwork by David Graham
Typeset by Fakenham Photosetting Ltd, Fakenham, Norfolk
Printed in Spain for Hodder Arnold, an imprint of Hodder Education, a division of Hodder Headline, 338 Euston Road, London NW1 3BH.

CONTENTS

INTRODUCTION

The aim of this book is to explain in simple language the basic topics that you may encounter during your first year of studying accounting. It is designed to help you understand the topics that may be examined at AS Level.

The chapter objectives identify the key points covered in the chapter you are about to read. There are references to the sections of the specification covered in the chapter.

Each time a new term is introduced it will appear in a definition box. Examination tips are also identified as the chapters progress. Each chapter will explain the topic then give examples of the way questions may be asked by the examiner. The example is followed by the answer. You are recommended to cover the answer with a spare sheet of paper and attempt the question yourself. If you get stuck you can then take a look at the answer and find how to proceed so that you can perhaps finish the question.

Throughout the text there are questions for practice purposes. The questions are graded, starting with simpler questions and building up to more complex questions as you progress through the chapter.

Odd-numbered questions have the answers at the end of the book. Even-numbered questions do not have the answers, so you could well find that they are the subject of homework!

In the main, even-numbered questions are very similar to the odd-numbered questions so in some cases you can use the odd-numbered answers as templates to help you answer the even-numbered questions.

It is important in your study of accounting that you gain as much practice as possible. You will need to learn, by heart, layouts and definitions so do not be afraid to revisit topic areas that you may have forgotten. You may also find it useful to go over certain examples and questions more than once as practice.

At the end of most chapters there are self-test questions. The answers to these questions can be arrived at through an examination of the chapter.

The examination at AS Level is of one hour duration and there will be between three and seven questions on each paper. All questions are compulsory so it is important that you do not skip over any topics.

'Accounting' is the term used loosely to cover book-keeping and accounting.

Book-keeping records all the financial transactions undertaken during a period. This is necessary in order that the owner can control how the business is performing. It is also necessary so that the owner has:

■ records of the information required by the Inland Revenue for tax purposes
■ records of the information required by Customs and Excise for VAT returns
■ records required by the suppliers of additional finance.

Book-keeping records the details of all:

■ expenditures incurred during the accounting period
■ incomes receivable during the accounting period
■ the profit (or loss) made during the period
■ amounts owed by debtors
■ amounts owed to creditors
■ the value of assets owned by the business and any changes in the values during the period
■ the value of liabilities owed by the business and any changes in the value during the period.

Accounting deals with the final presentation of the details gathered in the book-keeping system.

- It summarises the fine detail used.
- It deals with the classification of the information and presents the information in such a way that it will be useful to any readers and users of the information.
- It takes into account any standards laid down by the accounting bodies.
- It takes into account the legal requirements that must be adhered to.

Financial accounts are used by many groups of people so it is important that the information shown in the accounts should be:

- **relevant** – readers should be able to assess whether the business managers are using the resources at their disposal wisely. It is important that readers can also make informed economic decisions regarding the business.
- **reliable** – the financial information should be free from bias; it should be free of errors; and it must be prepared prudently.
- **comparable** – the use of appropriate accounting policies in the production and presentation of accounting information can identify similarities and differences that may account for differences in performance.
- **understandable** – the information presented in the accounts should be able to be understood by a reader with 'reasonable' knowledge of business and accounting.

The Balance Sheet

Most people who have read a newspaper or who have seen the news on television will have seen and heard the term 'balance sheet' at some time.

Some balance sheets are very complicated and a great deal of experience and technical know-how are needed to read and interpret them. Do not let this put you off. Everything appears daunting when first encountered. The first time you rode a bicycle, it was difficult. The first time that you tried to walk, you did not succeed!

Like all areas of study, accounting has its own jargon. When a new word or term is about to be introduced, an explanation will be given in a box like this:

> **Assets** are resources that are owned by an organisation. They are used to help the organisation survive and function.

Assets used in a business could include premises, machinery, vehicles, computers etc. Assets used in a rugby club might include the ground, lawnmowers, bar equipment etc.

> **Liabilities** represent the debts owed by an organisation.

The liabilities owed by a business could include a mortgage, and money owed to the suppliers of goods and services. For example, the liabilities of a local garage may include money owed to the Ford Motor Company for spare parts, to the supplier of electricity, to the supplier of office stationery etc. The liabilities of the rugby club could include money owed to a local garage for repairs to the mowers, money owed to the brewery for supplies of beer, money owed to the ground staff for last week's work etc.

A balance sheet simply lists all the assets that are owned by the organisation and all the liabilities that are owed by the organisation. A balance sheet can be prepared for a business, or a squash club, or you can even draw up your own personal balance sheet.

The only difference between your personal balance sheet and that of Barclays Bank plc is the types of assets owned and the magnitude of the figures used.

From now on, we will make most of our references to businesses.

QUESTION 1

Which items from the following list are liabilities of Anne's Mini-Market?

Stock; money owed to Kelloggs for the supply of breakfast cereals; a van used for collecting goods from the local cash and carry; an HP debt owed to Bent Finance Ltd for van purchase; three freezer cabinets; six display units; money owed by the Crown Hotel for goods supplied by Anne.

> **Trade debtors** are people (or organisations) that owe money to a business, because they are customers who have not yet paid for the goods or services provided.

Specification coverage:
AQA 10.4;
OCR 5.1.1.

By the end of this chapter you should be able to:
- prepare a simple balance sheet
- calculate capital
- solve problems associated with the accounting equation.

> **Trade creditors** are people (or organisations) that the business owes money to, because they have supplied goods and services that the business has received but as yet has not paid for.

Initially, you may get the terms 'debtors' and 'creditors' confused. Try to find a way of memorising which is which. In all subjects there are facts or concepts that simply have to be learned; accounting is no different.

QUESTION 2

You owe your Mum £10: is she a debtor or a creditor?

Your brother owes you £1: is he a debtor or a creditor?

Balance sheets are presented in two main ways. At the moment, we shall use what is known as the 'horizontal layout'. Later, we will use a 'vertical layout'.

The horizontal layout lists the assets of a business on the left of the page. It lists the liabilities opposite the assets on the right of the page.

Very straightforward!

EXAMPLE

A balance sheet for Anne's Mini-Market might look like this:

	£		£
Premises	45,000	Mortgage on premises	25,000
Van	16,000	Hire purchase owed on van	12,000
Shop fittings	18,000	Trade creditors	890
Stock	1,670		
Trade debtors	140		
Bank balance	900		

All balance sheets must 'balance'.

This means that the assets must add to the same total as the liabilities.

It is fairly obvious that Anne's balance sheet, as shown above, does not balance.

To make it balance we need to insert a missing figure on the liabilities side. If we include £43,820 as a liability, the two sides would add to the same total of £81,710.

What is this missing figure? What does it represent?

> **Capital** is the term used to describe how much a business is worth. It represents how much the owner(s) has/have invested in the business.

Anne's business is worth £43,820. The business has assets totalling £81,710; the business debts amount to £37,890.

If Anne decided to stop trading, she would sell her assets, settle her debts and take £43,820 out of the business.

£43,820 is the amount the business owes the owner. It is the amount invested in the business, by Anne, on the date the balance sheet was drawn up. This is Anne's capital.

[**Note:** this assumes that the business assets could be sold for their balance sheet values. In reality, the assets may be sold for more or less than their balance sheet values and we will consider this at a later stage in our studies.]

WORKED EXAMPLE

If we include the capital figure that we previously calculated, Anne's balance sheet will 'balance' and look like this:

	£		£
Premises	45,000	Mortgage on premises	25,000
Van	16,000	Hire purchase owed on van	12,000
Shop fittings	18,000	Trade creditors	890
Stock	1,670		
Trade debtors	140	CAPITAL	43,820
Bank balance	900		
	81,710		81,710

A balance sheet will always balance because the capital figure is always the 'missing figure'.

What does Anne's balance sheet show us?

- It shows us what Anne's business is worth.
- It shows us the resources (assets) that are in use in Anne's business
- It shows us who has provided the funds to acquire those resources.
- It shows Anne's capital.

The funds that have financed the acquisition of the assets used in the business have been provided by:

- the business providing the finance for the hire purchase
- the bank or building society
- the creditors and
- ANNE.

Notice that capital is a liability. Initially, this is quite difficult to come to terms with. Capital is what the business owes the proprietor.

If you are unsure about the calculation of the capital figure (or that capital is a liability), imagine that Anne decided to close her business down. The business assets would be sold; they should fetch £81,710. This would be used to pay off the hire purchase debt £12,000, the bank or building society £25,000 and the creditors £890. The cash left £43,820 is what Anne would receive.

Fixed assets +
Current assets

Current liabilities +
Long-term liabilities +
Capital

The **accounting equation** recognises that the assets owned by a business are always equal to the claims against the business.

One side of the equation shows in monetary terms the assets that are owned by an organisation.

The other side of the equation shows how these resources have been financed with funds provided by the owner(s) and others.

Balance sheets are the formal way of showing the accounting equation.

Liquid is the term used to describe how easily an asset can be turned into cash.

Stock is more liquid than premises. Stock can be turned into cash much more quickly than premises (ask anyone who has tried to sell a house!)

Machinery is less liquid than debtors. It is generally easier to obtain money from debtors than it is to obtain money from selling surplus machinery.

Fixed assets will be used by the business for more than one year.

Examples might include business premises; factory machinery; delivery vehicles.

Current assets are cash or assets that will be changed into cash in the near future.

Examples might include stock; debtors; bank balances; cash in the till.

Assets are classified in balance sheets according to:

■ how long they are likely to be used in the business, and
■ how liquid they are.

Long-term liabilities are debts owed by a business which need to be paid after more than one year.

Examples might include a bank loan that needs to be repaid in four years' time. A 25-year mortgage would fall under this heading (except in its final year!)

Current liabilities are debts owed by a business that need to be repaid within one year.

Liabilities are classified according to the time allowed by the creditor to settle the debt.

Examples might include suppliers who are owed money for goods supplied (trade creditors); or money owed to a landlord for overdue rent.

In reality, many current liabilities need to be paid much more quickly, eg a supplier of goods is unlikely to allow a business 365 days before the debt is settled.

THE ACCOUNTING EQUATION

$$\text{Fixed assets} + \text{Current assets} = \text{Long-term liabilities} + \text{Current liabilities} + \text{Capital}$$

If we know four of the parts that make up the accounting equation, then we should be able to find out the missing one by completing the accounting equation.

QUESTION 3

Required Fill in the missing figures in the following table. Use the accounting equation to work out your answers.

Fixed assets £	Current assets £	Long-term liabilities £	Current liabilities £	Capital £
70,000	16,000	20,000	8,000	?
?	24,000	20,000	4,000	60,000
20,000	3,000	0	8,000	?
55,000	9,000	15,000	?	45,000
30,000	?	20,000	10,000	15,000

If we use the above asset classifications, the left side of Anne's balance sheet will look like this:

EXAMPLE

Fixed assets	£	Comment
Premises	45,000	Usually used for many years.
Shop fittings	18,000	Usually used for, say, 10 years.
Van	16,000	Usually in use for, say, 4 or 5 years.
Current assets	£	
Stock	1,670	Should become cash in the next few months.
Trade debtors	140	Should settle their debts within 30 days.
Bank balance	900	Almost as good as cash.

The order in which assets appear under their headings is known as the 'reverse order of liquidity'. This means that the most liquid of the assets appears last while the least liquid appears first.

If we classify Anne's liabilities, the right side of her balance sheet would look like this:

Comment		£
Capital is usually the first item to appear.	Capital	43,690
Mortgage is generally owed for a long time period, as also would money borrowed to purchase a vehicle. However, both of these would be classified as current liabilities in the final year of the debt.	Long-term liabilities	
	Mortgage on premises	25,000
	Hire purchase owed on van	12,000
Suppliers will usually expect payment within 30 days of the debt being incurred.	Current liabilities	
	Trade creditors	890

Business transactions are usually recorded over a 12-month period. This is known as the business's **financial year**. The process is then repeated for each subsequent year.

A business's financial year can start at any time during the calendar year. The financial year of a business may run from 1 February until the following 31 January; another business may have 1 October until the following 30 September as its financial year.

A balance sheet is prepared at one moment in time, usually at the end of the business's financial year. Anne's Mini-Market has a financial year end of 31 March. The balance sheet can only be prepared at one moment in time since some of its components will change on an hourly basis. Money will be going in and out of the bank account each day; stock will be sold and reordered regularly, Anne will be paying creditors on a regular basis, and so on.

The date shown in the heading for a balance sheet will reflect the fact that it is prepared at the end of one day. The heading will show the name of the business and the date when the balance sheet was prepared.

EXAMPLES OF HEADINGS

Angel's Records

Balance sheet **as at** 30 June 20**

Bill's Burger Bar

Balance sheet **as at** 28 February 20**

Mrs Charlotte's Tea Room

Balance sheet **as at** 31 October 20**

One final point before the two sides of the balance sheet are put together: assets are recorded on balance sheets at their **original cost**. This does initially cause a problem for some students of accounting.

The reason for valuing assets at cost is quite simple. Cost is the only **objective** valuation that can be applied to the assets that are owned.

Consider the van that Anne uses in her business. She paid £16,000 for it three years ago. She intends to use it for another two years. How could she determine the 'correct' value to include on her balance sheet?

She could take the van to her local garage for a valuation. Sounds simple but . . .

- the value placed on it would depend on whether it was a straight sale or a trade-in
- if it was part of a trade-in deal, the value would also change according to the selling price of the new vehicle
- another garage could give a better or worse allowance on Anne's three-year-old van.

Valuing assets can prove to be a minefield. The problem is solved by valuing all assets at cost.

We can now put the two sides of Anne's completed balance sheet together. It would look like this:

Anne's Mini-Market
Balance sheet as at 31 March 20**

	£	£		£	£
Fixed assets			**Capital**		43,820
Premises at cost		45,000			
Shop fittings at cost		18,000	**Long-term liabilities**		
Van at cost		16,000	Mortgage	25,000	
		79,000	Hire purchase debt	12,000	
Current assets					37,000
Stock	1,670		**Current liabilities**		
Trade debtors	140		Trade creditors		890
Bank balance	900				
		2,710			
		81,710			81,710

Chapter summary

- Balance sheets are prepared on one day.
- Balance sheets show the assets being used by a business on that day.
- Liabilities represent the indebtedness of the business to people or organisations outside the business on that day.
- Capital represents the indebtedness of the business to the owner of the business.
- The two sides of a balance sheet must always balance because of the accounting equation.

Self-test questions

These questions are designed to test whether you have understood the new concepts that have been introduced in the text.

Answers can be found in the text.

- Define the term 'asset'.
- Explain why fixed assets are valued in a balance sheet at cost.
- What is meant by the term 'liability'?
- Give an example of a liability typically found in a retail shop selling DVDs.
- What is a debtor?
- What is a creditor?
- Why must a balance sheet always balance?
- What is the main difference between a fixed asset and a current asset?
- What is the main difference between a long-term liability and a current liability?
- Why is capital shown as a liability in a balance sheet?
- Could a business have a financial year end on 29 April?
- Could a business have a financial year which runs from 19 June until 30 May the following year?

TEST QUESTIONS

Even-numbered questions do not have answers at the back of the book.

QUESTION 4

Required Explain how one type of business can include a delivery van as a current asset on its balance sheet, and yet another type of business includes a similar delivery van as a fixed asset on its balance sheet.

QUESTION 5

Required Classify the following items into fixed assets and current assets for an electrical goods retailer:

	Fixed asset	Current asset
27 refrigerators for resale		
Delivery van		
Money owed by customers		
Money in till		
Display cabinets		
Checkout scanners		

QUESTION 6

Required Classify the following items into fixed assets, current assets and current liabilities for a garage:

	Fixed asset	Current asset	Current liability
Electronic tuning equipment			
Money owed to BP plc			
Second-hand cars on forecourt			
Typewriters			
Break-down vehicle			
Petrol			

QUESTION 7

Carole has the following assets and liabilities on 31 August 20*3:

machinery at cost £120,000; vehicles at cost £70,000; stock £20,000; debtors £10,000; creditors £8,000; bank balance £2,000.

Required Calculate the amount of Carole's capital as at 31 August 20*3.

QUESTION 8

Atul has the following assets and liabilities on 31 December 20*3:

premises at cost £60,000; equipment at cost £25,000; stock £5,000; debtors £4,000; creditors £8,000; money owed to the bank £6,000.

Required Calculate the amount of Atul's capital as at 31 December 20*3

QUESTION 9

The following information is provided by Sandeep, a painter and decorator, as at 31 January 20*3:

capital £4,300; vehicle at cost £8,000; tools at cost £250; bank loan repayable in four years' time £4,000; stocks of paint £110; money owed to suppliers of paint £60.

Required Prepare the balance sheet as at 31 January 20*3. Classify all assets and liabilities.

QUESTION 10

Archie, a newsagent, provides the following information, as at 30 September 20*3:

capital £45,300; premises at cost £73,000; mortgage on premises £48,000; shop fittings at cost £14,000; vehicle at cost £3,000; stock £4,500; debtors £300; creditors £900; bank overdraft £600.

Required Prepare the balance sheet as at 30 September 20*3. Classify all assets and liabilities.

QUESTION 11

Sandra has provided you with the following information which relates to her business, as at 31 March 20*3:

premises at cost £40,000; machinery at cost £10,000; office equipment at cost £4,000; vehicle at cost £9,000; long-term bank loan £18,000; debtors £1,200; stock £4,000; creditors £500; bank balance £800. She is unable to tell you what her capital is currently.

Required Prepare the balance sheet as at 31 March 20*3.

QUESTION 12

Andrew is a door-to-door salesman selling cosmetics. He gives you the following information, as at 28 February 20*3:

car at cost £12,400; bank overdraft £1,800; stock £240; debtors £180; creditors £400.

Required Prepare Andrew's balance sheet as at 28 February 20*3.

QUESTION 13

Your Uncle Jack has recently had his balance sheet prepared by a local accountant. He cannot understand why his capital account is shown as a liability. 'Surely my accountant has got this wrong', he says.

Required Explain to Uncle Jack whether the accountant is correct in showing the capital account as a liability.

QUESTION 14

Required Explain the circumstances that could result in a mortgage being shown as a current liability.

CHAPTER
TWO

Profits

Owners of businesses are interested in what their businesses are worth. As we have seen, this can be determined by preparing a balance sheet or by using the accounting equation.

QUESTION 1

Required Explain whether the owner of a business could prepare a balance sheet on 9 December, or 23 June, or today.

QUESTION 2

Required Explain what the * represents in the accounting equation:

$$\text{Assets} * \text{Liabilities} = \text{Capital}$$

Not only are the owners of a business interested in what their business is worth, they are also interested in how much their business is earning for them. They are interested in the **profitability** of their business.

We cannot tell whether a business is profitable by analysing a balance sheet; after all, it can only tell us what the business has in the way of assets and liabilities at one particular time.

Many teachers and textbooks have said that a balance sheet is rather like a photograph – it captures the moment.

However, over a financial year it is likely that a balance sheet will change. Assets may increase or decrease. Liabilities may increase or decrease. These changes will take place because of business activity.

Profit is the excess of income over expenditure. A **loss** occurs when expenditure exceeds income.

If a business is profitable, one would expect that the assets owned by the business would increase, unless the owner of the business takes more cash and/or goods from the business than the profits warrant. If a business is unprofitable, one would expect that the business assets would decrease.

EXAMPLE

Take a very simple example. A businesswoman purchases some goods costing £100 and incurs no other expenses. She sells these goods for £250. The profit earned is £150. Unless the woman withdraws some of that profit, the business assets must increase by £150.

If you do not spend all your allowance and/or the wage you earn from your part-time job, your assets will increase. Imagine that you earn £2,400 over a year and you spend only £2,000. What happens to the difference? Your assets will show an increase of £400.

The cash that you will have increased by £400 or your savings account may have increased.

Note: saving is what other people do when they accumulate money for the future!

> **Net assets** of a business are all assets less all liabilities, or:
> Fixed assets + current assets − (long-term liabilities + current liabilities) or
> **Net assets** = **capital** (check this by referring to the accounting equation).

Profits increase the net assets of a business.

The converse is also true. That is, if there is an increase in the net assets, then this must be because of the business being profitable.

The only exception to this rule would be if extra assets were introduced into the business from outside or if liabilities were paid off by money from outside the business. An example of this would be if the owner of the business injected more money into the business or if more assets were introduced into the business from another source.

How can we calculate the profits?

WORKED EXAMPLE

Barker Dog Foods has the following assets and liabilities as at 1 January 20*2:

fixed assets at cost £270,000; current assets £21,000; trade creditors £5,000.

One year later, on 1 January 20*3, the business had the following assets and liabilities:

Fixed assets at cost £290,000; current assets £27,000; trade creditors £8,000.

During the year there were no withdrawals or injections of money or assets by the owner.

Required Calculate the profit earned by Barker Dog Foods for the year ended 31 December 20*2.

Answer

		£
Barker Dog Foods' net assets as at 1 January 20*2	Fixed assets	270,000
	Current assets	21,000
		291,000
	less current liabilities	5,000
	Net assets (capital)	286,000
Barker Dog Foods' net assets as at 1 January 20*3	Fixed assets	290,000
	Current assets	27,000
		317,000
	less current liabilities	8,000
	Net assets (capital)	309,000

The net assets (capital) of the business have increased by £23,000 (£309,000 − £286,000) during the year. This is the profit that Barker Dog Foods has made during the year. It has to be profit since we were told that no money or assets had been introduced or withdrawn during the year.

> **Retained profits** are profits that are kept in a business for expansion purposes. They increase the net assets of a business. They are sometimes said to be '**ploughed back**'.

> **Drawings** is the term used to describe the withdrawal of resources (cash or goods) from the business by the proprietor for private use outside the business.

It is unrealistic to think that money or assets would not be injected into a business if this was necessary to safeguard the business or in order to expand the business.

It is also unrealistic to imagine that the owner of a business would not withdraw some cash from the business in order to pay for various items of private household expenditure during the year. This cash taken from the business is drawings.

It is also unrealistic to imagine that Brenda, who owns a garage, would send her car to another garage for servicing or for repairs. The value of servicing or repairing Brenda's car is drawings.

Any cash or goods taken from a business by the proprietor for private use are in fact withdrawals of profits!

In order to calculate business profits it is important that we consider only transactions that involve the business.

- So, money won on the National Lottery and paid into the business bank account should not be included in any calculations to determine profits.
- Cash taken from the business and used to buy the week's groceries from Tesco should not be used in our calculation of profits.
- The cheque for £2,300 drawn on the business bank account to pay Thomson for the family holiday is not part of the calculation.

WORKED EXAMPLE

Cora has been in business for a number of years. At 1 March 20*1 her business assets and liabilities were as follows: fixed assets at cost £40,000; current assets £10,000; current liabilities £5,000. One year later, on 28 February 20*2, her business assets and liabilities were: fixed assets, £45,000; current assets £9,000; and current liabilities £6,000.

During the year she withdrew from the business cash of £14,500 for private use.

Required Calculate Cora's business profits for the year ended 28 February 20*2.

Answer

	£
Cora's net assets as at 1 March 20*1 (£40,000 + £10,000 − £5,000)	45,000
Cora's net assets as at 28 February 20*2:	48,000
Increase in net assets over the year *(profits ploughed back into the business)*:	3,000

	£
Increase in net assets over the year	3,000
Drawings *(profits withdrawn during the year)*	14,500
Business profit earned during the year	17,500

WORKED EXAMPLE

Chang had business net assets on 1 August 20*1 of £16,000. On 31 July 20*2 his business net assets stood at £45,000. During the year his Uncle George died and left Chang £20,000. The legacy was paid into the business bank account.

Required Calculate the profit that Chang's business made for the year ended 31 July 20*2.

Answer

	£
Chang's net assets as at 1 August 20*1	16,000
Chang's net assets as at 31 July 20*2	45,000
Increase in net assets over the year	29,000

WORKED EXAMPLE *continued*

Some of the increase in net assets is due to Uncle George's legacy. This has to be disregarded if we wish to determine the profits generated by the business, so ...

	£
Increase in net assets over the year	29,000
Less capital introduced	20,000
Business profit earned during the year	9,000

WORKED EXAMPLE

Marc has been in business for a number of years. On 1 February 20*1 his capital account stood at £30,500. At 31 January 20*2 his business balance sheet showed the following: fixed assets at cost £45,000; current assets £18,000; long-term liability £20,000; current liabilities £7,000. During the year he paid into the business bank account a National Lottery win of £10,000. His drawings for the year amounted to £21,000.

Required   Calculate the profit or loss made by the business for the year ended 31 January 20*2.

Answer

	£
Marc's net assets (capital) as at 1 February 20*1	30,500
Marc's net assets (capital) as at 31 January 20*2	36,000
Increase in net assets over the year:	5,500
Add Drawings:	21,000
	26,500
Less Capital introduced:	10,000
Business profit for the year ended 31 January 20*2	16,500

WORKED EXAMPLE

Helen's balance sheet as at 1 May 20*1 showed: fixed assets at cost £16,000; current assets £4,000; current liabilities £3,500; capital £16,500. On 30 April 20*2 her balance sheet showed: fixed assets £30,000; current assets £5,000; current liabilities £6,000 and a long-term liability of £20,000. During the year Helen paid into the business bank account a legacy of £18,000. Her drawings for the year amounted to £14,000.

Required   Calculate the profit or loss made by Helen's business for the year ended 30 April 20*2.

Answer

	£	
Helen's net assets as at 1 May 20*1	16,500	
Helen's net assets as at 31 April 20*2	9,000	
Decrease in net assets over the year	(7,500)	(Negative numbers are
Add Drawings for the year	14,000	often shown in brackets.)
	6,500	
Less Capital introduced	18,000	
Loss made by Helen's business during the year	(11,500)	

Chapter summary

- Profit can be calculated quickly and accurately by comparing net assets held by a business at the end of a financial year with net assets held at the start of the year.
- Adjustments to the change shown have to be made by adding back drawings and eliminating any capital introduced during the year

Self-test questions

- Define the term 'profits'.
- Define the term 'loss'.
- Explain what is meant by the term 'net assets'.
- What is the connection between capital and net assets?
- Fixed assets £7,000; current assets £3,000; current liabilities £2,000. Calculate net assets.
- Fixed assets £100,000; current assets £20,000; long-term liabilities £40,000; current liabilities £9,000. Calculate capital.
- What is meant by the term 'drawings'?
- Give an example of drawings that the proprietor of an electrical goods store could make.
- Is it possible to make drawings that exceed the profit earned in a year?
- Explain what is meant by 'capital introduced'.

TEST QUESTIONS

Even numbers do not have answers in the back of the book.

QUESTION 3

Ben runs a general store. Which of the following items are drawings?

- Money taken from till to pay staff.
- Money taken from till to buy Ben's wife a bunch of flowers for her birthday.
- Money taken from till to purchase stamps to send out bills.
- Crisps taken from shop for children's lunch box.
- Vegetables taken from shop for evening meal.

QUESTION 4

A business shows an increase in its net assets over the year of £12,300. During the year the proprietor made drawings to the value of £16,000. Calculate the profit made during the year by the business.

QUESTION 5

A business's net assets reduced by £3,500 during the year. The proprietor's drawings amounted to £8,900. Calculate the profit or loss made by the business during the year.

QUESTION 6

A business shows an increase in its net assets over the year of £35,000. During the year the proprietor paid an inheritance of £25,000 into the business bank account. Calculate the profit or loss made by the business during the year.

QUESTION 7

A proprietor's capital account increased over the year by £12,700. She paid a £50,000 Premium Bond win into the business bank account during the year. Calculate the profit or loss made by the business during the year.

QUESTION 8

Over a year the capital account shown in a business balance sheet has increased by £17,800. During the year the proprietor paid a legacy of £4,000 into the business bank account. His drawings for the year amounted to £19,500. Calculate the profit or loss made by the business during the year.

QUESTION 9

The net assets of a business have increased over the year by £2,750. The proprietor paid into the business bank account £35,000 withdrawn from her personal building society account. During the year she withdrew £14,000 from the business for personal expenses. Calculate the profit or loss made by the business during the year.

QUESTION 10

On 1 February 20*2 the net assets of Becky's business were £83,000. During the year ended 31 January 20*3 she withdrew £18,000 for her private use; she also paid into the business bank account a Premium Bond win of £20,000. At 31 January 20*3 the net assets of Becky's business amounted to £79,000. Calculate the profit or loss made by Becky's business for the year ended 31 January 20*3.

QUESTION 11

On 1 November 20*1 the business assets of Charles were as follows: fixed assets £42,000; current assets £17,000. The current liabilities amounted to £14,000. A year later, on 31 October 20*2, the fixed assets of the business were £56,000; the current assets were £20,000; and the current liabilities were £15,000. In addition, the business had a long-term bank loan of £10,000 which is due to be repaid in 20*9. During the year ended 31 October 20*2 Charles paid a legacy of £12,000 into the business bank account. His personal drawings for the year amounted to £14,000. Calculate the profit or loss made by Charles' business for the year ended 31 October 20*2.

QUESTION 12

The following information relates to Boogies Boutique:

	at 1 January 20*2 £	at 31 December 20*2 £
Fixed assets	70,000	72,000
Current assets	26,000	27,000
Long-term liability	–	20,000
Current liabilities	18,000	23,000

During the year ended 31 December 20*2 the proprietor of Boogies Boutique introduced a further £9,500 from a private source; she also withdrew £16,500 for personal expenditure. Calculate the profit or loss for the year made by Boogies Boutique.

CHAPTER
THREE

The Trading Account

We have seen that we can calculate the profit or loss for a business over a period of time (usually a financial year), provided that we know:

- the net assets of the business at the start; and
- the net assets of the business at the end of the time period in question.

Profits are generally calculated over a financial year but they could be calculated for any time period. We could calculate the profits earned by a business for a week or a month, for two months or for 73 days if we wished to.

Many business owners calculate their profits half way through the year as well as at their financial year-end in order to plot the progress of their business.

QUESTION 1

Required Fill in the gaps:

Net assets of a business is the same as the owner's ....Capital....; both show how much the business is ....worth........ .

> **Final accounts** are the trading account, the profit and loss account and balance sheet of a business.

The final accounts are usually produced at the financial year-end, but they could be produced at any time they might be required by the owner or managers of a business.

> A **trading account** is a statement that calculates the **gross profit** that a business has made by buying and selling its goods during a particular period of time.

> **Gross profit** is sales less the cost of those sales.

Although the net asset method of calculating the net profit of a business does calculate the net profit **easily** and **accurately**, it does have a major drawback. It does not give us any details of how the profit (or loss) was arrived at.

The details of how a profit has been earned or why a loss has been incurred are important to both the owner and any external providers of finance:

- the owner will probably wish to make greater profits in the future
- lenders will wish to see that their investment is safe and that any interest or repayments due will be able to be met by the business.

> **Revenue expenditure** is spending on everyday expenses.

> **Capital expenditure** is spending on fixed assets or the improvement of fixed assets.

Specification coverage:
AQA 10.4, 12.2;
OCR 5.3.1; 5.1.3.

By the end of this chapter you should be able to:
- prepare a trading account
- distinguish between capital and revenue expenditure
- distinguish between capital and revenue receipts
- calculate cost of sales
- determine gross profit
- incorporate returns and payments for carriage into a trading account.

> **Revenue receipts** are incomes derived from the 'usual' activities of the business.

> **Capital receipts** are derived from transactions that are not the usual activities of the business.

QUESTION 2

Required Place an x in the column which classifies the following receipts and payments made by Bloggs' Garage:

	Revenue Expenditure	Capital Expenditure	Revenue Receipt	Capital Receipt
Loan of money from the bank				
Sale of break-down truck				
Petrol sales				
Assistant's wages				
Purchase of hydraulic jack				

Profits can be calculated by using the 'net asset method'. This method of discovering profit is like discovering a skeleton. We are unable to see the details of how the profit was arrived at just as we cannot determine whether the person was fat or thin or whether they were beautiful or plain from looking at their skeleton.

We need to put some flesh on our skeleton. We need to put some detail into our profit calculations.

The details of how profits are arrived at are shown in two statements:

■ the trading account; and
■ the profit and loss account.

Both of these statements are fairly easy to understand. (How often have you heard a teacher say that!)

THE TRADING ACCOUNT

The trading account shows how much it cost to buy the goods and how much they were sold for. The goods in question are the goods that the business buys and sells in its everyday activities.

The goods bought for resale are called 'purchases' (gosh!).

The goods that are sold are called 'sales' (an even bigger gosh!).

QUESTION 3

A clothes shop buys:

■ jeans
■ sweatshirts
■ trainers
■ a delivery van
■ leather jackets.

Required Identify the items above that are purchases.

QUESTION 4

A general store sells:

■ apples

- magazines
- a freezer cabinet that is no longer required
- fish fingers
- caramel toffees.

Required Identify the items above that are sales.

A simple trading account compares the purchases and sales for a financial period. The difference between the two is the **gross profit** earned for the period.

The trading account is generally prepared to show the gross profit earned for a financial year. However a trading account could be prepared for a week, a month, two months or 123 days.

EXAMPLES OF TRADING ACCOUNT HEADINGS

Brian Bains

Trading account **for the year ended** 31 December 20*3

Brenda Binks

Trading account **for the three months ended** 30 June 20*3

Boris Bruker

Trading account **for the half-year ended** 31 July 20*3

All the headings are for a **period** of time. The balance sheets we prepared earlier were prepared as at **one moment** in time.

WORKED EXAMPLE

Betty owns a business selling magazines and books. She is able to give you the following information relating to her business for the year ended 31 December 20*2:

	£
Purchases of magazines and books	32,500
Purchase of cash register	840
Sales of magazines and books	65,800
Sales of shop fittings	1,200

Required Prepare the trading account for the year ended 31 December 20*2.

Answer

Trading account for the year ended 31 December 20*2

	£		£
Purchases	32,500	Sales	65,800
Gross profit	33,300		
	65,800		65,800

Notes
- The figures included in the trading account are figures for a year; the heading tells us this.
- The purchase of the cash register has not been included – it is capital expenditure.
- The sale of shop fittings has not been included – it is a capital receipt.
- Purchases are revenue expenditure. They are part of the everyday costs associated with running Betty's business
- Sales are revenue receipts. These receipts are from Betty's normal trading activities.
- The gross profit is a balancing figure. It has been included to make the two sides of the trading

account balance, i.e. to add to the same total. You will have to calculate this figure by deducting the value of purchases from the value of the sales.
(Sales £65,800 − purchases £32,500 = gross profit £33,300.)

The trading account is prepared by using purchases and sales which are examples of revenue expenditure and revenue receipts.

> **Stock** (or **stock in trade**) is the term applied to goods bought for resale which have not been disposed of during the financial year. Like fixed assets, it is valued at cost price. (But see Chapter 17.)

The preparation of a trading account is so simple, there has to be a complication! There always is!

As you can appreciate, very few businesses sell all the goods that they purchase each day. At the end of every day there will be goods left on the shelves, in the display cabinets and in the stock room.

Generally, there will be stock left unsold at the end of any financial year. The last millisecond of the last day of the financial year is (almost) the same time as the first millisecond of the new financial year. So, the stock value at the end of one financial year is the stock value at the start of the following financial year:

- The stock held by a business at 31 May 20*1 is the stock held on 1 June 20*1.
- Stock as at 30 November 20*2 is stock as at 1 December 20*2.

The stocks held at the start of a financial year are sometimes referred to as 'opening stock'. The stocks held one year later at the end of the financial year are sometimes referred to as 'closing stock'.

What effect will opening and closing stock values have on a trading account?

We need to calculate the value of the goods that have been sold during the year.

> **Cost of sales** is deducted from net sales to calculate the gross profit earned by a business.
> Cost of sales = opening stock + purchases − closing stock.

I am on a diet! My wife (she never eats bread) is counting the number of slices of bread that I eat during the day. How does she find out how many slices I have eaten today?
She knows that there were 8 slices in the bread bin this morning. I bought a loaf
(only 14 slices) this afternoon and there are now 13 slices left.
How many slices have I eaten?
Answer: Too many for my diet! Actually, only 9 slices.

If you calculated my bread consumption accurately then the trading account should pose no problems for you.

Opening stock of bread	8 slices
Purchases of bread	<u>14 slices</u>
I could have eaten	22 slices
However, there were	<u>13 slices</u> left
So I must have eaten	9 slices

WORKED EXAMPLE

Becky has a market stall selling jeans. She provides the following information:

- Stock of jeans as at 1 September 20*2: £345
- Purchases of jeans for the year ended 31 August 20*3: £18,450
- Sales of jeans for the year ended 31 August 20*3: £42,750
- Stock of jeans as at 31 August 20*3: £400

Required Prepare the trading account for the year ended 31 August 20*3.

Answer
We first have to find the value of the jeans that Becky sold during the year. We do this by applying the technique that was used to find how many slices of bread I ate today.

WORKED EXAMPLE *continued*

	£	
Becky started the year with	345	worth of jeans
She bought a further	18,450	worth of jeans
So she could have sold	18,795	worth ... but she didn't ... she had
some left. She had	400	worth left.
So she must have sold ...	18,395	

How much did she sell these jeans for? £42,750. Her gross profit for the year was £24,355.

Talk yourself through this example a few times. It is important that you understand the process that you have gone through.

The actual trading account should be presented like this:

Becky
Trading account for the year ended 31 August 20*3

	£		£
Stock 1 September 20*2	345	Sales	42,750
Purchases	18,450		
	18,795		
Less Stock 31 August 20*3	400		
Cost of goods sold	18,395		
Gross profit	24,355		
	42,750		42,750

The description for £18,795 is 'cost of goods sold'. This is the value of the jeans that Becky sold during the year at cost price.

The figure is the monetary value of the jeans sold at the price she paid for them.

£42,750 is the monetary value of the **same** jeans at the price that the customers paid.

QUESTION 5

The following information relates to the business of Biddulph for the year ended 31 March 20*3:

stock as at 1 April 20*2 £4,560; stock as at 31 March 20*3 £5,050;
purchases for the year £47,800; sales for the year £84,350.

Required Prepare the trading account for the year ended 31 March 20*3.

QUESTION 6

Julie owns a small retail grocery store. She provides the following data:

purchase of goods for resale £49,000; purchase of delivery van £14,500; stock as at 30 June 20*3 £890; stock as at 1 July 20*2 £930; sale of unused shop fittings £320; sales of groceries £81,000.

Required Select the appropriate information and prepare a trading account for the year ended 30 June 20*3.

Note
■ You should not have included the purchase of the delivery van in your trading account because it is capital expenditure.
■ You should not have included the sale of unused shop fittings in your trading account because it is a capital receipt.

QUESTION 7

Clary provides the following information for the year ended 30 April 20*3:

stock as at 1 May 20*2 £340; stock as at 30 April 20*3 £530; purchases £23,560; sales £52,900.

Required Prepare trading account for the year ended 30 April 20*3.

QUESTION 8

Eddie provides the following information for the year ended 31 July 20*3:

stock as at 1 August 20*2 £12,907; stock as at 31 July 20*3 £10,987; purchases as at £143,673; sales £243,561.

Required Prepare a trading account for the year ended 31 July 20*3.

QUESTION 9

Joe provides the following information for the year ended 31 December 20*3:

stock as at 1 January 20*2 £238; stock as at 31 December 20*3 £432; purchases £34,930;

sales £54,760.

Required Prepare a trading account for the year ended 31 December 20*3.

The next step in the preparation of trading accounts is the one that seems to cause a lot of students a lot of headaches.

> **Sales returns** are goods that have been returned by the customer. They are also known as **returns in** or **returns inwards**.

> **Purchase returns** are goods that the business sends back to the supplier. They are also known as **returns out** or **returns outwards**.

Even in businesses that are extremely well run, some goods are returned by customers.

The way that these sales returns are treated in the trading account seems fairly obvious: the total of sales returns is deducted from the total sales for the year.

No matter how good and how careful suppliers are, there will inevitably be occasions when a business has to return goods. Again, our treatment of any purchase returns seems to be fairly obvious: the total of purchase returns is deducted from the total purchases for the year.

WORKED EXAMPLE

The following information relates to the business of Bunty:

stock as at 1 September 20*2 £1,200; stock as at 31 August 20*3 £1,500; purchases £48,000; sales £72,380; returns inwards £180; returns outwards £360.

Required Prepare the trading account for the year ended 31 August 20*3.

Answer

Bunty
Trading account for the year ended 31 August 20*3

	£	£		£
Stock as at 1 Sept 20*2		1,200	Sales	72,380
Purchases	48,000		less returns inwards	180
Less returns outwards	360	47,640		
		48,840		
Stock as at 31 Aug 20*3		1,500		
Cost of goods sold		47,340		
Gross profit		24,860		
		72,200		72,200

Note the way that the calculation to find the 'net' purchases figure has been set back from the main column; this is a device that accountants often use so that the main column does not get too cluttered. You will soon get the hang of this.

QUESTION 10

The following information relates to the year ended 30 April 20*3 for the business of Sahera Patel:

stock as at 1 May 20*2 £1,435; stock as at 30 April 20*3 £1,265; purchases £34,328; sales £72,548; returns inwards £459; returns outwards £671.

Required Prepare the trading account for the year ended 30 April 20*3.

QUESTION 11

The following information relates to the year ended 30 November 20*3 for the business of Rob Berry:

stock as at 1 December 20*2 £1,657; stock as at 30 November 20*3 £2,004; purchases £54,672; sales £98,651; returns inwards £421; returns outwards £803.

Required Prepare the trading account for the year ended 30 November 20*3.

QUESTION 12

Kim Reddy provides the following information for the year ended 28 February 20*3:

stock as at 1 March 20*2 £502; stock as at 28 February 20*3 £677; purchases £85,207; sales £137,503; returns inwards £506; returns outwards £109.

Required Prepare the trading account for the year ended 28 February 20*3.

> **Carriage inwards** is an expense incurred when a supplier charges for delivery on the goods purchased.

> **Carriage outwards** *is also an expense* which a business incurs when it pays for delivery of goods to a customer. It is sometimes referred to as **carriage on sales**.

Carriage inwards makes the goods that are purchased more expensive. It is added to the goods that appear as purchases on the trading account.

REVISION TIP

Carriage IN ... TradINg account.

Carriage outwards is an expense that will be dealt with later (see page 29).

WORKED EXAMPLE

The following figures relate to the business of Benji, who owns a hardware business:

stock as at 1 October 20*2 £5,300; stock as at 30 September 20*3 £4,900; purchases for the year £124,600; sales for the year £314,000; returns inwards for the year £930; returns outwards for the year £2,100; carriage inwards for the year £1,750.

Required Prepare the trading account for the year ended 30 September 20*3.

Answer

Benji
Trading account for the year ended 30 September 20*3.

	£	£		£
Stock as at 1 Oct 20*2		5,300	Sales	314,000
Purchases	124,600		*less* returns inwards	930
Less returns outwards	2,100			
	122,500			
Carriage inwards	1,750	124,250		
		129,550		
Stock as at 30 Sept 20*3		4,900		
Cost of goods sold		124,650		
Gross profit		188,520		
		313,170		313,170

This example shows the most complicated form that a trading account can take. No one can ask you to prepare a more complex trading account.

To make a more difficult example you could only be asked to manipulate larger numbers!

Note once more the use of the two columns. This has enabled us to get one figure for the total cost of net purchases £124,250 without lots of calculations in the main column.

When you attempt the test questions below you may have to refer to Benji's trading account to achieve a good layout. Don't worry about this. You will soon start to remember where to enter the various items.

Chapter summary

- The trading account is used to calculate gross profit by deducting the sales at cost price from the sales figure.
- Returns inwards are deducted from sales to find the net sales.
- Returns outwards are deducted from purchases to find the net purchases figure.
- Carriage inwards is an expense that makes purchases more expensive.
- Carriage outwards is also an expense but is not used in the trading account.

Self-test questions

- What is meant by the term 'final accounts'?
- Which statement would you prepare to calculate the capital of a business?
- Give two reasons why the owner of a business would prepare final accounts.
- Which statement would you prepare to calculate gross profit?
- Explain what is meant by the term 'revenue expenditure'.
- Give an example of a revenue receipt for a 'Chinese takeaway'.
- Which statement would you prepare to calculate net assets?
- Explain what is meant by the term 'capital receipts'.
- Give an example of capital expenditure for a plumber.
- Which is the only statement prepared in the final accounts of a business that contains capital expenditure?

TEST QUESTIONS

Even numbers do not have answers in the back of the book.

QUESTION 13

Required Match the titles and the dates:

- Profit and loss account
- Trading account
- Balance sheet

- as at 31 December 20*2
- for the year ended 30 June 20*2
- for the year ended 30 April 20*2

QUESTION 14

Required State whether the following headings are correct:

- Profit and loss account for the month ended 28 February 20*2 — Yes/No
- Balance sheet for the month ended 31 March 20*2 — Yes/No
- Trading account for the year ended 30 April 20*2 — Yes/No
- Balance sheet as at 31 May 20*2 — Yes/No
- Trading account as at 30 June 20*2 — Yes/No

QUESTION 15

Required Complete the equations:

Sales − cost of sales = ...

£230,000 − £120,000 = ...

QUESTION 16

Required Complete the equations:

Cost of sales + gross profit = ...

£67,000 + £56,000 = ...

QUESTION 17

Required State which of the following could be found in a trading account:

- capital expenditure
- returns inwards
- carriage inwards
- opening stock.

QUESTION 18

Required State which of the following items could be found in a trading account:

- capital receipts
- returns outwards
- carriage outwards
- closing stock.

QUESTION 19

Required State how the value of goods available for sale is calculated.

QUESTION 20

Required State what is meant by 'cost of goods sold'.

QUESTION 21

The following information is given for the year ended 30 June 20*3 for Trevor:

stock as at 1 July 20*2 £256; stock as at 30 June 20*3 £641; purchases £71,006; sales £108,975.

Required Calculate the value of goods available for sale at 30 June 20*3.

QUESTION 22

The following information relates to the year ended 28 February 20*3 for Rodney:

stock as at 1 March 20*2 £230; stock as at 28 February 20*3 £380; purchases £24,600; sales £39,400.

Required Prepare the trading account for the year ended 28 February 20*3 for Rodney.

QUESTION 23

The following information is given for the year ended 31 January 20*3 for Del:

stock as at 1 February 20*2 £970; stock as at 31 January 20*3 £1,050; purchases £35,780; sales £56,710.

Required Prepare the trading account for the year ended 31 January 20*3.

QUESTION 24

The following information relates to the year ended 31 March 20*3 for Belinda's business:

stock as at 1 April 20*2 £6,500; stock as at 31 March 20*3 £5,850; purchases £266,000; sales £412,000; purchase returns £470; sales returns £990; carriage inwards for the year £430; carriage outwards for the year £1,670.

Required Prepare the trading account for the year ended 31 March 20*3.

QUESTION 25

The following information relates to the business of Natalie:

stock 1 February 20*2 £1,560; stock as at 31 January 20*3 £1,640; purchases £65,090; sales £176,040; returns inwards £360; carriage inwards £960; returns outwards £770; carriage outwards £430.

Required Prepare the trading account for the year ended 31 January 20*3.

QUESTION 26

The following information is given for the year ended 31 October 20*3 for Elsie:

stock as at 1 November 20*2 £1,234; stock as at 31 October 20*3 £1,357; purchases £48,961; sales £88,552; returns inwards £508; returns outwards £469; carriage inwards £48; carriage outwards £1,486.

Required Prepare the trading account for the year ended 31 October 20*3.

QUESTION 27

The following information is given for the year ended 31 December 20*3 for Mao:

stock as at 1 January 20*3 £12,651; stock as at 31 December 20*3 £11,537; purchases £175,873; sales £342,960; returns inwards £4,532; returns outwards £1,364; carriage inwards £733.

Required Prepare the trading account for the year ended 31 December 20*3.

QUESTION 28

The following information is available for the year ended 30 June 20*3 for Jay:

stock as at 1 July 20*2 £12,641; stock as at 30 June 20*3 £10,673; purchases £132,785; sales £410,006; purchase of office equipment £3,450; returns inwards £421; returns outwards £650; carriage inwards £48; carriage outwards £769.

Required Prepare the trading account for the year ended 30 June 20*3.

CHAPTER
FOUR

The Profit And Loss Account

A person who is in business will endeavour to generate profits.

He or she will use some of those profits in order to pay for their housekeeping, their holidays, their hobbies etc. They may 'plough back' some of the profits to make the business more efficient so that greater profits may be generated in the future.

You may use all your allowance or wage from a part-time job to buy DVDs, CDs and computer games **or** you may spend it on every day living costs.

But do remember that sometimes things do not work out for the owner of a business and the business may actually run at a loss.

If your weekly income does not cover your weekly expenditure, what do you do? You draw some money from your savings (if you have any) or you may borrow sufficient money to tide you over until your income is sufficient to cover your spending.

The same principle applies to someone in business. If the business is unprofitable, the owner may have to live off his savings or borrow money to help the business to survive.

We have just seen how to calculate the gross profit of a trading business. Put simply, the gross profit is the difference between the cost of goods sold by a business and the amount that the goods have been sold for.

Clearly, there are expenses that have to be paid out of this gross profit in order that the business can continue to operate.

> **Net profit** is calculated by deducting all expenses incurred by the business from the gross profit that it has earned through buying and selling its goods.

Denise buys 1,000 CDs for £4,000 and she sells them all for £6,990. She has made a gross profit of £2,990 on the sale. However, she will have incurred some expenses in selling the CDs.

QUESTION

Can you list some expenses that Denise might have incurred?

Your answer could have included:

rent of a market stall; transport costs to get the CDs to the stall; wages of any sales assistants; wrapping materials etc.

When all other expenses incurred in the sales have been taken into account, the result is **net profit**.

If Denise ran the stall for a month and paid the following expenses:

- local council £400 for rent of the stall
- wages to her assistant £880
- wrapping materials £34
- electricity for lighting and heating £161

her net profit for the month would be £1,515.

Gross profit £2,990 − expenses £1,475

$$(400 + 880 + 34 + 161)$$

Specification coverage:
AQA 10.4;
OCR 5.3.1.

By the end of this chapter you should be able to:
- prepare a profit and loss account
- calculate net profit
- understand the different purposes for which accounts are prepared
- incorporate carriage outwards into the profit and loss account.

> A **profit and loss account** is a statement that calculates the net profit that a business has made for a period of time (usually a financial year).

A profit and loss account details the incomes and expenditure incurred by the business during the period of time.

Why do we need to prepare a trading account and a profit and loss account? We have seen that we can calculate profits accurately and fairly quickly by comparing the net assets of a business at the beginning of a time period with the net assets at the end of the period.

As we said earlier, calculating profit using the 'net asset' method is like finding a skeleton. Managers or owners of a business generally need to know more than just the net profit figure in isolation.

> The **stewardship function** of accounting.
> Final accounts are produced to show the providers of finance that their funds are being used wisely by the managers or owner of the business in question.

The managers or owner of a business often use other people's money (from banks, building societies, relatives etc.) to help provide some of the finance necessary to enable the business to operate.

A bank manager would not be able to say whether a profit of £12,765 would give him confidence that the money provided by his bank is secure and being used wisely. The profit figure in isolation does not show how the gross profit of the business is being used. Is does not answer the question of how much is the business spending on wages, rent, insurance etc.

> The **management function** of accounting.
> Final accounts are also produced to enable the managers or owner of a business to gauge how well the business has performed and to provide information that might highlight areas in which improvements can be made in the way that the business is run.

The managers of a business will wish to improve the performance of the business. A profit figure alone will not highlight areas of good practice and identify areas that need to be improved. Details of all expenditure might show that a business is paying a high rent or has a large amount of vehicle expenses. If these could be reduced then profits would rise.

QUESTION

How could the business reduce rent paid and spend less on vehicle expenses?

Answers could have included:

- moving to smaller premises (if present premises are too large)
- moving to 'out of town' premises (provided customers would not be lost) etc.
- using diesel vehicles
- charging delivery to some customers etc.

QUESTION 1

Required List six items of revenue expenditure that a supermarket would incur in an average month's trading.

QUESTION 2

Required State whether the following statements are true or false:

- Capital expenditure is included in a profit and loss account	True/False
- Capital expenditure is not included in a profit and loss account	True/False
- Revenue expenditure is included in a profit and loss account	True/False
- Revenue expenditure is not included in a profit and loss account	True/False
- Capital receipts are included in a profit and loss account	True/False
- Capital receipts are not included in a profit and loss account	True/False
- Revenue receipts are included in a profit and loss account	True/False

WORKED EXAMPLE

David owns and runs a greengrocer's shop. For the year ended 31 March 20*3 he made a gross profit of £21,500; during the same year he incurred the following expenditure:

	£
Rent and rates	750
Wages	8,000
Insurance	400
New weigh scales	2,340
Motor expenses	1,100
Light and heating expenses	500
Stationery and advertising	250
Bank charges	135
New delivery van	15,600
General expenses	185
Money spent on family holiday	2,300

Required Prepare David's profit and loss account for the year ended 31 March 20*3.

Answer

David
Profit and loss Account for the year ended 31 March 20*3

	£		£
Rent and rates	750	Gross profit	21,500
Wages	8,000		
Insurance	400		
Motor expenses	1,100		
Light and heating expenses	500		
Stationery and advertising	250		
Bank charges	135		
General expenses	185		
NET PROFIT	10,180		
	21,500		21,500

The weigh scales and the delivery van have not been included because they are both examples of capital expenditure. They will appear on David's balance sheet.

The money spent on the holiday has not been included since this is not a business expense. The profit and loss account refers only to business expenses.

The holiday would be drawings if the transaction had gone through the records of the business.

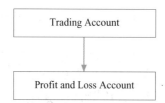

```
┌─────────────────────────┐
│     Trading Account     │
└─────────────────────────┘
            │
            ▼
┌─────────────────────────┐
│  Profit and Loss Account │
└─────────────────────────┘
```

It is usual for businesses to combine the profit and loss account with the trading account.

WORKED EXAMPLE

Danielle trades as a trader in furniture. She supplies the following information relating to the year ended 31 May 20*3:

	£
Stock as at 1 June 20*2	27,268
Stock as at 31 May 20*3	28,420
Purchases	481,690
Sales	748,381
Wages	132,471
Rent and rates	26,402
Advertising and insurance	8,327
Motor expenses	10,513
Office expenses	12,468
Lighting and heating	11,235

Required Prepare the trading and profit and loss account for the year ended 31 May 20*3 for Danielle.

Answer

Danielle
Trading and profit and loss account for the year ended 31 May 20*3

	£		£
Stock as at 1 June 20*2	27,268	Sales	748,381
Purchases	481,690		
	508,958		
Less Stock	28,420		
Cost of goods sold	480,538		
Gross profit	267,843		
	748,381		748,381
Wages	132,471	Gross profit	267,843
Rent and rates	26,402		
Advertising and insurance	8,327		
Motor expenses	10,513		
Office expenses	12,468		
Light and heat	11,235		
Net profit	66,427		
	267,843		267,843

The trading account determined the gross profit of £267,843.

The profit and loss account shows what is left of the gross profit when all expenses for the year have been taken into account.

Carriage outward is an expense borne by the business. It is sometimes referred to as carriage on sales. It is included in the *profit and loss account* with all other expenses incurred by the business.

REVISION TIP

Carriage out .... Profit and loss account

Carriage IN .... TradINg account

Chapter summary

- A profit and loss account calculates the net profit of a business.
- It lists revenue expenditure incurred.
- It provides detail for the stewardship and management functions of accounting.
- Carriage inwards appears in the trading account as an addition to purchases.
- Carriage outwards appears in the profit and loss account as an expense.

Self-test questions

- Why is it important to make the distinction between capital and revenue expenditure?
- Give an example of revenue expenditure for a furniture shop.
- Give an example of capital expenditure for a book shop.
- Under what circumstances might the purchase of a commercial oven/cooker constitute revenue expenditure?
- How is gross profit calculated?
- How is carriage inwards treated in a trading and profit and loss account?
- How is carriage outwards treated in a trading and profit and loss account?
- How is net profit calculated?
- Why is gross profit different to net profit?
- Complete the following equations:
  - Net profit + revenue expenditure = ...
  - Gross profit − revenue expenditure = ...
  - Gross profit − net profit = ...
- What do we mean by the term 'final accounts'?

TEST QUESTIONS

QUESTION 3

The following information is given for the year ended 31 December 20*3 for Pierre Roi:

stock as at 1 January 20*3 £613; stock as at 31 December 20*3 £770; purchases £14,661; sales £25,047.

Required Prepare the trading account for the year ended 31 December 20*3.

QUESTION 4

The following information relates to the year ended 31 July 20*3 for Pauline:

stock as at 1 August 20*2 £429; stock as at 31 July 20*3 £591; purchases £32,649; sales £71,544.

Required Prepare the trading account for the year ended 31 July 20*3.

QUESTION 5

Jack supplies the following information for the year ended 31 January 20*3:

gross profit £43,719; wages £15,437; motor expenses £2,864; rent and rates £1,442; insurance £3,669; general expenses £8,742.

Required Prepare the profit and loss account for the year ended 31 January 20*3.

QUESTION 6

The following information is given for the year ended 30 April 20*3 for Viv:

gross profit £45,892; wages £27,769; rent and rates £6,000; insurance £4,575; motor expenses £7,814; general expenses £2,390.

Required Prepare the profit and loss account for the year ended 30 April 20*3.

QUESTION 7

Terry supplies the following information for the year ended 31 May 20*3:

stock as at 1 June 20*2 £1,329; stock as at 31 May 20*3 £1,275; purchases £23,664; sales £65,782; wages £12,674; motor expenses £6,710; general expenses £441; heating and lighting expenses £1,375; advertising £2,674.

Required Prepare a trading and profit and loss account for the year ended 31 May 20*3.

QUESTION 8

Pablo supplies the following information for the year ended 28 February 20*3:

stock as at 1 March 20*2 £211; stock as at 28 February 20*3 £485; purchases £27,665; sales £74,882; wages £32,559; motor expenses £11,456; rates £674; general expenses £5,391.

Required Prepare a trading and profit and loss account for the year ended 28 February 20*3.

QUESTION 9

The following information is given for the year ended 30 November 20*3 for Gwenelle:

stock as at 1 December 20*2 £12,453; stock as at 30 November 20*3 £10,661; purchases £157,994; sales £325,007; wages £56,743; rates £6,740; heating and lighting £5,441; advertising £1,250; insurance £6,750; general expenses £7,531.

Required Prepare the trading and profit and loss account for the year ended 30 November 20*3.

QUESTION 10

Bill supplies the following information for the year ended 30 June 20*3:

stock as at 1 July 20*2 £438; stock as at 30 June 20*3 £541; purchases £54,763; sales £99,063; returns inwards £286; returns outwards £421; wages £17,539; motor expenses £6,882; advertising £480; heat and light £2,856; rates £1,165; general expenses £6,423.

Required Prepare the trading and profit and loss account for the year ended 30 June 20*3.

QUESTION 11

Helen supplies the following information for the year ended 31 March 20*3:

stock as at 1 April 20*2 £1,554; stock as at 31 March 20*3 £977; purchases £23,887; sales £51,311; returns inwards £367; returns outwards £541; wages £8,712; rates £2,350; heat and light £1,458; advertising £2,350; insurance £2,005; general expenses £4,637.

Required Prepare the trading and profit and loss account for the year ended 31 March 20*3.

QUESTION 12

The following information is given for the year ended 31 October 20*3 for Les:

stock as at 1 November 20*2 £3,419; stock as at 31 October 20*3 £3,491; purchases £43,771; sales £74,911; returns inwards £118; returns outwards £489; wages £12,562; telephone £782; rates £1,750; motor expenses £6,488; general expenses £7,869.

Required Prepare the trading and profit and loss account for the year ended 31 October 20*3.

QUESTION 13

The following information is supplied for the year ended 31 August 20*3 for Janice:

stock as at 1 September 20*2 £673; stock as at 31 August 20*3 £891; purchases £29,041; sales £93,673; returns inwards £276; returns outwards £450; carriage inwards £452; carriage outwards £772; wages £23,774; general expenses £5,675; motor expenses £2,563; rent £3,600; rates £895; telephone £779; advertising £1,250; heat and light £2,588.

Required Prepare the trading and profit and loss account for the year ended 31 August 20*3.

QUESTION 14

Attil provides the following information for the year ended 31 December 20*3:

stock as at 1 January 20*3 £207; stock as at 31 December 20*3 £870; purchases £43,672; sales £91,211; returns inwards £75; returns outwards £671; carriage inwards £317; carriage outwards £139; wages £23,649; rates £1,764; heating and lighting £2,785; telephone £1,476; insurance £579; general expenses £4,361.

Required Prepare the trading and profit and loss account for the year ended 31 December 20*3.

QUESTION 15

The following information relates to the year ended 31 March 20*3 for Catherine:

stock as at 1 April 20*2 £1,549; stock as at 31 March 20*3 £1,471; purchases £54,772; sales £127,773; returns inwards £321; returns outwards £84; carriage inwards £270; carriage outwards £129; wages £41,005; motor expenses £2,756; rent £4,750; rates £1,254; insurance £2,674; advertising £1,547; heat and light £2,541; telephone £3,428; general expenses £6,539.

Required Prepare the trading and profit and loss account for the year ended 31 March 20*3.

QUESTION 16

The following information relates to the year ended 28 February 20*3 for Fred:

stock as at 1 March 20*2 £2,765; stock as at 28 February £2,890; purchases £34,675; purchase of computer for shop £2,990; sales £71,320; returns inwards £276; returns outwards £100; carriage inwards £187; carriage outwards £908; wages £8,650; telephone £1,981; rent £6,000; heating and lighting £2,410; general expenses £7,845.

Required Prepare a trading and profit and loss account for the year ended 28 February 20*3.

CHAPTER
FIVE

The Final Accounts

Final accounts is the term often used to describe the trading account and profit and loss account and balance sheet produced by the owner of a business at the financial year-end.

A full set of final accounts is produced at the end of the financial year. This enables the owner of the business to see

- if the business has been running profitably during the year
- the assets and liabilities that the business owns at the end of the year.

Specification coverage:
AQA 10.4, 11.2;
OCR 5.3.1.

By the end of this chapter you should be able to:
- prepare a full set of final accounts
- understand the relationship between the trading account, the profit and loss account and the balance sheet.

WORKED EXAMPLE

Edward has given you the information in the table that relates to his DIY shop. All the figures in the list relate to the year ended 28 February 20*3. All that is, except the stock figure and the capital figure. These two figures are the value of the stock at the start of the year and Edward's capital at the start of the year.

Why? This will be explained later. Trust me – I'm an accountant!

The stock at 28 February 20*3 was valued at £24,560.

Required Prepare a set of final accounts for the year ended 28 February 20*3.

	£
Premises at cost	80,000
Fixtures at cost	14,200
Vehicle at cost	8,700
Purchases	211,640
Sales	408,830
Stock as at 1 March 20*2	26,480
Wages	152,610
Light and heat	8,420
Motor expenses	3,170
Drawings	18,500
Advertising	860
Insurance	1,540
General expenses	3,950
Debtors	1,340
Creditors	7,140
Bank balance	2,790
Capital as at 1 March 20*2	118,230

WORKED EXAMPLE *continued*

Answer

Edward
Balance sheet as at 28 February 20*3

Fixed assets			Current liabilities		
Premises at cost		80,000	Creditors		7,140
Fixtures at cost		14,200			
Vehicle at cost		8,700			
		102,900			
Current assets					
Stock	24,560				
Debtors	1,340		**Capital**		
Bank balance	2,790	28,690	(balancing figure)		124,450
		131,590			131,590

We have calculated the capital figure (net assets) as at the balance sheet date.

The list provided by Edward tells us that one year earlier Edward's capital (net assets) was £118,230.

Edward's business has £6,220 more net assets at the end of the year than at the start of the year. These assets have been provided by the profits retained in the business over the year.

	£
Net assets at 28 February 20*3	124,450
Less Net assets 31 March 20*2	118,230
Net profit retained in business	6,220

But, Edward has been withdrawing profits all through the year in order to finance his life outside the business. He has been making *drawings* during the year.

These profits need to be added to the retained profits to tell us the total profit generated by the business during the year.

	£
Net profit retained in the business	6,220
Net profit withdrawn by Edward	18,500
Total business profit for the year ended 28 February 20*3	24,720

This calculation does not provide us with the details that may be required for **management** and **stewardship** reasons. For this we must prepare a trading and profit and loss account for the year.

Edward
Trading and profit and loss account for the year ended 28 February 20*3

	£		£
Stock as at 1 March 20*2	26,480	Sales	408,830
Purchases	211,640		
	238,120		
Less Stock as at 28 February 20*3	24,560		
Cost of goods sold	213,560		
Gross profit	195,270		
	408,830		408,830
Wages	152,610	Gross profit	195,270
Light and heat	8,420		
Motor expenses	3,170		
Advertising	860		
Insurance	1,540		
General expenses	3,950		
Net profit	24,720		
	195,270		195,270

Hopefully, you are now aware that if a business is making profits the net assets of a business will increase provided those profits are reinvested ('ploughed back') into the business, and are not withdrawn from the business.

You should also be aware that if the business is running at a loss, the net assets will reduce.

Spend a little time running through this in your mind. It is quite sensible.

If you don't spend all of your income, the surplus must show up in your net assets.

REVISION TIP

When you have studied a topic, ask yourself this question:

'Could I explain what I have just learned to a relative who is not an accountant?'.

If the answer is 'Yes, I think I could', then you do understand the topic.

If the answer is 'No way!', then further work is required on your part.

Now for a small change in the presentation of the work that has already been covered.

Accountants generally present their final accounts in a set order.

You should be reasonably confident on the preparation of the three statements that make up the final accounts.

The three statements are usually presented in this order:

- the **trading account** for the year
- the **profit and loss account** for the year
- the **balance sheet** as at the end of the year.

To help in the preparation of the three statements you may find it useful to go down the list of information and indicate alongside where each item will be used.

● EXAMINATION TIP

Always give a full heading. Use the business name then the heading.

WORKED EXAMPLE

	£
Purchases	123,932
Sales	427,109
Wages	96,452
Drawings	23,600
Machinery at cost	100,000
Mortgage on premises	80,000
Carriage inwards	675
Carriage outwards	490

Required   Indicate where each of the items shown above would be found in a set of final accounts.

Answer

Purchases	*Trading a/c*
Sales	*Trading a/c*
Wages	*P & L a/c*
Drawings	*Balance sheet*
Machinery at cost	*Balance sheet*
Mortgage on premises	*Balance sheet*
Carriage inwards	*Trading a/c*
Carriage outwards	*P & L a/c*

WORKED EXAMPLE

Erica owns and runs a small repair garage. She supplies the information in the table for the year ended 31 May 20*3.

Erica has valued her stock on 31 May 20*3 at £1,045.

Required Prepare a trading and profit and loss account for the year ended 31 May 20*3 and a balance sheet as at 31 May 20*3.

	£
Premises at cost	180,000
Break-down truck at cost	24,000
Office furniture at cost	8,000
Debtors	3,450
Creditors	1,673
Stock as at 1 June 20*2	945
Purchases	48,620
Sales	92,431
Wages and general expenses	23,789
Rates	872
Insurance	2,150
Advertising	450
Stationery	357
Mortgage on premises	160,000
Drawings	15,750
Bank balance	849
Capital	55,128

Answer

Erica
Trading and profit and loss account for the year ended 31 May 20*3

	£		£
Stock as at 1 June 20*2	945	Sales	92,431
Purchases	48,620		
	49,565		
Less Stock as at 31 May 20*3	1,045		
Cost of goods sold	48,520		
Gross profit	43,911		
	92,431		92,431
Wages	23,789	Gross profit	43,911
Rates	872		
Insurance	2,150		
Advertising	450		
Stationery	357		
Net profit	16,293		
	43,911		43,911

Balance sheet as at 31 May 20*3

	£	£		£
Fixed assets			**Capital**	55,671
Premises at cost		180,000	(Balancing figure)	
Break-down truck at cost		24,000		
Office furniture at cost		8,000		
		212,000	**Long-term liability**	
Current assets			Mortgage on premises	160,000
Stock	1,045			
Debtors	3,450		**Current liabilities**	
Bank balance	849	5,344	Creditors	1,673
		217,344		217,344

We can check to see whether or not we have arrived at the correct figure for Erica's profit.

In Chapter 2 we used the net asset method of calculating profit. We shall use it to check the net profit that we calculated using the profit and loss account.

	£
Closing capital as at 31 May 20*3	55,671
Less Opening capital as at 1 June 20*2	55,128
Profits retained in Erica's business	543
Plus Profits taken out of the business (drawings)	15,750
Total profits generated by the business	16,293

These details are an important source of information so they are usually incorporated into the balance sheet and from now on we shall include them in any balance sheet that is prepared.

The way that the information is presented on the balance sheet is as follows:

	£	
Opening capital	55,128	[The worth of the business at the start of the year]
Add Profit	16,293	[The increase in worth over the year]
	71,421	
Less Drawings	15,750	[The decrease in worth during the year because of drawings of profits]
Closing capital	55,671	[The worth of the business at the end of the year]

Talk yourself through this new layout. It should make sense!

O EXAMINATION TIP

If an examination question asks you to **calculate** net profit, use the net asset method because it is much quicker (you will probably have insufficient information to use any other method).

If the question asks you to prepare a trading and profit and loss account then that is precisely what the answer must show!

WORKED EXAMPLE

Drew has been trading as a florist for some years. The information in the table relates to his financial year-end as at 31 August 20*3.

The stock as at 31 August 20*3 has been valued at £210.

Required Prepare the trading and profit and loss account for the year ended 31 August 20*3 and a balance sheet as at that date.

	£
Purchases	58,400
Sales	97,260
Stock as at 1 September 20*2	230
General expenses	4,260
Rent and rates	5,500
Light and heat	2,300
Stationery and wrapping materials	8,700
Fixtures and fittings at cost	3,400
Van at cost	7,500
Debtors	85
Creditors	432
Drawings	13,200
Cash in hand	87
Balance at bank	990
Capital	6,960

WORKED EXAMPLE *continued*

Answer

Drew
Trading and profit and loss account for the year ended 31 August 20*3

	£		£
Stock as at 1 September 20*2	230	Sales	97,260
Purchases	58,400		
	58,630		
Less Stock as at 31 August 20*3	210		
Cost of goods sold	58,420		
Gross profit	38,840		
	97,260		97,260
General expenses	4,260	Gross profit	38,840
Rent and rates	5,500		
Light and heat	2,300		
Stationery and wrapping materials	8,700		
Net profit	18,080		
	38,840		38,840

Balance sheet as at 31 August 20*3

Fixed assets				Capital as at 1 September 20*2	6,960
Fixtures and fittings at cost		3,400		*Add* Profit	18,080
Van at cost		7,500			25,040
		10,900		*Less* Drawings	13,200
Current assets					11,840
Stock	210				
Debtors	85			**Current liabilities**	
Balance at bank	990			Creditors	432
Cash in hand	87	1,372			
		12,272			12,272

Chapter summary

- Final accounts comprise the trading account; the profit and loss account; and the balance sheet.
- They are interconnected. Gross profit is transferred from the trading account to the profit and loss account. The net profit is transferred from the profit and loss account to the balance sheet.

Self-test questions

- Identify the three statements that make up the final accounts of a business.
- Which statements are prepared for the year?
- Name the only statement in the final accounts that is prepared for one day of the financial year.
- You have been using a list of figures to prepare final accounts; which stock figure appears in this list?
- Why are assets shown on a balance sheet at cost?
- Define 'drawings'.
- Sales − cost of sales = ?
- Sales − cost of sales − expenses = ?
- Opening capital − closing capital + drawings = ?
- List three items that could be classified as current liabilities.

TEST QUESTIONS

QUESTION 1

Ashley Peacock provides the following information for the year ended 30 June 20*3:

	£
Capital	108,044
Premises at cost	150,000
Machinery at cost	45,000
Motor van at cost	17,500
Stock as at 1 July 20*2	7,854
Debtors	13,563
Creditors	8,734
Bank balance	1,245
Purchases	70,031
Sales	175,672
Wages and general expenses	38,962
Repairs and renewals	7,459
Rent and rates	5,350
Insurance and advertising	5,312
Motor expenses	13,674
Drawings	16,500
Long-term loan	100,000
Stock as at 30 June 20*3	9,004

Required Prepare a trading and profit and loss account for the year ended 30 June 20*3 and a balance sheet as at that date.

QUESTION 2

Frank Sert provides the following information for the year ended 31 March 20*3:

	£
Land and buildings at cost	115,000
Machinery at cost	35,700
Vehicles at cost	52,500
Debtors	7,342
Creditors	6,721

	£
Stock as at 1 April 20*2	3,572
Bank balance	2,775
Drawings	14,000
Purchases	42,782
Sales	121,649
Carriage inwards	541
Wages	34,669
Insurance	1,560
Motor expenses	5,231
Advertising	3,672
General expenses	4,759
Capital	199,305
Stock as at 31 March 20*3	3,885

Required Prepare the trading and profit and loss account for the year ended 31 March 20*3 and a balance sheet as at that date.

QUESTION 3

Leslie Harris provides the following information for the year ended 31 December 20*3:

	£
Machinery at cost	85,750
Vehicles at cost	50,000
Stock as at 1 January 20*3	3,691
Debtors	5,367
Creditors	3,753
Purchases	48,775
Sales	102,367
Carriage inwards	693
Carriage outwards	528
Wages and salaries	28,570
Motor expenses	6,371
Heat and light	2,448
Advertising and insurance	3,691

	£
General expenses	7,999
Drawings	21,700
Bank overdraft	872
Long-term loan	100,000
Capital	58,591
Stock as at 31 December 20*3	4,187

Required Prepare the trading and profit and loss account for the year ended 31 December 20*3 and a balance sheet as at that date.

QUESTION 4

Joan Hornby supplies the following information for the year ended 30 September 20*3:

	£
Stock as at 1 October 20*2	6,500
Purchases	205,985
Sales	450,064
Returns inwards	412
Rent	5,480
Rates	3,420
Insurance	1,740
Light and heat	4,532
Wages	61,439
Motor expenses	5,300
General expenses	5,331
Carriage inwards	461
Carriage outwards	793
Debtors	34,671
Creditors	29,870
Land and buildings at cost	110,000
Plant and machinery at cost	43,500
Vehicles at cost	35,000
Bank balance	3,874
Cash in hand	769
Bank loan (repayable in 2020)	50,000

	£
Drawings	23,760
Capital	82,773
Stock as at 30 September 20*3	7,439

Required Prepare the trading and profit and loss account for the year ended 30 September 20*3 and a balance sheet as at that date.

QUESTION 5

The following information is available for the year ended 31 March 20*3 for Dvatesh Narowal:

	£
Motor vehicles at cost	35,000
Office equipment at cost	18,750
Premises at cost	65,000
Purchases	48,661
Sales	102,453
Returns inwards	743
Returns outwards	911
Carriage inwards	1,539
Carriage outwards	332
Salaries	28,749
Drawings	24,675
Motor expenses	5,673
Advertising	1,350
Insurances	3,764
Heat and light	2,479
Rates	1,245
General expenses	941
Debtors	4,601
Creditors	1,955
Stock as at 1 April 20*2	995
Bank overdraft	351
Long-term bank loan	40,000
Capital	98,827
Stock at 31 March 20*3	1,007

Required Prepare the trading and profit and loss account for the year ended 31 March 20*3 and a balance sheet as at that date.

QUESTION 6

The following information relates to the year ended 28 February 20*3 for Rita Shah:

	£
Sales	438,965
Purchases	117,671
Carriage inwards	563
Returns inwards	631
Carriage outwards	793
Returns outwards	1,451
Drawings	24,700
Wages and salaries	74,378
Rent, rates and insurance	8,765
Advertising and stationery	4,611
Motor expenses	11,453
General expenses	4,358
Premises at cost	91,000
Machinery at cost	42,000
Office equipment at cost	14,650
Motor vehicles at cost	47,000
Debtors	2,865
Creditors	3,428
Stock as at 1 March 20*2	8,531
Bank balance	4,662
Capital	14,787
Stock at 28 February 20*3	8,002

Required Prepare the trading and profit and loss account for the year ended 28 February 20*3.

CHAPTER SIX

Double-entry Book-keeping

In the previous chapters you were presented with figures. Some of these figures were used to prepare balance sheets; some were used to prepare trading accounts that showed the gross profit; some figures were used to prepare profit and loss accounts so that the net profit of a business could be determined.

In the 'real world' these figures will be derived from the transactions undertaken by a business on a daily basis. There are two main ways in which businesses record their financial transactions. They use either

- a double-entry book-keeping system; or
- a single-entry book-keeping system.

This chapter looks at the double-entry system that provides the accountant with the information needed in order to provide the data required to prepare the final accounts.

As the name implies, double-entry book-keeping recognises that there are two sides or aspects to every business transaction.

I fill my car with £20 diesel. The two aspects of this transaction are:

- I receive the diesel
- the filling station gives me the diesel.

I buy a pair of trainers costing £53:

- I receive the trainers
- the sports shop gives me the trainers.

There are two more aspects to these transactions.

When I give the filling station attendant my £20 note:

- she receives the cash
- I give the cash.

When I give the shop assistant my £53:

- he receives the cash
- I give the cash.

This way of recording both sides of any transaction is known as the **dual aspect** principle of accounting.

> An **account** contains the detailed record of financial transactions undertaken by a business.

All financial transactions involving the business are recorded in a format called an **account**.

You would find each account on a separate page in the ledger. In fact, if a great many transactions of a similar nature were undertaken, an account may spread over several pages.

> The **ledger** is the book where all accounts are kept.

For convenience's sake, this one book is divided into several smaller books. You can imagine that large businesses like Marks and Spencer or McDonald's could not possibly keep all their financial records in one book.

Initially, to make our task a little simpler, we shall keep all our records together. Later, the other

Specification coverage:
AQA 10.1;
OCR 5.1.1.

By the end of this chapter you should be able to:
- use double-entry book-keeping to record financial transactions
- enter financial transactions into the ledger
- understand the purpose of the ledger
- understand and use debit and credit entries
- understand why the ledger is divided into three parts.

books will be introduced and you will see that it does make sense to split the ledger into several different parts.

Don't worry if all this seems a little strange. You will soon get the hang of it but it does require practice. The key to success in accounting is practice.

An account looks like this:

Each account has two sides:

- the **left** side is known as the **debit** side
- the **right** side is known as the **credit** side.

An account	
DEBIT	CREDIT
The **debit** side of an account is always the **receiving** side or the side that shows **gains in value**. 'Debit' is often abbreviated to 'Dr'.	The **credit** side of an account is always the **giving** or **losing** side or the side that shows **value given**. 'Credit' is often abbreviated to 'Cr'.

Dr	An account	Cr
	RECEIVES or GAINS	GIVES or LOSES

An account in the ledger would be headed thus:

Dr	******* account	Cr

Note that there should always be a heading; if the account shown is not a personal account, the heading should include the word 'account'.

> **Purchases** are any items that are purchased with the intention of selling them to customers. They are revenue **expenditure**.

> **Sales** are any items that are sold in the normal course of business to customers. They are revenue **income**.

The golden rule of the game of 'double entry' is that every time you enter something on the debit side (left side) of an account, you must enter an equivalent amount on the credit side (right side) of another account.

'Fairly straightforward', I hear you say, **but** it does require practice.

WORKED EXAMPLE

Barbara owns a butchery business.

During one week, the following financial transactions take place:

1   She purchases meat £210 from Scragg and Co. She will pay for the meat in a couple of weeks.
2   Barbara's cash sales for the week amount to £742.
3   Barbara supplies meat to the Grand Hotel £217. It will pay for the meat at the month end.
4   Barbara pays her shop rent £75.
5   She pays her telephone bill £43.

Required Enter the transactions in Barbara's ledger.

Answer

1   Barbara receives meat ... and Scragg and Co. 'loses' meat:

Dr	Purchases account	Cr		Dr	Scragg and Co.	Cr
	210					210

2   Barbara 'loses' (sells) meat ... and she gains cash:

Dr	Sales account	Cr		Dr	Cash account	Cr
		742		742		

3   Barbara 'loses' meat ... the Grand Hotel gains meat:

Dr	Sales account	Cr		Dr	Grand Hotel	Cr
		217		217		

4   Barbara gains the use of her premises ... and she 'loses' (pays) cash:

Dr	Rent account	Cr		Dr	Cash account	Cr
	75					75

This is a tricky entry because we are used to talking about 'paying rent'.

Barbara does not pay rent – she pays money to a landlord for the use of his building.

Barbara receives/gains the use of the premises.

In cases like this, think of the cash entry first, then put in the second entry.

5   Barbara gains the use of her telephone ... and she loses cash:

Dr	Telephone account	Cr		Dr	Cash account	Cr
	43					43

Another tricky entry.

QUESTION 1

Trevor Smith owns and runs a general store. The following transactions took place last week:

1   Trevor's cash sales for the week amount to £1,634.
2   He pays wages for the week £899 in cash.
3   Trevor takes £180 cash from the business for his own private use.
4   He pays £328 cash for servicing his delivery van.
5   Trevor sells meat, rolls etc. £65 to the local squash club for a function; the treasurer will pay Trevor next week.

Required   Enter the transactions in Trevor Smith's ledger.

If there are a number of transactions that need to be recorded in the same account, we do just that. We enter them all in that one account.

> # WORKED EXAMPLE
>
> Greta Teer owns and runs a newsagent's. The following transactions took place over the past few days:
>
> 1   Cash sales of newspapers amounted to £68.
> 2   Cash sales of chocolate and sweets amounted to £151.
> 3   Greta purchased sweets, chocolates, crisps and soft drinks £135 from her wholesaler.
> 4   She paid £160 for rates.
> 5   Greta sold four boxes of crisps for cash £30 to St Agnes youth club.
>
> Required   Enter the transactions in Greta's ledger.
>
> Answer
>
> | Dr | Sales account | Cr |
> |----|---------------|-----|
> | | | 68 |
> | | | 151 |
> | | | 30 |
>
> | Dr | Cash account | Cr |
> |----|--------------|-----|
> | 68 | | 135 |
> | 151 | | 160 |
> | 30 | | |
>
> | Dr | Purchases account | Cr |
> |----|-------------------|-----|
> | 135 | | |
>
> | Dr | Rates account | Cr |
> |----|---------------|-----|
> | 160 | | |
>
> Note that all the transactions involving cash have been entered in one cash account. All the sales transactions have also been entered in one account

QUESTION 2

Ben Chan owns and runs a Chinese take-away. The following transactions are for his business:

1 Ben pays wages £312.
2 Cash sales amount to £321.
3 Ben pays cash for rent £200.
4 Ben pays £62 cash for rice, potatoes and meat.
5 Ben withdraws cash £250 for holiday spending money.

Required Enter the transactions in Ben's ledger.

It should be obvious that as well as keeping money in the business till, businesses will bank money and will pay many bills by means of cheques.

So, as well as having a cash account in the ledger, the business would also keep a bank account too.

WORKED EXAMPLE

Sven Drax owns and runs a hotel. He supplies the following information:

1 Sven purchases a deep freeze £415, paying by cheque.
2 He purchases for cash £127 fruit and vegetables for the hotel restaurant.
3 Sven purchases petrol £45 cash for the hotel mini-bus.
4 He pays for a family holiday £1,500, using a business cheque.
5 He pays £2,178 cash takings into the bank account.

Required Enter the transactions into the hotel ledger.

Answer

Dr	Deep freeze account	Cr		Dr	Bank account	Cr
415				2,178		415
						1,500

Dr	Purchases account	Cr		Dr	Cash account	Cr
127						127
						45

Dr	Motor expenses account	Cr		Dr	Drawings account	Cr
45				1,500		

Dr	Takings (or sales) account	Cr
		2,178

Note: The deep freeze is not a purchase – it is capital expenditure. There was not already an account . . . so . . .

when in doubt, open an account.

The cheque paid out to the holiday company is drawings – it is not a business expense.

QUESTION 3

Gladys Voisin owns a shop selling games, DVDs, CDs and videos. The following transactions have just taken place:

1 Gladys purchases games from her wholesaler £350, paying by cheque.
2 She banks a day's takings £671.
3 Gladys pays her shop insurance £478 by cheque.
4 She sells an old display unit for £15 cash.
5 Gladys purchases a DVD player for use in the shop £345, paying by cheque.

Required Enter the transactions in Gladys's ledger.

> **Credit customers** are people (or businesses) that we sell goods to; they will pay for their goods at some time in the future. The are goods sold on **credit**.
> Until credit customers pay for the goods they have purchased, they will be **debtors**.

> **Credit suppliers** are people (or businesses) that we purchase goods from; we will settle the debt that we owe at some future date. The goods are purchased on **credit**.
> Until we pay for the goods that we have purchased, the credit suppliers will be **creditors**.

All accounts are entered in one book called the ledger.

Because the number of accounts could run into many hundreds, it is obviously more convenient to split the ledger into a number of different books.

Can you think of how you might split the ledger to make it more manageable?

What we do is to put:

■ all credit customers' accounts together
■ all credit suppliers' accounts together and
■ all other accounts in another ledger.

■ All transactions involving **credit customers** will be found in the **sales ledger** (also known as the debtors' ledger).
■ All transactions with **credit suppliers** will be found in the **purchases ledger** (also known as the creditors' ledger).
■ All **other** transactions will be found in the **general ledger**. (For those of you who may be computer experts, the general ledger is often called the 'nominal ledger' on computer programs.)

Initially, you will make mistakes when asked which accounts would appear in which ledger; don't worry about this – we have all made similar mistakes in the past.

The tricky ones are:

■ the sales account, which is **not**, I repeat, **not** found in the sales ledger. The sales ledger is reserved for the accounts of our credit customers. The sales account would be found in the general ledger.
■ the purchases account will not be found in the purchases ledger. The purchase ledger is reserved for the accounts of credit suppliers only. The purchases account would be found in the general ledger.
■ We only record credit transactions in sales ledger and purchases ledger.

If a sale is made for cash, it is not entered in the sales ledger.

If something is purchased for cash, it is not entered in the purchases ledger.

These transactions appear in the general ledger.

WORKED EXAMPLE

Jill purchases goods for resale £73; she pays cash.

She sells goods £19 for cash.

Required List the two entries for each transaction that are required in Jill's ledger.

Answer

Debits	Credits
Purchases	Cash
Cash	Sales

When you go to a take-away and you order your meal, the proprietor does not open an account for you; he simply takes your money and gives you your meal.

- He debits – cash (the sale of your meal would be included in his total sales for the day).
- He credits – sales (using the same total sales figure for the day).

The splitting of the ledger makes sense. It is sensible that you keep your CDs separate from your socks. You keep your bike parts separate from your jeans etc. (Well, most people seem to.)

Ledger accounts may be classified under the following headings:

- **Personal** – these are accounts that record transactions with credit customers and credit suppliers.
- **Nominal** accounts, **real** accounts and **liability** accounts will all be found in the general ledger.
- **Nominal** accounts record expenses, profits, losses and gains.
- **Real** accounts record the acquisition and disposal of fixed assets like land, buildings, equipment and vehicles.
- **Liability** accounts record the acquisition and repayment of loans and overdrafts.

Remember that each account would be in a different ledger, according to the classification we have discussed.

Each account would be shown on a separate page in the ledger.

There is not enough space in this book to afford such a luxury. We will write the accounts on the same page.

QUESTION 4

In which ledger would you expect to find the following accounts? Tick the appropriate box.

Account name	Purchases ledger	Sales ledger	General ledger
Tamsin; a credit customer		✓	
Frank; a supplier to be paid next month	–		
Returns inwards account			–
Cash sales account			✓
Rent account			–
Bank account			–
Capital account			✓
Credit sales account			✓
Drawings account			✓
Motor expenses account			✓
Purchases account			–

WORKED EXAMPLE

Siobhan Murphy provides the following information for the last few days:

1   Siobhan returns faulty goods £41 to Declan.
2   She purchases a fixed asset £1,450 from Jock on credit.
3   Siobhan sells goods £77 to Fiona who pays by cheque.
4   She purchases goods for resale £510 from Tom on credit.
5   She purchases goods for resale £65 from Joan for cash.

Required Enter the transactions in Siobhan's ledger (indicate in which ledger each account could be found).

Answer

Dr Returns outwards account (GL) Cr		Dr Declan (PL) Cr	
	41	41	

Dr Fixed assets account (GL) Cr		Dr Jock (PL) Cr	
1450			1450

Dr Sales account (GL) Cr		Dr Bank account (GL) Cr	
	77	77	

Dr Purchases account (GL) Cr		Dr Tom (PL) Cr	
510			510
65			

Dr Cash account (GL) Cr	
	65

Note

- That customers' and suppliers' accounts appear in the sales ledger and in the purchases ledger – but only if the transactions are on credit
- The accounts that are not personal accounts are found in the general ledger
- That all debits have a corresponding credit
- That all credits have a corresponding debit.

Those students who have bank accounts will observe that money paid out of the account is entered in the left column (debit) of the bank statement, while moneys received into the account are entered in the right column (credit).

This causes problems for students initially.

After what we have said above, this might seem to be the wrong way round.

So, who is right?

Well, both the bank and I are correct.

You need to remember that the bank statement is written from the bank's point of view, not yours.

More details will be given on this later.

QUESTION 5

In the table, enter the account that should be debited and the account that should be credited.

Transaction	Debit	Credit
Rent paid with cash	Rent account	Cash account
Goods for resale purchased from Knight on credit	P	k...
Cash sales	C	S
Wages paid by cheque	W	B
Purchase of fixed asset by cheque	FA	B
Carriage inward paid with cash	CI	C
Goods for resale purchased from Day, with cash	P	D
Vehicle service paid by cheque	V	B
Drawings of cash	D	C
Purchase of a fixed asset on credit from Lock	FA	Lock
Carriage outward paid by cheque	B	CO

Chapter summary

- All financial transactions are recorded in accounts.
- All accounts are found in the ledger.
- Every debit entry in the ledger must have a corresponding credit entry.
- Every credit entry in the ledger must have a corresponding debit entry.
- The ledger is divided into three parts because it is easier and more convenient to use in this form.
- The purchases ledger contains the accounts of suppliers with credit accounts.
- The sales ledger contains the accounts of customers with credit accounts.
- The general ledger contains nominal, real and liability accounts.

Self-test questions

- Complete the sentence: 'Every . . . needs a corresponding credit'.
- Name the book in which all financial transactions are entered.
- List the three divisions of the book.
- What is the alternative name given to the purchases ledger? What is the alternative name given to the sales ledger?
- Define the term 'account'.
- Explain the meaning of 'personal' accounts.
- Name two 'real' accounts found in the books of account.
- Name two 'nominal' accounts found in the books of account.
- Name two 'liability' accounts.
- Which side of an account is the 'receiving' side?
- Which side of an account is the 'giving' side?

TEST QUESTIONS

QUESTION 6

The following information is given for the business of Derek:

1 Derek purchases goods for resale £48 for cash.
2 He purchases goods for resale £120 from Nita; he pays cash.
3 Derek sells goods to Sadie £11 for cash.
4 He purchases a fixed asset £2,780 for use in the business; he pays cash.
5 Derek sells goods £58 to Doris for cash.

Required Enter the transactions in the ledger accounts.

QUESTION 7

Harriet provides the following information relating to her business:

1 Harriet pays cash wages £349.
2 She sells goods £211 for cash to Albert.
3 Harriet pays her telephone bill £62 with cash.
4 She purchases goods for resale £109 for cash.
5 Harriet draws £210 cash from the business for private use.

Required Enter the transactions in the ledger accounts.

QUESTION 8

The following information relates to the business of Selena, a greengrocer:

1 Selena purchases fruit and vegetables £104 on credit from Docker.
2 She purchases a set of scales £270 on credit from Waites.
3 Selena purchases potatoes £60 for cash from A. Farmer.
4 Her cash sales for the week amounted to £643.
5 Selena sells fruit £58 on credit to the Towers Hotel.

Required Enter the transactions in the ledger accounts.

QUESTION 9

Bhinda owns and runs a garage. The following information relates to her business:

1 Cash petrol sales amount to £1,287.
2 Bhinda purchases a break-down vehicle £42,500 on credit from W. Rekers.
3 She purchases £3,538 worth of petrol on credit from Esso.
4 Bhinda services the car fleet of I. Hurry £1,473; the amount due will be paid next month.
5 Bhinda purchases a new cash register £2,650 from NCR; she pays by cheque.

Required Enter the transaction in the ledger accounts. Indicate the ledger in which the account will be found.

QUESTION 10

Raymond is hairdresser. He provides the following information:

1 Raymond purchases new hairdryers £125 on credit from B. Lowav.
2 He purchases colours and perms £72 from T. Int, paying cash.
3 Raymond purchases cosmetics £212 from B. Lush, paying by cheque.
4 He pays his week's receipts £963 into the business bank account.
5 Raymond pays his business electricity bill £142 by cheque.

Required Enter the transactions in the ledger accounts. Indicate the ledger in which the account will be found.

QUESTION 11

Arnold owns and runs an electrical goods store. He provides the following information:

1 Sales for the week £3,642 paid into the business bank account.
2 Wages paid in cash £784.

3 Arnold repairs plasma screen television in 'Hitters Squash Club' £188. The club will settle the bill next month.
4 Arnold purchases spare parts for repairing electrical goods £340 from Dorak Ltd. on credit.
5 Telephone bill paid by cheque £166.
6 Repairs to Arnold's family car £320 paid with business cheque.
7 Arnold returns faulty parts £24 to Dorak Ltd.

Required Enter the transactions in the ledger accounts. Indicate the ledger in which the account will be found.

QUESTION 12

Celia owns owns and runs a painting and decorating business. The following information relates to the business:

1 Cash receipts for work done amount to £2,653.
2 She purchases paint £157 from B. Rush on credit.
3 Celia pays wages £530 in cash.
4 Celia pays a private telephone bill £79 using business cash.
5 Celia purchases a van £21,750 from Ardale Motors. She will pay for the van next month.
6 She purchases fuel for her van £32; she pays cash.
7 Celia returns paint £18 to B. Rush.

Required Enter the transactions in the ledger accounts. Indicate the ledger in which the account will be found.

QUESTION 13

Bupesh owns and runs a supermarket. The following business transactions have taken place:

1 Bupesh purchases goods for resale £457 from John, paying cash.
2 His cash sales amount to £759.
3 Bupesh purchases goods £265 from Noel on credit.
4 Bupesh reeives a cheque £395 for goods sold to Jacqui.
5 He sells goods £511 to Daser Ltd on credit.
6 Bupesh returns faulty goods £43 to Noel.
7 He pays wages £421 by cheque.
8 Daser Ltd returns goods £165.

Required Enter the transactions in the ledger accounts. Indicate the ledger in which the account will be found.

SEVEN

Books of Prime Entry

The **books of prime entry** are also known as **books of original entry** and **subsidiary books**. These terms are interchangeable.

- The books of prime entry are used as a convenient way of entering transactions into the double-entry system.
- It is less efficient to make entries as they arise. It is too time consuming and that means it is generally more costly.
- It is better to collect the entries and categorise them into bundles of similar types and then to post from these books in bulk.

When a person is washing up, they don't wash one plate, then dry it, then put it away then come back, wash another plate, dry it and put it away, then wash a fork, dry it and put it away – I am sure that you can see where this is going.

It is much better to wash everything in one go, to dry everything in one go, separate the washing-up into plates, cups, knives and forks and then put them away.

Similarly, when repairing the car; a person does not go to the garage, get a screwdriver, use it, put it away, come back to the car, see that a spanner is needed, go to the garage and pick a spanner up.

It is more efficient to get all the tools out at once; do the job; and put all the tools away at the end of the job.

Transactions are listed in the subsidiary books.

Each subsidiary book is a list of similar types of transaction. The items are listed in the book of prime entry until it is worthwhile to post the list to the ledger. Some of this sounds very confusing but hopefully, when you have seen how the books work things will become very clear.

All transactions must be entered in one of the books of prime entry before the transaction can be entered in the ledger.

> **Posting** is the term used by accountants for entering transactions into the ledger accounts of the business.

The double-entry system is like a game of football.

In order to be able to watch the game, you must first get into the stadium.

The only way into a football stadium is by presenting a ticket.

You need a ticket (a source document) to gain access to the double-entry game.

One entrance into the stadium is reserved for a player (the cash book). So the cash book can be used to get into the stadium and will also play its part in the game.

Specification coverage:
AQA 10.1;
OCR 5.1.1.

By the end of this chapter you should be able to:
- identify and use the six books of prime entry
- understand how financial transactions are entered in the books of prime entry
- post from the books of prime entry to the ledger.

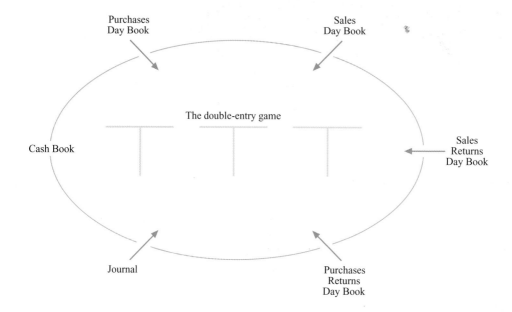

There are six books of prime entry, which will now be discussed.

PURCHASES DAY BOOK

(Also known as the purchases book or the purchases journal.)

When a purchase invoice is received from a supplier of goods showing the goods that have been purchased and the price charged, the details are listed in the purchases day book.

The purchases day book is a list of credit purchases made. The source documents are the purchase invoices received.

When it is convenient (this could be daily, weekly or monthly, depending on the volume of purchases made by the business) the list of purchases is totalled and the total is posted to the debit side of the purchases account in the general ledger because the goods have been received.

Each individual supplier's ledger account in the purchases ledger is credited with the value of goods purchased (showing that the supplier has 'lost' the goods).

SALES DAY BOOK

(Also known as the sales book or the sales journal.)

When good are sold, the supplier sends a sales invoice to the customer. The sales invoice itemises the goods that have been sold and the price of those goods. A copy of this invoice will be retained by the seller.

The copy sales invoice is the source document from which the sales day book is written up.

The sales day book is a list of the copy sales invoices sent to customers.

When it is convenient (this could be daily, weekly or monthly, depending on the volume of sales made by the business) the list is totalled and the total is posted to the credit of the sales account in the general ledger because the goods have been 'lost'.

Each individual customer's ledger account in the sales ledger is debited with the value of goods sold to them (indicating that the customer has received the goods).

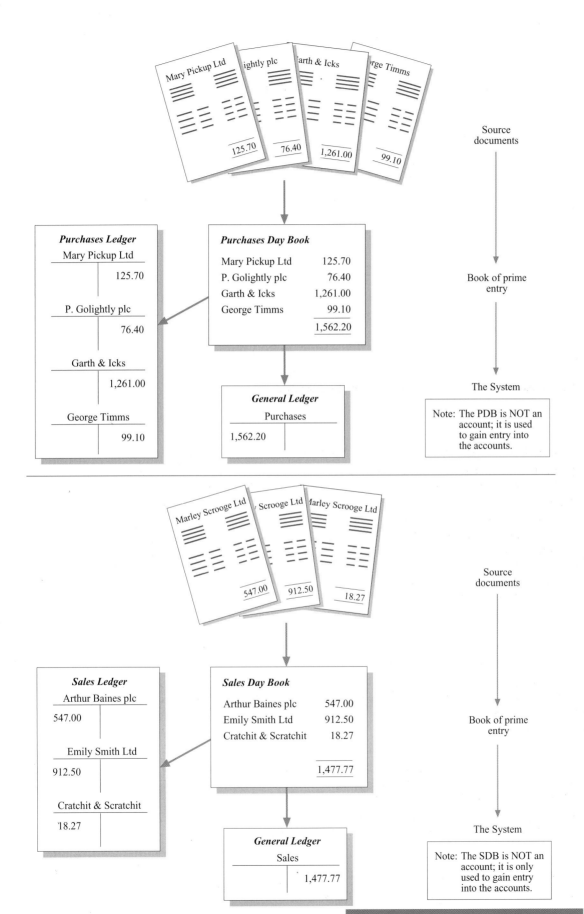

		Source documents
	Purchases Day Book	
	Mary Pickup Ltd	125.70
	P. Golightly plc	76.40
	Garth & Icks	1,261.00
	George Timms	99.10
		1,562.20

Purchases Ledger

Mary Pickup Ltd

125.70

P. Golightly plc

76.40

Garth & Icks

1,261.00

George Timms

99.10

Book of prime entry

General Ledger

Purchases

1,562.20

The System

Note: The PDB is NOT an account; it is used to gain entry into the accounts.

Source documents

Sales Day Book

Arthur Baines plc   547.00
Emily Smith Ltd   912.50
Cratchit & Scratchit   18.27

1,477.77

Sales Ledger

Arthur Baines plc

547.00

Emily Smith Ltd

912.50

Cratchit & Scratchit

18.27

Book of prime entry

General Ledger

Sales

1,477.77

The System

Note: The SDB is NOT an account; it is only used to gain entry into the accounts.

SALES RETURNS DAY BOOK

(Also known as the sales returns book or sales returns journal.)

Sales that are not acceptable are returned by the customer and a credit note is sent.

A copy of the credit note will be retained and this is the source document from which the sales returns day book is written up.

When convenient the list is added and the total is posted to the debit of the sales returns account (the goods have been received). The sales returns account is sometimes known as the returns inward account.

Each individual entry in the sales returns day book is posted to the credit of the customer who returned the goods (they have 'lost' the goods).

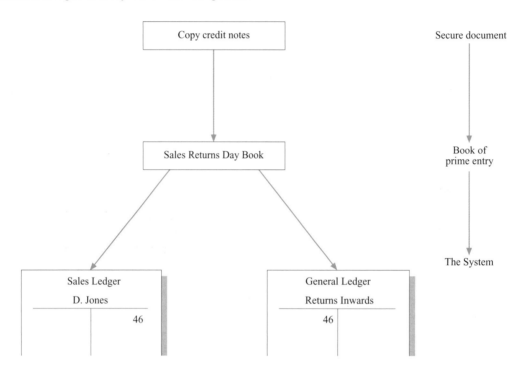

PURCHASES RETURNS DAY BOOK

(Also known as the purchases returns book or purchases returns journal.)

Sometimes, goods that have been purchased turn out to be faulty, the wrong colour, the wrong size or not useful in some other way. These goods will be returned to the supplier. The supplier in due course will send a credit note.

The credit notes are the source documents from which the purchases returns day book is written up.

The purchases returns day book is a list of all the credit notes received from suppliers. When it is convenient, the list is added and the total is posted to the credit of the purchases returns account sometimes known as the returns outwards account (the returns have been 'lost').

Each individual entry in the purchases returns day book is then posted to the debit of the respective suppliers account in the purchases ledger (the suppliers receive the goods).

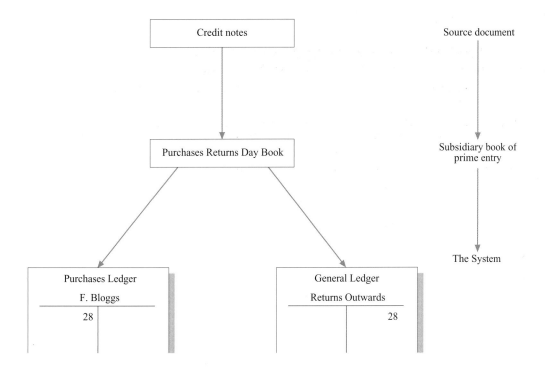

JOURNAL

(Also known as the journal proper.)

This book often gives students a hard time. Don't worry: its uses are very limited and it is not as difficult as we often assume when we first come into contact with it.

It is very useful as a revision aid.

Its use is also a popular examination topic favoured by examiners at all levels in accounting.

The journal is used when we cannot comfortably find another book of prime entry to use.

Its layout is different from the day books described above.

<table>
<tr><th colspan="5">JOURNAL</th></tr>
<tr><th>Date</th><th>Particulars</th><th>Folio</th><th>Debit</th><th>Credit</th></tr>
<tr><td>The date of the entries</td><td>The account to be debited

The account to be credited</td><td>Ledger and page</td><td>Amount to be debited</td><td>
Amount to be credited</td></tr>
<tr><td colspan="5">A description of why the transaction was necessary. Referred to as the 'narrative'.</td></tr>
</table>

EXAMPLE

Note that in examination questions the 'folio' columns are often omitted.

The journal has six uses:

1. When fixed assets are purchased on a credit basis.
2. When fixed assets are sold on credit.
3. When a business first comes into existence.
4. When a business finally closes.
5. For the correction of errors.
6. For recording inter-ledger transfers.

The source documents used to write up the journal would include:

- purchase invoices for capital expenditure
- sales invoices for sales of capital items.

Other source documents will be encountered as we progress with our studies.

WORKED EXAMPLE OF USE 1

On 23 April 20*3 Tina purchased machine xtr/397 £12,600 for use in her factory from Dextel Ltd. on credit.

Required The entry in Tina's journal to record the transaction.

Answer

Date	Particulars	Folio	Dr £	Cr £
23 April	Machinery	GL23*	12,600	
	Dextel Ltd	PL26		12,600

Purchase of machine xtr/ 397 on credit from Dextel Ltd.

*Page numbers in the ledgers are for illustrative purposes.

WORKED EXAMPLE OF USE 2

On 6 September 20*3 Hussain sold vehicle P341 FTX to Greg's Garage for £230. Greg will settle the debt on 31 October 20*3.

Required The entry in Hussain's journal to record the transaction.

Answer

Date	Particulars	Folio	Debit £	Credit £
6 September	Greg's Garage	SL42	230	
	Vehicles	GL11		230

Sale of vehicle P341 FTX to Greg's Garage.

WORKED EXAMPLE OF USE 3

Marlene started in business on 1 January 20*3 by paying £14,000 into her business bank account.

Required The entry in Marlene's journal to record the transaction.

Answer

Date	Particulars	Folio	Debit £	Credit £
1 January	Bank	GL1	14,000	
	Capital	GL2		14,000
Capital introduced by Marlene				

The other three uses will be dealt with later.

◯ EXAMINATION TIP

If you find it difficult to prepare journal entries, try drawing up 'T' accounts as you did in Chapter 6. Then, from the accounts, draw up the journal.

Really, the journal should be done first as it is the book of prime entry,

WORKED EXAMPLE

On 2 August Jared purchases, on credit, a new lathe for his business (£5,400) from Factre Ltd.

Required The entries in Jared's journal to record the transaction.

Answer

Imagine that you were unsure how to tackle this question. Draw up the 'T' accounts.

Jared gains a lathe   Factre Ltd 'loses' the lathe

Dr	Lathe	Cr	Dr	Factre Ltd	Cr
5,400					5,400

Which account has been debited? Which account has been credited?

If you can do this, then you can draw up the journal:

Date	Particulars	Folio	Debit £	Credit £
2 August	Machinery	GL19	5,400	
	Factre Ltd	PL 41		5,400
Purchase of new JY/317 lathe from Factre Ltd.				

The final book of prime entry is the cash book.

CASH BOOK

This book will be dealt with in more detail in Chapter 11.

It is sufficient to say at this stage that any cash (or bank) transactions will be entered in the cash book.

The five other books of prime entry deal with credit transactions only.

The cash book is not only part of our double-entry system; it is also a book of prime entry.

The source documents used to write up the cash book would include:

■ cheque book counterfoils
■ receipts received from suppliers who have dealt in cash
■ copy receipts given to customers
■ cash register till rolls.

Other source documents used to write up the cash book will be encountered later.

Chapter summary

- All transactions must be entered into a book of prime entry before they can be entered in the double-entry system.
- There are six books of prime entry.
- Five deal with credit transactions:
  - purchases day book
  - sales day book
  - purchases returns day book
  - sales returns day book
  - journal.
- The five are lists from which ledger entries are compiled.
- The cash book deals with all cash and bank transactions.

Self-test questions

■ Give another name for the sales book.
■ Give another name for the journal.
■ Name the source document used to prepare the purchases day book
■ Name the source document used to prepare the sales returns day book.
■ Which two ledger accounts are prepared from entries in the sales day book?
■ Which two accounts are prepared from entries in the purchases returns day book?
■ Give another name for returns inward.
■ Give another name for returns outward.
■ Which book of prime entry is also part of the double-entry system?
■ Name one use for the journal.

TEST QUESTIONS

QUESTION 1

The purchase day book for Ghito is shown:

Purchases day book

	£
Andrew	460
Zara	34
Kijah	593
Peter	742
	1,829

Required Prepare the ledger accounts from the entries in the purchases day book.

QUESTION 2

The purchases day book of Reg is given:

Purchases day book

	£
Collins	599
O'Malley	43
Otis	777
Bradley	75
	1,494

Required Prepare the ledger accounts from the entries in the purchases day book.

QUESTION 3

Bertrand receives the following purchase invoices:

Invoice no.	Supplier's name	Amount of invoice £
1	Froot	213
2	Acme	54
3	Dixon	730
4	Gold	107

Required Prepare the day book and post the entries to the ledger accounts. Indicate the ledger used.

QUESTION 4

Charlotte receives the following purchase invoices:

Invoice no.	Supplier's name	Amount of invoice £
5	Garewal	513
6	Shaddon	78
7	Schmidt	920
8	Brax	703

Required Prepare the day book and post the entries to the ledger accounts. Indicate the ledgers used.

QUESTION 5

The sales day book for Rab is given:

Sales day book

	£
Parker	439
Clive	51
Gray	882
Fitton	29
	1,401

Required Prepare the ledger accounts from the entries in the sales day book.

QUESTION 6

The sales day book for Mandy is given:

Sales day book

	£
Sacks	510
Baggs	409
Perce	67
Walls	111
	1,097

Required Prepare the ledger accounts from the entries in the sales day book.

QUESTION 7

Keith has the following copy sales invoices:

Sales invoice no.	Customer name	Amount of invoice £
34	Rowan	91
35	Ash	631
36	Holly	76
37	Berry	522

Required Prepare the day book and post the entries to the ledger accounts. Indicate the ledgers used.

QUESTION 8

Alice has the following copy sales invoices:

Sales invoice no.	Customer name	Amount of invoice £
175	Russell	9
176	Cavendish	1,563
177	O'Toole	57
178	Green	63

Required Prepare the day book and post the entries to the ledger accounts. Indicate the ledgers used.

QUESTION 9

The following purchases returns day book for Gwen is given:

Purchases returns day book

	£
Samson	23
Tardy	54
Suchard	14
	91

Required Prepare the ledger accounts from the purchases returns day book. Indicate the ledgers used.

QUESTION 10

The following purchases returns day book for Jane is given:

Purchases returns day book

	£
Felix	34
Catt	12
Gnort	134
	180

Required Prepare the ledger accounts from the purchases returns day book. Indicate the ledgers used.

QUESTION 11

The following sales returns day book for Harold is given:

Sales returns day book

	£
Randall	38
Hamilton	15
Frame	103
	156

Required Prepare the ledger accounts from the sales returns day book. Indicate the ledgers used.

QUESTION 12

The following sales returns day book for Anders is given:

Sales returns day book

	£
Snood	46
Dores	17
Voisin	39
	102

Required Prepare the ledger accounts from the sales returns day book. Indicate the ledgers used.

QUESTION 13

On 15 June Grant purchased a delivery van £35,000 on credit from Fogg's Garage.

Required Prepare the journal entries to record this transaction.

Remember, a narrative is always used.

QUESTION 14

On 7 November Phillipa purchased a deep freeze for her shop £1,200 from Icecold Ltd. She will pay for the deep freeze at the end of December.

Required Prepare the journal entries to record this transaction.

QUESTION 15

On 6 January Branch sold a machine for £200 to Tippers Ltd. Tippers will settle the debt at the end of January.

Required Prepare the journal entries to record this transaction.

QUESTION 16

On 29 April Briggs, a welder, sold an electric generator for £300 on credit to Cox.

Required Prepare the journal entries to record this transaction.

QUESTION 17

Complete the table by stating, for each transaction, the book of prime entry to be used; the account to be debited; and the account to be credited.

The first row has been completed for you.

Transaction	Book of prime entry	Account debited	Account credited
Goods sold on credit	Sales day book	Customer	Sales
Fixed asset sold for cash			
Goods for resale purchased on credit			
Cash sales			
Purchase of goods for resale paid cash			
Cheques received from customers			
Money withdrawn for personal use			
Insurance premium paid with cash			
Fixed asset sold, payment to be received next month			
Wages paid by cash			

QUESTION 18

Complete the table by stating, for each transaction, the book of prime entry to be used; the account to be debited; and the account to be credited.

Transaction	Book of prime entry	Account debited	Account credited
Electricity bill paid by cheque			
Fixed asset sold on credit			
Purchases made on credit			
Receipts paid into bank			
Credit sale of goods			
Fixed assets purchased on credit			
Goods returned to supplier			
Fixed asset sold for cash			
Goods returned from customer			
Purchases paid for with cash			

QUESTION 19

Identify the book of prime entry to be written up from the following source documents:

- invoice received for purchase of goods for resale
- cash register till roll

- copy credit note set to customer
- invoice received for purchase of new warehouse.

QUESTION 20

Identify the book of prime entry to be written up from the following source documents:

- copy sales invoice
- receipt for cash sale of old delivery van
- credit note received from supplier
- cheque book counterfoil
- cash receipt for purchase of goods for resale.

CHAPTER
EIGHT

Value Added Tax

Value added tax (VAT) is described in SSAP 5 as 'tax on the supply of goods and services which is eventually borne by the final consumer but collected at each stage of the production and distribution chain'.

Specification coverage:
AQA 10.2;
OCR 5.1.1.

By the end of this chapter you should be able to:
■ calculate VAT on invoices and credit notes
■ post from the books of prime entry to the ledger accounts
■ calculate VAT
■ calculate VAT when cash discount is included.

A trader acts as a collector of VAT and so the tax should not be included in any of the incomes or expenditures of the business. It must be recorded separately from the transactions that affect the business.

At the moment, VAT is levied on most goods and services at 17.5%. This is the VAT rate that will be used in all examples in this chapter.

When a trader purchases goods or a service from a supplier to the value of £100 he will actually receive an invoice for £117.50. The invoice will be itemised as follows:

	£	
	100.00	for the goods, and
	17.50	for the VAT charged on those goods by the supplier
The invoice total is	117.50	

When a trader sells goods or a service to a customer to the value of £200, the trader will send his customer a sales invoice for £235. This invoice will show the following details:

	£	
	200.00	for the goods, and
	35.00	for the VAT charged to the customer
The invoice total is	235.00	

If we need to calculate the amount of VAT to be added to the value of goods to reach the final invoice total, we use the formula:

FORMULA

Value of goods $\times \dfrac{17.5}{100}$ = VAT to be added to the value of the goods.

An alternative formula is:

Value of goods $\times$ 0.175 = VAT to be added to the value of the goods.

📌 REVISION TIP

Have a go at using both of these methods. Choose the method you feel most comfortable with and **use it always**. Do not use one version one day and the other version the following day. If you do this you will get the two versions mixed up and get your calculation wrong.

WORKED EXAMPLE

A trader sells goods with a value of £349.

Required Calculate the amount of VAT that should be added to the goods to arrive at the invoice total.

Answer
£61.08

Workings

$$£349 \times \frac{17.5}{100} = £61.08 \quad \text{(or £349} \times 0.175\text{)}$$

WORKED EXAMPLE

A trader sells goods with a value of £12,562.

Required Calculate the amount of VAT that should be added to the goods to arrive at the invoice total.

Answer
£2,198.35

Workings

$$£12\,562 \times \frac{17.5}{100} = £2198.35 \quad \text{(or £12 562} \times 0.175\text{)}$$

QUESTION 1

The following information is given:

- sales of £276
- sales of £871
- sales of £670
- sales of £197
- sales of £395.

Required Calculate the VAT to be charged on each of the sales.

QUESTION 2

The following sales have been made:

- sales of £239
- sales of £2,876
- sales of £23
- sales of £464
- sales of £57.

Required Calculate the amount of VAT to be charged on each of the sales.

If the total amount of an invoice (including VAT at 17.5%) is known, the amount of VAT added to the value of the goods can be found by using the formula:

FORMULA

$$\frac{17.5}{117.5} \times \text{Total invoice price} = \text{VAT added to the invoice}$$

$$\text{or } \frac{7}{47} \times \text{Total invoice price} = \text{VAT added to the invoice}$$

WORKED EXAMPLE

A trader receives an invoice totalling £300.80.

Required Calculate the amount of VAT (at 17.5%) included in the invoice.

Answer   £44.80

Workings
$\frac{17.5}{117.5} \times £300.80 = £44.80$ or $\frac{7}{47} \times £300.80 = £44.80$

WORKED EXAMPLE

An invoice totalling £3,839 including VAT is received.

Required Calculate the amount of VAT included in the invoice total.

Answer   £571.77

Workings
$\frac{17.5}{117.5} \times £3,839 = £571.77$ or $\frac{7}{47} \times £3,839 = £571.77$

QUESTION 3

Three purchase invoices are received from suppliers:

- purchase invoice 1 totals £4,298
- purchase invoice 2 totals £49
- purchase invoice 3 totals £12,786.

Required Calculate the amount of VAT included in the total of each purchase invoice.

QUESTION 4

Four sales invoices are sent to credit customers:

- sales invoice 1 totals £23
- sales invoice 2 totals £13,650
- sales invoice 3 totals £719
- sales invoice 4 totals £1,844.

Required Calculate the amount of VAT included in the total of each sales invoice.

If the VAT is known, we can calculate the value of the goods by deducting the VAT from the total of the invoice. Using the examples from above:

- If the VAT included in the invoice total of £300.80 is £44.80 then the goods must have a value of £256 (£300.80 − £44.80).
- The invoice totaling £3,839 includes VAT of £571.77 so the goods must have a value of £3,267.23 (£3,839 − £571.77).

QUESTION 5

The following purchase invoice totals include VAT at 17.5%:

- purchase invoice 4 totals £3,016.23
- purchase invoice 5 totals £77.32
- purchase invoice 6 totals £42,602.68
- purchase invoice 7 totals £8.11
- purchase invoice 8 totals £383.56.

Required (a) Calculate the amount of VAT included in each total.

(b) Calculate the value of the goods purchased that has been included on the invoice.

QUESTION 6

The following sales invoice totals include VAT at 17.5%:

- sales invoice 5 totals £1,599.64
- sales invoice 6 totals £270.25
- sales invoice 7 totals £484.92
- sales invoice 8 totals £763.75
- sales invoice 9 totals £106.50.

Required (a) Calculate the amount of VAT included in each total.

(b) Calculate the value of the goods sold that has been included on the invoice.

RECORDING VAT ON PURCHASES IN THE PURCHASES DAY BOOK AND IN THE LEDGERS

We have already seen that the purchases day book is simply a list of the purchases made by a business.

It is used as the prime entry (first entry) before entering the information into the double-entry system.

The purchases day book is written up from the purchase invoices received from the supplier. These invoices will show the value of the goods purchased plus the VAT that the supplier charges (and will collect) on behalf of Her Majesty's Customs and Excise.

We need to include an extra column in the purchase day book to record the VAT charged by the supplier.

WORKED EXAMPLE

Gabriel Angelo received the following purchase invoices from his suppliers during the week 6–13 April 20*3:

Date		Net value £	VAT £	Invoice total £
6 April	A. Barton	170.64	29.86	200.50
8 April	C. Dixon	87.43	15.30	102.73
10 April	E. Frear	98.26	17.20	115.46
13 April	G. Hamal	128.90	22.56	151.46

Required Prepare the purchases day book for the period 6–13 April.

Answer

Purchases Day Book (page 26*)

Date	Particulars	Invoice no.*	Purchases	VAT	Total
6 April	A. Barton	382/46	170.64	29.86	200.50
8 April	C. Dixon	19684	87.43	15.30	102.73
10 April	E. Frear	bh/341	98.26	17.20	115.46
13 April	G. Hamal	341	128.90	22.56	151.46
			485.23	84.92	570.15

* given for illustrative purposes

As we saw earlier, the day books are used **before** we post the information to the ledgers.

The same is true with the day books that also show VAT.

Each individual entry in the day book is entered in the purchase ledger.

Instead of having only one list showing purchases, we now have three lists, showing totals for:

- purchases
- VAT and
- the whole invoice.

- The total of the purchases column is posted to the debit of the purchases account.
- The total of the VAT column is posted to the debit of the VAT account.
- The total of the total column will be used when control accounts are prepared (Chapter 15).

WORKED EXAMPLE

Use the information for Gabriel Angelo above.

Required Using the purchases day book shown above, record the entries in:

(a) the purchases ledger
(b) the general ledger.

Answer
(a)

Purchases Ledger

Dr	A. Barton			Cr
	6 April Purchases	PDB 26	200.50

Dr	C. Dixon			Cr
	8 April Purchases	PDB 26	102.73

Dr	E. Frear			Cr
	10 April Purchases	PDB 26	115.46

Dr	G. Hamal			Cr
	13 April Purchases	PDB 26	151.46

General Ledger

Dr	Purchases account			Cr
13 April Sundry creditors	PDB 26	485.23		

Dr	VAT account			Cr
13 April Creditors	PDB 26	84.92		

You should be able to see that we have a total of £570.15 on the debit side of the general ledger and £570.15 on the credit side of the purchase ledger.

RECORDING VAT ON PURCHASES RETURNS IN THE PURCHASE RETURNS DAY BOOK AND IN THE LEDGERS

We have seen how to record credit purchases in the ledgers. We now need to consider again how to deal with goods that are returned to the supplier because they are not required. This time, as in real life, there is the problem of VAT.

As previously mentioned, the purchases returns day book is merely a list of goods that have been returned to the supplier. We compile the list from the credit notes that the supplier sends us when he receives the goods.

WORKED EXAMPLE

On 4 May Gabriel Angelo returned, to C. Dixon, goods with a total invoiced price (including VAT) of £5.64. The following day he returned to G. Hamal goods valued at £23.00 (excluding VAT).

Required Prepare the purchases returns day book for Gabriel and post the entries to the general ledger and the purchases ledger

Answer

Purchases returns day book (Page 8)

Date	Particulars	Credit note	Returns	VAT	Total
4 May	C. Dixon	487/bh	4.80	0.84	5.64
5 May	G. Hamal	86745	23.00	4.03	27.03
			27.80	4.87	32.67

Workings

C. Dixon £5.64 $\times \dfrac{17.5}{117.5} = £0.84$ or £5.64 $\times \dfrac{7}{47} = £0.84$

G. Hamal £23.00 $\times \dfrac{17.5}{100} = £4.03$ or £23.00 $\times \dfrac{7}{47} = £4.03$

Purchases ledger

Dr			C. Dixon			Cr
4 May Purchase returns	PRDB 8	5.64	8 April Purchases		PDB 26	102.73

Dr			G. Hamal			Cr
5 May Purchase returns	PRDB 8	27.03	13 April Purchase		PDB 26	151.46

General ledger

Dr			Purchases returns account			Cr
			10 May Sundry creditors	PRDB 8		27.80

Dr			VAT account			Cr
13 April Creditors	PDB 26	84.92	10 May Creditors		PRDB 8	4.87

QUESTION 7

Dorian Chakiris owns a clothing shop.

The following transactions took place in the first week of November. Invoices and credit notes have been received. The details of these are shown as follows:

2 November	Purchased cloth from Datf plc total invoice price (including VAT) £349.03
3 November	Purchased cloth £151.90 (net of VAT) from Halifax Fabrics. Returned one length of cloth to Datf plc £82.40 (including VAT)

6 November   Purchased threads etc from Fred's Threads £26.40 (including VAT)
7 November   Returned faulty threads to Fred's Threads £2.35 (net of VAT)

Required (a) Prepare the purchases day book.
(b) Prepare the purchases returns day book.
(c) Post the entries in both day books to the relevant ledger accounts in the general ledger and the purchases ledger.

RECORDING VAT ON SALES AND SALES RETURNS DAY BOOKS AND IN THE LEDGERS

As we have just seen, a business is charged VAT on its purchases.

When the business sells some of its products, it must charge VAT on its sales.

The calculation involved in calculating the VAT to be charged was explained earlier in the chapter.

WORKED EXAMPLE

Required (a) Calculate the VAT chargeable on sales with a value of:
- £468.32
- £52.78
- £17,641.60.

(b) Calculate the total invoice price on sales with a value of:
- £90.84
- £23,719.00
- £5.68.

Answer
(a) VAT chargeable on sales totalling £468.32 is £81.96.

Workings
£468.32 × $\frac{17.5}{100}$ or £468 × 0.175

VAT chargeable on sales totalling £52.78 is £9.24.

Workings
£52.78 × $\frac{17.5}{100}$ or £52.78 × 0.175

VAT chargeable on sales totalling £17,641.60 is £3,087.28.

(b) The total invoice price on sales with a value of £90.84 is £106.74.

Workings
£90.84 × $\frac{117.5}{100}$ or £90.84 × 1.175

The total invoice price on sales totalling £23,719.00 is £27,869.83.

Workings
£23,719.00 × $\frac{117.5}{100}$ or £23,719.00 × 1.175

The total invoice price on sales of £5.68 is £6.67.

WORKED EXAMPLE

Gabriel Angelo has made the following sales during the week ended 27 April 20*3.

He has not yet included VAT on the total for each invoice.

- 20 April goods sold to M. Thompson £417.00
- 23 April goods sold to A. Hakim Ltd £458.82
- 26 April goods sold to F. Rank £1,674.80
- 27 April goods sold to M. Wong £54.20.

Required (a) Calculate the total of each invoice.
(b) Record the invoices in Gabriel's sales day book.
(c) Make the necessary ledger entries.

Answer

Sales day book

Date	Particulars	Invoice number	Sales	VAT	Total
20 April	M. Thompson	731	417.00	72.98	489.98
23 April	A. Hakim Ltd	732	458.82	80.29	539.11
26 April	F. Rank	733	1,674.80	293.09	1,967.89
27 April	M. Wong	734	54.20	9.49	63.69
			2,604.82	455.85	3,060.67

Workings

$$£417.00 \times \frac{17.5}{100} = £72.98$$

$$£458.82 \times \frac{17.5}{100} = £80.29$$

$$£1674.80 \times \frac{17.5}{100} = £293.09$$

$$£54.20 \times \frac{17.5}{100} = £9.49$$

Sales ledger

Dr		M. Thompson		Cr
20 April Sales	SDB1	489.98		

Dr		A. Hakim Ltd		Cr
23 April Sales	SDB1	539.11		

Dr		F. Rank		Cr
26 April Sales	SDB1	1,967.89		

Dr		M. Wong		Cr
27 April Sales	SDB1	63.69		

General ledger

Dr	Sales account			Cr
		27 April Sundry debtors	SDB1	2604.82

Dr	VAT account			Cr
		27 April Debtors	SDB1	455.85

Note that there are debits totaling £3,060.67 in the sales ledger. There are also credits totalling £3,060.67 in the general ledger; this completes our double entry.

RECORDING VAT ON SALES RETURNS IN THE SALES RETURNS DAY BOOK

As previously shown, the sales returns day book is a list of goods sent back to the business by customers. When these goods are received, a credit note will be sent to the customer. The purchases returns day book is written up from the copies of these credit notes. The credit note will show the value of the goods returned. It will also show the VAT that was originally charged on the goods.

The VAT calculations are exactly the same as the calculations we used when calculating the amounts to be entered on sales invoices.

WORKED EXAMPLE

The following goods have been returned to Gabriel during the week ended 18 May 20*3:

- 13 May goods totalling £32.30 returned by A. Hakim Ltd
- 18 May goods totalling £17.40 returned by M. Wong.

Required (a) Calculate the sales returns and the VAT on the returns.
(b) Enter your figures in the sales returns day book.
(c) Post the entries from the sales returns day book to the appropriate ledger accounts.

Answer

Sales returns day book

Date	Particulars	Credit note	Sales returns	VAT	Total
13 May	A. Hakim	142	32.30	5.65	37.95
18 May	M. Wong	143	17.40	3.05	20.45
			49.70	8.70	58.40

Sales ledger

Dr			A. Hakim			Cr
23 April Sales	SDB1	539.11	13 May Sales returns	SRDB1	37.95	

Dr			M. Wong	Cr		
27 April Sales	SDB1	63.69	18 May Sales returns	SRDB1	20.45	

General ledger

Dr			Sales returns			
18 May Sundry debtors	SRDB1	49.70				

Dr			VAT			Cr
18 May Debtors	SRDB1	8.70	27 April Debtors	SDB1	455.85	

The VAT account in the general ledger would shows all the entries made between 13 April and 18 May in the two examples used above.

The VAT account would look like this:

Dr			VAT			Cr
13 April Creditors	PDB26	84.92	10 May Creditors	PRDB8	4.87
18 May Debtors	SRDB1	8.70	27 April Debtors	SDB1	455.85

QUESTION 8

Jock Murphy owns a wholesale grocery store.

The following sales took place during April. The details of copy sales invoices and copy sales credit notes are as follows. All totals include VAT at 17½%.

12 April	sold goods to Trevor Vines £329.00
	sold goods to Art Newvo plc £4,512.90
13 April	sold goods to Vera Wert £83.68
14 April	goods returned by Trevor Vines £12.60
	sold goods to Atul Patel £549.04
	sold goods to Dorian Blue £906.54
15 April	sold goods to Zerot Ltd £21.88
18 April	goods returned by Atul Patel £126.46

Required (a) Prepare the sales day book.
(b) Prepare the sales returns day book.
(c) Post the entries in both day books to the relevant ledger accounts in the general ledger and the sales ledger.

TRADE DISCOUNT

Trade discount is a reduction in price charged by a supplier to a customer who is in the same line of business.

Extrav plc sells a range of kitchen cupboards to the general public for £1,200.
Howard Sellers is a kitchen designer and fitter. He can purchase the same kitchen cupboards from Extrav plc, to fit into a customer's kitchen, for £800.
Howard gets trade discount of £400.
The trade discount as a percentage is 33⅓%.
In this case the trade discount allowed to Howard was £400 as a percentage of £1200.

WORKED EXAMPLE

Given on the following page are prices charged to the general public by Extrav plc, a wholesaler, and the rate of trade discount allowed to different retail businesses in the same trade.

WORKED EXAMPLE *continued*

Name of trade customer	Goods	Retail price charged to the general public £	Rate of trade discount %
G. Harris plc	XZ/439	1,490	25
I. Jarvis	XZ/537	630	10
Kath Lean Ltd	VB/552	4,600	50
Max E. Mum	NJ/145	6,780	70
O. Prune	VB/530	138	30

Required Calculate the discounted price charged to the trade customer by the wholesaler on each of the goods listed.

Answer

	Goods	Trade discount price £
G. Harris plc	XZ/439	1,117.50
I. Jarvis	XZ/537	567.00
Kath Lean Ltd	VB/552	2,300.00
Max E. Mum	NJ/145	2,034.00
O. Prune	VB/530	96.60

Workings

XZ/439 £1,490 $\times \dfrac{25}{100}$ = £372.50   £1,490.00 − £372.50 = £1,117.50

XZ/537 £630 $\times \dfrac{10}{100}$ = £63.00   £630.00 − £63.00 = £567.00

The calculation has been done in two stages:

■ Firstly, the trade discount was calculated.
■ Secondly, the trade discount was deducted from the wholesale price charged to the public.

There is a short-cut.

If the rate of trade discount is deducted from 100%, this will tell us the proportion of the original price that will be charged to the trade customers.

WORKED EXAMPLE

For G. Harris plc the discounted price is 75% of the non-discounted price
(100% − 25%):

£1,490 $\times \dfrac{75}{100}$ = £1,117.50

For I. Jarvis the discounted price is 90% of the non-discounted price (100% − 10%):

£630 $\times \dfrac{90}{100}$ = £567.00

Now try this method with the three other types of goods.

You should have multiplied by 50% or $\dfrac{50}{100}$ for Kath Lean Ltd,

In the sales day book the actual value of the sales are recorded net of any trade discount. So, the sales day book of Extrav plc would record the above transactions as follows:

EXAMPLE

Date	Particulars	Invoice no.	Sales £	VAT £	Total £
17 August	G. Harris plc	1,278	1,117.50	195.56	1,313.06
17 August	I. Jarvis	1,279	567.00	92.23	666.23
18 August	Kath Lean Ltd	1,280	2,300.00	402.50	2,702.50
20 August	Max E. Mum	1,281	2,304.00	403.20	2,707.20
21 August	O. Prune	1,282	96.60	16.91	113.51
			6,385.10	1,110.40	7,502.50

Similarly, in the purchases day books of the customers of Extrav plc, the amount net of trade discount would be entered.

In I. Jarvis's purchase day book, we would find: purchases of £567.00; VAT charged £92.23; totalling £666.23.

The postings to the sales ledger and the general ledger would follow the lines of the entries shown in Chapter 7.

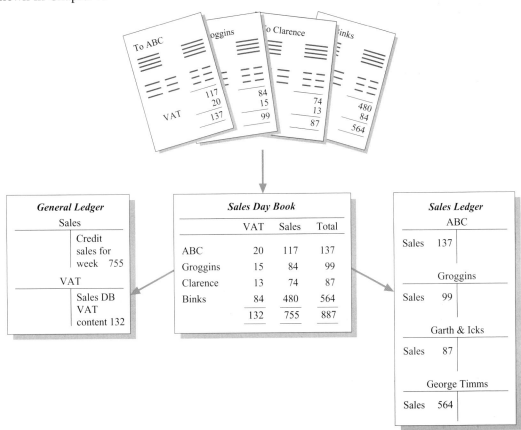

	General Ledger	
	Sales	
	Credit sales for week	755
	VAT	
	Sales DB VAT content	132

Sales Day Book			
	VAT	Sales	Total
ABC	20	117	137
Groggins	15	84	99
Clarence	13	74	87
Binks	84	480	564
	132	755	887

Sales Ledger	
ABC	
Sales 137	
Groggins	
Sales 99	
Garth & Icks	
Sales 87	
George Timms	
Sales 564	

They would look like this:

WORKED EXAMPLE

<table>
<tr><td colspan="4" align="center">Sales ledger</td></tr>
<tr><td>Dr</td><td colspan="2" align="center">G. Harris plc</td><td align="right">Cr</td></tr>
<tr><td>17 August Sales</td><td>SDB 7</td><td>1,313.06</td><td></td></tr>
<tr><td>Dr</td><td colspan="2" align="center">I. Jarvis</td><td align="right">Cr</td></tr>
<tr><td>17 August Sales</td><td>SDB 7</td><td>666.23</td><td></td></tr>
<tr><td>Dr</td><td colspan="2" align="center">Kath Lean Ltd</td><td align="right">Cr</td></tr>
<tr><td>18 August Sales</td><td>SDB 7</td><td>2,702.50</td><td></td></tr>
</table>

WORKED EXAMPLE

<table>
<tr><td>Dr</td><td colspan="2" align="center">Max E. Mum</td><td align="right">Cr</td></tr>
<tr><td>20 August Sales</td><td>SDB 7</td><td>2,707.20</td><td></td></tr>
<tr><td>Dr</td><td colspan="2" align="center">O. Prune</td><td align="right">Cr</td></tr>
<tr><td>21 August Sales</td><td>SDB 7</td><td>113.51</td><td></td></tr>
<tr><td colspan="4" align="center">General Ledger</td></tr>
<tr><td>Dr</td><td colspan="2" align="center">Sales</td><td align="right">Cr</td></tr>
<tr><td></td><td colspan="3">21 August Sundry debtors   SDB 7   6,385.10</td></tr>
<tr><td>Dr</td><td colspan="2" align="center">VAT</td><td align="right">Cr</td></tr>
<tr><td></td><td colspan="3">21 August Debtors   SDB 7   1,110.40</td></tr>
</table>

QUESTION 9

F. Pitt is a builders' merchant selling materials to the building trade. He provides the following list of trade customers for 3 May:

Customer's name	Value of materials sold	Trade discount allowed
H. Odd	£3,490	20%
T. Rowell	£630	30%
B. Rick	£1,200	25%
M. Ortar	£320	50%

Required (a) Calculate the amount of trade discount allowed to each customer.
(b) Calculate the amount that should be entered in Pitt's sales day book net of trade discount.

QUESTION 10

B. Rush sells materials to painters and decorators.

She provides the following list of trade customers for 17 June:

Customer's name	Value of materials sold	Trade discount allowed
S. Tippel	£260	10%
D. Lux	£1,000	25%
V.R. Nish	£420	15%
N. Dercot	£480	20%

Required (a) Calculate the amount of trade discount allowed to each customer.
(b) Calculate the amount to be entered in Rush's sales day book net of trade discount.

QUESTION 11

Olly Branch is a wholesale fruit and vegetable dealer.

He supplies a list of goods sold to him on 23 January:

Supplier's name	Value of goods received	Trade discount allowed to Olly
O. Range	£340	20%
P. Omme	£1,200	25%
P. Ear	£630	33⅓%
F. Root	£265	20%

Required (a) Calculate the amount of trade discount allowed to Olly by his suppliers.
(b) Calculate the amounts to be entered in Olly's purchases day book.
(c) Show the entries in Olly's purchases day book, including the VAT column.

QUESTION 12

Drecker Ltd supplies goods to hotels and restaurants.

The following is a list of goods sold by Drecker's on 19 February:

Customer's name	Value of goods sold	Trade discount allowed by Drecker Ltd
Grand Hotel	£1,500	33⅓%
Joe's Café	£46	15%
Mooney's	£300	20%
Patel Bros	£280	25%

Required (a) Calculate the amount of trade discount allowed by Drecker Ltd to its customers.
(b) Calculate the amounts to be entered in Drecker's sales day book.
(c) Show the entries in Drecker's sales day book, including the VAT column.

Cash discount is a reduction in the price charged for goods when a credit customer settles the debt within a time stipulated by the supplier.

Remember that Howard Sellers bought £800 of kitchen cupboards from Extrav plc to fit into a customer's kitchen.
Extrav plc's terms are that if Howard settles his debt before the end of the month then he may deduct 5% cash discount.
If Howard does settle his debt before the month-end stipulated by Extrav plc then he need pay only £760.
Howard would deduct £40 which is 5% of the £800 owed by him.

WORKED EXAMPLE

Given below are examples of amounts owed to Extrav plc by some cutomers and the rates of cash discount allowed to the customers if their debt is settled within 30 days of receipt of the sales invoice from Extrav plc:

Customer	Amount owed £	Rate of cash discount allowed £
V. Watts	346.00	5%
Xavier Alton Ltd	90.50	2.5%
B. Clowes	760.00	5%
Dean Egg plc	18.60	2.5%
Fred Gregg	9,761.50	5%

Required Calculate the amount to be paid by the customers if they settle their debt within the 30 days allowed by Extrav plc.

WORKED EXAMPLE

Answer

Customer	Amount to be paid £
V. Watts	328.70
Xavier Alton Ltd	88.24
B. Clowes	722.00
Dean Egg plc	18.14
Fred Gregg	9,273.42

Workings

V. Watts £346.00 $\times \dfrac{5}{100}$ = £17.30   £346.00 − £17.30 = £328.70

Xavier Alton Ltd £90.50 $\times \dfrac{2.5}{100}$ = £2.26   £90.50 − £2.26 = £88.24

The calculation has been done in two stages:

- Firstly, the cash discount was calculated.
- Secondly, the cash discount was then deducted from the amount owed.

There is a short-cut.

If the rate of cash discount is deducted from 100%, this will tell us the proportion of the debt that may be paid by the customer.

V. Watts owed £346.00 if advantage was taken of the cash discount offered only 95% of the outstanding debt needs to be paid (100% − 5%).

So, £346.00 $\times \dfrac{95}{100}$ = £328.70 may be paid if the debt is settled within the stipulated time, i.e. 30 days.

Xavier Alton Ltd owed £90.50. If advantage is taken of the cash discount offered, only 97.5% of the outstanding debt needs to be paid (100% − 2.5%).

So, £90.50 $\times \dfrac{97.5}{100}$ = £88.24 may be paid if the debt is settled within the stipulated time, i.e. 30 days.

Now try this method with the remaining three debts.

You should have multiplied the outstanding debts by 95% or $\dfrac{95}{100}$ for B. Clowes and Fred, and by 97.5% or $\dfrac{97.5}{100}$ for Dean Egg plc.

If the discount only has to be calculated then the amount outstanding should be multiplied by the discount rate.

You may have noticed the way that the answers have been worded: *'if advantage is taken of the discount offered'.*
Surely everyone offered a cash discount should take advantage of the reduction? Not if there is a better way of using the money.

A business has a bank balance of £3,560.
The business's wages amounting to £3,400 are due to be paid at the month end and a cash discount of £190.00 can be obtained if a debt is cleared by the month-end.

I think that the wage bill would take priority over the settling of the debt.

WORKED EXAMPLE *continued*

Cash discount is recorded in the books of account.

Remember: trade discount is not recorded.

If all the debts listed above were paid within the stipulated time at the beginning of July, the entries in the sales ledger to record the payments made above would be:

Sales ledger

Dr		V. Watts		Cr
	3 July	Bank		328.70
		Discount allowed		17.30

Dr		X. Alton		Cr
	3 July	Bank		88.24
		Discount allowed		2.26

Dr		B. Clowes		Cr
	4 July	Bank		722.00
		Discount allowed		38.00

Dr		Dean Egg plc		Cr
	4 July	Bank		18.14
		Discount allowed		0.46

Dr		Fred Gregg		Cr
	4 July	Bank		9,273.42
		Discount allowed		488.08

The debit entries are in the bank column of the cash book, and in the discount allowed account in the general ledger.

Cash book

3 July	V Watts	328.70
3 July	X Alton	88.24
4 July	B. Clowes	722.00
4 July	D. Egg	18.14
4 July	F. Gregg	9,273.42

General ledger
Discount allowed account

3 July	V. Watts	17.30
3 July	X. Alton	2.26
4 July	B. Clowes	38.00
4 July	D. Egg	0.46
4 July	F. Gregg	488.08

You can imagine that if we had to go through every account in the sales ledger to determine the total amount of discount that has been allowed it would be a mammoth task. There is a short-cut to gain the total of discount allowed and discount received which will be dealt with in the chapter dealing with the three-column cash book.

When cash discount is offered by the seller of goods we encounter the problem of how to calculate VAT.

Her Majesty's Customs and Excise Department expects the shrewd businessman or businesswoman to take advantage of any cash discount allowed by a seller of goods. So VAT is calculated on the price of goods less any cash discount.

WORKED EXAMPLE

The following information is given:

(a) Goods with a selling price of £200; a cash discount of 5% is offered.
(b) Goods with a selling price of £150; a cash discount of 2½% is offered.
(c) Goods with a selling price of £300; a cash discount of 1% is offered.

Required Calculate the amount on which VAT will be calculated.

Answer
(a) £190.00   *Workings £200 × 95%*   *or £200 × 0.95*
(b) £146.25   *Workings £150 × 97.5%*   *or £150 × 0.975*
(c) £297.00   *Workings £300 × 99%*   *or £300 × 0.99.*

QUESTION 13

The following information relates to credit sales that have taken place on 27 October:

(a) Goods sold to Rick £278.
(b) Goods sold to Doug £290.
(c) Goods sold to Celia £36.
(d) Goods sold to Doris £1,490.

Terms are that if debts are settled before the end of November, 5% cash discount will be allowed.

Required Calculate the amounts due if all debts were settled during November.

QUESTION 14

The following information relates to credit sales that have taken place on 25 August:

(a) Goods sold to Larry £28; cash discount offered for prompt payment 1%.
(b) Goods sold to Mary £270; cash discount offered for prompt payment 3%.
(c) Goods sold to Tanjinder £2,490; cash discount offered for prompt payment 5%.
(d) Goods sold to Kim £180; cash discount offered for prompt payment 2½%.

Even if the purchaser of the goods does not take advantage of the cash discount offered, the VAT is still calculated on the amount that has been calculated as if they had taken advantage of the cash discount.

Note that trade discount is disregarded.

So if Jean buys goods with a retail value of £750 and is allowed trade discount of 33⅓%, her purchase price is £500. If she is allowed cash discount of 10% the VAT on the order is calculated on £450. (Workings £500 − 10% = £450.)

The VAT to be charged on the goods itemised on this invoice will be £78.75

Health Warning

- This is probably the most difficult calculation dealing with VAT that you will come across in an examination.
- You need to learn how to do this calculation.
- Practise it several times. This is the secret to getting a good grade in any examination.
- It is worth spending some time mastering it. The marks gained will separate you from other candidates.
- Remember the old saying: 'practice makes perfect' . . . or nearly always!

Work through the two examples that follow.

They may seem difficult at first, but with a little practice and perseverance you should be able to do them.

WORKED EXAMPLE

Marcel Maursy sells £900.00 of goods on credit to André Boult. Marcel's terms are:

- trade discount 25% and
- cash discount 5% if André settles his account within 30 days.

Required Calculate the total value of the sales invoice sent to André.

Answer
The total value of the invoice is £787.22.

Workings

	£		£
Price of goods	900.00		
Less Trade discount	225.00		
Selling price (to André)	675.00		675.00
		Value of cash discount	33.75
		Amount André would pay	641.25
		before the addition of VAT	
		if he took advantage of	
		the cash discount.	
VAT on £641.25	112.22		
Total invoice value	787.22		

EXAMPLE

Marcel sells £2,370 goods on credit to Carole Singer. The terms are:

- trade discount 33⅓% and
- cash discount 7½% if Carole settles her account within 30 days.

Required Calculate the total of the sales invoice sent to Carole.

Answer
The total value of the invoice is £1,835.77

Workings

	£		£
Price of goods	2,370.00		
Less Trade discount	790.00		
Selling price (to Carole)	1,580.00		1,580.00
		Value of cash discount	118.50
		Amount Carole would pay	1,461.50
		before the addition of VAT	
		if she took advantage of	
		the cash discount	
VAT on £1,461.50	255.77		
Total invoice price	1,835.77		

QUESTION 15

Tammy sells £1,572 of goods on credit to Darren.

The terms are:

- trade discount 25%
- cash discount 2½% if Darren settles his account within 30 days.

Required Calculate the total of the sales invoice sent to Darren.

QUESTION 16

Ferdie sells £120 goods on credit to Anne.

The terms are:

- trade discount 33⅓%
- cash discount 2% if Anne settles her account within 30 days.

Required Calculate the total of the sales invoice sent to Anne.

QUESTION 17

Portia sells £299 goods on credit to Alec.

The terms are:

- trade discount 33⅓%
- cash discount 5% if Alec settles his account within 30 days.

The total of the sales invoice sent to Alec is:

A £99.67
B £199.33
C £232.47
D £284.05.

Required Select the correct answer from those given above.

QUESTION 18

Hibo sells £1,450 of goods on credit to Natalie.

Her terms are:

- trade discount 20%
- cash discount 2½% if Natalie settles her account within 30 days.

The total of the sales invoice sent to Natalie is:

A £1,328.93
B £1,363.00
C £1,357 .93
D £1,703.75.

Required Select the correct answer from those given above.

THE LEDGER ENTRIES TO RECORD PURCHASES, SALES, PURCHASES RETURNS AND SALES RETURNS

The entries are very similar to those we encountered earlier in the chapter.

WORKED EXAMPLE

Alvin makes the following credit purchases during July:

Date	Supplier's name	Purchases £	Trade discount allowed %	Cash discount allowed if account settled in 30 days %
3 July	Thomson	1,440	25	5
4 July	Frood Ltd	760	20	Nil
6 July	Grant	450	10	2
7 July	Rickman	1,280	15	2½

Required (a) Enter the transactions in the purchase day book.
(b) Post the entries from the day book to the appropriate accounts in the general ledger and the purchases ledger.

Answer
(a)

Purchase day book

Date	Particulars	Invoice no.	Purchases	VAT	Total
3 July	Thomson	56/834	1,080.00	179.55	1,259.55
4 July	Frood Ltd	20345	608.00	106.40	714.40
6 July	Grant	DL/342	405.00	69.46	474.46
7 July	Rickman	312	1,088.00	185.64	1,273.64
			3,181.00	541.05	3,722.05

Did you remember to deduct any cash discount allowable before calculating the VAT?

I do hope so!

- Thomson's VAT was calculated on £1,026 (£1,080 less £54 (5%) cash discount).
- Grant's VAT was calculated on £396.90 (£405 less £8.10 (2%) cash discount).
- Rickman's VAT was calculated on £1,060.80 (£1,088 less £27.20 (2%) cash discount).

(b)
Purchases ledger

Dr	Thomson	Cr	Dr	Frood Ltd	Cr
	3 July Purchases 1,259.55			4 July Purchases 714 .40	

Dr	Grant	Cr	Dr	Rickman	Cr
	6 July Purchases 474.46			7 July Purchases 1,273.64	

General ledger

Dr	Purchases account	Cr	Dr	VAT account	Cr
7 July Sundry creditors 3,181.00			7 July Sundry creditors 541.05		

88   INTRODUCING ACCOUNTING FOR AS

WORKED EXAMPLE *continued*

Additional information
Alvin paid all outstanding creditors by cheque on 31 July.

Required Enter the payments made by Alvin in the appropriate accounts.

Answer

Purchases ledger

Dr	Thomson		Cr		Dr	Frood		Cr
31 July Bank	1,205.55	3 July Purchases	1,259.55		31 July Bank	714.40	4 July Purchases	714.40
31 July Dis Rec	54.00							
	1259.55		1259.55					

Dr	Grant		Cr		Dr	Rickman		Cr
31 July Bank	466.36	6 July Purchases	474.46		31 July Bank	1,246.44	7 July Purchases	1,273.64
31 July Disc Rec	8.10				31 July Disc Rec	27.20		
	474.46		474.46			1,273.64		1,273.64

Dr	Cash Book	Cr
	31 July Thomson	1,205.55
	31 July Frood	714.40
	31 July Grant	466.36
	31 July Rickman	1,246.44

General ledger

Dr	Discount received account	Cr
	31 July Thomson	54.00
	31 July Grant	8.10
	31 July Rickman	27.20

QUESTION 19

Dick has made the following credit purchases during February:

Date	Supplier's name	Purchases £	Trade discount allowed %	Cash discount allowed if account settled within 30 days %
16 Feb	Sharan	450	33⅓	5
18 Feb	Frere & Son	1,530	20	2½
18 Feb	Cuvee	560	25	1
20 Feb	Sagoo	1,800	15	5

Required (a) Enter the transactions in Dick's purchases day book.
(b) Post the entries in the day book to the appropriate ledger accounts.

Additional information
Dick settled all outstanding creditor accounts by cheque on 5 March.

Required (c) Enter the payments made by Dick in the appropriate ledger accounts.

QUESTION 20

Ruth makes the following credit sales:

	£
3 May Blair	438
3 May Duncan	530
5 May Kennedy	128
6 May Smith	462

All customers have the same terms of trade: trade discount 25%
cash discount 5% if debts settled within 30 days.

Required (a) Prepare the entries in the sales day book.
(b) Post the entries in the sales day book to the appropriate accounts in the sales ledger and the general ledger.

Additional information
Duncan and Kennedy both settled their accounts by cheque on 28 May.

Smith settled his account by cheque on 15 August.

Blair settled by cheque on 3 September after many reminders.

Required Enter the cheques received in the appropriate accounts.

Returns are dealt with in a similar way. They are entered in the appropriate returns book which has analysis columns showing the VAT included in the total value of the goods returned.

WORKED EXAMPLE

Jim Brown returns faulty goods to the suppliers:

Date	Supplier's name	Invoice price of goods returned (inclusive of VAT) £
7 March	S. Windler	109.00
17 March	F. Aulty	64.64

Required (a) Enter the returns in the appropriate day book.
(b) Post the entries in the day book to the appropriate ledger accounts.

Answer
(a)   Purchases returns day book

Date	Particulars	Credit note	Purchase returns £	VAT £	Total £
7 March	S. Windler	tg/245	92.77	16.23	109.00
17 March	F. Aulty	454	55.01	9.63	64.64
			147.78	25.86	173.64

Workings
The VAT included in Windler's and Aulty's returns must be calculated:

Windler £109.00 $\times \frac{17.5}{117.5}$ = £16.23 or £109.00 $\times \frac{7}{47}$ = £16.23

Aulty £64.64 $\times \frac{17.5}{117.5}$ = £9.63 or £64.64 $\times \frac{7}{47}$ = £9.63

WORKED EXAMPLE *continued*

(b) **Purchases ledger**

Dr	S. Windler	Cr	Dr	F. Aulty	Cr
7 March Returns outwards 109.00			17 March Returns outwards 64.64		

General ledger

Dr	Returns outward account	Cr	Dr	VAT account	Cr
		17 March Sundry creditors 147.78			17 March Sundry creditors 25.86

WORKED EXAMPLE

Customers have returned faulty goods to Ifor during December. The details are as follows:

Date	Customer's name	Price shown on invoice (inclusive of VAT) £
12 December	Talwar & Co.	341.56
14 December	Tread Ltd	54.98
20 December	Jinto Bros	128.51

Required (a) Enter the returns in the sales returns day book.
(b) Post the entries in the sales returns day book to the appropriate ledger accounts.

Answer
(a) **Sales returns day book**

Date	Particulars	Credit note	Returns	VAT	Total
12 December	Talwar & Co.	256	290.69	50.87	341.56
14 December	Tread Ltd	257	46.79	8.19	54.98
20 December	Jinto Bros	258	109 37	19.14	128.51
			446.85	78.20	525.05

(b) **Sales ledger**

Dr	Talwar	Cr	Dr	Tread Ltd	Cr
		12 Dec Returns inwards 341.56			14 Dec Returns inwards 54.98

Dr	Jinto Bros	Cr
		20 Dec Returns inwards 128.51

General ledger

Dr	Returns inwards account	Cr	Dr	VAT account	Cr
20 Dec Sundry debtors 446.85			20 Dec Sundry debtors 78.20		

QUESTION 21

During April the following transactions took place:

Returns outwards			
Date	Supplier's name	Credit note no.	Invoice price of returns (inclusive of VAT) £
7 April	Boon & Co.	45/67	127.46
8 April	Slump	d/439	42.32
11 April	Rage Ltd	23	56.44

Returns inwards			
4 April	Gosling	143	30.54
9 April	Vickers	144	15.77

Required (a) Enter the returns in the appropriate day books.
(b) Post the entries in the day books to the appropriate ledger accounts.
(You should use only one VAT account.)

QUESTION 22

During November the following transactions took place:

Returns outwards			
Date	Supplier's name	Credit note no.	Invoice price of returns (inclusive of VAT) £
3 November	Innit Ltd	rt/54	12.82
9 November	Dunnit & Co.	658	72.80

Returns inwards			
Date	Customer's name	Credit note no.	Invoice price of returns (inclusive of VAT)
5 November	Hendry	762	90.43
14 November	Davies	763	42.06
14 November	Drago	764	128.00

Required (a) Enter the returns in the appropriate day books.
(b) Post the entries in the day books to the appropriate ledger accounts.

QUESTION 23

The following transactions have taken place during September:

Credit sales

Date	Customer's name	Invoice no.	Price shown on invoice (**exclusive** of VAT) £
3 September	J. Oliver	528	385.78
9 September	F. Wingett	529	341.34
21 September	W. Lowther	530	110.49
27 September	R. Shears	531	761.97

Purchases on credit

Date	Supplier's name	Invoice no.	Price shown on invoice (**inclusive** of VAT) £
5 September	J. Knowsley	63	45.83
7 September	J. Lewis	b/521	45.76
12 September	L. Franks	t/45	34.88
23 September	L. Pritchard	129	132.34

Sales returns

Date	Customer's name	Credit note no.	Invoice price (**inclusive** of VAT) £
6 September	S. Welter	435	56.77
7 September	J. Oliver	436	21.33

Purchase returns

Date	Supplier's name	Credit note no.	Invoice price (**exclusive** of VAT)
14 September	I. Williams	4/67	43.62
26 September	J. Lewis	b/623	56.00

Required (a) Enter the transactions in the appropriate day book.
(b) Post the transactions from the day book to the relevant ledger accounts.

QUESTION 24

The following transactions have taken place during August:

Credit sales			
Date	Customer's name	Invoice no.	Price shown on invoice (**exclusive** of VAT) £
1 August	U. Stare	782	637.92
7 August	I. Coff	783	439.07
16 August	D. Alnami	784	54.01
27 August	F. Trott	785	139.63

Purchases on credit			
Date	Supplier's name	Invoice no.	Price shown on invoice (**inclusive** of VAT) £
8 August	P. Oborne	er/56	62.72
8 August	E. Compton	34/uy	348.20
10 August	T. Ronto	4456	139.73
26 August	M. Nixon	tp/459	532.90

Sales returns			
Date	Customer's name	Credit note no.	Invoice price (**inclusive** of VAT) £
22 August	I. Coff	349	12.86
27 August	T. Lynes	350	43.93

Purchase returns			
Date	Supplier's name	Credit note no.	Invoice price (**exclusive** of VAT)
2 August	S. Bhatia	sb/78	54.00
24 August	E. Compton	zx453	42.66
25 August	J.Thaker	25	101.00

Required (a) Enter the transactions in the appropriate day books.
(b) Post the transactions from the day books to the relevant ledger accounts.

The Trial Balance

We have seen that every time that we make a debit entry into our double-entry system, we must also make a credit entry.

If we follow this rule, then the total of all debit entries must equal the sum of all credit entries.

A trial balance is a summary of all the entries in the double-entry system.

It checks that each transaction has been entered once on the debit side of an account and once on the credit side of another account.

A balancing figure is an amount that needs to be included in the debit side or credit side of an account to make the debit side equal to the credit side.

Specification coverage:
AQA 10.3; OCR 5.1.2, 5.2.1.

By the end of this chapter you should be able to:
■ prepare a trial balance
■ identify errors not revealed by a trial balance
■ prepare and use a suspense account
■ calculate the effect that errors will have on gross and net profits.

EXAMPLE

Dr	An account	Cr
	23	45
	41	
	16	

The debit side of the account adds to £80.

The credit side adds to £45.

To make the account balance we need to insert £35 into the credit side.

The account looks like this:

Dr	An account	Cr
	23	45
	41	35
	16	
	80	80

The account balances.

This process makes it look as though the debit entries were exactly the same amounts as the credit entries – not true!

The debit side was £35 heavier. We need to reflect this when we start the account again.

We carry the balance down.

We start anew with an opening balance of £35:

Dr	An account	Cr
	23	45
	41	35
	16	
	80	80
	35	

The rules of our double-entry game say that every time we include a debit entry in the system, we must also include a credit entry.

We have done just that. We inserted a credit entry to make the account balance.

Our debit entry starts us off again.

WORKED EXAMPLE

The following accounts are given:

Dr	Zog	Cr		Dr	Melvyn	Cr		Dr	Tan	Cr
23		53		12		34		71		90
13		41		25		37		27		38
		8		73				91		

Required Balance the accounts and carry down any balances.

Answer

Dr	Zog	Cr		Dr	Melvyn	Cr		Dr	Tan	Cr
23		53		12		34		71		90
13		41		25		37		27		38
_66_		_8_		_73_		_39_		_91_		_61_
102		102		110		110		189		189
		66		39				61		

When a balance is described as a debit balance or a credit balance, we are describing the balance required to start the account up again; the balance that has been brought down.

In the example above:

- Zog's account has a credit balance of £66
- Melvyn's account has a debit balance of £39 and
- Tan's account has a debit balance of £61.

QUESTION 1

The following accounts are given:

Dr	Albert	Cr		Dr	Annie	Cr		Dr	Arthur	Cr
14		56		28		9		79		52
34		67		51		7		17		34
61						49		70		

109

Required Balance the accounts and carry down any balances.

QUESTION 2

The following accounts are given:

Dr	Rent account (GL)	Cr		Dr	Sales account (GL)	Cr		Dr	Tungi (SL)	Cr
450	*1350*					723		46		44
450						218		39		2
450						109				13

1350   1350

1390

Required Balance the accounts and carry down any balances.

We prepare a trial balance by balancing all the ledger accounts and carrying down any outstanding balances on each account.
We then list all the debit balances under a debit column of the trial balance and we list each credit balance in a column headed 'credit'.
The debit column is totalled; the credit is totalled.
The two columns should have the same total.

If we extract a trial balance and the two sides total to the same figure we can say with some certainty that every debit has a corresponding credit.
If the trial balance totals do not agree, then we can say with some certainty that there are some errors in the double-entry system.

Here are a couple of simple double-entry examples using 'T' accounts followed by a very simple trial balance.

WORKED EXAMPLE

The following tránsactions are for Gary's business:

1   Gary purchased goods for resale £153 from Dora on credit.
2   He sold goods £29 to Chris on credit.
3   Gary sold goods for cash £296.
4   He paid motor expenses £68, paying cash.

Required   Enter the transactions in Gary's ledger, carry down any balances and check the entries by extracting a trial balance.

Answer

Dr	Purchases account	Cr		Dr	Dora	Cr
	153					153

Dr	Sales account	Cr		Dr	Chris	Cr
		29			29	
		296				

Dr	Cash account	Cr		Dr	Motor expenses account	Cr
	296	68			68	

Trial balance

	£	£	
Purchases	153		The ledger shows a debit balance; the trial balance shows a debit balance.
Dora		153	The ledger shows a credit balance; the trial balance shows a credit balance.
Sales		325	Sales have credit entries totalling 325; the trial balance shows this balance.
Chris	29		
Cash	228		The debit side is 'heavier'; the trial balance shows the debit balancing figure.
Motor expenses	68		
	478	478	

The trial balance has shown that we have entered our transactions accurately.

WORKED EXAMPLE

The following ledger accounts have been extracted from a ledger:

Dr	Cash account	Cr	Dr	Bank account	Cr
42		100	365		534
534		458	912		141
		12			69

Dr	Rent account	Cr	Dr	Wages account	Cr
100			458		

Dr	Sales account	Cr	Dr	Purchases account	Cr
		42	141		
		365	69		
		912	12		

Required Balance the accounts; carry down any balances and extract a trial balance to check the accuracy of the ledger accounts.

Answer

Dr	Cash account	Cr	Dr	Bank account	Cr
42		100	365		534
534		458	912		141
		12			69
		6			533
576		576	1,277		1,277
6			533		

Dr	Rent account	Cr	Dr	Wages account	Cr
100			458		

Dr	Sales account	Cr	Dr	Purchases account	Cr
		42	141		
		365	69		
1,319		912	12		222
1,319		1,319	222		222
		1,319	222		

Trial balance

	£	£
Cash	6	
Bank	533	
Rent	100	
Wages	458	
Sales		1,319
Purchases	222	
	1,319	1,319

WORKED EXAMPLE

Sharon owns and runs a clothes shop. The following transactions have taken place:

1   Sharon's cash sales amount to £612.
2   She purchases jeans from Cath £129 on credit.
3   Sharon sells a shirt and jeans to Ursula £76 on credit.
4   She pays the shop rent £250 using cash.
5   She purchases trainers £345 on credit from Rocky.
6   Sharon pays wages £166 using cash.

Required Enter the transactions in Sharon's ledger.

Carry down any balances.

Extract a trial balance to check the accuracy of your entries.

Answer

Dr	Cash account (GL)	Cr		Dr	Sales account (GL)	Cr
(1) 612		250				612 (1)
		166				76

Dr	Purchases account (GL)	Cr		Dr	Cath (PL)	Cr
129						129
345						

Dr	Ursula (SL)	Cr		Dr	Rent account (GL)	Cr
76				250		

Dr	Rocky (PL)	Cr		Dr	Wages account (GL)	Cr
		345		166		

Trial balance

	£	£
Cash	196	
Sales		688
Purchases	474	
Cath		129
Ursula	76	
Rent	250	
Rocky		345
Wages	166	
	1,162	1,162

QUESTION 3

The following information is given for Timmy:

1   Timmy sells goods for cash £750.
2   He pays rent £100 cash.
3   Timmy sells goods on credit £48 to Chas.
4   He pays wages £78 cash.
5   Timmy purchases goods for resale £330 on credit from Duncan.
6   He purchases goods for resale £69 from Vera, paying cash.

Required Enter the transactions in Timmy's ledger.

Carry down any balances.

Extract a trial balance to check the accuracy of the entries.

QUESTION 4

Malcolm provides the following information:

1. Malcolm purchases a delivery vehicle £12,650 on credit from Drest Motors.
2. He purchases fuel for his vehicle £35 cash.
3. Malcolm purchases goods for resale £542 on credit from S. Unset.
4. He sells goods for cash £212.
5. Malcolm purchases goods for resale £239 on credit from S. Unset.
6. He sells goods £360 on credit to Ovis.
7. Malcolm withdraws £50 cash for personal use.
8. He pays insurance premium £340 cash.

Required Enter the transactions in Malcolm's ledger.

Carry down any balances.

Extract a trial balance to check the accuracy of the entries.

The trial balance is made up of the balances extracted from the ledger.

It summarises the balances.

If you consider the few trial balances that have been prepared, a pattern has started to emerge:

DEBIT BALANCES

- Assets are always debit balances. Examples above are cash balances (an asset); debtors like Ursula (an asset) – she owes money to Sharon.
- Expenses are always debit balances. Examples above are the balance on the rent account; the balance on the wages account; the balance on the purchases account.

CREDIT BALANCES

- Incomes and benefits are always credit balances. The example above is the balance on the sales account.
- Liabilities are always credit balances. The examples above are Cath and Rocky; they are creditors – Sharon owes them money.

A trial balance will show balances thus:

Debit balances	Credit balances
Assets	Liabilities
Expenses	Incomes
	Benefits

EXAMPLE

The following is a list of account headings found in Tricia's ledger.

Place a tick in the appropriate columns to show the category into which each item falls.

Indicate whether a balance on the account would appear in the debit or credit column of her trial balance.

Account name	Asset	Expense	Liability	Income or benefit	Debit	Credit
Wages						
Premises						
Creditor						
Advertising						
Sales						
Bank overdraft						

QUESTION 5

Wendy owns and runs a card and stationery shop. The following is a list of accounts found in Wendy's ledgers.

State the name of the ledger in which the account would be found.

Place a tick in the appropriate columns to show the category into which each item falls.

Indicate whether a balance on the account would appear in the debit or credit column of her trial balance.

Account name	Ledger	Asset	Expense	Liability	Income or benefit	Debit	Credit
Motor vehicles							
Rates							
Mortgage							
Carriage inward							
Premises							
Quentin – a credit customer							
Capital							
Tara – a credit supplier							
Purchases							
Insurance							
Sales							
Carriage outward							

WORKED EXAMPLE

The following balances have been extracted from the ledgers of Lionel on 30 April 20*3:

buildings at cost £120,000; fixtures and fittings at cost £45,000; van £14,500; motor expenses £4,160; rent £7,000; rates £2,400; insurance £2,100; cash in hand £120; balance at bank £3,670; debtors £850; creditors £1,200; sales £260,000; purchases £140,000; capital £78,600.

Required Prepare a trial balance at 30 April 20*3.

WORKED EXAMPLE *continued*

Answer

Lionel
Trial balance as at 30 April 20*3

	Dr £	Cr £
Buildings at cost	120,000	
Fixtures at cost	45,000	
Van at cost	14,500	
Rent	7,000	
Rates	2,400	
Insurance	2,100	
Motor expenses	4,160	
Cash in hand	120	
Balance at bank	3,670	
Debtors	850	
Creditors		1,200
Sales		260,000
Purchases	140,000	
Capital		78,600
	339,800	339,800

WORKED EXAMPLE

The following balances have been extracted from the ledgers of Leigh on 31 August 20*3:

purchases £87,000; sales £140,000; vehicles at cost £18,000; motor expenses £4,200; rent £8,600; rates £1,500; insurance £2,400; repairs £940; cash £310; bank £4,460; debtors £1,680; creditors £240; drawings £16,500; capital £5,350.

Required Prepare a trial balance at 31 August 20*3 for Leigh.

Answer

Leigh
Trial balance as at 31 August 20*3

	Dr £	Cr £
Purchases	87,000	
Sales		140,000
Vehicles at cost	18,000	
Motor expenses	4,200	
Rent	8,600	
Rates	1,500	
Insurance	2,400	
Repairs	940	
Cash	310	
Bank	4,460	
Debtors	1,680	
Creditors		240
Drawings	16,500	
Capital		5,350
	145,590	145,590

Do you recognise the trial balance?

It is the 'list' that you used to prepare balance sheets, trading accounts and profit and loss accounts in earlier chapters.

We have divided it into debit balances and credit balances from the ledgers.

Note
- The debit and credit column totals are the same. So we can say with some certainty that whoever did the double-entry book-keeping probably made a debit entry for every credit entry. ('Probably' means that there could be some missing debit and/or credits of the same total value – these are known as 'compensating errors'. But more of errors later!)
- The debit column of the trial balance contains only assets and expenses; the credit column of the trial balance contains only liabilities and incomes or benefits.

USES OF THE TRIAL BALANCE

The trial balance has only one function and that is: to check the arithmetic accuracy of the double-entry system. However, as you have already seen in earlier chapters, the trial balance can be used as a list from which to prepare the final accounts. It is generally used to prepare the trading account, the profit and loss account and the balance sheet.

LIMITATIONS OF THE TRIAL BALANCE

The trial balance has certain limitations. Even if the trial balance totals do agree, that is no guarantee that there are no mistakes in the system. There are six types of error that will not show in an incorrect trial balance. These will be listed in a moment.

If the totals of a trial balance disagree, you must run through a few checks in order to see that you have not made a simple error:

1. Check that you have added the debit column up correctly and also that you have added the credit column correctly.
2. Check that there are lots more entries in the debit column than there are in the credit column.
   The debit column should contain only assets and expenses. The credit column should contain only liabilities and incomes or benefits.
3. If you cannot find the error, look at the totals. If the debit column is smaller than the credit column total, check that you have not missed a debit balance. If the credit column total is the smaller of the two, check that you have not missed a credit balance.
4. If the error has not been found by going through the three previous points, divide the difference in the totals by two. Then look to see if an asset has been incorrectly placed in the credit column or if a liability has been placed in the debit column, because items in the incorrect column will double the mistake.
5. If you divide the error by 9 and your answer is a whole number, then the error could be what is known as a 'transposition error': e.g. £123 entered as £132 or £96 written as £69.

ERRORS THAT ARE NOT REVEALED WHEN EXTRACTING A TRIAL BALANCE

There are six errors that are not revealed by extracting a trial balance:

1. errors of commission
2. complete reversal of entries
3. errors of omission
4. errors of principle
5. errors of original entry
6. compensating errors.

Learn the names of these errors. This is a popular examination topic.

- You may use a mnemonic to help remember facts.
- You could remember the types of errors as 'CROPOC'
- A letter for each type of error: **C**ommision, **R**eversal, **O**mission, **P**rinciple, **O**riginal entry, **C**ompensating.

THE TYPES OF ERRORS IN DETAIL

1. Errors of commission

Errors of commission arise when the correct amount is entered on the correct side of the wrong account.

If £600 rent was paid by cheque and the rates account was debited with £600, this would not be revealed by the trial balance.

2. Complete reversal of entries

This occurs when the correct figures are used but both entries are entered on the wrong side of the accounts used.

For example, if £70 of goods were purchased from P. Smith, and P. Smith was debited with £70, and the purchases account was credited with £70, no error would be revealed.

3. Errors of omission

These errors occur when a transaction is completely missed from the ledgers. If a purchase invoice was destroyed, there would be no entry in the purchase day book, therefore the purchases account in the general ledger would not contain the transaction; neither would the supplier's account contain the transaction.

The debit entry is zero; the credit entry is zero. The debit and credit entries agree.

4. Errors of principle

These errors occur when a transaction is posted to the incorrect class of account. For example, if a new vehicle were to be purchased on credit and was inadvertently entered into the motor expenses account, this would not be revealed by the trial balance.

Some readers may be confused by the difference between an error of commission and an error of principle:

- an error of **commission** will not affect profits or the validity of the balance sheet
- an error of **principle** will affect the profit of the business and will either understate or overstate the entry on the balance sheet.

You may wish to use this rule when trying to decide whether an incorrect posting is an error of commission or an error of principle.

If a vehicle costing £23,500 is posted to the motor expenses account, the profit will be understated by £23,500. The fixed assets shown on the balance will be understated by £23,500 also.

5. Errors of original entry

If a credit sale sale for £176 was entered in the sales day book as £167 then a debit entry of £167 would be recorded in the customer's account in the sales ledger and a credit entry of £167 would be entered in the sales account in the general ledger.

The debit entry is £167; the credit entry is £167. The debit and credit entries agree.

6. Compensating errors

Compensating errors cancel each other out. If the debit side of an account is totalled incorrectly and is £100 too much and another totally separate account with credit entries is incorrectly totalled by £100, then no error will be revealed.

WORKED EXAMPLE

Identify the types of errors listed below.

1   Vehicle repair paid by cheque £649:

       Debit entry   **Credit entry**
      Bank account £649   Motor expenses account £649.

2   Machine sold for £4,000:

       Debit entry   **Credit entry**
      Bank account £4,000   Sales account £4,000

3   Goods purchased £29 from Trip & Co. on credit:

       Debit entry   **Credit entry**
     Purchases account £29   Prit & Co. £29.

4   Goods sold £76 on credit to Ricket:

       Debit entry   **Credit entry**
     Ricket account £67   Sales account £67.

Answer
1   Complete reversal of entries.
2   Error of principle.
3   Error of commission.
4   Error of original entry.

QUESTION 6

The following errors have been discovered in the ledgers of Howard:

1   Howard had recently purchased shop fittings £3,700 on credit from Minser.
   The item had been recorded in Howard's journal as:

	Dr £	Cr £
Shop fittings	7,300	
Minser		7,300

2   Repairs to his vehicle (£560), paid by cheque, had been entered as a debit in the vehicles account.
3   A purchase invoice for £281 had been destroyed and had not been entered in the purchase day book.
4   A cheque for £33 received from Roter had been entered as a credit in R. Oter's account.
5   Repairs carried out on Mrs Howard's car £612 had been entered in the business motor expenses account.

Required   Identify the types of errors discovered in Howard's ledger.

Although the prime function of a trial balance is to test the accuracy of our double-entry system, we often use a trial balance as a list from which we prepare our final accounts. This saves us much time.

However, if the trial balance fails to balance then we can rest assured that our final accounts will not balance.

When the trial balance fails to balance, the difference between the total of the debit side and the total of the credit side is placed in a temporary account called a 'suspense account'.

If the debit column of the trial balance has a smaller total than the credit column we insert an item 'Suspense account' in the debit column in order that the two columns will have the same total. If the total of the credit column of the trial balance is smaller than the total of the debit column then the amount for 'Suspense account' would be inserted in the credit column.

WORKED EXAMPLE

Lara has extracted a trial balance. The totals of the debit and credit columns do not agree:

	Debit column total £	Credit column total £
	123,456	132,546
Lara inserts a Suspense account to make the trial balance balance	9,090	
	132,546	132,546

WORKED EXAMPLE

Lawrence has extracted a trial balance from his ledgers. The totals of the debit and credit columns do not agree:

	Debit column total £	Credit column total £
	890,321	889,617
Lawrence inserts a Suspense account to make the trial balance balance		704
	890,321	890,321

We can then prepare a set of draft final accounts safe in the knowledge that they will balance (provided **we** do not make any errors in the preparation).

In the draft final accounts, a suspense account shown as a debit balance in the trial balance will be shown as a current asset on the balance sheet.

If the suspense account has been included as a credit balance in the trial balance, it should be shown as a current liability on the balance sheet.

● EXAMINATION TIP

- A word of warning: if you prepare a set of final accounts as an answer in an examination and those accounts do not balance, run through the checks mentioned earlier. If you do not find the error, do not make the balance sheet balance by inserting a suspense item.
- This wastes time and you are merely drawing attention to the fact that you have made an error in your answer.

How would Lara's suspense account be shown in her final accounts?
How would Lawrence's suspense account be shown in his final accounts?

Lara's suspense account balance would be shown as a current asset £9,090 on her draft balance sheet.
Lawrence's suspense account balance would be shown as a current liability £704 on his draft balance sheet.

When the errors that have prevented the trial balance from balancing are found and corrected, the draft accounts are amended and should be correct according to the information given.

When errors affecting the balancing of the trial balance are found they will be entered in the suspense account (and in another account since we are using a double-entry system).

Casting is a term used by accountants for adding. **Undercast** means that a total is lower than it ought to be. **Overcast** means that a total is greater than it ought to be.

Remember:

- that not all errors affect the balancing of the trial balance
- when the errors are entered in the suspense account, the suspense account balance should be eliminated.

WORKED EXAMPLE

On 31 March 20*3 Vincent's trial balance failed to balance. The debit column total was £20,500, the credit column was £21,000. The difference was entered in a suspense account.

Since extracting the trial balance, the following errors have been found:

1. The purchases account was undercast by £1,000.
2. Goods sold on credit to J. Latimer £500 were debited to J. Latimer but had not been included in the sales day book.

Required Prepare:

      (a) the journal entries to correct the errors; and
      (b) the suspense account after the corrections have been made.

If journal entries are required, we ask ourselves the questions:

In the first example:
- Which account was debited? Answer – purchases account.
- Which account was credited? Answer – suspense account.

In the second example:
- Which account was debited? Answer – suspense account.
- Which account was credited? Answer – sales account

Answer
(a)

JOURNAL

		Dr £	Cr £
1.	Purchases account	1,000	
	Suspense account		1,000

Correction of error. Purchase day book undercast by £1,000.

2.	Suspense account	500	
	Sales account		500

Correction of error. Sale of goods to Latimer not included in sales day book.

(b) **Dr**   **Suspense account**   **Cr**

Trial balance difference	500	Purchases	1,000
Sales account	500		
	1,000		1,000

WORKED EXAMPLE

On 30 November 20*3 Maureen's trial balance failed to agree. The debit column total £230,161; the credit column totalled £189,521. The difference was entered in a suspense account. On further examination of the books of account, the following errors were found:

1. Motoring expenses £1,700 had been entered in the van account.
2. The total of the sales day book for July £16,320 had been posted to the debit side of the purchases account.
3. The total of rent received for the year £4,000 had been entered as a debit entry in the rent payable account.
4. Maureen had withdrawn goods for her own use £4,700 during the year. These goods had been entered on the debit of the purchases account.

Required Prepare:
        (a) the journal entries to correct the errors
        (b) the suspense account.

Answer
(a)

JOURNAL

	Dr £	Cr £
Motor expenses	1,700	
Van		1,700

Error of principle. Motor expenses included as capital expenditure.

Suspense account	32,640	
Sales		16,320
Purchases		16,320

Posting error. Sales posted incorrectly to purchases account.

Suspense account	8,000	
Rent receivable		4,000
Rent payable		4,000

Posting error. Rent receivable entered incorrectly in the rent payable account.

Drawings	4,700	
Purchases		4,700

Posting error. Drawings entered as purchases.

(b) **Dr**   **Suspense account**   **Cr**

Sales account	16,320	Trial balance difference	40,640
Purchases account	16,320		
Rent receivable	4,000		
Rent payable	4,000		
	40,640		40,640

Any errors occurring in the double-entry system will generally have an effect on either

- the profit and loss account or
- the balance sheet.

Errors that affect the component parts of the trading account will affect both

- gross profit and
- net profit.

Errors that affect the component parts of the profit and loss account will affect the net profit. (Any change in net profit will also affect the balance sheet in that net profit affects capital.)

Examination questions frequently ask candidates to correct errors and then to work on a draft net profit to arrive at a corrected net profit for the period.

WORKED EXAMPLE

The following accounts contain errors:

- rates account
- sales account
- wages account
- returns inward account
- horace's account – a debtor's account.

Required Complete the table showing changes to gross profit and net profit when corrections are made

Account	Gross profit	Net profit
Rates account	ne	Low
Sales account	Yes	yes
Wages account	no	Yes
Returns inward account	Yes	Yes
Horace's account	no	no

Answer

Account	Gross profit	Net profit
Rates account	No change	Change
Sales account	Change	Change
Wages account	No change	Change
Returns inward account	Change	Change
Horace's account	No change	No change

QUESTION 7

The following accounts contain errors:

- Rent account
- Mortgage account
- Insurance account
- Drawings account
- Advertising account
- Returns outward
- Carriage outward
- Purchases account.

Required Complete the table showing changes to gross profit and net profit when corrections are made.

Account	Gross profit	Net profit
Rent account		
Mortgage account		
Insurance account		
Drawings account		
Advertising account		
Returns outward account		
Carriage outward account		
Purchases account		

After any errors are discovered:

- the journal should be used to effect the changes
- the ledger accounts should be corrected
- gross profit should be adjusted
- net profit should be adjusted and
- changes to balance sheet items should be made.

WORKED EXAMPLE

The trial balance of Gordon Brannen failed to balance on 31 March 20*3. The difference was entered in a suspense account. A set of draft final accounts was prepared before the errors were discovered. The draft net profit was £27,864.

The following errors were discovered:

1. The purchase day book had been overcast by £100.
2. A payment made to M. Dixon £121 had been posted to the incorrect side of her account.
3. Fixtures purchased for £2,340 had been entered in the purchase day book.
4. Goods sold on credit to B. Hoyle £97 had been completely omitted form the books of account.
5. An insurance payment for £430 had been correctly entered in the cash book but had not been entered in the insurance account.

Required Prepare:
(a) journal entries to correct the error
(b) a suspense account after the errors have been corrected
(c) a statement showing the corrected net profit.

Answer
(a)
                          JOURNAL

	Dr £	Cr £
Suspense	100	
Purchases		100

Correction of error. Purchase day book overcast by £100.

| Dixon | 242 | |
| Suspense | | 242 |

Payment of £121 posted to the incorrect side of Dixon's account.

WORKED EXAMPLE *continued*

Fixtures	2,340		
Purchases		2,340	

Fixtures incorrectly entered in Purchases account.

B Hoyle	97		
Sales		97	

Sale of goods to Hoyle omitted from ledgers.

Insurance	430		
Suspense		430	

Insurance premium omitted from insurance account.

(b)   Suspense account

Purchases	100	Dixon	242
*Trial balance difference	572	Insurance	430
	672		672

Note the amount of the difference on the trial balance * was not given in the question.

It must be assumed to be the amount necessary to make the suspense account balance since all the errors have been corrected.

(c) Statement of corrected net profit

		£
Profit as per draft accounts		27,864
1	Decrease in purchases	100
3	Decrease in purchases	2,340
4	Increase in sales	97
5	Increase in insurance	(430)
Corrected net profit		29,971

Error 2 does not affect the net profit; it would, however, affect the total of creditors which appears on the balance sheet. It would reduce current liabilities.

◯ EXAMINATION TIP

If a transaction has no effect, tell the examiner this. If you don't say, the examiner does not know whether you have omitted the transaction because this is the correct treatment or because you don't know what the effect is.

When correcting a draft net profit, remember that:

- any expense account that is debited in the journal will reduce draft net profit
- any expense account that is credited in the journal will increase draft net profit

Notes to the answer

- Always use headings. They often carry marks; don't throw these marks away!
- Always give a precise narrative to each journal entry.
- You may have to calculate the trial balance difference to enter in the suspense account.
- Identify any items you have not used in the statement of adjusted profit – if you don't, an examiner does not know whether you have missed the transaction out deliberately because you do not know how to treat the item.

Chapter summary

- A trial balance is extracted from the three ledgers.
- It is a summarised version of all the accounts extracted from the three ledgers.
- The debit column of a trial balance lists assets and expenses.
- The credit column of a trial balance lists liabilities and incomes and benefits.
- A trial balance checks the arithmetical accuracy of the double-entry book-keeping system.
- If the trial balance balances, it is not a guarantee that the system is free of errors.
- There are six types of error that will not be disclosed by extracting a trial balance.
- The trial balance can also be used as a useful list from which to prepare the final accounts of the business.
- A suspense account is used to make the debit column total agree with the credit column total if the trial balance does not balance.
- When errors are rectified the suspense account should 'disappear'.

Self-test questions

- The debit side of an account totals £242; the credit side totals £200. What is the balance on the account?
- Generally, which side of a trial balance will have the most entries?
- Liabilities are shown on the .... side of a trial balance. Fill in the gap.
- Incomes are shown on the .... side of a trial balance. Fill in the gap.
- From which ledger are the figures used in a trial balance extracted?
- In which ledger would you expect to find the account of Gerald, a supplier of goods on credit?
- In which ledger would you expect to find the returns inwards account?
- The trial balance balances, so there are no mistakes in the double-entry system. True or false?
- What is the main use of a trial balance?
- What is an error of commission?
- What does the mnemonic 'CROPOC' mean?
- The debit column of a trial balance totals £230,150 and the credit column totals £230,000; what amount will be entered in a suspense account?
- What does the term 'overcast' mean?
- Would an error in the carriage inwards account affect gross profit or net profit?
- Would an expense account credited in the journal increase or decrease net profit?

TEST QUESTIONS

QUESTION 8

The following information is given for Boris Klien as at 31 July 20*3:

capital as at 1 August 20*2 £387; motor vehicle £18,000; machinery £21,000; premises £75,000; wages 23,471; rent £8,500; rates £1,342; purchases £68,577; sales £202,767; returns inwards £312; returns outwards £928; stock as at 1 August £4,968; debtors £14,307; creditors £8,942; bank balance £2,160; mortgage £25,000.

Required Prepare a trial balance as at 31 July 20*3.

QUESTION 9

The following information is given for Sue Lycett as at 31 December 20*3:

Trial balance as at 31 August 20*3.

	Dr £	Cr £
Capital	45,578	
Vehicles at cost	43,500	
Office equipment at cost	17,600	
Debtors		4,656
Creditors	2,873	
Stock as at 1 September 20*2	4,502	
Purchases	56,221	
Sales		132,448
Wages	34,662	
Motor expenses	3,189	
Rent and rates	4,692	
Insurances		1,634
Advertising	2,654	
General expenses	4,654	
Carriage inwards	543	
Carriage outwards		511
Returns inwards		1,985
Returns outwards	588	
Bank balance	346	
Cash in hand	138	
	218,205	141,580

Required Redraft the trial balance making any corrections deemed necessary.

QUESTION 10

The following information is available for Malcolm Troqueer:

Trial balance as at 31 January 20*3

	Dr £	Cr £
Capital	7,486	
Premises at cost	60,000	
Office equipment at cost	12,000	
Delivery vehicle at cost		8,000
Mortgage on premises	30,000	
HP debt on vehicle		2,000
Purchases		83,904
Sales		181,657
Wages	34,000	
General expenses		16,471
Debtors	9,384	
Creditors	7,168	
Bank overdraft	1,477	
Cash in hand	236	
Stock as at 1 February 20*2		4,577
Suspense	1,216	
	162,967	296,609

Required Redraft the trial balance making any corrections deemed necessary.

QUESTION 11

The following information is available:

1. Rent account has been overcast £300.
   Wages account has been undercast £150.
   Sales account has been overcast £150.
2. Returns inwards £219 has been debited to Sales account.
3. Purchase of delivery vehicle £19,650 has been debited to motor expenses.
4. Purchase of one ball point pen 17 pence has not been included in the books of account because it is such a trivial amount.

Required Identify the types of errors described.

QUESTION 12

The following information is available:

1. Business motor expenses for the week £82 have been entered in the cash book as £28.
2. Capital introduced by the proprietor 4,000 has been entered in the sales account.
3. A credit sale to Danny £49 has been credited to Dani's account.
4. The cost of an advertisement to sell the motorbike of the son of the proprietor £28 has been included in the advertising account.

Required Identify the types of errors described.

QUESTION 13

After extracting a trial balance, Ralph has discovered the following errors in his double entry system:

1. Rent £200 has been entered in the rates account.
2. The wages account has been undercast by £400.
3. Payment made to Tom £146 entered in cash book but not in Tom's account.
4. Payment for insurance £273 debited in cash book and credited to insurance account.

Required (a) Prepare journal entries showing the corrections necessary to correct the errors.
(b) Prepare a suspense account to correct the errors, showing the original trial balance difference.
(c) State which side of the trial balance was the larger before the discovery of the errors.

QUESTION 14

After extracting a trial balance Jeanne discovered the following errors:

1. Bank charges £149 have not been entered in any books of account.
2. The sales day book has been undercast by £1,100.
3. A car service £550 on Jeanne's private car has been included in motor expenses.
4. Carriage inwards £48 has been included in the carriage outwards account.

Required (a) Prepare journal entries showing the entries necessary to correct the errors.
(b) Prepare a suspense account to correct the errors, showing the original trial balance difference.
(c) State which side of the trial balance was the larger before the discovery of the errors.

QUESTION 15

The following errors have been discovered in the books of Monirul. He has already prepared a draft trading and profit and loss account. These have revealed a gross profit of £48,712 and a net profit of £13,467.

1. Purchases £321 from Beatrice have been debited to her account.
2. The sales returns day book has been undercast by £100.
3. VAT on purchases £1,461 has been omitted from the general ledger.
4. The sales day book has been overcast by £1,010.

Required (a) Prepare journal entries necessary to correct the errors.
(b) Prepare a suspense account to correct the errors, showing the original trial balance difference.
(c) State which side of the trial balance was the larger before the discovery of the errors.
(d) Prepare a statement showing the gross profit after correcting the errors.
(e) Prepare a statement showing the net profit after correcting the errors.

QUESTION 16

The following errors have been discovered in the books of Jenni:

She has already prepared a draft trading and profit and loss account. These have revealed a gross profit of £107,648 and a net profit of £23,614.

1. A cheque £217 paid to G. Ray has been debited to Gray.
2. Carriage inwards £126 has been debited to carriage outwards.
3. VAT on sales £572 has been credited to the VAT account as £752.
4. Jenni's drawings £432 have been included in wages as £342.
5. Wages account has been overcast by £1,200.

Required Prepare:
   (a) Prepare journal entries necessary to correct the errors.
   (b) Prepare a suspense account to correct the errors, showing the original trial balance difference.
   (c) State which side of the trial balance was the larger before the discovery of the errors.
   (d) Prepare a statement showing the gross profit after correcting the errors.
   (e) Prepare a statement showing the net profit after correcting the errors.

CHAPTER
TEN

The Ledger Accounts in Detail

Up to now we have used 'T' accounts to record the two sides of a transaction. This is fine and it will give us the information that we require.

However, it would be more useful if the 'T' accounts gave us more details of each transaction.

■ It would be useful to know **when** the transaction took place.
■ It would also be useful to be able to follow the whole transaction through to its **completion**, especially when a problem occurs in the system.

These problems are rectified by simple means.

Each entry should be preceded by:

■ the **date** of the transaction; and
■ a **description** stating where the corresponding entry can be located
■ the appropriate **folio number** of the 'other' entry.

An entry in a ledger account may look like this:

Dr			An account	Cr
7 April Sales	GL 17	217		

The transaction took place on 7 April. The 'opposite' entry, i.e. the credit entry, is in the sales account and the credit entry can be found on page 17 of the general ledger.

Dr	Another account			Cr
	12 Sept Purchases	GL 28	416	

The transaction took place on 12 September. The debit entry is in the purchases account which is on page 28 of the general ledger.

○ EXAMINATION TIP

If you are ever asked to prepare a ledger account then it must have all the details to score all of the marks – however, when you are working things out you may use 'T' accounts because this is faster and just as accurate.

Many accountants and teachers use 'T' accounts to solve tricky problems and for general workings.

REVISION TIP

Try jotting down your workings using 'T' accounts. When you gain confidence in their use you will find that you can use them as a revision tool and for solving problems.

The information shown in ledger accounts is derived from one of the books of prime entry.

WORKED EXAMPLE

The following transactions took place during the first week in October (ignore VAT):

1 1 October Purchased goods for resale on credit from Arkimed plc £120.
2 1 October Sold goods on credit to Morris & Co. £600.
3 2 October Purchased vehicle on credit from Pooley Motors plc £17,400.
4 4 October Sold goods on credit to Nelson plc £315.
5 4 October Purchased goods for resale on credit from Bain & Co. £450.
6 4 October Purchased goods for resale on credit from Darth & Son £170.
7 7 October Sold goods on credit to Olivia Ltd £1,340.
8 7 October Returned damaged goods £38 to Arkimed plc.
9 7 October Purchased goods for resale on credit from Charlene £320.

Required (a) Identify the source document that has been used in each case to write up the book of prime entry.
          (b) Write up the books of prime entry.
          (c) Show the entries as they appear in each ledger account.

Answer

(a) Purchase invoices   Copy sales invoices   Credit note
     Transactions 1, 3, 5, 6, 9.   Transactions 2, 4, 7.   Transaction 8.

(b)

Purchase day book

		£
1 Oct	Arkimed plc PL 1	120
4 Oct	Bain & Co. PL 2	450
4 Oct	Darth & Son PL 3	170
7 Oct	Charlene PL 4	320
		1,060

Sales day book

		£
1 Oct	Morris plc SL 1	600
4 Oct	Nelson plc SL 2	315
7 Oct	Olivia Ltd SL 3	1,340
		2,255

Purchase returns day book

		£
7 Oct	Arkimed plc PL 1	38

Journal

		£	£
2 Oct	Vehicles GL 4	17,400	
	Pooley Motors plc PL 5		17,400
	Purchase of vehicle from Pooley Motors plc.		

(c)

Purchase ledger

Dr   Arkimed plc   Cr

| 7 Oct Returns outward PRDB 1 | 38 | 1 Oct Purchases | PDB 1 | 120 |

Dr   Bain & Co.   Cr

| | | 4 Oct Purchase | PDB 1 | 450 |

Dr   Darth & Son   Cr

| | | 4 Oct Purchases | PDB 1 | 170 |

Dr   Charlene   Cr

| | | 7 Oct Purchases | PDB 1 | 320 |

Dr   Pooley Motors plc   Cr

| | | 2 Oct Vehicles | J 1 | 17,400 |

Sales ledger

Dr			Morris plc		Cr
1 Oct Sales	SDB 1	600			

Dr			Nelson plc		Cr
4 Oct Sales	SDB 1	315			

Dr			Olivia Ltd		Cr
7 Oct Sales	SDB 1	1,340			

General ledger

Dr			Purchases account		Cr
7 Oct Sundry creditors PDB 1		1,060			

Dr			Sales account		Cr
			7 Oct Sundry debtors	SDB 1	2,255

Dr			Returns outward account		Cr
			7 Oct Sundry creditors	PRDB 1	38

Dr			Vehicles account		Cr
2 Oct Pooley motors plc PDB 5		17,400			

How can we check the accuracy of our book-keeping entries?

We can check the (arithmetical) accuracy of the entries in the double-entry system by extracting a trial balance.

The trial balance extracted from the ledgers above shows:

	Dr	Cr
Creditors		
Arkimed		82
Bain & Co.		450
Darth & Son		170
Charlene		320
Pooley Motors plc		17,400
Debtors		
Morris plc	600	
Nelson plc	315	
Olivia	1,340	
Purchases	1,060	
Sales		2,255
Returns outward		38
Vehicle	17,400	
	20,715	20,715

We can say that the book-keeping entries are arithmetically correct.

The cash book is a book of prime entry.

It contains the business cash account and the business bank account.

We will consider the cash book in much more detail later.

The following example uses the cash book as a book of prime entry:

WORKED EXAMPLE

The following transactions took place during December:

- 1 December paid rent using cash £250.
- 2 December paid rates by cheque £110.
- 6 December paid wages using cash £1,782.
- 13 December paid wages using cash £1,780.
- 17 December paid insurance premium by cheque £240.
- 20 December paid wages using cash £1,780.
- 27 December paid wages using cash £1,781.
- 31 December paid rent by cheque £250.

Required (a) Enter the transactions in a book of prime entry.
(b) Show the necessary ledger accounts.

Answer
(a)

Cash book

Dr   **Cash account**   **Cr**

1 Dec	Rent	GL 1	250
6 Dec	Wages	GL 4	1,782
13 Dec	Wages	GL 4	1,780
20 Dec	Wages	GL 4	1,780
27 Dec	Wages	GL 4	1,781

Dr   **Bank account**   **Cr**

2 Dec	Rates	GL 2	110
17 Dec	Insurance	GL 3	240
31 Dec	Rent	GL 1	250

(b)   **General ledger**

Dr   **Rent account**   **Cr**

1 Dec Cash	CB 1	250	
31 Dec Bank	CB 1	250	

Dr   **Rates account**   **Cr**

2 Dec Bank	CB 1	110	

Dr   **Insurance account**   **Cr**

17 Dec Bank	CB 1	240	

Dr   **Wages account**   **Cr**

6 Dec Cash	CB 1	1,782	
13 Dec Cash	CB 1	1,780	
20 Dec Cash	CB 1	1,780	
27 Dec Cash	CB 1	1,781	

Entering transactions in the books of prime entry and then the ledgers is not a difficult task; it just takes patience and the ability to enter transactions twice – once on the debit side of an account and once on the credit side of another account.

Remember: practice makes perfect.

Chapter summary

- Ledger accounts must show date; details of 'opposite' entry; folio details; and amount of transaction.
- 'T' accounts must be used only for revision purposes or as part of workings.
- All transactions must be entered in a book of prime entry before being posted to a ledger.

TEST QUESTIONS

QUESTION 1

Explain which book of prime entry would be used to enter the following transactions:

1. goods for resale purchased on credit from Dast
2. goods returned to Berks
3. purchase of office equipment from Cronin for cash
4. goods sold to Perks on credit
5. cash sales.

QUESTION 2

Which book of prime entry would be used to enter the following transactions?:

1. goods returned by Marshall
2. purchase of computer for use in the office on credit from Offo Ltd
3. goods sold to Barker on credit
4. goods for resale purchased for cash from Tinto
5. petrol purchased from Clive Road Garage for cash
6. purchase of office equipment from Desks & Co. for cash.

QUESTION 3

The following transaction took place during March 20*3:

March		£
2	Sold goods on credit to Fallon	217
6	Purchased goods on credit from Westby	179
19	Purchased goods on credit from Rawstron	731
23	Sold goods on credit to Slee	52
24	Sold goods on credit to Earley	770
31	Purchased goods on credit from Coulson	229

Required (a) Enter the transactions in the books of prime entry.
(b) Show the necessary entries in the ledgers.

QUESTION 4

The following transactions took place during August 20*3:

August		£
4	Purchased goods for resale from Dillon	551
6	Purchased goods for resale from Black	901
11	Sold goods on credit to Adder	510
23	Purchased goods on credit from Breem	56
30	Sold goods on credit to Goody	190
31	Sold goods on credit to O'Shea	77

Required (a) Enter the transactions in the books of prime entry.
(b) Show the necessary entries in the ledgers.

QUESTION 5

The following credit transactions took place during February 20*3:

February		£
1	Sold goods to Davidson	59
5	Purchased goods from Sellars	911
6	Purchased goods from Garewal	187
7	Purchased goods from Chan	67
15	Sold goods to Nixon	563
23	Goods retuned by Davidson	19
27	Goods returned to Sellars	45
28	Sold goods to Nismo	518
28	Goods returned to Garewal	12

Required (a) Enter the transactions in the books of prime entry.
(b) Show the necessary entries in the ledgers.

QUESTION 6

The following credit transactions took place during April 20*3:

April		£
1	Sold goods to Marks	458
3	Sold goods to Henry	121
4	Goods retuned by Marks	59
7	Purchased goods from Binns	72
8	Sold goods to Shaw	923
9	Purchased goods from Baxter	777
21	Purchased goods from Spencer	43
25	Goods returned by Henry	21
28	Sold goods to Marks	631
29	Goods returned to Binns	55

Required (a) Enter the transactions in the books of prime entry.
(b) Show the necessary entries in the ledgers.

QUESTION 7

The following credit transactions took place during October 20*3:

October		£
3	Sold goods to Clements	456
5	Purchased delivery van from Austen Motors	23,580
8	Sold goods to Lycett	53
12	Purchased goods from Crosby	598
13	Goods returned by Clements	34
14	Sold goods to Clements	437
21	Purchased goods from Cox	674
22	Purchased goods from Patel	771
29	Purchased goods from Frear	50
30	Goods returned to Crosby	140

Required (a) Enter the transactions in the books of prime entry.
(b) Show the necessary entries in the ledgers.

QUESTION 8

The following credit transactions took place during December 20*3:

December		£
4	Purchased goods from Taylor	632
5	Sold goods to Butcher	562
8	Purchased shop fiitings from Archer	7,600
11	Sold goods to Gravinski	87
14	Returned goods to Taylor	135
15	Sold goods to Bush	908
18	Goods returned by Butcher	99
20	Purchased goods from Lim	412
29	Goods sold to McDuff	138
30	Purchased goods from Taylor	44

Required (a) Enter the transaction in the books of prime entry.
(b) Show the necessary entries in the ledgers.

QUESTION 9

Jim Kelly owns and runs a clothes shop.

The following transactions took place during June 20*3:

June		£
1	Goods sold on credit to Thomas	97
4	Goods purchased on credit from Tunk Ltd	573
7	Display units purchased on credit from Sheep Ltd.	3,750
8	Cash sales for the week	752
12	Goods returned by Thomas	97
14	Goods purchased on credit from Tupp	880
15	Cash sales for week	893
22	Cash sales for week	439
23	Goods sold to Shah on credit	254
27	Goods returned to Tupp	108
29	Cash sales for week	1,065
30	Goods purchased from Rult on credit	349

Required (a) Enter the transactions in the books of prime entry.
(b) Show the necessary entries in the ledgers.

QUESTION 10

Rebecca owns and runs a garage.

The following transactions took place during March 20*3:

March		£
2	Goods purchased on credit from Spanners plc	452
4	Credit sales to Drodlet.	290
6	Goods purchased for cash from Lygett	740
9	Credit sales to Drodlet	540
11	Purchase of hydraulic jack from Upps Ltd	5,250
12	Cash sales to Corston	230
16	Goods returned to Spanners plc	27
19	Goods returned by Drodlet	53
23	Goods purchased on credit from Fox	993
27	Cash sale to Bishop	450
28	Goods returned to Lygett	18
30	Goods purchased on credit from Fadley	651
31	Goods sold on credit to Mundy	511

Required (a) Enter the transactions in the books of prime entry.
(b) Show the necessary entries in the ledgers.

CHAPTER
ELEVEN

The Two-column Cash Book

We have looked in some detail at the five books of prime entry used to gain entry into the double-entry system.

The sixth and final book of prime entry is the cash book. The other five books were concerned with **credit** transactions. The cash book records all transactions concerning **money**. Money can be in the form of cash, cheques, credit and debit card transactions.

In a previous chapter we used a cash account and a bank account and you would then quickly have noticed that those accounts were used very frequently and as a result became very full with entries.

Generally, in business, these accounts are used more frequently than any other accounts. This means that is sensible to remove these two accounts from the general ledger and keep them apart from the other accounts.

The cash and bank accounts are kept separately in one book – the cash book.

Because it is such an important and sensitive area of the business, all cash and cheque transactions are usually the responsibility of one senior or well-qualified person – the cashier.

The accounts in the cash book work on double-entry principles like all other accounts:

■ the debit (or receiving) side is found on the left
■ the credit (or giving) side is on the right.

The only difference in the layout of the cash book is that the debit entries are distanced from the credit entries by extra columns and information and that the debit entries, generally, take up the whole of the left page while the credit entries take up the whole of the right page.

The layout is the same on both sides of the cash book:

Specification coverage:
AQA 10.1;
OCR 5.1.1.

By the end of this chapter you should be able to:
■ write up a two-column cash book
■ make entries involving cash and cheques received
■ make entries involving cash and cheque payments
■ make contra entries in the cash book.

EXAMPLE

The debit side of the cash book looks like this:

Cash book				
Date	Particular	Folio	Cash	Bank

The credit side of the cash book looks like this:

Cash book				
	Date	Particulars	Folio	Cash	Bank

The whole cash book looks like this:

Cash book									
Date (1)	Particulars (2)	Folio (3)	Cash (4)	Bank (5)	Date (6)	Particulars (7)	Folio (8)	Cash (9)	Bank (10)

The columns are used in the same way that the ledger columns were used:

(1) and (6) give the date on which the transaction occurred.
(2) and (7) identify the account where the corresponding entry can be found.
(3) and (8) show the page of the ledger where the corresponding entry can be found.
(4) all cash received is entered in this column.
(5) all monies paid into the business bank account are recorded in this column.
(9) all cash payments made are recorded in this column.
(10) all payments made by cheque are recorded in this column.

WORKED EXAMPLE

Joe Flint maintains a two-column cash book. The following transactions have taken place:

1 September	Joe paid R. Serth £34 cash
2 September	he paid T. Horse £167 cash
5 September	he paid V. Dole £78 cash.

Required Enter the transactions in Joe Flint's cash book.

Answer

Cash book

Date	Particulars	Folio	Cash	Bank	Date	Particulars	Folio	Cash	Bank
					1 Sept	R. Serth	PL9	34	
					2 Sept	T. Horse	PL6	167	
					5 Sept	V. Dole	PL 2	78	

WORKED EXAMPLE

Fred Baggs maintains a two-column cash book. The following transactions have taken place:

3 February	Fred paid rent £400 by cheque
7 February	he paid Gary £67 by cheque
9 February	he paid wages £832 by cheque.

Required Enter the transactions in Fred's cash book.

Answer

Cash book

Date	Particulars	Folio	Cash	Bank	Date	Particulars	Folio	Cash	Bank
					3 Feb	Rent	GL8		400
					7 Feb	Gary	PL9		67
					9 Feb	Wages	GL15		832

WORKED EXAMPLE

Rageh maintains a two-column cash book. The following transactions have taken place:

4 May	Cash received from Nigel £213
5 May	Cash received from Harry £92
9 May	Cash received from Hilary £729.

Required Enter the transactions in Rageh's cash book.

Answer

Cash book

Date	Particulars	Folio	Cash	Bank	Date	Particulars	Folio	Cash	Bank
4 May	Nigel	SL12	213						
5 May	Harry	SL 7	92						
9 May	Hilary	SL 8	729						

WORKED EXAMPLE

Bertha maintains a two-column cash book. The following transactions have taken place:

2 January	Cheque received from Steve £249
3 January	Cash sales banked £851
11 January	Cheque received from Mustaf £29.

Required Enter the transactions in Bertha's cash book.

Answer

Cash book

Date	Particulars	Folio	Cash	Bank	Date	Particulars	Folio	Cash	Bank
2 Jan	Steve	SL5		249					
3 Jan	Cash sales	GL23		851					
11 Jan	Mustaf	SL7		29					

WORKED EXAMPLE

Garibaldi maintains a two-column cash book. The following transactions have taken place:

2 April	Cash received from Xavier, a customer, £458
4 April	Motor repairs £530 paid by cash
6 April	Cash received from Milly, a customer £77
7 April	Rent £210 paid by cash
9 April	Insurance premium £156 paid by cash
12 April	Cash sales £743.

Required Enter the transactions in Garibaldi's cash book.

Answer

Cash book

Date	Particulars	Folio	Cash	Bank	Date	Particulars	Folio	Cash	Bank
2 Apr	Xavier	SL 4	458		4 Apr	Motor exps	GL23	530	
6 Apr	Milly	SL 13	77		7 Apr	Rent	GL 8	210	
12 Apr	Cash sales	GL 2	743		9 Apr	Insurance	GL11	156	

WORKED EXAMPLE

Hertz maintains a two-column cash book. The following transactions have taken place:

3 October	Price, a supplier, paid £350 by cheque
6 October	Hertz receives a cheque for £450, an overpayment of rent
9 October	Takings paid into bank £2187
11 October	Bliff, a customer, paid by cheque £639
12 October	A cheque received from Box £93 paid into the bank
17 October	Rates £219 paid by cheque.

Required Enter the transactions in Hertz's cash book.

Answer

Cash book

Date	Particulars	Folio	Cash	Bank	Date	Particulars	Folio	Cash	Bank
6 Oct	Rent	GL 6		450	3 Oct	Price	SL4		350
9 Oct	Sales	GL17		2,187	11 Oct	Bliff	SL23		639
12 Oct	Box	PL14		93	17 Oct	Rates	GL7		219

It is now simply a matter of putting cash payments and cash receipts in the same book as cheque payments and monies paid into the bank.

WORKED EXAMPLE

Matthew maintains a two-column cash book. The following transactions have taken place:

1 November	Cheque from Norman, a customer, £288 paid into bank
2 November	Motor expenses paid by cheque £311
5 November	Matthew draws a cheque for private use £150
10 November	Cash takings £2,390
15 November	Motor fuel purchased with cash £42
21 November	Cheque paid into bank for rates rebate £273
29 November	Paid wages in cash £1,309
30 November	Takings £5,630 paid directly into bank.

Required Enter the transactions in Matthew's cash book.

Answer

Cash book

Date	Particulars	Folio	Cash	Bank	Date	Particulars	Folio	Cash	Bank
1 Nov	Norman	SL 4		288	2 Nov	Motor expenses	GL 12		311
10 Nov	Sales	GL9	2,390		5 Nov	Drawings	GL23		150
21 Nov	Rates	GL11		273	15 Nov	Motor expenses	GL12	42	
30 Nov	Sales	GL9		5,630	29 Nov	Wages	GL7	1,309	

QUESTION 1

Miller maintains a two-column cash book. The following **cash** transactions have taken place:

1 February	Cash received from Cling, a cutomer, £76
3 February	Cash paid to cleaner £94
5 February	Cash takings £522
6 February	Motor fuel purchased for cash £51

7 February   Cash received from Laker £83
8 February   Wages paid in cash £317.

Required Enter the transactions in the cash book.

QUESTION 2

Pratesh maintains a two-column cash book. The following **cash** transactions have taken place:

1 May   Cash received from Knight, a customer, £102
2 May   Cash takings £760
5 May   Stationery purchased for cash £75
6 May   Cash received from McGough £54
7 May   Brunton, a supplier, paid with cash £68
8 May   Part-time worker paid cash £49.

Required Enter the transactions in the cash book.

QUESTION 3

Allen maintains a two-column cash book. The following transactions have taken place using the business **bank account**:

1 July   Insurance premium paid by cheque £548
4 July   Wages paid by cheque £752
6 July   Cheque received from Hanks £138
7 July   Allen withdraws money for personal use by cheque £150
8 July   Cash sales banked £2,693
9 July   Cheque received from Kann £198.

Required Enter the transactions in the cash book.

QUESTION 4

Glaze maintains a two-column cash book. The following transactions have taken place:

1 April   Received rates refund by cheque £450
2 April   Cash sales £2,490
2 April   Rent paid by cheque £650
3 April   Cash sales paid directly into the bank £787
4 April   Paid wages in cash £236
4 April   Received loan £12,000, paid directly into bank
4 April   Purchased motor van, paid by cheque £9,800
6 April   Paid Trew, a supplier, cash £23.

Required Enter the transactions in the cash book.

The source documents used to write up the cash book are:

■ Debit side – copy receipts
              till rolls
              paying-in book counterfoils

■ Credit side – receipts
              paying-in book counterfoils
              cheque book counterfoils.

A further source of information to be used to write up the cash book is the bank statements sent out by the bank showing a copy of the details of transactions made using the business – but more of this source later.

> **Cash in hand** is the term used to describe the amount of cash held by a business at any one time. The cash in hand in a shop would be found in the tills. In a larger business it could, perhaps, be found in the safe.

■ At the end of an appropriate length of time, the cash book should be balanced [the time when balancing takes place will generally depend on the size of the business and the number of transactions that are included in the cash book].

- Both of the balances in the cash book should be verified.
- How could you verify the cash balance brought down?
- How could you verify the bank balance that you brought down?

- The balance brought down in the cash column should agree with the cash in hand at that date.
- The bank balance in the cash book can be verified by reference to the bank statement.
- The cash and bank columns of the cash book are balanced in the same way that ledger accounts are balanced.
- The balances are brought down to start the 'new' time period.
- Remember: the cash balance will always be brought down as a debit. The bank balance brought down could be either a debit or a credit balance.

WORKED EXAMPLE

The cash book of Grey is shown:

Cash book

Date	Particulars	Folio	Cash	Bank	Date	Particulars	Folio	Cash	Bank
1 Nov	Reid	SL6		1,439	4 Nov	Wages	GL4		428
6 Nov	Sales	GL9	1,270		7 Nov	Hunt	PL6	73	
8 Nov	Gong	SL23		451	11 Nov	Rent	GL6		600
14 Nov	Potts	SL14		349	16 Nov	Trig	PL16	38	

Required Balance the cash and bank columns of the cash book on 16 November and carry any balances down.

Answer

Cash book

Date	Particulars	Folio	Cash	Bank	Date	Particulars	Folio	Cash	Bank
1 Nov	Reid	SL6		1,439	4 Nov	Wages	GL4		428
6 Nov	Sales	GL6	1,270		7 Nov	Hunt	PL6	73	
8 Nov	Gong	SL23		451	11 Nov	Rent	GL6		600
14 Nov	Potts	SL14		349	16 Nov	Trig	PL16	38	
					16 Nov	*Balances*	c/d	1,159	1,211
			1,270	2,239				1,270	2,239
17 Nov	Balances b/d		1,159	1,211					

Note
- Make sure that all four totals are on the same line.
- Balance the cash columns first; then balance the bank columns. Don't try to do them both at the same time.

● EXAMINATION TIP

Always bring balances down; if you don't, you will lose at least one mark in an examination

QUESTION 5

The cash book of Rowe is shown:

					Cash book				
Date	**Particulars**	**Folio**	**Cash**	**Bank**	**Date**	**Particulars**	**Folio**	**Cash**	**Bank**
2 Jan	Hatters	SL17	238		9 Jan	Postages	GL21	45	
5 Jan	Cash sales	GL7	1,458		11 Jan	Blagg	PL25		347
9 Jan	Ffunders	SL34		2,376	14 Jan	Wages	GL6	905	
15 Jan	Rodders	SL10		349	16 Jan	Defroux	PL13		312

Required Balance the cash and bank columns of the cash book on 16 January and carry any balances down.

> A transaction that appears on both the debit and credit sides of the double-entry system is called a **contra entry**.

Contra entries have no effect on the wellbeing of the business.

Clearly, it is unsafe to keep large amounts of cash and cheques on the business premises for prolonged periods of time. The cashier will arrange for the monies received to be taken to the bank and deposited when the amount in the till or safe warrants it.

WORKED EXAMPLE

The following is an extract from the cash book of Grant:

					Cash book				
Date	**Particulars**	**Folio**	**Cash**	**Bank**	**Date**	**Particulars**	**Folio**	**Cash**	**Bank**
4 Jul	Cash sales	GL32	4,397		5 Jul	Purchases	GL7	48	
4 Jul	Bradley	SL51	74						

Grant has more than £4,000 cash on his premises – this represents a security risk. He pays £4,000 into the business bank account on 5 July.

Talk yourself through this transaction.

Grant takes £4,000 from the till ... the cash column loses £4,000.

5 July Bank   C   4,000

Note
- The date of the transaction.
- The particulars telling where the 'opposite' entry is to be found (in the bank column).
- 'C' is for 'contra', showing that Grant's business is neither better nor worse off because of the transaction.
- £4,000 in the cash column shows that cash has been 'lost'.

Grant takes the money to the bank and the bank receives the money.

5 July   Cash   C   4,000

Again note:
- the date of the transaction
- the particulars telling where the opposite entry is to be found (in the cash column)
- 'C' is for 'contra', showing that Grant's business is neither better nor worse off because of the transaction
- £4,000 in the bank column shows that money has been received into the bank account.

The effect on the business is the same as the effect on your finances that would occur if you moved a five pound note out of one pocket into another pocket.

Another common contra entry in the cash book is the withdrawal of cash from the bank for use in the business. This transaction often occurs when cash wages need to be paid and the business has insufficient cash in the safe to make up the necessary wage packets.

[Because of security measures, many larger businesses now pay wages and salaries directly into staff bank accounts so that large amounts of cash do not need to be transported from the bank and then kept on the business's premises.]

WORKED EXAMPLE

The following is an extract from the cash book of Dan:

						Cash book			
Date	Particulars	Folio	Cash	Bank	Date	Particulars	Folio	Cash	Bank
12 Aug	Robson	SL32		4,574	11 Aug	Machinery	GL6	2,350	
16 Aug	Nkomo	SL79		5,490					

Wages amounting to £4,529 have to be paid in cash on 18 August. Dan withdraws this sum from the bank on 17 August.

If we talk ourselves through the process, the entries become clear . . .

Dan goes to the bank and withdraws £4,529:

17 Aug	Cash	C		4,529

He returns to his business premises and puts the cash in the safe:

17 Aug	Bank	C	4,529	

QUESTION 6

On 17 December Phil draws £27,300 from the business bank account to pay the wage bill due on 20 December.

On 23 December he pays £4,768 cash receipts into the bank account.

Required Show the entries necessary to complete both transactions:

Date	Particulars	Folio	Cash	Bank	Date	Particulars	Folio	Cash	Bank
17 Dec					17 Dec				
23 Dec					23 Dec				

Many larger businesses now keep a cheque payments book and a cash receipts and lodgement book. This is certainly the case where the bulk of transactions are conducted through the bank account. Any cash payments with this form of recording are entered in a cash account and a petty cash book. In such a system the petty cash book would have a substantial float for the imprest.

Chapter summary

- The cash book is both a book of prime entry and a part of the double-entry system.
- All transactions that involve cash are entered in the cash book.
- All cash transactions are entered in the cash columns.
- All transactions involving cheques are entered in the bank columns.
- Contra items have no effect on the worth of the business.
- Any balance shown in the cash column must be a debit balance.
- Balances shown in the bank column could be either a debit or a credit balance.

Self-test questions

- Draw out the headings used in a two-column cash book.
- What does the word 'contra' mean?
- Complete the sentence: 'The cash book is not only a book of prime entry; it is also part of the …………….. ……………… system.'
- In which column would a cash sale be entered?
- In which column would a cheque for the payment of rates be entered?
- Complete the sentence: 'Money taken from the safe and deposited in the bank would be …………. in the cash column of the cash book and be …………… in the bank column.' (Enter 'debit' or 'credit'.)
- Which book of prime entry would you use to record a sale of goods on credit?
- Name two source documents used to write up the cash book.
- Is it possible to have a credit balance in the cash column of the cash book?
- Is it possible to have a credit balance in the bank column of the cash book?
- Complete the sentence: 'Money withdrawn from the bank for use in the business would be ………. in the cash column of the cash book and be …………. in the bank column.' (Enter 'debit' or 'credit'.)

TEST QUESTIONS

QUESTION 7

The following transactions relate to the business of Martin:

1 May	Cash sales £349
2 May	Electricity bill paid by cash £163
3 May	Received cheque £561 from Ed, a customer
6 May	Cash sales £670
6 May	Cash paid into the bank £500
7 May	Paid wages by cheque £471
8 May	Purchased stationery £112 by cash.

Required (a) Enter the transactions in the cash book.
(b) Balance the cash book as at 7 May.

QUESTION 8

The following transactions relate to the business of Silver:

3 October	Cheque received £540 from Benedict
4 October	Cash sales £469
7 October	Cash received £591 from Frout
8 October	Telephone bill paid £261 by cheque
8 October	Gas bill paid £171 cash
8 October	Cash paid into bank £750
9 October	Cheque received £347 from Neal.

Required (a) Enter the transactions in the cash book.
(b) Balance the cash book as at 9 October.

QUESTION 9

The following transactions relate to the business of Hunter:

2 April	Cash sales £1,792
3 April	Cash paid into bank £1,500
4 April	Cheque received from Burgess £286
6 April	Rent paid by cheque £240
7 April	Insurance premium £110 paid by cash
8 April	Cheque paid for repairs £892
8 April	Cash sales £135.

Required (a) Enter the transactions into the cash book.
(b) Balance the cash book as at 8 April.

QUESTION 10

The following transactions relate to the business of Lamb:

3 November	Cash sales £452
5 November	Cash withdrawn by Lamb for private use £125
6 November	Cash sales £2,380
6 November	Cash paid into bank £2,500
8 November	Wages paid by cheque £1,432
9 November	Cheque paid to Ripon, a supplier, £475
10 November	Cash paid for cleaning materials £28.

Required (a) Enter the transactions in the cash book.
(b) Balance the cash book as at 10 November.

QUESTION 11

The following transactions relate to the business of Golightly:

2 January	Cash sales paid directly into bank £3,487
3 January	Cash received from Thompson, a customer, £172
3 January	Motor expenses paid by cheque £345
5 January	Rates paid by cheque £210
6 January	Cash sales £1,372
7 January	Cash paid into bank £1,000
9 January	Motor fuel purchased £48 cash.

Required (a) Enter the transactions in the cash book.
(b) Balance the cash book as at 9 January.

QUESTION 12

The following transaction relate to the business of Dublin:

3 May	Cash sales £4,268
3 May	Cash paid into bank £4,000
5 May	Rates paid by cheque £245
6 May	Cheque received from Marks, a customer, £2,120
7 May	£2,467 withdrawn from the bank for use in the business
8 May	Wages paid £2,467 cash.

Required (a) Enter the transactions in the cash book.
(b) Balance the cash book as at 8 May.

QUESTION 13

The following transactions relate to the business of York:

19 October	Cash sales £2,380
20 October	Stationery purchased £120 cash
21 October	Motor fuel purchased £38 cash
21 October	£1,950 paid into bank
22 October	Cash sales paid directly into bank £2,785
23 October	Cheque paid to Todd, a supplier, £490

| 24 October | Cash withdrawn from bank £2,500 |
| 25 October | Wages paid £1,988 cash. |

Required (a) Enter the transactions in the cash book.
(b) Balance the cash book as at 25 October.

QUESTION 14

The following transactions relate to the business of Robin:

23 May	Cash sales £2,887
24 May	Telephone bill paid £176 cash
24 May	Vehicle repair paid £483 by cheque
25 May	Wages paid £1,784 cash
27 May	Cash sales £2,590
28 May	Cheque received from Retop Ltd £674
29 May	Cash paid into bank £2,000
30 May	Robin withdraws £275 cash from bank for personal use.

Required (a) Enter the transactions in the cash book.
(b) Balance the cash book as at 30 May.

CHAPTER
TWELVE

The Petty Cash Book

A **float** is an amount of money put in the petty cash box at the start of the period to enable daily payments to be made.

Imprest is the system generally used to maintain a cash float from which small cash expenses can be paid.

Specification coverage:
AQA 10.1;
OCR 5.1.1.

By the end of this chapter you should be able to:
■ write up a petty cash book
■ use an imprest system
■ analyse petty cash payments.

The petty cash book records the many small items of expenditure that may occur on a daily basis. The main work of the cashiers would be interrupted if they were to be asked frequently for money for postages, small items of stationery, travel expenses etc. It would also take up much space in the main cash book if many trivial transactions were to be recorded.

The petty cashier is responsible for the payment of petty (small) amounts and for entering the payments into the petty cash book. Although it is a responsible position, it is generally an additional role given to a receptionist or personal assistant.

An amount of money (the imprest) is advanced to the petty cashier to enable payments for small amounts of expenditure to be made.

THE ADVANTAGES OF USING AN IMPREST SYSTEM

1. It saves the time of the main cashiers who may be very busy dealing with the main functions of the business.
2. It gives junior members of staff responsibility for a limited amount of cash and encourages accuracy in accounting for it.
3. The imprest is fairly small and unlikely to be the subject of fraudulent activities.
4. It saves time in the posting of small items to the main ledgers since the analysis columns collects and summarises these.

THE IMPREST SYSTEM

The basic idea of the system is that the main cashier will give the petty cashier an amount of cash sufficient to cover expenses for the ensuing period.

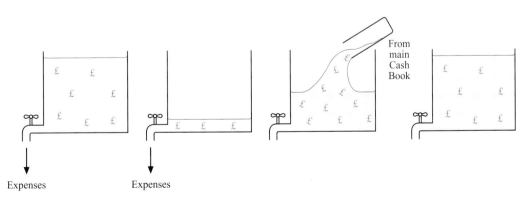

When the petty cash 'float' is low the main cashier will 'top up' the petty cash float to its original level.

P.C. Float	50
P.C. Expenses	<u>37</u>
	13
Cash from Cashier to reimburse	<u>37</u>
	<u>50</u>

All money paid out by the petty cashier should be supported by a petty cash voucher showing who received the money and for what reason. It should be signed by the recipient.

The petty cash book is an extension of the main cash book and as such is part of the double-entry system.

There are, generally, very few debit entries in the petty cash book and the layout reflects this.

> **Petty cash vouchers** are filled in each time money is taken from the petty cash float. The voucher should be signed by the person receiving the cash. Any receipts obtained should be attached to the voucher.

SOURCE DOCUMENTS USED TO PREPARE THE PETTY CASH BOOK ARE

- Receipts gained when the person spending the money has paid for the items, for example receipts for postages from the local post office, petrol receipts from the garage, receipts for drawing pins or envelopes etc.
- Petty cash vouchers – the person spending the money should fill in the voucher with the nature of the expenditure and should sign it.
- Clearly, where possible, receipts should be supplied to the petty cashier since the money spent can be verified as a genuine expense.

HOW OFTEN WILL THE IMPREST BE RESTORED TO ITS ORIGINAL AMOUNT?

It is difficult to answer this question precisely. The imprest will be restored when the petty cashier feels that he or she has insufficient funds to pay any requests for expenses incurred the following day. Clearly, this could be every few days in some businesses while in others the 'topping up' of the imprest may occur less frequently.

HOW LARGE WILL THE IMPREST BE?

Once again, it is difficult to answer this question with precision. In, say, a transport business the imprest would be fairly large since drivers will require cash to pay for overnight accommodation, meals and vehicle fuel. In the case of a small business where staff incur very few out-of-pocket transactions on behalf of the business, the imprest need not be very large.

BALANCING THE PETTY CASH BOOK

The difficult part of preparing the petty cash book occurs when the imprest is restored.

[There are a number of alternative book-keeping methods used but my advice is to use only one method and to learn this thoroughly – use the same method every time.]

WORKED EXAMPLE

Aslam Shoaib maintains a petty cash book as well as a main cash book.

The imprest for the petty cash book is £100. During the first week of September the following monies were paid out by the petty cashier:

1 September	£8 paid for postages
2 September	£16 paid for flowers for a sick colleague
3 September	£20 paid for petrol
4 September	£6 paid for envelopes
5 September	£10 paid to plumber for repairing tap in washroom
6 September	£23 paid to Post Office for mailing a parcel.

Required   Balance the petty cash book and show the entries necessary to restore the imprest to £100.

Answer

Receipts £	Folio	Date	Details	Voucher no.	Payment £	
100.00	CB5	1 Sept	Cash			
		1 Sept	Postages	1	8.00	
		2 Sept	Sundries	2	16.00	
		3 Sept	Petrol	3	20.00	
		4 Sept	Stationery	4	6.00	
		5 Sept	Repairs	5	10.00	
		6 Sept	Postages	6	23.00	
					83.00	*has been spent*
		6 Sept	Balance	c/d	17.00	*left in float*
100.00					100.00	
17.00		7 Sept	Balance	b/d		*left in float*
83.00	CB12	7 Sept	Cash			*amount received from main cashier to restore the imprest*

WORKED EXAMPLE

Reine Polydor owns and runs a transport business. She maintains a petty cash book with an imprest of £300. She provides the following information relating to petty cash transactions:

5 May	Overnight accommodation for driver £48
5 May	Paid for petrol £20
6 May	Postages £12
6 May	Overnight accommodation £96
7 May	Postage paid for parcel £8
7 May	Stationery purchased £25
8 May	Overnight accommodation £52.

Required   Balance the petty cash book and show the entries necessary to restore the imprest to £300.

WORKED EXAMPLE *continued*

Answer

Receipts	Folio	Date	Details	Voucher no.	Payment
300	CB41	5 May	Cash		
		5 May	Accommodation	23	48
		5 May	Petrol	24	20
		6 May	Postages	25	12
		6 May	Accommodation	26	96
		7 May	Postage	27	8
		7 May	Stationery	28	25
		8 May	Accommodation	29	52
					261
		8 May	Balance	c/d	39
300					300
39		9 May	Balance	b/d	
261	CB47	9 May	Cash		

QUESTION 1

Nancy Ng maintains a petty cash book with an imprest of £100.

The following transactions have taken place using petty cash during July:

1 July	Cash received from main cashier £100
6 July	Cleaning materials purchased £22
13 July	Stamps purchased £15
22 July	Petrol paid for £28
23 July	Postage on parcel £11.

Required Balance the petty cash book and show the entries necessary to restore the imprest.

QUESTION 2

John James maintains a petty cash book with an imprest of £250.

The following transactions took place using petty cash during February:

1 Feb	Accommodation for salesperson £80
3 Feb	Petrol paid for £20
9 Feb	Cleaning materials purchased £15
11 Feb	Accommodation for salesperson £65
15 Feb	Postages £22
16 Feb	Envelopes and computer disks purchased £12
21 Feb	Coffee, tea, milk and sugar for staff £16.

Required Balance the petty cash book and show the entries necessary to restore the imprest.

QUESTION 3

How much cash would the petty cashier require from the main cashier to restore the imprest of £100 in the following cases?

1 The petty cashier has spent £96.
2 Petty cash in hand is £18.
3 The petty cashier has spent £69.
4 Petty cash in hand is £22.

QUESTION 4

How much cash would the petty cashier require from the main cashier to restore the imprest of £250 in the following cases?

1 Petty cash in hand is £19.
2 Petty cash in hand is £21.

3 The petty cashier has spent £247.
4 The petty cashier has spent £188.
5 Petty cash in hand is £7.
6 The petty cashier has spent £191.

ANALYSIS COLUMNS IN THE PETTY CASH BOOK

The credit side of the petty cash book is generally kept using analysis columns. This means that instead of posting each item of expenditure separately to the general ledger, a number of items are posted at once.

WORKED EXAMPLE

Frank Org maintains a petty cash book using the imprest system. The imprest is £100. The following transactions have taken place:

2 March	Petrol for delivery van £32
4 March	Postages £12
7 March	Postages £8
14 March	Cleaning materials £23
15 March	Postages £6.

Required Prepare the analytical petty cash book, balance the book and show the entries necessary to restore the imprest to £100.

Answer

Receipts	Folio	Date	Details	Voucher no.	Total	Motor expenses	Postages	Cleaning
100	CB29	1 Mar	Cash					
		2 Mar	Petrol	23	32	32		
		4 Mar	Postages	24	12		12	
		7 Mar	Postages	25	8		8	
		14 Mar	Cleaning	26	23			23
		15 Mar	Postages	27	6		6	
					81	32	26	23
		15 Mar	Balance	c/d	19	gl 13	gl 15	gl 16
100					100			
19		16 Mar	Balance	b/d				
81	CB37	16 Mar	Cash					

- The total of the motor expenses column is posted to the debit of the motor expenses account which can be found on page 13 in the general ledger.
- The total of the postages column is posted to the debit of the postages account which can be found on page 15 in the general ledger.
- The total of the cleaning column is posted to the debit of the cleaning account which can be found on page 16 in the general ledger.

Hopefully, you can see that this process is more efficient than posting individual amounts to the general ledger as and when they arise.

Also, note that the petty cash book is a book of prime entry like the main cash book.

WORKED EXAMPLE

Doreen Bishop keeps an analytical petty cash book using the imprest system.

Her imprest is £200. On 4 June the petty cash in hand amounted to £18. The following transactions have taken place during the first week of June:

4 June	Motor expenses £30
5 June	Employee's bed and breakfast £38
5 June	Motor expenses £24
6 June	Postages £25
8 June	Cleaning materials £21
9 June	Employee's bed and breakfast £38.

Required Prepare the analytical petty cash book, balance the book and show the entries necessary to restore the imprest.

Answer

Receipts	Folio	Date	Details	Voucher no.	Total	Motor exps	Accdn	Postages	Cleaning
18		4 June	Balance	b/d					
182	CB87	4 June	Cash						
		4 June	Motor exps	13	30	30			
		5 June	Bed and breakf	14	38		38		
		5 June	Motor exps	15	24	24			
		6 June	Postages	16	25			25	
		8 June	Cleaning mats	17	21				21
		9 June	Bed and breakf	18	38		38		
					176	54	76	25	21
		9 June	Balance	c/d	24	gl 19	gl 3	gl 27	gl 8
200					200				
24		10 June	Balance	b/d					
176	CB95	10 June	Cash						

To summarise: the petty cash book is balanced off each time the petty cashier feels that there are insufficient funds left to meet the next day's requirements.

- A line is drawn underneath the total and analysis columns on the credit side of the book. These columns are totalled.
- As a check, the totals of the analysis columns should add across and equal the amount shown in the total column.
- The analysis columns are closed with the usual double underlining.
- The cash in hand is calculated and included in the total credit column as a balance to be carried down.
- The debit amount column and the credit total column must agree and they should be closed (by double underlining!).
- The balance is carried down to the debit side.
- The imprest is restored by an amount (equal to the expenditure incurred by the petty cashier) received from the main cashier.
- All the analysis columns are posted to the debit side of the appropriate ledger account in the general ledger (and in some instances the purchase ledger).

Note

There may be some entries on the debit side of the petty cash book. However, these are rare and are generally not examined.

Examples of debit entries could include the money paid by a member of staff who has purchased a stamp for private use, or a payment from a member of staff who has made a private telephone call and has paid the petty cashier for the call.

WORKED EXAMPLE

Tommy Cubby keeps an analytical petty cash book. His imprest is £50.

On 19 October the petty cash in hand amounted to £7. The following transactions have taken place:

19 October	Postages £15
20 October	Travelling expenses £3
26 October	Postage for parcel £7
27 October	Money received from member of staff for private telephone call £2
28 October	Stationery £17.

Required Prepare the petty cash book, balance the book and show the entries necessary to restore the imprest.

Answer

Receipts	Folio	Date	Details	Voucher no.	Total	Travel exps	Postage	Stationery
7		19 Oct	Balance	b/d				
43	CB 16	19 Oct	Cash					
		19 Oct	Postage	54	15		15	
		20 Oct	Travelling	55	3	3		
		26 Oct	Postage	56	7		7	
2	gl 17	27 Oct	Telephone					
		28 Oct	Stationery	57	17			17
					42	3	22	17
		28 Oct	Balance	c/d	10			
52					52			
10		28 Oct	Balance	b/d				
40	CB 23	28 Oct	Cash					

Chapter summary

- The petty cash book is used to record small items of expenditure. If these small items were included in the main cash book it would soon become full of insignificant entries that would all need to be posted to the ledgers individually rather than as totals of the petty cash book analysis columns

QUESTION 5

Divya Talwar keeps an analytical cash book. Her imprest is £200. On 23 January her petty cash in hand was £32. Payments out of petty cash were:

23 January	Travelling expenses £45
24 January	Postages £20
24 January	Cleaning expenses £19
24 January	Travelling expenses £30
26 January	Travelling expenses £51
28 January	Parcel post £8.

Required Prepare the petty cash book with analysis columns for travelling expenses, postages and cleaning. Balance the book and show the entries necessary to restore the imprest.

QUESTION 6

The following is a summary of petty cash transactions of Barclay Froom. He maintains an imprest of £100. At 7 August Barclay had petty cash in hand of £12.

7 August	Travel £18
7 August	Postages £12
8 August	Stationery £26

9 August	Cleaning materials £16
10 August	Travel £16
11 August	Postages £10.

Required Prepare the petty cash book with analysis columns for travel, postages, stationery and cleaning. Balance the book and show any entries necessary to restore the imprest.

QUESTION 7

Tom Nixon keeps an analytical petty cash book. He maintains an imprest of £500. At 17 July Tom had petty cash in hand of £68. The following transactions have taken place:

17 July	Motor expenses £56
18 July	Overnight accommodation £107
18 July	Postages £30
21 July	Overnight accommodation £88
23 July	Cleaning materials £19
23 July	Overnight accommodation £102
24 July	Postages £15
25 July	Overnight accommodation £54.

Required Prepare the petty cash book with analysis columns for motor expenses, accommodation, postages and cleaning. Balance the book and show any entries necessary to restore the imprest.

QUESTION 8

Joyce McTavish maintains an analytical petty cash book. She has an imprest of £150.

At 29 April Joyce had petty cash in hand of £17. The following transactions have taken place:

29 April	Postages £16
29 April	Motor expenses £18
30 April	Cleaning materials £26
2 May	Petrol for delivery van £15
3 May	Postages £12
4 May	Cleaner's wage £32
5 May	Petrol for van £18
5 May	Postages £5.

Required Prepare the petty cash book with analysis columns for postages, motor expenses and cleaning. Balance the book and show any entries necessary to restore the imprest.

CHAPTER
THIRTEEN

The Three-column Cash Book

DISCOUNTS

There are two types of discount available to businesses.

1 Trade discount is a reduction in the price of goods charged by a manufacturer or distributer to a retailer.

Trade discount is not recorded in the double-entry books of account.

Specification coverage:
AQA 10.1;
OCR 5.1.1.

By the end of this chapter you should be able to:
- write up a three-column cash book
- distinguish between trade discount and cash discount
- account for VAT in the cash book
- account for VAT in the petty cash book.

EXAMPLE

Six beds having a retail price of £800 each are sold by a manufacturer to a retailer at a trade discount of 40%.

The retailer records purchases of £2,880 (6 × £480) (£800 per bed less £320 trade discount). The manufacturer records sales of £2,880 also.

2 Cash discounts are available to encourage a debtor to settle a debt due promptly.

EXAMPLE

A customer owes £100.

A retailer may indicate that if the debt is settled before the month-end a cash discount of 5% will allowed.

The debtor pays before the month-end so only £95 needs to be paid – £100 less £5 cash discount.

However, both the receipt of the money and the discount are recorded by the retailer and the customer.

These two types of discount were considered in Chapter 11 on Value Added Tax.

To record cash discounts:

WORKED EXAMPLE

On 1 August Sahera has three debtors. Her settlement terms allow a cash discount of 5% to customers who settle their debts before the end of August.

Debtor	Amount owed	Date of payment by cheque
Geoff	£2,800	23 August
Edward	£80	17 September
Fiona	£360	29 August

WORKED EXAMPLE *continued*

Required Prepare the ledger accounts record the settling of the debts due. (For illustrative
purposes only: Sahera does not keep a cash book.)

Answer

Sales ledger

Dr			Geoff			Cr
		23 Aug Bank		GL1	2,660.00	
		23 Aug Discount allowed	GL 2	140.00		

Dr			Edward			Cr
		17 Sept Bank		GL1	80.00	

Dr			Fiona			Cr
		29 Aug Bank		GL1	342.00	
		29 Aug Discount allowed	GL2	18.00		

General ledger

Dr			Bank account		Cr
23 Aug Geoff	SL1	2,660.00			
29 Aug Fiona	SL3	342.00			
17 Sept Edward	SL2	80.00			

Dr			Discount allowed account		Cr
23 Aug Geoff	SL1	140.00			
29 Aug Fiona	SL3	18.00			

So you can see that discount allowed is credited to the customer's account, thus reducing the
amount to be paid in settlement. It is debited to the discount allowed account in the general
ledger.

WORKED EXAMPLE

Sahera has three creditors on 1 August (for illustrative purposes only: Sahera does not
keep a cash book).

Supplier	Amount owed £	Cash discount available if payment made before 31 August %
Arbuckle & Co.	400	2
BTQ plc	7,400	5
Carot Ltd	200	3

Sahera settled the amounts she owed by cheque on 26 August.

Required The ledger accounts in Sahera's books of account recording the payments made
by Sahera.

WORKED EXAMPLE *continued*

Answer

Dr		**Arbuckle & Co.**	**Cr**

26 Aug Bank	GL3	392.00	
26 Aug Discount received	GL4	8.00	

Dr		**BTQ plc**	**Cr**

26 Aug Bank	GL3	7,030.00	
26 Aug Discount received	GL4	370.00	

Dr		**Carot Ltd**	**Cr**

26 Aug Bank	GL3	194.00	
26 Aug Discount received	GL4	6.00	

General ledger

Dr		**Bank account**	**Cr**

	26 Aug	Arbuckle & Co.	PL1	392.00
	26 Aug	BTQ plc	PL2	7,030.00
	26 Aug	Carot Ltd	PL3	194.00

Dr		**Discount received account**	**Cr**

	26 Aug	Arbuckle & Co.	PL1	8.00
	26 Aug	BTQ plc	PL2	370.00
	26 Aug	Carot Ltd	PL3	6.00

You can see that discount received is debited to the supplier's account, thus reducing the amount that Sahera has to pay in settlement. The discounts are credited to the discount received account in the general ledger.

To summarise: discount allowed is debited to the discount allowed account in the general ledger and is credited to the customer's account in the sales ledger.

Discount received is credited to the discount received account in the general ledger and is debited to the supplier's account in the purchase ledger.

Memorandum columns record information that is not part of the double-entry system.

To write up the discount accounts in the general ledger in the way outlined above means that all the accounts in the sales ledger must be scrutinised and all the accounts in the purchase ledger must also be examined and lists must be made of all the discounts allowed and discounts received in order to post them to the general ledger.

This could be a mammoth task. We simplify our work by adding an extra column to those already found in the cash book.

We have already used a 'two-column' cash book (cash columns and bank columns). The principles used still hold good. We introduce a third column on the debit and credit for discounts. We now have – yes – a three-column cash book. The three-column cash book headings look like this:

Date	Particulars	Folio	Discount	Cash	Bank	Date	Particulars	Folio	Discount	Cash	Bank

The discount columns are memorandum columns; they record the discounts but are not part of the double-entry system. This is a much more efficient way of collecting the information necessary to write up the discount accounts in the general ledger rather than examining every account in the sales ledger and every account in the purchase ledger.

THE THREE-COLUMN CASH BOOK 145

Note that we will now dispense with the folio columns in most examples and questions. Folios are very rarely required in examination answers.

The entries to record the above transactions in Sahera's cash book would look like this:

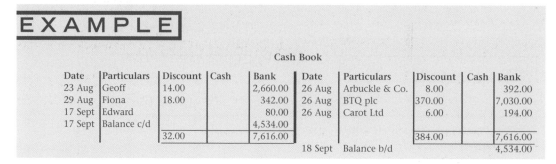

EXAMPLE

Cash Book

Date	Particulars	Discount	Cash	Bank	Date	Particulars	Discount	Cash	Bank
23 Aug	Geoff	14.00		2,660.00	26 Aug	Arbuckle & Co.	8.00		392.00
29 Aug	Fiona	18.00		342.00	26 Aug	BTQ plc	370.00		7,030.00
17 Sept	Edward			80.00	26 Aug	Carot Ltd	6.00		194.00
17 Sept	Balance c/d			4,534.00					
		32.00		7,616.00			384.00		7,616.00
					18 Sept	Balance b/d			4,534.00

The cash and bank columns in the cash book are balanced as they were in the two-column version of the cash book.

The discount columns are totalled. They are *not* compared and balanced since there is no connection between the two columns. One column refers to customers' accounts; the other column refers to suppliers' accounts.

The discount columns are MEMORANDUM columns only – they are not part of the double-entry system.

The totals of the discount columns are then posted to the respective discount allowed and discount received accounts in the general ledger.

The purchase ledger accounts and the sales ledger accounts are the same as previously shown, however, the discount accounts would look like this:

EXAMPLE

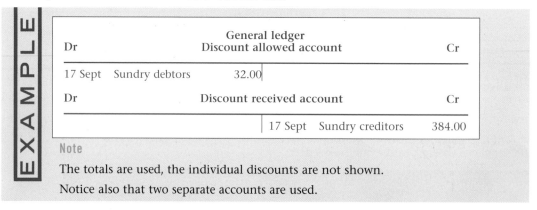

General ledger

Dr	Discount allowed account		Cr
17 Sept Sundry debtors	32.00		

Dr	Discount received account		Cr
		17 Sept Sundry creditors	384.00

Note

The totals are used, the individual discounts are not shown.

Notice also that two separate accounts are used.

VAT IN THE CASH BOOK

Input tax is the VAT that a business pays to a supplier based on the total invoice price less any cash discount that might be available for prompt payment.

Output tax is the VAT that a business charges its customers based on the total invoice price less any cash discount that might be available for prompt payment.

VAT is charged on all goods sold, as we have already seen in the sales day book. However, cash sales are not entered in the sales day book. The book of prime entry for cash transactions is the cash book. VAT on cash sales must therefore be accounted for in the cash book.

VAT is charged on all purchases of goods. Purchases for cash are not entered in the day books they are entered in the cash book. VAT on cash purchases must therefore be accounted for in the cash book.

When a business sells goods for cash and purchases goods for cash we need to include some extra analysis columns in the cash book.

The analysis columns help us identify how much of the

- money received is from sales and how much is VAT
- money paid is for purchases and how much is VAT.

WORKED EXAMPLE

The information given relates to the business of R. Gray:

1 January   Cash in hand was £150 and the balance at bank was £2,130
The following transactions took place in January:
2 January   Cash sales (inclusive of VAT) £846
2 January   Cheque received from P. Grady (£144) in settlement of £160 debt
2 January   Cheque paid to VXQ Ltd (£1,900) in settlement of £2,000 owed.
3 January   Cash sales (inclusive of VAT) £717
4 January   Purchases for cash (inclusive of VAT) £248
5 January   Cheque received from T. Sunker £380 in settlement of £400 debt
7 January   Cheque paid to T. Baggs £425 in settlement of £436 owed
8 January   Purchases for cash (inclusive of VAT) £373
8 January   £1,000 cash paid into bank account.

Required (a) Prepare Gray's cash book for the period 1 January to 8 January.
          (b) Post the transactions to the appropriate ledger accounts.

Answer

Dr   Cash book   Cr

Date	Details	Disc.	Cash	Bank	Sales	VAT	Date	Details	Disc.	Cash	Bank	Purchases	VAT
1 Jan	Bal b/d		150	2,130			2 Jan	VXQ Ltd	100		1,900		
2 Jan	Sales		846		720	126	4 Jan	Purchases		248		211	37
2 Jan	P Grady	16		144			7 Jan	T. Baggs	11		425		
3 Jan	Sales		717		610	107	8 Jan	Purchases		373		317	56
5 Jan	T. Sunker	20		380			8 Jan	Bank C		1,000			
8 Jan	Cash C			1,000			8 Jan	Bal c/d			92	1,329	
		36	1,713	3,654	1,330	233			111	1,713	3,654	528	93
9 Jan	Bal b/d		92	1,329									

Sales ledger   Purchase ledger

Dr	P. Grady	Cr		Dr	VXQ Ltd	Cr
	2 Jan Bank	144		2 Jan Bank	1,900	
	Disc. alld	16		Disc. recd	100	

Dr	T. Sunker	Cr		Dr	T. Baggs	Cr
	5 Jan Bank	380		7 Jan Bank	425	
	Disc. alld	20		Disc. recd	11	

General ledger

Dr	Sales account	Cr		Dr	Purchases account	Cr
	8 Jan Cash	1,33		8 Jan Cash	528	

Dr	Discount allowed account	Cr		Dr	Discount received account	Cr
8 Jan Cash	36				8 Jan Cash	111

Dr	VAT	Cr
8 Jan Cash	93	8 Jan Cash 233

TREATMENT OF VAT IN THE PETTY CASH BOOK

The principles used in the treatment of VAT in the main cash book are applied when writing up the petty cash book.

We need an extra column to record the VAT.

WORKED EXAMPLE

Derek Porter maintains a petty cash book with an imprest of £200. The following transactions have taken place during June:

1 June   £200 float received from the cashier.
Payments made:
2 June   £25 paid for postages
3 June   £38 paid for the purchase of cleaning materials
5 June   £40 paid for petrol
6 June   £15 paid for postages
7 June   £32 paid for stationery
7 June   £26 paid for the purchase of cleaning materials
8 June   £10 paid for postages.

Required (a) Prepare the petty cash book with analysis columns for VAT, cleaning, motor expenses, postages and stationery.
(b) Balance the book and show any entries necessary to restore the imprest.

Answer

Petty cash book

Receipts	Date	Particulars	Voucher no.	Total	VAT	Cleaning	Motor expenses	Postages	Stationery
£				£	£	£	£	£	£
200.00	1 June	Bank	CB27						
	2 June	Postages	12	25.00				25.00	
	3 June	Cleaning	13	38.00	5.66	32.34			
	5 June	Petrol	14	40.00	5.96		34.04		
	6 June	Postages	15	15.00				15.00	
	7 June	Stationery	16	32.00	4.77				27.23
	7 June	Cleaning	17	26.00	3.87	22.13			
	8 June	Postages	18	10.00				10.00	
				186.00	20.26	54.47	34.04	50.00	27.23
	8 June	Balance	c/d	14.00					
200.00				200.00	gl 2	gl 7	gl 16	gl 9	gl 19
14.00	9 June	Balance	b/d						
186.00	9 June	Bank	CB32						

To complete the double entry there will be debit entries in the general ledger for:

- VAT (page 2)
- Cleaning (page 7)
- Motor expenses (page 16)
- Postages (page 9) and
- Stationery (page 19).

There will be a credit entry in the main cash book (page 27) for £200.00 on 1 June and another credit entry will appear for £186.00 on page 32 on 9 June.

Chapter summary

- Trade discount is not recorded in the books of account.
- Cash discount is a reward for prompt payment.
- Cash discount allowed is credited in the debtor's account and debited to the discount allowed account in the general ledger.
- Cash discount received is debited to the creditor's account and credited to the discount received account in the general ledger.
- To save time, both types of cash discount are listed in the cash book. The totals of the two columns are posted separately to the two discount accounts in the general ledger.
- The discount columns in the cash book are memorandum columns only – they are not part of the double-entry system.
- VAT must be shown in the cash book and the petty cash book when transactions have not been entered in another book of prime entry.

Self-test questions

- Explain the term 'cash discount'.
- Explain the term 'trade discount'.
- Discount .... is debited to the discount .... account in the general ledger. Fill in the gaps.
- Discount .... is credited to the discount .... account in the general ledger. Fill in the gaps.
- On which side of the cash book would you find the discount allowed column?
- On which side of the cash book would you find the discount received column?
- Which columns of the cash book are balanced off regularly?
- Which columns of the cash book are not balanced off?
- What is meant by the term 'memorandum column'.
- Under what circumstances do we write 'C' for 'contra' against transactions in the cash book?

TEST QUESTIONS

QUESTION 1

Tom Cunningham had cash in hand £217 and a balance at bank £1,132 at 1 February.

The following transactions took place during February:

1 February	Cash sales £912 (including £136 VAT)
1 February	Paid Mowlem £834 by cheque
2 February	Received cheque from McAllister £138
3 February	Cash sales £468 (including £70 VAT)
4 February	Received cheque from Tyson £1,172
4 February	Paid Laker £137 by cheque
4 February	Purchased goods for cash £126 (including £19 VAT)
5 February	Purchased goods for cash £488 (including £73 VAT)
5 February	Paid £750 cash into the bank account.

Required (a) Prepare Tom's cash book for the period 1 February to 5 February.
(b) Post the entries in the cash book to the appropriate ledger accounts

QUESTION 2

B. Branden had cash in hand £861 and a balance at bank £1,307 at 1 November.

The following transactions took place during November:

3 November	Purchased goods for cash £677 (including £100 VAT)
3 November	Paid A. Capp £317 by cheque
4 November	Cash sales £709 (including £105 VAT)
5 November	Cash sales £487 (including £73 VAT)
6 November	Paid C. Nesta £288 by cheque
7 November	Paid wages £836 by cheque

7 November	Cash sales £369 (including £55 VAT)
7 November	Paid T. Richards £412 by cheque
8 November	Received cheque £279 from J. Bond.
8 November	Received cheque £97 from L. Earl.
8 November	Paid £1,000 cash into the bank account.

Required (a) Prepare B. Branden's cash book for the period 1 November to 8 November.
(b) Post the entries in the cash book to the appropriate ledger accounts.

QUESTION 3

Sven David had cash in hand £88 and a balance at bank £376 on 1 May.

The following transactions took place during May:

1 May	Cheque received from Gholar £600; he has deducted £30 cash discount
2 May	Purchased goods for cash £308 (including VAT)
3 May	Purchased goods for cash £613 (including VAT)
3 May	Cash sales £845 (including VAT)
3 May	Cheque received from Tempest £210; she has deducted £12 cash discount
4 May	Cheque received from Trevor £120; he has deducted £8 cash discount
6 May	Paid Breem £40 by cheque
7 May	Cash sales £466 (including VAT)
7 May	Paid £250 cash into the bank account.

Required (a) Prepare Sven's cash book for the period 1 May to 7 May.
(b) Post the entries in the cash book to the appropriate ledger accounts.

QUESTION 4

Roy Becker had cash in hand £281 and a balance at bank £834 on 6 December.

The following transactions took place in December:

6 December	Cheque received from Healy £765 (including VAT)
7 December	Cash sales £3,276 (including VAT)
7 December	Purchased goods for cash £234 (including VAT)
8 December	Cheque received from Callaghan £480; she has deducted £30 cash discount
8 December	Goods purchased for cash £801 (including VAT)
8 December	Cheque received from Wilson £26
9 December	Paid Heath £712 by cheque after deducting £38 cash discount
10 December	Goods purchased for cash £523 (including VAT)
11 December	Cash sales £930 (including VAT)
12 December	Paid Bassi £750 by cheque after deducting £40 cash discount
12 December	Paid £2,500 cash into the bank account.

Required (a) Prepare Roy's cash book for the period 6 December to 12 December.
(b) Post the entries in the cash book to the appropriate ledger accounts.

QUESTION 5

Bjorn Tyke maintains a petty cash book with an imprest of £150. On 1 August a balance of £13.28 was brought down from 31 July and the imprest was restored with a receipt from the main cashier.

The following payments were made:

1 August	£20.00 paid for postages
2 August	£17.84 paid for stationery (including VAT)
3 August	£3.61 paid for cleaning materials (including VAT)
4 August	£25.00 paid for postages
4 August	£40.00 paid for petrol for delivery vehicle (including VAT)
5 August	£7.84 paid for stationery (including VAT)
5 August	£9.16 paid for cleaning materials (including VAT)
5 August	£20.00 paid for petrol for delivery vehicle (including VAT).

Required (a) Prepare the petty cash book with analysis columns for VAT, motor expenses, postages, stationery and cleaning.
(b) Balance the book and show any entries necessary to restore the imprest.

QUESTION 6

Albert Frost maintains a petty cash book with an imprest of £100. On 16 April a balance of £7.84 was brought down from 15 April and the imprest was restored with a receipt from the main cashier. The following payments were made:

16 April	£8.20 paid for stationery (including VAT)
18 April	£7.50 paid for postages
18 April	£12.00 paid for flowers for receptionist who is ill (including VAT)
20 April	£14.37 paid for staff coffee, tea, milk and sugar (including VAT)
21 April	£8.20 paid for stationery (including VAT)
23 April	£25.00 paid for petrol for delivery vehicle (including VAT).

Required (a) Prepare the petty cash book with analysis columns for VAT, stationery, postages, motor expenses and sundries.
(b) Balance the book and show any entries necessary to restore the imprest.

CHAPTER
FOURTEEN

Bank Reconciliations

We have seen that the whole double-entry system can be checked by extracting a trial balance.

Remember that even if the trial balance does balance, it does not necessarily mean that there are no errors in the double-entry system.

All you can be sure of is that the double-entry system is arithmetically correct.

Can you remember the six types of errors that are not revealed by extracting a trial balance? Remember CROPOC?

If not, refer back to page 103.

Altogether, we use four checks to verify the accuracy of the system. Three we do at frequent intervals throughout the year. The fourth, the trial balance, is generally prepared at the year-end, although a trial balance could be extracted every day to see if the system is arithmetically correct.

Let us first look at the two checks that are used to verify the entries in the **cash book**.

Specification coverage:
AQA 10.3.

By the end of this chapter you should be able to:
- update the bank columns of a cash book
- identify unpresented cheques
- identify lodgements not yet credited
- prepare a bank reconciliation statement.

CHECKING THE ACCURACY OF THE CASH BALANCE SHOWN IN THE CASH BOOK

We check the cash balance shown in the cash columns of the cash book very frequently.

[We cannot be any more precise than this because it would be impossible to say exactly how often the cash would be checked in any particular business.] Some businesses, like the corner shop, would perhaps only check the cash balances on a weekly basis whereas some very large organisations may check the cash balances in the tills much more frequently.

How often would you check the cash balances in your tills if you were the owner of a shop? It might depend on how much cash goes through each till. It might depend on how many staff had access to the tills and how trustworthy those members of staff are.

HOW DO WE CHECK THE CASH?

We add all the money that is in the till and check it against the till roll total. The two should be the same. It is done fairly frequently, because if there is a discrepancy it is much easier to remember what might have caused any difference. For example, money may have been taken from the till to pay the window cleaner and no note has been made of the payment. It is much easier to remember this immediately after the event than, say, some four months later.

The cash in the till should not only agree with the till roll total but also should agree with the total of the cash columns in the cash book kept by the business.

This is the first check and most frequent check undertaken by businesses. It is fairly straightforward and very easy to do.

CHECKING THE ACCURACY OF TRANSACTIONS RECORDED IN THE BANK COLUMNS OF THE CASH BOOK

This frequently gives students a few problems.

> The **drawer** is the person (or business) using the cheque for payment.

> The **payee** is the person to whom the cheque is made payable.

How are the bank columns written up?

The bulk of banking transactions are undertaken by the bank on instructions given by the managers of the business. The instructions to undertake transactions involving the use of the banking system are given to the bank by:

1   cheque – cheques are simply instructions given to the bank to take money from an account and give the money to someone else
2   paying-in slip – these slips record the amount of cash and cheques paid into the business account.

When any bank transaction is undertaken, two records are kept of the transaction. One is recorded by the business in the cash book. The other record is kept by the bank. The two records kept are taken from different parts of the source document.

When money is paid into the high street bank the person paying in the money will fill in a slip showing the numbers and amounts of each type of coin and note deposited plus a list of all the cheques that are being paid in. They fill in a counterfoil which duplicates this information. The money and cheques are handed to the bank cashier who checks the amounts for accuracy and then stamps the paying-in slip and the duplicate (counterfoil or stub). From this counterfoil, the debit entries are made in the cash book so this is one of the source documents used to write up the cash book.

The bank uses the actual paying-in slip to show the money and cheques that have been deposited in the business bank account. These entries will appear as credit entries on the business bank statement, which is a copy of the bank's records.

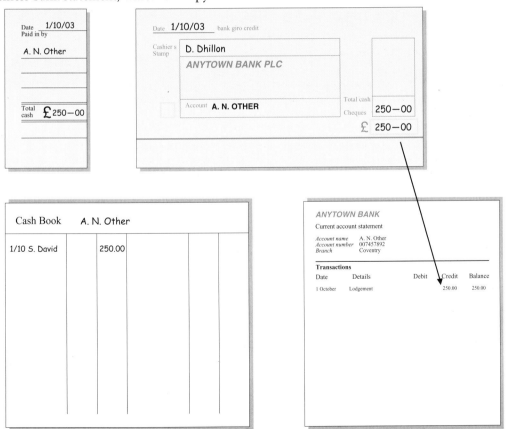

When payment is made by cheque, the cheque is filled out with the payee's name, the date and the amount in both words and figures and then the drawer signs the cheque and sends it to the creditor (the person who has been owed the money).

The cheque counterfoil is used as the source document to write up the credit bank column in our cash book.

The bank uses the cheque that has been sent to the payee (the creditor) to enter withdrawals from the business account. These withdrawals will be shown on the debit side of the bank statement.

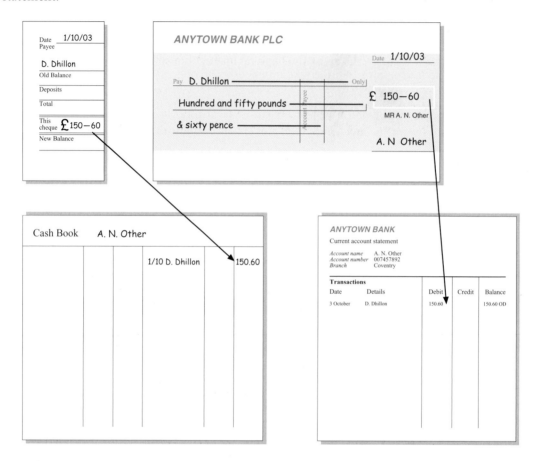

Note the third column on the bank statement showing a running balance figure.

A statement will be sent to the businessman or businesswoman on a frequent basis, usually at the end of every month but in the case of very large businesses the bank statement may be sent to the business on a weekly basis.

Standing orders are payments made automatically by a bank on behalf of customers. They are set amounts and may be paid weekly, monthly or annually.

Direct debits are payments made by the bank on behalf of customers. The authority to withdraw money from the account is given to the payee. The amounts withdrawn from the account is generally variable.

Bank charges are made by banks to cover the costs of maintaining the drawer's account.

Interest on overdrafts: the interest charged by banks when an account is overdrawn.

> **Credit transfers** are amounts paid into an account directly through the banking system instead of by issuing a cheque.

> **Dishonoured cheques** are cheques that have not gone through the drawer's bank account. Often this may be because the drawer has insufficient funds in their account to honour (pay) the cheque.

⊙ EXAMINATION TIP

Learn these definitions. They are frequently asked for in examinations. They are frequently answered poorly!

The bank statement and the cash book should be identical since the cash book is prepared from the counterfoils which are duplicates of the original documents from which the bank draws up its bank statement.

Can you think of any reasons why these two should not be identical?

- The counterfoil might not actually agree with the cheque. The cheque might say '£110' but the cheque counterfoil could say '£101', so our cash book will say '£101' and the bank statement will say '£110'. Which amount is correct? The bank will have taken £110 out of the account so this is the correct amount and our counterfoil and cash book should be changed.

- The counterfoil might not have been filled in at all. The amount shown in the bank statement should be entered in the cash book.

- The bank may have made payments from the account on a standing order and the payment from the account has for the moment been overlooked by the drawer and not yet included in the business cash book. The amounts should be entered as a payment in the credit bank column of the cash book.

- The bank may have made payment from the account by direct debit and the payment from the account has been overlooked by the drawer. The amount should be entered as a payment in the credit bank column of the cash book.

- The bank may have taken money from the account as bank charges and this amount has not yet been included in the business cash book. The amount should be included as a payment in the credit bank column of the cash book.

- The bank may have made an interest charge for times when the bank statement shows a debit balance (i.e. the account has been overdrawn). The amount of interest charged should be entered as a payment in the credit bank column of the cash book.
- The bank may have received deposits on behalf of the business directly through the banking system. Any credit transfers should be entered as receipts by debiting the bank column in the cash book.

- When a cheque is received the cheque will be banked. It is entered in the debit bank column of the cash book. If, subsequently, the cheque is dishonoured this fact will be shown on the bank statement. (This is referred to colloquially as a cheque that has 'bounced'.) The trader cannot debit his or her bank account until the bank informs the trader. If it is not also shown in the cash book the dishonoured cheque should be entered as a payment in the credit bank column of the cash book

- The trader can make the following errors:
  - addition errors in either bank column of the cash book
  - entering the incorrect amount from the cheque and paying-in counterfoils
  - entering the correct amount on the incorrect side of the cash book.
- The bank could make the following errors:
  - Entering a withdrawal that should have been debited to the account of someone else
  - Entering a deposit that should have been credited to the account of someone else.

Note
It is highly unlikely that addition errors will take place in bank statements since they are computer-generated.

QUESTION 1

The following transactions have taken place:

1   A cheque paid to Watkins for £200.
2   The total of cash sales for the day £1,730.
3   A payment by cheque to Smith for £200 less 5% cash discount.
4   £3,430 cash sales paid into the business bank account.
5   Payment of £435 cash to a supplier.
6   £2,000 cash withdrawn from the bank for business use.

Required Explain how each transaction should be treated in the cash book.

> **Lodgements** are payments made into the bank account.

We have seen how entries using the banking system are recorded in the cash book.

Cheques received are shown in the debit bank column of the cash book.

Cheques paid to suppliers of goods and services are shown in the credit bank columns of the cash book.

QUESTION 2

Required Explain:
  (a) the types of transactions that would increase the bank balance
  (b) the types of transactions that would decrease the bank balance.

The amounts withdrawn from the bank account by cheque should appear as identical amounts on the credit bank columns of the cash book and the debit columns of the bank statement.

Amounts paid in should appear as identical amounts in the debit bank columns of the cash book and the credit columns of the bank statement.

We have already listed reasons why the cash book kept by a business and the record kept by the bank may be different. If we correct the differences, all should be well.

Why is there a need to prepare a bank reconciliation statement?

We need to check that:

(a) all transactions using banking facilitites have been recorded
(b) all transactions have been recorded accurately by both the business and the bank and
(c) that all transactions have gone through the bank account kept at the bank.

> **Clearing** a cheque refers to the passage of a cheque through the banking system. It involves the transfer of money from one account to another. This can take a few days if the accounts are held at different banks.

When a trader pays a supplier by cheque this should be entered in the credit bank column (using the counterfoil as the source document) on the same date that the cheque was written.

However, the bank will not show the cheque on the bank statement until several days later – this could be as much as a week later (days in the post plus days in the clearing system).

When the trader pays money into the business bank account, it will be recorded immediately in the trader's bank column in his/her cash book. However, the bank will not credit it to the trader's bank account until the cheque is cleared.

[NOTE: the bank statement is prepared from the actual cheques and paying-in slips received by the bank. If an error is made on the counterfoil, two different amounts will be recorded by the bank and by the trader.]

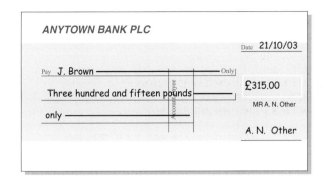

Which is correct?

The bank will react to its instructions which are to remove £315 from the account and pay it to someone else.

After all the necessary adjustments have been made, the cash book should contain exactly the same information as the bank statement.

Or should it?

Well, it could, but in real life the likelihood of this happening is fairly remote because of the reasons outlined in (c) on page 156.

Some cheques paid out by the trader and entered in the cash book will still be in the postal system, in the payee's office or in the bank clearing system. These cheques have yet to be presented at the trader's bank – they are called '**unpresented cheques**'.

Some deposits made by the trader on the day the bank statement is produced by the bank may not yet be recorded on the statement. These items are called '**lodgements not yet credited by the bank**'.

So we have to reconcile (bring together) the two different amounts.

This is done in the bank reconciliation statement. The statement is set out thus:

EXAMPLE

Bank reconciliation as at ... [the date when the reconciliation is taking place]

Balance at bank as per cash book

Add Unpresented cheques

Less Lodgements not yet credited by the bank

Balance at bank as per bank statement

○ EXAMINATION TIP

Learn the layout for a bank reconciliation statement. It is a popular examination topic.

PROCEDURE USED IN PREPARING A BANK RECONCILIATION STATEMENT

1   **Balance the cash book.**
Remember only the cash and bank columns are balanced the discount columns are totalled.

2   **Compare the bank columns of the cash book with the bank statement.**
Tick all the entries shown in the cash book and their corresponding entries in the bank statement.

3   **Bring the cash book up to date by:**
(a) entering payments made by the bank, but not yet entered in the cash book, in the credit bank column of the cash book (standing orders, direct debits, bank charges, fees and interest and dishonoured cheques)
(b) entering amounts received by the bank, but not entered in the cash book, in the debit bank column of the cash book.

4   **Correct any errors discovered in the bank columns of the cash book.**

5   **If the bank statement contains errors, inform the bank, make note of the error and ask the bank for an adjusted bank statement balance.**

6   **Prepare the bank reconciliation statement.**

Bank Reconciliation Statement as at XX XX XX [date]

Balance as per cash book

Add Unpresented cheques   _____

Less Lodgements not yet credited by the bank   _____

Balance at bank as per the bank statement XX XX XX [date]   _____

Note
The adjusted balance shown in the bank columns of the cash book is the balance to be shown in:

(a) the trial balance and
(b) the balance sheet.

Remember to post all the items entered in the cash book adjustments to the appropriate accounts since it is highly likely that these errors have been entered in the appropriate ledger accounts.

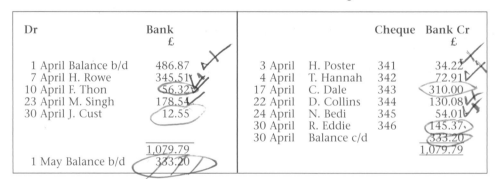

WORKED EXAMPLE

The bank columns of P. Court's cash book shows the following details:

Dr	Bank £				Cheque	Bank Cr £
1 April Balance b/d	486.87		3 April	H. Poster	341	34.22
7 April H. Rowe	345.51		4 April	T. Hannah	342	72.91
10 April F. Thon	56.32		17 April	C. Dale	343	310.00
23 April M. Singh	178.54		22 April	D. Collins	344	130.08
30 April J. Cust	12.55		24 April	N. Bedi	345	54.01
			30 April	R. Eddie	346	145.37
			30 April	Balance c/d		333.20
	1,079.79					1,079.79
1 May Balance b/d	333.20					

She received her bank statement on 3 May.

WORKED EXAMPLE *continued*

Date	Details	Debit £	Credit £	Balance £
1 April	Balance			486.87
7 April	Lodgement		345.51	832.38
9 April	342	72.91		759.47
10 April	341	34.22		725.25
	Lodgement	56.32		781.57
15 April	Direct debit (Insurance)	45.66		735 91
17 April	Credit transfer (M.Cox)		61.00	796.91
23 April	Lodgement		178.54	975.45
29 April	344	130.08		845.37
	345	54.01		791.36
30 April	Bank charges	6.43		784.93

Required (a) Make any necessary adjustments to P. Court's cash book.
(b) Prepare a bank reconciliation statement as at 30 April.

Answer

Workings
'Tick' all the items that appear both in Court's cash book and her bank statement.

The item that remains unticked in the debit bank column of the cash book is:

Cust £12.55

The items that remain unticked in the credit bank column of the cash book are:

Dale £310.00

Eddie £145.37

The item that remains unticked in the credit column of the bank statement is:

Cox £61.00

The items that remain unticked in the debit column of the bank statement are:

Direct debit for insurance £45.66

Bank charges £6.43.

It is important that Court's cash book is updated.

The cash book is a vital part of her double-entry records so it should be correct and contain all the transactions relating to the business.

The three transactions remaining unticked on the bank statement **have taken place**.

They remain unticked because **she has not yet recorded them**.

The first task is to **record them** in the cash book.

In real life the cash book would simply be extended for a few lines to enable the entries to be made.

WORKED EXAMPLE *continued*

(a)

Dr			Cash book			Cr
1 May	Balance b/d	333.20	15 April	Insurance		45.66
17 April	M. Cox	61.00	30 April	Bank charges		6.43
			30 April	Balance c/d		342.11
		394.20				394.20
1 May	Balance b/d	342.11				

The balance shown is the balance to be entered on Court's trial balance; it is also the balance to be shown as a current asset on her balance sheet.

We should not forget to complete the double entry for these transactions:

Dr		Cox (SL)		Cr
		17 April	Bank	61.00

Dr	Insurance account (GL)	Cr	Dr	Bank charges account (GL)	Cr
15 April Bank 45.66			30 April Bank 6.43		

[Purely for illustrative purposes, as this was not asked for.]

◯ EXAMINATION TIP

Do not give the examiner more than he asks for. You will not score extra marks. You will penalise yourself by taking more time to answer the question.

(b) **Bank reconciliation statement as at 30 April**

	£	£
Balance at bank as per the cash book		342.11
Add Unpresented cheques		
Dale	310.00	
Eddie	145.37	455.37
		797.48
Less Lodgements not yet credited		
Cust		12.55
Balance at bank as per bank statement		784.93

We have reconciled the bank balance shown in the cash book with that shown in the bank statement.

We can say with certainty that the transactions recorded in the bank columns of the cash book are accurate.

WORKED EXAMPLE

The bank columns of D. Dhillon's cash book are shown:

Dr			Cash book				Cr
		£					£
1 Oct	Balance b/d	127.63	2 Oct	M. Vaughan	673	272.61	
7 Oct	D. Paster	367.42	4 Oct	C. Chan	674	81.13	
15 Oct	T. Henley	84.56	11 Oct	M. Vere	675	364.42	
15 Oct	B. Tain	97.42	27 Oct	D Perth	676	182.09	
31 Oct	M. Sond	216.84	29 Oct	N. Lister	677	12.13	
31 Oct	Balance c/d	18.51					
		912.38				912.38	
			1 Nov	Balance b/d		18.51	

He received his bank statement on 4 November.

ANYTOWN BANK PLC

Current account statement

Account name	D. DHILLON
Account number	007457892
Branch	Coventry

Transactions

Date	Details	Debit	Credit	Balance
1 October	Balance			127.63
3 October	Lodgement		367.42	495.05
7 October	674	81.31		413.74
	Lodgement		84.56	498.30
10 October	Lodgement		97.42	595.72
15 October	675	364.42		231.30
16 October	673	272.61		41.31 OD
31 October	Credit transfer G. Jackson		41.99	0.68
	Stdg order Loan repmt	150.00		149.32 OD
	Dishonoured cheque	12.48		161.80 OD
	Bank charges	27.56		189.36 OD

81.31
− 81.13

Required (a) Make any adjustments to Dhillon's cash book.

(b) Prepare a bank reconciliation statement as at 31 October.

Answer

(a)

Dr			Cash book		Cr
31 Oct	Credit transfer G. Jackson	41.99	31 Oct	Balance b/d	18.51
			4 Oct	Correction – C. Chan	0.18
			31 Oct	s/o Loan repayment	150.00
			31 Oct	Dishonoured cheque	12.48
			31 Oct	Bank charges	27.56
31 Oct	Balance c/d	166.74			
		208.73			208.73
			31 Oct	Balance b/d	166.74

■ Note how the amount paid to Chan has been increased – the bank has paid him £81.31 so the cash book has to record the payment.

WORKED EXAMPLE *continued*

- Note that the dishonoured cheque has been credited in the cash book.
- Notice also that the opening balance is a credit balance on the bank statement, indicating that Dhillon has money in the bank; at the end of October a debit balance is shown on the bank statement, indicating that Dhillon is overdrawn.

(b) **D. Dhillon**

Bank reconciliation as at 31 October

	£		
Balance at bank as per cash book		166.74 OD	
Add Unpresented cheques			
D. Perth	182.09		
N. Lister	12.13	194.22	[this positive
		27.48	amount added to a
			negative amount
			gives this positive
			result]
Less Lodgements not yet credited			
M. Sond		216.84	[this amount
			deducted gives a
			negative result]
Balance at bank as per bank statement		189.36 OD	

Once more we can say that all the transactions recorded in the bank columns of the cash book have been recorded accurately.

Chapter summary

- Bank reconciliations are used to check the accuracy of transactions recorded in the bank columns of the cash book.
- It is a two-stage operation – the cash book is updated first then the actual reconciliation is prepared by adjusting the balance shown in the cash book for unpresented cheques and lodgements not yet credited in the bank statement.

Self-test questions

- Why would a trader prepare a bank reconciliation statement?
- How often is a bank reconciliation statement prepared?
- Explain the term 'drawer'.
- What is a standing order?
- What is the difference between a standing order and a direct debit?
- What is meant by the term 'overdrawn'?
- Why are credit transfers often missing from the bank columns of the cash book?
- Fill in the gaps

Bank reconciliation statement .... 31 March 20*3

	£
Balance at bank as per cash book	210
.... unpresented cheques	156
	......
.... lodgements not yet credited	99
Balance at bank as per bank statement	.....

TEST QUESTIONS

QUESTION 3

The bank columns of Philip Robb's cash book are as follows:

Dr			Cash book				Cr
		£					£
1 July	Bal	320	2 July	Stone	86		126
17 July	AVT Ltd	630	5 July	Baines	87		417
24 July	B. Rush	420	19 July	Brown	88		326
			31 July	Edge	89		312
			31 July	Bal c/d			189
		1,370					1,370
1 Aug	Bal c/d	189					

Philip receives his bank statement on 5 August.

ANYTOWN BANK PLC

Current account statement

Account name P. ROBB
Account number 943436192
Branch Sheffield

Transactions

Date	Details	Debit	Credit	Balance
1 July				320
5 July	86	126		194
17 July	Lodgement		630	824
23 July	88	326		498
24 July	Lodgement		420	918
28 July	87	417		501

Required Prepare a bank reconciliation statement as at 28 July.

QUESTION 4

The bank columns of Tim Robson's cash book are as follows:

Dr			Cash book					Cr
		£						£
2 Apr	Bal b/d	721	3 Apr	T. Galloway	314			291
10 Apr	S. Tay	560	12 Apr	G. Ayre	315			438
27 Apr	R. Stock	186	14 Apr	M. Beam	316			17
			23 Apr	H. Misty	317			146
			29 Apr	T. Beck	318			132
			30 Apr	Bal c/d				443
		1,467						1,467
1 May	Bal b/d	433						

Tim Robson received his bank statement on 3 May.

ANYTOWN BANK PLC

Current account statement

Account name	T. ROBSON
Account number	205104012
Branch	Reading

Transactions

Date	Details	Debit	Credit	Balance
1 April	Bal b/d			721
8 April	314	291		430
19 April	Lodgement		560	990
26 April	317	146		844
26 April	316	17		827
27 April	Lodgement		186	1,013

Required Prepare a bank reconciliation statement as at 27 April.

QUESTION 5

The bank columns of Lucy Hill's cash book are as follows:

Dr			Cash book					Cr
		£						£
2 Nov	Bal b/d	261	4 Nov	P. Charles	77			211
10 Nov	A. Zargreb	384	8 Nov	S. Fence	78			14
27 Nov	V. Campbell	29	12 Nov	C. Mutt	79			137
			17 Nov	T. Parker	80			58
			23 Nov	G. Bowden	81			169
			30 Nov	Bal c/d				85
		674						674
1 Dec	Bal b/d	85						

Lucy receives her bank statement on 4 December.

```
ANYTOWN BANK PLC

Current account statement

Account name      L. HILL
Account number    396106600
Branch            Oxford
```

Transactions

Date	Details	Debit	Credit	Balance
2 Nov	Bal b/d			261
9 Nov	77	211		50
10 Nov	Lodgement		384	434
21 Nov	80	58		376
23 Nov	79	137		239
28 Nov	81	169		70
29 Nov	78	14		56

Required   Prepare a bank reconciliation statement as at 29 November.

QUESTION 6

The bank columns of Rebecca Florin's cash book are as follows:

Dr		£			Cash book		Cr £
1 Mar	Bal b/d	1,287 ✓		5 Mar	M. Waters	414	97 ✓
21 Mar	P. Dobie	716 ✓		9 Mar	S. Gonzalez	415	238 ✓
31 Mar	J. Porage	128		14 Mar	C. Batt	416	41 ✓
				14 Mar	D. Bundle	417	562 ✓
				17 Mar	L. French	418	125 ✓
				31 Mar	Bal c/d		1,068
		2,131					2,131
1 Apr	Bal b/d	1,068					

Rebecca receives her bank statement on 2 April.

```
ANYTOWN BANK PLC

Current account statement

Account name      R. FLORIN
Account number    566193640
Branch            Manchester
```

Transactions

Date	Details	Debit	Credit	Balance
1 March				1,287
10 March	414	97		1,190
13 March	415	238		952
20 March	416	41		911
29 March	Lodgement		716	1,627
29 March	417	562		1,065
30 March	418	125		840

Required   Prepare a bank reconciliation statement as at 31 March.

QUESTION 7

The bank columns of Lily Baxter's cash book are as follows:

Dr			£			Cr	£
1 Jan	Bal b/d	93		4 Jan	B. George	612	236
15 Jan	H. Young	1,438		6 Jan	T. Gorman	613	541
29 Jan	G. Bralter	412		7 Jan	L. Smith	614	82
				11 Jan	D. Tan	615	176
				29 Jan	P. Vent	616	456
				30 Jan	Bal c/d		452
			1,943				1,943
1 Feb	Bal b/d	452					

Lily receives her bank statement on 2 December.

ANYTOWN BANK PLC

Current account statement

Account name   L. BAXTER
Account number   451341201
Branch   Liverpool

Transactions

Date	Details	Debit	Credit	Balance
1 Jan				93
10 Jan	612	236		143 OD
12 Jan	614	82		225 OD
15 Jan	Lodgement		1,438	1,213
19 Jan	613	541		672
20 Jan	615	176		496

Required   Prepare a bank reconciliation statement as at 28 January.

QUESTION 8

The bank columns of Leslie Vine's cash book are as follows:

Dr			£			Cr	£
1 June	Bal b/d	734		2 June	T. Royal	931	261
8 June	P. Time	368		4 June	T. Hassan	932	147
16 June	V. Sass	541		11 June	R. Peal	933	298
30 June	T. Chinois	432		11 June	W. Rooney	934	75
				12 June	Z. Nex	935	611
				15 June	O. Preston	936	181
				30 June	Bal c/d		502
			2,075				2,075
1 July	Bal b/d	502					

Leslie receives his bank statement on 29 June.

ANYTOWN BANK PLC

Current account statement

Account name   L. VINE
Account number   731834149
Branch   Stockport

Transactions

Date	Details	Debit	Credit	Balance
8 June	931	261		473
8 June	Lodgement		368	841
15 June	934	75		766
16 June	935	611		155
16 June	Lodgement		541	696
22 June	932	147		549

Required Prepare a bank reconciliation statement as at 30 June.

QUESTION 9

The bank columns of Vera Dawson's cash book are as follows:

Dr			Cash book			Cr
		£				£
			1 Jan	Balance b/d		267.42
3 Jan	N. Orbert	446.27	3 Jan	O. Lever	127	38.56
7 Jan	S. Brown	290.42	4 Jan	B. Render	128	129.81
16 Jan	J. Smythe	312.46	8 Jan	C. Dunn	129	1,264.36
31 Jan	T. Recks	530.22	12 Jan	P. Green	130	8.40
31 Jan	Bal c/d	146.44	18 Jan	G. Wright	131	17.26
		1,725.81				1,725.81
			1 Feb	Bal. B/d		146.44

Vera receives her bank statement on 4 February

ANYTOWN BANK PLC

Current account statement

Account name   V. DAWSON
Account number   674832198
Branch   Bristol

Transactions

Date	Details	Debit	Credit	Balance
				267.42 OD
3 Jan	Lodgement		446.27	178.85
5 Jan	127	38.56		140.29
7 Jan	Lodgement		290.42	430.71
15 Jan	Direct debit			
	Electricity	246.38		184.33
16 Jan	Lodgement		312.46	496.79
18 Jan	129	1,264.36		767.57 OD
21 Jan	130	8.40		775.97 OD
31 Jan	Bank charges	12.52		788.49 OD
31 Jan	Interest on overdraft	26.78		815.27 OD

Required (a) Make any adjustments to Vera Dawson's cash book.
(b) Prepare a bank reconciliation statement as at 31 January.

QUESTION 10

The bank columns of Matthew Carter are as follows:

Dr		£			Cash book		Cr £
1 Oct	Bal b/d	127.63	2 Oct	M. Vaughan	673	272.61
3 Oct	D. Parker	367.42	4 Oct	C. Chan	674	81.13
7 Oct	T. Henley	84.56	11 Oct	M. Vere	675	364.42
15 Oct	B. Tain	97.42	27 Oct	D. Perth	676	182.09
31 Oct	M. Sand	216.84	29 Oct	N. Lister	677	12.13
	Bal c/d	18.51				
		912.38				912.38
			1 Nov	Bal b/d		18.51

ANYTOWN BANK PLC

Current account statement

Account name   M. CARTER
Account number   457839018
Branch   Ipswich

Transactions

Date	Details	Debit	Credit	Balance
1 Oct	Balance			127.63
3 Oct	Lodgement		367.42	495.05
6 Oct	Standing order			
	—loan repayment	150.00		345.05
7 Oct	Lodgement		84.56	429.61
8 Oct	674	81.31		348.30
10 Oct	673	273.61		74.69
15 Oct	Lodgement		97.42	172.11
17 Oct	675	364.42		192.31 OD
31 Oct	Bank charges	12.48		204.79 OD
	Bank overdraft interest	27.56		232.35 OD

Required (a) Make any necessary adjustments to Matthew's cash book.
                (b) Prepare a bank reconciliation statement as at 31 October.

QUESTION 11

On 30 April 20*3 Pat Nicholson received her bank statement. It showed a credit balance of £858. The bank columns of her cash book showed a debit balance of £180.

On the same date it was found that:

■ a lodgement of £200 had not been entered in the cash book
■ a cheque lodged in the bank £460 had been entered in the cash book as £640
■ a credit transfer £165 had not been entered in the cash book
■ cheques amounting to £493 had not been presented to the bank.

Required (a) Make any necessary adjustments to Pat's cash book.
                (b) Prepare a bank reconciliation statement as at 30 April 20*3.

QUESTION 12

On 31 August 20*3 Bernard Drouin received his bank statement. It showed a credit balance of £210. The bank columns of his cash book showed a debit balance of £170.

On the same date it was found that:

- a cheque paid into the bank account £109 had not been entered in the cash book
- a standing order for insurance £245 had not been entered in the cash book
- cheques amounting to £348 had not been presented to the bank
- lodgements amounting to £172 had not yet been credited by the bank.

Required (a) Make any necessary adjustments to Bernard's cash book
              (b) Prepare a bank reconciliation statement as at 31 August 20*3.

QUESTION 13

On 31 March 20*3 the cash book of Nancy Best showed a bank overdraft of £590.

On the same date it was found that:

- cheques amounting to £938 had not been presented at the bank for payment
- a standing order for loan interest £83 had not been entered in the cash book
- a direct debit for water rates for £31 had not been entered in the cash book
- a credit transfer from Thelma Rodders for £66 had not been entered in the cash book
- lodgements of £206 had not yet been credited to Nancy's account by the bank.

Required (a) Make any necessary adjustments to Nancy's cash book.
              (b) Prepare a bank reconciliation as at 31 March 20*3, showing clearly the balance at
                   bank as per Nancy's bank statement.

QUESTION 14

On 31 December 20*3 Tracy Beddow's cash book showed a balance of £374.

On the same date it was found that:

- cheques amounting to £236 had not been presented at the bank for payment
- a direct debit for electricity £99 had not been entered in the cash book
- bank overdraft interest £103 had not been entered in the cash book
- bank charges £86 had not been entered in the cash book
- a standing order £46 for a trade magazine had not been entered in the cash book
- a cheque received from Traster Ltd for £85 had been entered in the cash book as £58
- lodgements amounting to £487 had not yet been credited to Tracy's account by the bank.

Required (a) Make any necessary adjustments to Tracy's cash book.
              (b) Prepare a bank reconciliation as at 31 December 20*3, showing clearly the balance
                   at bank as per Tracy's bank statement.

CHAPTER
FIFTEEN

Control Accounts

We have already seen that the arithmetical accuracy of the whole double-entry book-keeping system is checked by extracting a trial balance.

We said that although in theory there is only one book used to record all double-entry transactions, the ledger is actually divided into three.

QUESTION 1

Required Name the three ledgers.

QUESTION 2

Some of the accounts in Theresa's ledger are listed:

■ sales account
■ purchases account
■ the account of Abdul, a credit customer
■ the account of Bart, a credit supplier
■ sales returns account
■ purchase returns account
■ the account of Chel, a supplier
■ cash sales account
■ the account of Dodd, a credit customer
■ sales returns account.

Required Identify the ledger in which the accounts would be found

The bulk of all entries in the double entry system are in the personal ledgers:

■ the sales ledger
■ the purchase ledger.

Because there are so many entries in these two ledgers, there is great potential for errors to be made.

Control accounts are used to check the accuracy of the entries made in each of the sales ledgers and each of the purchases ledgers.

A control account is prepared for each ledger, each month. In this way errors can be identified as being in one particular ledger in the month that they have occurred.

The control account summarises all the individual entries that have been made in the sales ledgers and the purchases ledgers in any particular month. **Any** entry in **any** ledger account will be duplicated in the control account.

If a business has a vast number of credit customers it may divide the sales ledger according to the geographical areas, customers of particular sales persons, alphabetically etc.

The sales day book would reflect any divisions of the sales ledger.

Memorandum accounts record financial information in account form but they are not part of the double-entry system.

Some businesses use control accounts as part of their double-entry system

Specification coverage
AQA 10.3
OCR 5.2.2.

By the end of this chapter you should be able to:
■ check the accuracy of entries in the sales ledger
■ check the accuracy of entries in the purchases ledger
■ explain how debit balances can occur in the purchases ledger
■ explain how credit balances can occur in the sales ledger.

They maintain personal credit customers accounts in detail as memorandum accounts. These memorandum accounts are used:

(a) to send out monthly statements
(b) for credit control purposes, i.e. identifying bad debts and potential doubtful debtors.

They maintain personal credit suppliers' accounts in detail as memorandum accounts. These memorandum accounts are used:

(a) to check monthly statements received and
(b) for credit control purposes.

Other businesses use the detailed sales and purchases ledger accounts as part of their double-entry system. They maintain control accounts as memorandum accounts.

○ EXAMINATION TIP

For the purposes of examination technique the construction of control accounts is the same whether or not they are maintained as part of the double-entry system or as memorandum accounts.

Schedule of debtors is a list of debtors balances extracted from the sales ledger.

Schedule of creditors is a list of creditor balances extracted from the purchase ledger.

PREPARATION OF SALES LEDGER CONTROL ACCOUNTS

The sales ledger control account is a replica in total of all the entries made in the individual sales ledger accounts. Here is a simple illustration:

WORKED EXAMPLE

Sales ledger

Dr	Clogg	Cr	Dr	Saddler	Cr
1 May Sales 50	9 May Cash 48		7 May Sales 60	12 May Returns inward 29	
	9 May Disc Alld 2			14 May Bank 20	
50	50			14 May Bal c/d 11	
				60	
			60		
			15 May Bal b/d 11		

Required Prepare a sales ledger control account at 15 May for the ledger shown.

Answer

Dr	Sales ledger control account		Cr
1 May Sales	50	9 May Cash	48
7 May Sales	60	9 May Discount allowed	2
		12 May Returns inward	29
		14 May Bank	20
		14 May Balance c/d	11
	110		110
15 May Balance b/d	11		

The control account is an exact replica of all the ledger accounts.

If you can remember this you should not get the items required in preparing the control account on the wrong side.

(This, of course, assumes that you understand on which side each of the entries appears in an individual account!)

● EXAMINATION TIP

The most common error that students make when answering an examination question is to reverse the control account.

We cannot in reality look at every individual account in the sales ledger and copy them into the sales ledger control account. Or add each of the different categories of entries together – it would be too time-consuming.

We can, however, get the necessary figures in total by using the books of prime entry.

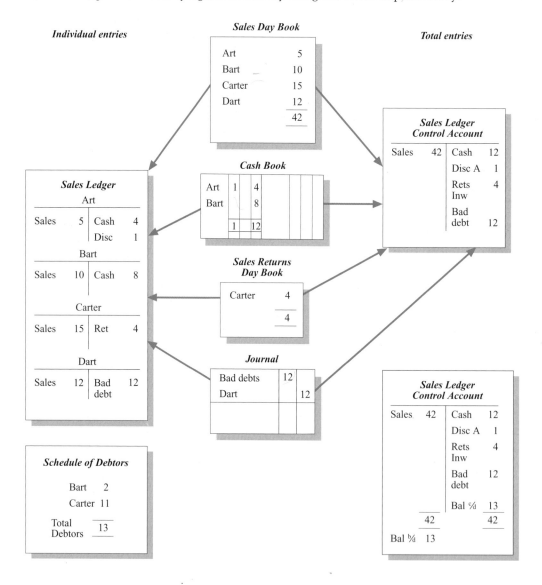

WORKED EXAMPLE

Petra started business in May 20*3. She provides the following totals from her books of prime entry on 31 May 20*3:

credit sales £7,300; cash sales £2,100; sales returns £420; monies received from debtors £5,400.

A schedule of debtors extracted from Petra's sales ledger totals £1,480.

Required A sales ledger control account for May 20*3 for Petra.

Answer

Dr			Sales ledger control account		Cr	
31 May	Sales	7,300	31 May	Returns inward	420	
			31 May	Cash	5,400	
			31 May	Balance c/d	1,480	[figure included to make control account balance]
		7,300			7,300	
1 June	Balance b/d	1,480				

The debtors at the end of May, according to the control account, should be £1,480. This figure should agree with the total of balances listed on the schedule of debtors – it does, so we can say that the sales ledger is arithmetically correct for the month of May 20*3.

- I hope that you did not include the £2,100 cash sales – these do not appear in the sales ledger – the sales ledger is reserved only for credit customers.
- I also hope that you brought down the £1,480 debit balance on the sales ledger control account.

WORKED EXAMPLE

At the end of her second month of trading, Petra provides you with the following information which she has extracted from her books of prime entry on 30 June 20*3:

credit sales £9,400; cash sales £2,750; monies received from debtors £6,200; discount allowed to credit customers £610; sales returns £240. (Bring forward the debtors' balance from the May sales ledger control account.)

Required Prepare a sales ledger control account for June 20*3.

Answer

Dr			Sales ledger control account		Cr	
1 June	Balance b/d	1,480	30 June	Cash	6,200	
30 June	Sales	9,400	30 June	Discount allowed	610	
			30 June	Returns inward	240	
			30 June	Balance c/d	3,830	
		10,880			10,880	
1 July	Balance b/d	3,830				

QUESTION 3

Petra provides the following information which has been extracted from her books of prime entry on 31 July 20*3:

	£
Credit sales	9,600
Cash sales	2,350
Monies received from debtors	7,200
Discount allowed	910
Returns inwards	340
Returns outwards	400

She is also able to provide the following information:

Debtors 1 July 20*3	3,830
Schedule of debtor's total	4,980

NOTE
Returns <u>in</u>wards are goods that have been returned by credit customers and have been received <u>into</u> Petra's business.
Returns <u>out</u>wards are goods that have been returned and have gone <u>out</u> of Petra's business.

Required Prepare a sales ledger control account for the month of July 20*3.

QUESTION 4

Petra provides the following information which has been extracted from her books of prime entry on 31 August 20*3:

	£
Debtors 1 August 20*3	3,380
Credit sales	10,100
Cash sales	2,450
Monies received from debtors	7,400
Discount allowed	870
Dishonoured cheque	360
Returns inwards	600
Returns outwards	550

She is also able to provide the following information:

Debtors 1 August	3,380
Schedule of debtors total	4,870

The dishonoured cheque for £360 was originally part of the monies received and because it has now been 'returned' should be entered on the debit side of the control account.

Required (a) Sales ledger control account for the month of August 20*3.
(b) Explain what the control account reveals.

Do not forget to bring balances down – if you fail to do this, it will cost you valuable marks.

PREPARATION OF PURCHASE LEDGER CONTROL ACCOUNTS

The purchase ledger control account is a replica of all the entries made in the individual purchase ledger accounts.

Here is a simple illustration:

EXAMPLE

Dr	Saleem		Cr	Dr		Toshak		Cr
13 July Cash	347	1 July Purchases	350	19 July Cash	20	7 July Purchase		125
Discount received	3			31 July Bal c/d	123	24 July Returns outwards		18
	350		350		143			143
						1 Aug Balance b/d		123

Dr	Purchase ledger control account		Cr
13 July Cash	347	1 July Purchases	350
13 July Discount received	3	7 July Purchases	125
19 July Cash	20	24 July Returns outwards	18
31 July Balance c/d	123		
	493		493
		1 Aug Balance b/d	123

Once again, this simple but effective illustration relies on the fact that you must understand what an individual account in the purchase ledger looks like.

We cannot look at every individual account in the purchase ledger and total them.

We use totals that can be found in the books of prime entry.

WORKED EXAMPLE

EXAMPLE 1

Yip started in business in February 20*3. He provides the following totals from his books of prime entry on 28 February 20*3:

credit purchases £9,430; cash purchases £1,790; purchase returns £105; monies paid by Yip to creditors £8,100; a schedule of creditors extracted from the purchase ledger on 28 February totals £1,225.

Required Prepare a purchase ledger control account for February 20*3.

Answer

Dr	Purchase ledger control account			Cr
28 February	Returns outward	105	28 February Purchases	9,430
28 February	Cash	8,100		
28 February	Balance c/d	1,225		
		9,430		9,430
			1 March Balance b/d	1,225

WORKED EXAMPLE *continued*

The creditors at the end of February, according to the control account, should amount to £1,225. This agrees with Yip's schedule of creditors, so we can say that his purchase ledger is arithmetically correct.

Did you include the cash purchases? Of course you didn't – they do not appear in the purchase ledger – the ledger is used to record only Yip's transactions with his credit suppliers.

EXAMPLE 2

Yip provides you with the following information which has been extracted from his books of prime entry for March 20*3, his second month of trading:

credit purchases £8,600; cash purchases £2,930; monies paid by Yip to creditors £6,800; discount received from creditors £460; purchase returns £120.

(Bring forward the creditors' balance from the February purchase ledger control account.)

Required Prepare a purchase ledger control account for March 20*3.

Answer

Dr			Purchase ledger control account			Cr
31 March	Cash	6,800	1 March	Balance b/d	1,225
31 March	Discount received	460	31 March	Purchases	8,600
31 March	Returns outwards	120			
31 March	Balance c/d	2,445			
		9,825			9,825
			1 April	Balance b/d	2,445

QUESTION 5

Yip provides the following information from his books of prime entry for April 20*3:

	£
Credit purchases	9,200
Cash purchases	3,150
Monies paid to creditors by Yip	9,300
Discount received	700
Returns inward	610
Returns outward	150

He is also able to provide the following information:

Creditors 1 April 20*3	2,445
Schedule of creditors total 30 April 20*3	1,495

Required Prepare a purchase ledger control account for the month of April 20*3 for Yip.

QUESTION 6

Yip provides the following information from his books of prime entry for May 20*3:

	£
Credit purchases	9,350
Cash purchases	4,075
Monies paid to creditors by Yip	7,900
Discount received	460
Returns inward	670
Returns outward	170

He is also able to provide the following information:

Creditors 1 May 20*3	1,495
Schedule of creditors total 31 May 20*3	2,335

Required   (a)   Prepare a purchase ledger control account for May 20*3.
            (b)   Explain what the control account reveals.

CREDIT BALANCES IN THE SALES LEDGER

Usually, any closing balance in the account of an individual credit customer will be a debit. However, it is possible that an individual debtor account may end with a credit balance. How can this possibly happen?

WORKED EXAMPLE

EXAMPLE 1

Petra sells £720 goods to Claude on 3 October.

On 23 October Claude sends Petra a cheque for £720.

On 29 October Claude returns £30 of goods which have proved to be faulty.

Required   Prepare the account of Claude as it would appear in Petra's sales ledger at 31 October 20*3.

Answer
The question asks for the account so it must be produced in detail, not as a 'T' account.

Dr			Claude		Cr
3 October	Sales	720	23 October	Bank	720
			29 October	Returns inward	30

You can see that at 31 October there is a credit balance in Claude's account although this account is contained in Petra's sales ledger (debtors ledger).

In Petra's list of outstanding balances in the sales ledger at 31 October 20*3 she will have to show this balance on Claude's account as a creditor. It will also feature in the sales ledger control account for October as a creditor.

Do not deduct this amount from Petra's total debtors. It must be included in a trial balance as at 31 October 20*3 and a balance sheet prepared as at 31 October 20*3 with other creditors.

EXAMPLE 2

Toddy will be a regular customer of Petra. He has paid £50 on the 24th of each month to Petra by standing order since 24 May 20*3. On 6 September Petra sells £230 of goods to Toddy.

Required   Prepare the account of Toddy as it would appear in Petra's sales ledger at 30 September 20*3.

Answer

Dr			Toddy			Cr
6 September	Sales	230	24 May	Bank		50
			24 June	Bank		50
			24 July	Bank		50
			24 August	Bank		50
30 September	Balance c/d	20	24 September	Bank		50
		250				250
			1 October	Balance b/d		20

In Petra's list of outstanding balances in her sales ledger at 30 September the balance standing on Toddy's account will be shown as a credit of £20 – he is a creditor at that date – and this should be shown accordingly on a trial balance extracted on 30 September or any balance sheet prepared at 30 September.

A credit balance could also appear in a debtor's account if the customer had made an overpayment or was allowed additional cash or trade discount after the account had been settled.

DEBIT BALANCES IN THE PURCHASE LEDGER

Similar circumstances could result in debit balances appearing on the list of balances extracted from a purchase ledger.

Debit balances would appear in the purchase ledger if a trader:

(a) settled his account with a supplier then returned faulty goods
(b) pays a fixed amount each month which in total exceeds the amount of purchases made
(c) was allowed additional discount after settling his/her account
(d) had overpaid an outstanding balance.

■ Any credit balances in the sales ledger at a month-end will be shown as credit balances in the sales ledger control account for that month.
■ Any debit balances in the purchase ledger at a month-end will be shown as debit balances in the purchase ledger control account for that month.

WORKED EXAMPLE

Harvey provides the following information from his books of prime entry at 31 July 20*3:

	£
Credit sales for July	6,930
Monies received from debtors during month	5,100
Discount allowed	450
Returns inwards	180

He provides the following additional information:

- Debit balances appearing in the sales ledger at 1 July 20*3 2,100
- Credit balances appearing in the sales ledger at 1 July 20*3 30
- Creditor appearing in sales ledger schedule of debtors total at 31 July 20*3 90

Required Prepare the sales ledger control account for July 20*3 for Harvey.

Answer

Dr			Sales ledger control account			Cr
1 July	Balance b/d	2,100	1 July	Balance b/d		30
31 July	Sales	6,930	31 July	Cash		5,100
			31 July	Discount allowed		450
			31 July	Returns inward		180
31 July	Balance c/d [given]	90	31 July	Balance c/d [missing figure]		3,360
		9,120				9,120
1 August	Balance b/d	3,360	1 August	Balance b/d		90

CONTRA ENTRIES (SOMETIMES CALLED 'SET-OFFS')

WORKED EXAMPLE

A business may well be both a customer of and a supplier to another business. For example, B. Neal had supplied Hoole with fabrics valued at £4,300 on credit. Neal purchased £700 worth of curtains for his business on credit from Hoole.

This would appear in Neal's books of account thus:

	Sales ledger			Purchases ledger	
Dr	Hoole	Cr	Dr	Hoole	Cr
Sales	4,300			Purchases	700

It would not seem sensible for Neal to send £700 to Hoole while demanding that Hoole pay £4,300. The usual procedure in cases like this is to transfer the smaller amount from one ledger to the other. The entries are:

	Sales ledger	
Dr	Hoole	Cr
	Transfer to purchases ledger	700

WORKED EXAMPLE *continued*

Purchases ledger

Dr		Hoole		Cr
Transfer from Sales ledger	700			

This will close one account (in the purchase ledger) and reduce the balance owed by Hoole (in the sales ledger). The account now looks like this:

Sales ledger

Dr		Hoole		Cr
Sales	4,300	Transfer to purchases ledger	700	

Purchases ledger

Dr		Hoole		Cr
Transfer from Sales ledger	700	Purchases	700	

All transactions should be recorded in a book of prime entry. Entries involving transfers should be entered in the journal:

Journal

		Dr £	Cr £
Hoole	PL 26	700	
Hoole	SL 15		700

Transfer of credit balance in Hoole's account in Purchase ledger to Hoole's account in Sales ledger

- All entries in the personal ledgers must also be shown in the control accounts.
- There will be an entry on the credit side of Neal's sales ledger control account.
- There will also be an entry on the debit side of Neal's purchase ledger control account reflecting the entries in the two personal ledgers.

WORKED EXAMPLE

In Rodney's books Ernie has a debit balance of £100 in Rodney's sales ledger and a credit balance of £30 in Rodney's purchase ledger.

Required Show the contra entries(set-offs) as they would appear in both Rodney's sales ledger control account and his purchase ledger control account.

Answer

Dr	Rodney sales ledger control account		Cr
		Transfer from purchases ledger	30

Dr	Rodney purchase ledger control account		Cr
Transfer to sales ledger	30		

180   INTRODUCING ACCOUNTING FOR AS

WORKED EXAMPLE *continued*

EXAMPLE

In Derek's books, Eric has a debit balance of £710 in Derek's sales ledger and a credit balance of £1,400 in Derek's purchase ledger.

Required Show how the contras (set-offs) would appear in both Derek's sales ledger control account and his purchase ledger control account.

Answer

Dr	Sales ledger control account	Cr
	Transfer to purchases ledger	710

Dr	Purchases ledger control account		Cr
Transfer from sales ledger	710		

Note
It does not matter whether the debit balance or the credit balance is greater. When showing the contra in the control accounts:

- the sales ledger control account is always credited and
- the purchase ledger control account is always debited.

[In the personal ledgers the smaller balance is the balance that is transferred.]

WORKED EXAMPLE

Damien provides the following information taken from his books at 30 November 20*3:

sales ledger balances 1 November £6,340; purchase ledger balances 1 November 20*3 £3,960; credit sales for November £140,100; credit purchases for November £64,300; monies received from debtors for November £139,570; monies paid to creditors in November £63,030; discounts allowed £350; discounts received £180; returns inward £900; returns outward £600; transfers from sales ledger to purchase ledger £440.

Required (a) Prepare a sales ledger control account showing clearly the closing balance of outstanding debtors at 30 November 20*3.
(b) Prepare a purchase ledger control account showing clearly the closing balance of outstanding creditors at 30 November 20*3.

Answer

Dr			Sales ledger control account			Cr
1 November	Balance b/d	6,340	30 November	Cash		139,570
30 November	Sales	140,100	30 November	Discount allowed		350
			30 November	Returns inward		900
			30 November	Transfer to purchases ledger		440
			30 November	Balance c/d		5,180
		146,440				146,440
1 December	Balance b/d	5,180				

WORKED EXAMPLE *continued*

Dr	Purchases ledger control account				Cr
30 November	Cash	63,030	1 November	Balance b/d	3,960
30 November	Discount received	180	30 November	Purchases	64,300
30 November	Returns outward	600			
30 November	Transfer from sales ledger	440			
30 November	Balance c/d	4,010			
		68,260			68,260
			1 December	Balance b/d	4,010

VAT is included in all purchases and sales that are posted to the personal accounts in the sales ledger and the purchases ledger.

When preparing control accounts it is necessary to use the totals from the books of prime entry that are inclusive of VAT.

Provision for doubtful debts is not included in a sales ledger control account.

The provision is not entered in specific individual debtors' accounts.

Only transactions that appear in the ledger accounts appear in the control accounts.

Therefore if the provision does not appear in a personal ledger account … it will not appear in the control account

REVISION TIP

Practise preparing individual accounts from the sales ledger and the purchase ledger – control accounts are similar but use larger amounts of money.

ADVANTAGES OF USING CONTROL ACCOUNTS

1. They act as a check on the accuracy of all the postings made to the personal ledgers and this checks the reliability of the ledger accounts.
2. They enable some errors in the ledgers to be located quickly.
3. If the trial balance does not balance, the control accounts may indicate which personal ledger(s) contain(s) the error(s).
4. Total amounts owed by debtors and total amounts owing to creditors can be ascertained quickly enabling a trial balance and/or a balance sheet to be prepared quickly.
5. They may be used to give responsibility to staff by making them responsible for sections of the ledger.
6. They may be used as a check on the honesty of staff. The control account should be prepared by a member of staff who is not involved in the maintenance of the ledger being checked.

LIMITATIONS ON USING CONTROL ACCOUNTS

The main limitation of using control accounts as a means of verifying the accuracy of the personal ledgers rests on the fact that not all errors in the ledgers will be revealed by the preparation of a control account.

Within the ledger there could be:

- compensating errors plus errors of:
- omission
- commission
- original entry and
- reversal errors.

The details of how these errors could arise arise can be found in Chapter 8, 'The Trial Balance'.

QUESTION 7

The following information relates to the purchase ledger of Tricia Clott for the month of October 20*3:

	£
Total creditors on 1 October 20*3	3,741
Credit purchases	10,452
Cash paid to creditors	9,779
Discounts received	1,230

Required Prepare a purchase ledger control account for the month of October 20*3.

QUESTION 8

The following information relates to the creditors' ledger of Phillip Tyke for the month of February 20*3:

	£
Total creditors on 1 February 20*3	6,813
Credit purchases	18,734
Total cash purchases	2,451
Cash paid to creditors	19,003
Discounts received	872

Required Prepare a creditors' ledger control account for the month of February 20*3.

QUESTION 9

The following information relates to the sales ledger of Frew Niell for the month of December 20*3:

	£
Total debtors on 1 December 20*3	1,006
Credit sales	5,408
Cash received from debtors	4,921
Discounts allowed	561

Required Prepare a sales ledger control account for the month of December 20*3.

QUESTION 10

The following information relates to the debtors ledger of Martin Daley for the month of July 20*3:

	£
Total debtors on 1 July 20*3	4,110
Credit sales	16,882
Cash received from debtors	18,530
Discounts allowed	1,451

Required Prepare a debtors ledger control account for the month of July 20*3.

QUESTION 11

The following information is given for May 20*3 for Greg Trout:

	£
Total creditors on 1 May 20*3	22,556
Credit purchases	117,004
Cash purchases	4,662
Cash paid to creditors	109,621
Discounts received	3,551
Discounts allowed	3,239
Returns outwards	1,572
Returns inwards	1,422

Required Prepare a purchase ledger control account for the month of May 20*3.

QUESTION 12

The following information is given for September 20*3 for Ted Brester:

	£
Total creditors on 1 September 20*3	2,921
Credit purchases	6,443
Cash purchases	2,091
Cash paid to creditors	4,220
Discounts received	622
Discounts allowed	428
Returns outwards	1,261
Returns inwards	720

Required Prepare a purchase ledger control account for the month of September 20*3.

QUESTION 13

Claire Drov supplies the following information for August 20*3:

	£
Total debtors on 1 August 20*3	456
Credit sales	10,674
Cash sales	4,441
Cash received from debtors	8,634
Discounts received	3,001
Discounts allowed	1,329
Returns outwards	358
Returns inwards	566

Required Prepare a sales ledger control account for the month of August 20*3.

QUESTION 14

Dick Dresden supplies the following information for March 20*3:

	£
Total debtors on 1 March 20*3	5,127
Credit sales	11,439
Cash sales	3,771
Cash received from debtors	9,528
Discounts received	1,994
Discounts allowed	2,331
Returns outwards	731
Returns inwards	841

Required Prepare a debtors ledger control account for the month of March 20*3.

QUESTION 15

Xiu Jin supplies the following information for October 20*3:

	£
Credit balances in purchases ledger on 1 October 20*3	3,551
Debit balances in purchases ledger on 1 October 20*3	37
Credit purchases	15,338
Cash purchases	4,119
Cash paid to creditors	12,440
Discounts received	1,084

	£
Discounts allowed	936
Returns outwards	32
Returns inwards	631
Debit balances in purchases ledger on 31 October 20*3	154

Required Prepare a purchase ledger control account for the month of October 20*3.

QUESTION 16

Melodie Clyde supplies the following information for November 20*3:

	£
Debit balances in debtors ledger on 1 November 20*3	5,308
Credit balances in debtors ledger on 1 November 20*3	650
Credit purchases	5,773
Cash purchases	3,411
Credit sales	11,453
Cash sales	2,766
Cash paid to creditors	4,720
Cash received from debtors	9,539
Discounts received	393
Discounts allowed	197
Returns outwards	671
Returns inwards	777
Credit balances in debtors ledger on 30 November 20*3	240

Required Prepare a debtors ledger control account for the month of November 20*3.

QUESTION 17

Rory McDuff supplies the following information for the month of December 20*3:

	£
Debit balances in sales ledger on 1 December 20*3	7,449
Debit balances in purchases ledger on 1 December 20*3	342
Credit balances in sales ledger on 1 December 20*3	247
Credit balances in purchases ledger on 1 December 20*3	4,552
Credit sales	43,650
Credit purchases	20,005
Cash sales	8,643
Cash purchases	4,571
Cash received from credit customers	39,754
Cash paid to credit suppliers	19,003
Discounts received	251
Discounts allowed	166
Returns outwards	543
Returns inwards	510
Transfers from sales ledger to purchases ledger	300
Provision for doubtful debts on 31 December 20*3	150
Debit balances in purchases ledger on 31 December 20*3	45
Credit balances in sales ledger on 31 December 20*3	188

Required Prepare:
(a) a sales ledger control account for the month of December 20*3
(b) a purchases ledger control account for the month of December 20*3.

QUESTION 18

Ifor Jones supplies the following information for the month of February 20*3:

	£
Debit balances in sales ledger on 1 February 20*3	18,539
Debit balances in purchases ledger on 1 February 20*3	341
Credit balances in sales ledger on 1 February 20*3	450
Credit balances in purchases ledger on 1 February 20*3	9,557
Credit sales	123,921
Credit purchases	47,509
Cash sales	34,652
Cash purchases	18,674
Cash received from credit customers	112,659
Cash paid to credit suppliers	45,620
Discounts received	762
Discounts allowed	673
Returns outwards	1,290
Returns inwards	732
Transfers to purchases ledger from sales ledger	489
Provision for doubtful debts on 28 February 20*3	340
Debit balances in purchases ledger on 28 February 20*3	65
Credit balances in sales ledger on 28 February 20*3	138

Required Prepare:
(a) a sales ledger control account for the month of February 20*3
(b) a purchases ledger control account for the month of February 20*3.

SIXTEEN

Accruals and Pre-payments

So far in our studies we have assumed that money spent and money received exactly matched the time period under review.

- We have assumed that rent paid in February was for the use of premises in February.
- We have assumed that wages paid in July was payment for work done in July.
- We have assumed that the figures shown in the trial balance prepared at 31 December 20*3 showed all the incomes and all the expenses for the year ended 31 December 20*3; nothing more and nothing less.

When calculating profits, as accountants, we are interested in accounting for the resources that the business has used during the financial year to generate the revenue receipts for that same year.

The **accruals concept** recognises the difference between the actual payment of cash and the legal obligation to pay cash.

> **EXAMPLE**
>
> Larry runs a small newsagent's shop. He has signed a tenancy agreement with his landlord stating that he can use the shop for the next five years on payment of a rental of £6,000 per annum payable quarterly in advance on 1 January, 1 April, 1 July and 1 October.
>
> At 31 December 20*3, Larry's financial year-end, Larry has only paid his landlord £4,500 (ie he still owes the rent that was due to be paid on 1 October).
>
> The amount shown on Larry's profit and loss account for rent is £6,000 since Larry has had the use of a resource (the shop) worth £6,000 to help him generate his profits.

When preparing a trading and profit and loss account, a trader must include all items of expenditure paid and payable.

The accruals concept also recognises the distinction between the receipt of cash and legal right to receive cash.

This sounds a little strange at first but you will soon get the hang of this.

So from now on when we prepare a set of final accounts we shall include all the items that apply to the accounting period under consideration.

Some expenses listed in the trial balance are always paid in advance:

- insurance has to be paid in advance
- business rates are paid in advance.

Other expenses listed on the trial balance might not be paid up to date:

- part of Larry's rent payable had not been paid
- wages earned for work already done may not be due to be paid until next month.

Specification coverage:
AQA 12.2;
OCR 5.1.5.

By the end of this chapter you should be able to:
- explain the accruals concept
- make appropriate entries for accruals and pre-payments in the final accounts.

DEALING WITH ACCRUED EXPENSES

> **Trade creditors** are amounts owed to the suppliers of goods for resale.

> **Trade debtors** are amounts owed by credit customers who have not yet settled their accounts.

Remember Larry?

An extract from his trial balance as at 31 December 20*3 would show:

	Dr £	Cr £
Rent payable	4,500	

When we prepare the profit and loss account for the year ended 31 December 20*3 the entries shown above would show:

Dr	Profit and loss account for the year ended 31 December 20*3	Cr
	£	£
Rent payable	6,000	

But this cannot be totally correct.

Larry has increased his debit entries by £1,500, with no corresponding increase in his credit entries.

Probably a sending-off offence in the double-entry game!

He needs to include an extra credit in his final accounts ...
                                   ... rent payable owed at the year-end.

In the balance sheet prepared at the year-end, trade creditors represent amounts to owed to suppliers that have supplied goods but who have not yet been paid.

Since the rent payable is owed at the balance sheet date, this too must be a creditor.
Larry has used his premises and not yet paid for the use.
Rent payable must be shown as a current liability along with the trade creditors.

Note
- The balance sheet has not been credited.
- The balance sheet is not part of the double-entry system; it is merely a sheet showing balances outstanding at the end of the financial year.
- The outstanding rent is included in current liabilities with other credit balances (eg the trade creditors).

The balance sheet as at 31 December 20*3 would show:

	£		£
Current liabilities			
Accrued expenses (rent)			1,500

QUESTION 1

The following items are shown on a trial balance extracted on 30 June 20*3:

	£
Wages	43,000
Motor expenses	8,600
Telephone	2,400
Advertising	1,800
Heating and lighting expenses	2,000

At the year-end the following amounts remained outstanding and unpaid:

	£
Wages	872
Motor expenses	750
Telephone	280
Advertising	560
Heating and lighting	391

Required Complete the table below, showing the amounts to be included as an expense in the profit and loss account for the year ended 30 June 20*3 and the amount to be shown as a current liability in the balance sheet as at 30 June 20*3.

Answer

Expense	Profit and loss entry	Current liability
Wages		
Motor expenses		
Telephone		
Advertising		
Heating and lighting		

DEALING WITH PREPAID EXPENSES

Sometimes a business will pay for services before it actually receives the service:

■ insurance has to be paid for before cover is provided
■ local authority business rates must also to be paid before the period for which they are due.

Since we are accounting for resources used in the period covered by the final accounts any amounts paid in advance must be disregarded.

WORKED EXAMPLE

An extract from Larry's trial balance as at 31 December 20*3 shows:

	£	£
Insurance	2,300	
Business rates	1,200	

Insurance paid for January 20*4 amounts to £100.

Business rates paid for the three months ending 31 March 20*4 amount to £300.

Required Prepare a profit and loss extract for the year ended 31 December 20*3, showing the entries for insurance and business rates.

Answer

Larry

Dr Profit and loss account extract for the year ended 31 December 20*3 Cr		
	£	£
Insurance	2,200	
Business rates	900	

Larry does not include the £100 paid for *next year's insurance cover* or the £300 for *next year's rates bill.*

He only includes the payments made to acquire the resources that have been used to run his business this year.

But it cannot be right to reduce the two expenses without corresponding entries.

We reduce debits by increasing credits (check this out – it is correct).

In effect, Larry has credited insurance with £100; he has credited business rates with £300.

He needs to include two extra debits – two extra debtors.

Larry's balance sheet as at 31 December 20*3 will show:

	£	£
Current assets		
Amounts prepaid – insurance	100	
business rates	300	

QUESTION 2

The following items appear in a trial balance extracted on 31 August 20*3:

	£
Rent	7,500
General expenses	5,412
Insurance	1,872
Salaries	45,670
Rates	1,750

The following additional information is available as at 31 August 20*3:

		£
Amounts owing	Rent	500
	General expenses	521
	Salaries	729
Amounts paid for the year ending 31 August 20*4:		
	Insurance	341
	Rates	812

Required Complete the table. Indicate the amount to be included in the profit and loss account for the year ended 31 August 20*3 and the amount to be shown on the balance sheet as at 31 August 20*3.

Answer

Expense	Profit and loss account entry	Current asset	Current liability
Rent			
General expenses			
Salaries			
Insurance			
Rates			

DEALING WITH OUTSTANDING REVENUES

When revenue has been earned during a financial year but has not yet been paid, the revenue due must be included in the final accounts.

EXAMPLE

Larry sub-lets the rooms above his shop to Dan for a rental of £50 per week. At 31 December Dan owes two weeks' rent.

Larry's profit and loss account would show a full year's rental income of £2,600 even though he has actually received only £2,500 from Dan.

When preparing a trading and profit and loss account, a trader must include all items of revenue received or receivable for the time period under review.

QUESTION 3

Malcolm works on a commission basis for Hijah Ltd. He earns 10% commission on all goods sold. Sales for the year ended 30 November 20*3 were £87,750. Malcolm has received commission amounting to £7,000 in the year ended 30 November 20*3.

Required Fill in the missing amounts in Malcolm's final accounts.

Answer

Malcolm

Dr Profit and loss account extract for the year ended 30 November 20*3	Cr
	£
Commission receivable	——

Balance sheet extract as at 30 November 20*3

Current assets	£
Commission receivable owing	——

QUESTION 4

Gilly sub-lets part of her premises at an annual rental of £3,900. At the financial year end 31 December 20*3 Gilly's tenant owes £225 for three weeks' unpaid rent.

Required Fill in the missing amounts in Gilly's final accounts.

Answer

Gilly

Dr Profit and loss account extract for the year ended 31 December 20*3	Cr
	£
Rent receivable	——

Balance sheet extract as at 31 December 20*3

Current assets	£
Rent receivable owing	——

Sometimes commission receivable and rent receivable may be paid in advance. The amounts relating to *next year* will not be included in *this year's* final accounts.

WORKED EXAMPLE

Horace works on commission for Henri. Horace has earned £5,320 commission for the year ended 31 January 20*3. At 31 January 20*3 Horace has received commission payments of £6,000.

Required State:
(a) The amount to be entered in Horace's profit and loss account for the year ended 31 January 20*3.
(b) The amount to be shown in the balance sheet as at 31 January 20*3.

Answer
The amount to be shown in the profit and loss account is £5,320. This should be shown as an addition to the gross profit.

£680 is shown under current liabilities in the balance sheet (Horace owes Henri £680 at the end of the year).

WORKED EXAMPLE

Kim sub-lets part of her premises to Colin for £6,240 per annum. At Kim's financial year-end, 31 July 20*3, Colin had paid £6,600 rent.

Required State:
(a) The amount to be entered in Kim's profit and loss account for the year ended 31 July 20*3.
(b) The amount to be shown in the balance sheet as at 31 July 20*3.

Answer
The amount shown in the profit and loss account is £6,240. This should be added to gross profit.

£360 is shown as a current liability in the balance sheet.

Amounts **owed**, for **expenses**, by a business at the financial year-end are usually totalled and entered in the balance sheet as a current liability.

The total is known as one of the following:

- accruals
- accrued expenses
- expense creditors
- expenses owing.

Amounts **paid in advance**, for **expenses**, by the business at the financial year-end are usually totalled and entered in the balance sheet as a current asset.

The total is known as one of the following:

- pre-payments
- pre-paid expenses
- payments in advance.

Amounts **owed** to a business for **commission receivable** and **rent receivable** are usually added to pre-payments as accrued income.

Amounts **received in advance** for **commission receivable** and **rent receivable** are usually added to accruals.

Chapter summary

- We account for resources used during a financial year, not money paid to acquire resources.
- The accruals concept recognises the difference between the actual payment of cash and the legal obligation to pay cash. Accruals are current liabilities. Pre-payments are current assets.
- The concept also recognises the distinction between the actual receipt of cash and the legal right to receive cash. Cash received before it is due is a current liability. Cash owed but not yet paid is a current asset.

Self-test questions

- The accruals concept is sometimes known as the .... concept.
- Define an 'accrual'.
- Identify two other terms used to describe an accrual in a balance sheet.
- Define a 'pre-payment'.
- Identify two other terms used to describe a pre-payment in a balance sheet.
- The amount of an expense on the trial balance is always entered in the profit and loss account. True or false?
- A prepayment is a current asset. True or false?
- An accrued expense is a current asset. True or false?
- Money paid for the next financial year's rent is a current asset. True or false?
- Money received from a tenant for next year's rent is a current asset. True or false?

TEST QUESTIONS

QUESTION 5

Ben Trent provides the following trial balance extracted from his books of account on 31 March 20*3 after his first year of trading:

	Dr £	Cr £
Sales		123,563
Purchases	44,832	
Rent	5,600	
Rates	2,340	
Wages	47,892	
Motor expenses	2,357	
General expenses	7,459	
Capital		26,061
Drawings	14,670	
Debtors	8,564	
Creditors		5,430
Bank balance	1,340	
Equipment at cost	8,000	
Delivery van at cost	12,000	
	155,054	155,054

Additional information
Stock as at 31 March 20*3 was valued at £8,459; accrued wages amount to £874.

Required Prepare:
(a) a trading and profit and loss account for the year ended 31 March 20*3
(b) a balance sheet as at 31 March 20*3.

QUESTION 6

Lottie Chum provides the following trial balance extracted from her books of account on 31 October 20*3 after her first year of trading:

	Dr £	Cr £
Capital		92,112
Drawings	17,500	
Purchases	67,431	
Sales		165,997
Motor expenses	5,700	
Wages	84,532	
Heating and lighting	4,632	
Rates	1,280	
General expenses	8,349	
Premises at cost	45,000	
Equipment at cost	18,000	
Van at cost	6,500	
Debtors	4,673	
Creditors		5,342
Bank overdraft		376
Cash in hand	230	
	263,827	263,827

Additional information
Stock as at 31 October 20*3 was valued at £11,096; heating and lighting is accrued by £329.

Required Prepare:
(a) a trading and profit and loss account for the year ended 31 October 20*3
(b) a balance sheet as at 31 October 20*3.

QUESTION 7

Toby Moore provides the following trial balance extracted from his books of account on 31 July 20*3:

	Dr £	Cr £
Stock as at 1 August 20*2	8,756	
Sales		134,908
Purchases	54,731	
Returns inwards	453	
Returns outwards		612
Drawings	25,000	
Capital		76,810
Wages	34,770	
Motor expenses	1,443	
Insurance	880	
General expenses	4,119	
Premises at cost	65,000	
Machinery at cost	16,000	
Vehicle at cost	7,400	
Debtors	811	
Creditors		2,678
Bank overdraft		4,637
Cash in hand	282	
	219,645	219,645

Additional information
Stock as at 31 July 20*3 was valued at £9,315; insurance has been pre-paid £58 at 31 July 20*3.

Required Prepare:
(a) a trading and profit and loss account for the year ended 31 July 20*3
(b) a balance sheet as at 31 July 20*3.

QUESTION 8

Natasha Bedi provides the following trial balance extracted from her books of account on 31 January 20*3:

	Dr £	Cr £
Purchases	112,754	
Sales		232,987
Returns inwards	458	
Returns outwards		2,610
Stock as at 1 February 20*2	8,503	
Capital		82,911
Long-term loan		50,000
Drawings	34,675	
Wages	73,097	
Rates	2,540	
Telephone	670	
Motor expenses	7,904	
General expenses	12,554	
Debtors	23,564	
Creditors		9,432
Bank balance	4,672	
Cash in hand	549	
Premises at cost	54,000	
Office equipment at cost	23,500	
Delivery vehicle at cost	18,500	
	377,940	377,940

Additional information as at 31 January 20*3
Stock was valued at £10,564; rates paid in advance £320.

Required Prepare:
  (a) a trading and profit and loss account for the year ended 31 January 20*3
  (b) a balance sheet as at 31 January 20*3.

QUESTION 9

Seok Chin provides the following trial balance extracted from her books of account on 30 April 20*3:

	Dr £	Cr £
Long-term loan		120,000
Capital		72,318
Drawings	26,500	
Premises at cost	80,000	
Equipment at cost	23,000	
Vehicles at cost	84,000	
Purchases	238,056	
Sales		407,843
Returns inwards	1,453	
Returns outwards		573
Carriage outwards	1,323	
Rates	1,660	
Wages	73,009	
Motor expenses	32,540	
Telephone	3,760	
General expenses	8,116	
Stock as at 1 May 20*2	23,510	
Debtors	34,534	
Creditors		23,665
Bank overdraft		7,439
Cash in hand	377	
	631,838	631,838

Additional information as at 30 April 20*3
Stock was valued at £26,449; wages owing amounted to £2,007; rates have been prepaid £342.

Required Prepare:
  (a) a trading and profit and loss account for the year ended 30 April 20*3
  (b) a balance sheet as at 30 April 20*3.

QUESTION 10

Sol Jensen provides the following trial balance extracted from his books of account on 31 December 20*3:

	Dr £	Cr £
Sales		211,901
Purchases	116,754	
Returns inwards	453	
Returns outwards		509
Stock as at 1 January 20*3	20,064	
Carriage inwards	2,431	
Carriage outwards	1,342	
Wages	78,549	
Drawings	24,650	
Rent and rates	4,352	
Advertising	2,649	
Loan interest	1,250	
Insurance	4,380	
Office expenses	5,672	
General expenses	12,879	
Premises at cost	72,500	
Office equipment at cost	24,000	
Debtors	18,901	
Creditors		8,005
Bank balance	345	
Cash in hand	476	
Capital		126,232
Long-term bank loan		45,000
	391,647	391,647

Additional information as at 31 December 20*3

Stock was valued at £18,593; loan interest owing £250; office expenses owing £329; rates paid in advance £183; insurance paid in advance £465.

Required Prepare:
(a) a trading and profit and loss account for the year ended 31 December 20*3
(b) a balance sheet as at 31 December 20*3.

QUESTION 11

Julie Wreak provides the following trial balance extracted from her books of account on 31 May 20*3:

	Dr £	Cr £
Capital		95,894
Long-term loan		250,000
Premises at cost	240,000	
Lorry at cost	45,000	
Office equipment at cost	17,000	
Drawings	34,700	
Purchases	239,075	
Sales		407,563
Returns inwards	1,554	
Returns outwards		658
Carriage inwards	347	
Carriage outwards	1,453	
Wages	84,342	
Motor expenses	34,527	
Stationery	3,642	
Rent receivable		2,300
Rates	2,480	
Insurance	4,673	
Loan interest	2,400	
Bank overdraft		2,457
Cash in hand	754	
Stock as at 1 June 20*2	36,734	
Debtors	28,976	
Creditors		18,785
	777,657	777,657

Additional information as at 31 May 20*3

Stock was valued at £34,897; wages amounting to £6,238 had not been paid; £600 loan interest remains unpaid; the tenant owes £700 rent receivable; £562 insurance has been paid for the year ending 31 May 20*4; rates paid in advance amounts to £135.

Required Prepare:
(a) a trading and profit and loss account for the year ended 31 May 20*3
(b) a balance sheet as at 31 May 20*3.

QUESTION 12

Tonya Gook provides the following trial balance extracted from her books of account on 30 November 20*3:

	Dr £	Cr £
Capital		53,660
Drawings	32,784	
Equipment at cost	28,000	
Vehicle at cost	22,000	
Purchases	79,842	
Sales		196,432
Returns inwards	571	
Returns outwards		615
Carriage inwards	460	
Carriage outwards	1,386	
Stock as at 1 December 20*2	7,968	
General expenses	3,968	
Wages	79,870	
Rent payable	5,600	
Insurances	1,610	
Advertising	3,330	
Motor expenses	22,361	
Electricity charges	2,467	
Rates	2,590	
Long-term loan		45,000
Loan interest payable	3,500	
Rent receivable		2,815
Commission receivable		4,800
Creditors		11,370
Debtors	14,628	
Bank	1,725	
Cash in hand	32	
	314,692	314,692

Additional information as at 30 November 20*3

Stock was valued at £6,236; accrued wages £368; advertising owing amounted to £267; commission receivable paid in advance was £150; insurance has been pre-paid £142; rates have been pre-paid £240; rent receivable owing amounted to £85.

Required Prepare:
(a) a trading and profit and loss account for the year ended 30 November 20*3
(b) a balance sheet as at 30 November 20*3.

CHAPTER SEVENTEEN

Closing Down the Double-entry System

We have already seen how the double-entry system works. The system relies on the basic principle:

'Every debit must have a corresponding credit'.

Can you remember the three checks that we use throughout the year to verify the accuracy of parts of the double-entry system?

- Count the cash in hand and compare it with the balance shown in the cash column of the cash book.
- Prepare a bank reconciliation statement to check the accuracy of the entries made in the bank columns of the cash book.
- Prepare control accounts to check the accuracy of the transactions recorded in the purchases and sales ledgers.

Name the fourth and final check that we undertake before preparing the final accounts.

That's right – we prepare a trial balance.

We have seen that we consistently check the whole double-entry system by extracting a trial balance.

This means that when we prepare the 'final accounts' we know that they will balance. (That is, providing we do not make fundamental errors in their preparation.)

Specification coverage:
AQA 12.2, 12.3;
OCR 5.1.5.

By the end of this chapter you should be able to:
- close the nominal accounts in the general ledger
- prepare detailed trading and profit and loss accounts
- make entries in the stock account
- value stock using the lower of cost or net realisable value.

WORKED EXAMPLE

The following transactions took place during the year ended 31 August 20*3. All transactions were paid by cheque.

26 September 20*2 purchase of vehicle £17,500; 30 September 20*2 payment for rent £700; 11 October 20*2 purchase of vehicle £16,900; 17 October 20*2 paid for advertising £120; 1 November 20*2 paid wages £13,200; 23 November 20*2 paid for advertising £2,600; 31 December 20*2 paid rent £700; 1 February 20*3 paid wages £13,700; 31 March 20*3 paid rent £700; 31 March 20*3 paid rates £1,300; 1 May 20*3 paid wages £12,900; 17 June 20*3 paid advertising £340; 30 June 20*3 paid rent £700; 1 August 20*3 paid wages £14,600.

Required Prepare the wages, rent and rates, advertising and vehicles accounts for the year ended 31 August 20*3.

Answer

Dr	Vehicles account	Cr		Dr	Rent account	Cr
26 Sept Bank 17,500				30 Sept Bank 700		
11 Oct Bank 16,900				31 Dec Bank 700		
				31 Mar Bank 700		
				30 June Bank 700		

Dr	Advertising account	Cr		Dr	Wages account	Cr
17 Oct Bank 120				1 Nov Bank 13,200		
23 Nov Bank 2,600				1 Feb Bank 13,700		
17 June Bank 340				1 May Bank 12,900		
				1 Aug Bank 14,600		

Dr	Rates account	Cr
31 Mar Bank 1,300		

The credit entries corresponding to all the debit entries shown would appear in the bank account.

The arithmetical accuracy of the double-entry system is checked by extracting a trial balance at the end of each financial year before preparing a trading account, a profit and loss account and a balance sheet.

If the totals of each column in the trial balance are the same, we can prepare our final accounts safe in the knowledge that they should balance – if our final accounts do not balance then the error must lie in our preparation.

Do remember that there could be errors in the double-entry system that would not be revealed by extracting a trial balance (CROPOC!).

Up to now we have used the trial balance not only to check the arithmetical accuracy of our double-entry system; we have also used it as a list of information from which we can prepare our final accounts.

We will always continue to use our trial balance for both these purposes.

At the end of each financial year, we need to close down any accounts that we have finished with for the year in question.

Not all accounts will be closed down. Some accounts contain information that is relevant to the business's activity in the future. In fact, we only close down the nominal accounts in the general ledger since the information they contain will be used to calculate the year's profits.

The real accounts will remain, to carry their information through into the following year.

Private ledger contains accounts of a sensitive nature that the owner of a business does not wish others to see.

How are the nominal accounts closed?

The nominal accounts are closed by transferring the balances on each account to two further accounts found in the general ledger. The two further accounts are:

■ the trading account
■ the profit and loss account.

Yes, they are accounts and they ought to be in the general ledger.

In reality, they are rarely kept in the general ledger. The information contained in both accounts is of a sensitive nature and so they will be kept separate from the rest of the general ledger, in a private ledger.

A private ledger is part of the general ledger that is kept apart for obvious reasons.

QUESTION

Can you think of other accounts that the owner of a business might wish to keep in a private ledger?

Answer

The accounts could include the drawings account; loan account etc.

The accounts shown in the example above would be closed thus . . .

The nominal accounts are transferred to the trading account or the profit and loss account. The transfers will close the accounts for the year in question and will leave them clear to start a fresh new year.

The accounts shown in the above example will be used to illustrate the point.

Dr	Vehicles account		Cr		Dr		Rent account		Cr
26 Sept Bank	17,500				30 Sept	Bank	700		
11 Oct Bank	16,900				31 Dec	Bank	700		
					31 Mar	Bank	700	31 Aug P&La/c	
					30 June	Bank	700		2,800
							2,800		2,800

Dr	Advertising account		Cr		Dr		Wages account		Cr
17 Oct Bank	120	31 Aug P&La/c			1 Nov	Bank	13,200		
23 Nov Bank	2,600		2,720		1 Feb	Bank	13,700		
	2,720		2,720		1 May	Bank	12,900	31 Aug P&La/c	
					1 Aug	Bank	14,600		54,400
							54,400		54,400

Dr	Rates account		Cr		Dr	Bank account		Cr
31 Mar Bank	1,300	31 Aug P&La/c				26 Sep Veh	17,500	
			1,300			30 Sep Rent	700	
	1,300		1,300			11 Oct Veh	16,900	
						17 Oct Adv	120	
						1 Nov Wages	1,200	
						23 Nov Adv	2,600	
						31 Dec Rent	700	
						1 Feb Wages	13,700	
						31 Mar Rates	1,300	
						31 Mar Rent	700	
						1 May Wages	12,900	
						30 Jun Rent	700	
						1 Aug Wages	14,600	

Profit and loss account		
Rent	2,800	
Advertising	2,720	
Wages	54,400	
Rates	1,300	

Notice that credit entries are made using double-entry principles; each credit in a nominal account is matched by a debit in the profit and loss account.

Note that the vehicle account and the bank account stay open since we will use these accounts next year.

Note: The purchases, sales, purchases returns and sales returns accounts will be closed using the same technique but the balances on those accounts are transferred to the trading account.

Not only does the closing of the nominal accounts provide us with information to enable us to calculate the profits made by the business; it also enables us to have a fresh start in the general ledger nominal accounts next year.

Imagine if we did not tidy out these accounts on an annual basis; some accounts would have hundreds of thousands of entries after 20 years or so!

The rule is that all accounts providing us with information that is relevant to one financial year are closed down at the end of that year – the other accounts remain in the books as balances to start up the system again next year. All these balances are shown on the sheet for balances – the balance sheet on the final day of the financial year.

The profit and loss account is also balanced off and closed down. We can then prepare the next year's profit and loss account in a year's time.

WORKED EXAMPLE

The following trial balance has been extracted from the books of Patel, a trader, after his first year of trading:

Trial balance as at 31 December 20*3		
	£	**£**
Purchases	41,600	
Sales		103,110
Land and buildings at cost	60,000	
Furniture and fittings at cost	7,000	
Vehicles at cost	21,000	
Rent, rates and insurance	5,430	
Lighting and heating	7,980	
Motor expenses	9,260	
Repairs and renewals	1,780	
Wages	14,320	
Trade debtors	1,740	
Trade creditors		1,490
Drawings	2,170	
Capital		70,000
Cash	480	
Bank	1,840	
	174,600	174,600

Stock as at 31 December 20*3 £1,010.

Required (a) Place a tick in the end column of the trial balance showing which accounts will be closed down at the end of the financial year by posting the amounts to the profit and loss account.
(b) Prepare a trading and profit and loss account for the year ended 31 December 20*3.
(c) Prepare a balance sheet as at 31 December 20*3.

Answer
(a) Purchases sales, rent, rates and insurance, lighting and heating, motor expenses, repairs and renewals and wages should all be ticked. The remainder should not be ticked.
(b)

Patel trading and profit and loss account for the year ended 31 December 20*3			
	£		**£**
Purchases	41,600	Sales	103,110
Less Stock	1,010		
Cost of sales	40,590		
Gross profit	62,520		
	103,110		103,110

The trading account is 'closed off' by inserting a debit of £62,520 (gross profit).

The rules of the double-entry game say that we must have a credit ...

WORKED EXAMPLE *continued*

So ...

The credit is entered in the profit and loss account:

	£		£
Rent and rates	5,430	Gross profit	62,520
Lighting and heating	7,980		
Motor expenses	9,260		
Repairs and renewals	1,780		
Wages	14,320		
Net profit	23,750		
	62,520		62,520

The profit and loss account is 'closed off' by inserting a debit of £23,750.

The rules of the double entry game say that we must have a credit of £23,750 ...

So ...

The credit is entered in the capital account:

(c)   **Balance sheet Patel as at 31 December 20*3**

	£	£		£
Fixed assets			**Capital**	70,000
Land and buildings at cost		60,000	*Add* Profit	23,750
Furniture and fittings at cost		7,000		93,750
Vehicles at cost		21,000	*Less* Drawings	2,170
		88,000		91,580
Current assets			**Current liabilities**	
Stock	1,010		Trade creditors	1,490
Trade debtors	1,740			
Bank	1,840			
Cash	480	5,070		
		93,070		93,070

Draft – an attempt to prepare a statement or document which might need to be amended before it can be said to be a perfect copy.

WORKED EXAMPLE

The following draft trial balance has been extracted from the books of account of McDougal on 30 June 20*3 after her first year of trading.

There are three missing figures.

The accounts that will provide the missing figures are shown below the trial balance.

WORKED EXAMPLE *continued*

Trial balance as at 30 June 20*3

	£	£
Purchases	128,360	
Sales		317,830
Premises at cost	?	
Fixtures and fittings at cost	17,000	
Vehicles at cost	34,000	
Wages	119,000	
Rent and rates	14,670	
Motor expenses	21,630	
Repairs	?	
Lighting and heating	9,710	
General expenses	?	
Trade debtors	2,460	
Trade creditors		5,400
Drawings	26,300	
Capital		150,000
Bank	3,510	
Cash in hand	640	

Stock 30 June 20*3 £6,480.

Dr	Repairs account		Cr
3 Apl	Bank	348	
19 May	Cash	56	
12 June	Bank	1,319	
27 June	Bank	737	

Dr	General expenses account		Cr
7 Sept	Cash	1,467	
24 Nov	Bank	1,672	
3 Jan	Bank	4,381	
17 Feb	Cash	419	
9 May	Bank	2,318	
7 June	Bank	3,233	

Dr	Premises account		Cr
1 July Bal ¼ 80,000			

Required (a) Complete the trial balance and ensure that it balances.
(b) Close the nominal accounts shown.
(c) Prepare a trading and profit and loss account for the year ended 30 June 20*3.
(d) Prepare a balance sheet as at 30 June 20*3.

Answer
(a) The trial balance totals are £473,230.
(b) Repairs closed by credit entry £2,460; general expenses closed by credit entry £13,490.

The premises account should not be closed down – the premises will be used by the business in subsequent years.

WORKED EXAMPLE *continued*

(c)

McDougal

Trading and profit and loss account for the year ended 30 June 20*3

	£		£
Purchases	128,360	Sales	317,830
Less Stock	6,480		
Cost of sales	121,880		
Gross profit	195,950		
	317,830		317,830
Wages	119,000	Gross profit	195,950
Rent and rates	14,670		
Motor expense	21,630		
Repairs and renewals	2,460		
Lighting and heating	9,710		
General expenses	13,490		
Net profit	14,990		
	195,950		195,950

(d)

Balance sheet as at 30 June 20*3

	£	£			£
Fixed assets			**Capital**		150,000
Premises at cost		80,000	*Add* Profit		14,990
Fixtures and fittings at cost		17,000			164,990
Vehicles at cost		34,000	*Less* Drawings		26,300
		131,000			138,690
Current assets			**Current liabilities**		
Stock	6,480		Trade creditors		5,400
Trade debtors	2,460				
Bank	3,510				
Cash	640	13,090			
		144,090			144,090

McDougal's capital account in the general ledger would look like this:

Dr			Capital account			Cr
30 June 20*3	Drawings	26,300	1 July 20*2	Bank		150,000
30 June 20*3	Balance b/d	138,690	30 June 20*3	Profit and loss account		14,990*
		164,990				164,990
			1 July 20*3	Balance b/d		138,690

The debit £14,990 (net profit) entered on the profit and loss account needed a credit entry. The credit entry is in McDougal's capital account marked *.

It is useful and usual to show all the details contained in the capital account in the balance sheet as we have done above and in previous examples.

⊙ EXAMINATION TIP

If a question asks you to show a capital account it should be in account form. Not a list as it would appear in a balance sheet.

QUESTION 1

The following accounts appear in Theresa Gorton's general ledger. (The dates of the transactions have been omitted.)

Dr	Advertising account		Cr
Cash	120		
Bank	340		
Bank	720		
Cash	160		

Dr	Rates account		Cr
Bank	1,400		
Bank	1,400		

Dr	Motor expenses account		Cr
Bank	2,160		
Bank	814		
Bank	932		

Dr	Rent receivable account		Cr
		Bank	600
		Bank	600
		Bank	600
		Bank	600

Dr	Purchases account		Cr
Purchases day book	9,000		
Purchases day book	2,000		
Purchases day book	3,000		

Dr	Machinery account		Cr
Bank	14,000		
Bank	12,000		

Dr	Discount received account		Cr
		Cash	121
		Cash	72
		Cash	36

Dr	Sales account		Cr
		Sales day book	4,000
		Sales day book	12,000
		Sales day book	7,000
		Sales day book	4,500

Required (a) Close down the relevant accounts in the general ledger.
(b) Show how these entries would appear in the appropriate final accounts.

QUESTION 2

The following accounts appear in Ben Halliday's general ledger. (The dates of the transactions have been omitted.)

Dr	Premises account		Cr
Bank	125,000		

Dr	Purchases account		Cr
Purchases day book	1,320		
Purchases day book	4,581		
Purchases day book	1,007		

Dr	Sales account		Cr
		Sales day book	3,729
		Sales day book	4,516
		Sales day book	7,819

Dr	Rent payable account		Cr
Bank	150		
Bank	150		
Bank	150		

Dr	Discount allowed account		Cr
Cash	124		
Cash	64		

Dr	Purchase returns account		Cr
		PRDB	43
		PRDB	51

Dr	Insurance account		Cr
Cash	254		
Bank	2,440		
Cash	120		

Dr	Vehicles account		Cr
Bank	25,690		
Bank	18,450		

Required (a) Close down the relevant accounts in Ben's general ledger.
(b) Show how these entries would appear in the appropriate final accounts.

STOCK

Up to now, the businesses that we have looked at have, in the main, been in the first year of trading.

As part of our trading account and our closing balance sheet we have had to consider stock.

Stocks are the goods that remain unsold at the end of the financial year.

Stock is valued physically at the end of each financial year. Even if a trader keeps manual or computerised stock records, the figures produced are not used in the end-of-year accounts. Why not?

Despite what you might think, stock records kept manually or on a computerised system will be inaccurate! Why?

Because stock gets stolen, it gets damaged and it deteriorates; these phenomena are not shown in our manual or computerised records.

The most accurate way to value our stock is to count it manually and then value it – but more of that later.

After the trial balance is extracted, a value is placed on closing stock. Hence closing stock appears as an afterthought to the trial balance.

The closing stock figure is used to calculate the cost of sales figure for the year. Closing stock is a current asset and must be shown on the balance sheet at the end of the financial year.

Closing stock at the **end** of a financial year is opening stock at the start of the **next** financial year.

Year 1	Year 2	Year 3	Year 4
Closing stock is opening stock			
£1,000	£1,000		
	Closing stock is opening stock		
	£2,000	£2,000	
		Closing stock is opening stock	
		£3,000	£3,000
			Closing stock is opening stock
			£4,000 £4,000

This is fairly straightforward but hardly double-entry book keeping!

How is stock recorded in the double-entry system?

We need to open a stock account. Which ledger do we use?

■ Is stock a customer? No!
■ Is stock a supplier? No!

So the stock account appears in the **general ledger**.

WORKED EXAMPLE

Dr	Year 1 Stock account	Cr
Yr1 Trading a/c 1,000		

Stock is an asset so it is debited. The account stays open so the Balance is shown on the Balance sheet

Dr	Year 2 Stock account	Cr
Yr1 Trading a/c	1,000	

At the end of Year 2 the stock account is closed by crediting the account with £1,000 and debiting the Year 2 trading account.

Where is the credit entry?

Dr	Trading account	Cr
	Stock end year 1	1,000

This is the credit entry.
Note the two descriptions stating where the other entry is.

Dr	Stock account		Cr
Yr1 Trading a/c	1,000	Yr2 Trading a/c	1,000

At the end of Year 2, stock is valued and entered in the stock account as an asset

Dr	Stock account	Cr
Yr 2 Trading a/c 2,000		

Stock is an asset so a debit entry. The account is still open at the end of the year so the balance is shown on the balance sheet as a current asset.

The stock account and the trading account now look like this:

Dr	Stock account		Cr
Yr1 Trading a/c	1,000	Yr 2 Trading a/c	1,000
Yr 2 Trading a/c	2,000		

Dr	Trading account	Cr
Opening stock 1,000	Closing stock 2,000	

WORKED EXAMPLE *continued*

Year 3

Dr   Stock account   **Cr**

Dr		Cr	
Yr1 Trading a/c	1,000	Yr2 Trading a/c	1,000
Yr2 Trading a/c	2,000		

At the end of Year 3 the stock account is closed by crediting £2,000 to the account and debiting the Year 3 trading account with £2,000.

Dr   Stock account   **Cr**

Dr		Cr	
Yr1 Trading a/c	1,000	Yr2 Trading a/c	1,000
Yr2 Trading a/c	2,000	Yr3 Trading a/c	2,000

At the end of Year 3 stock is valued and entered in the stock account as an asset.

Dr   Stock account   **Cr**

Dr		Cr	
Yr 1 Trading a/c	1,000	Yr2 Trading a/c	1,000
Yr 2 Trading a/c	2,000	Yr3 Trading a/c	2.000
Yr 3 Trading a/c	3,000		

Stock is an asset so a debit entry is needed. The account is still open at the end of the year so the balance is shown on the balance sheet as a current asset.
The stock account and the trading account now look like this:

Dr   Stock account   **Cr**

Dr		Cr	
Yr1 Trading a/c	1,000	Yr2 Trading a/c	1,000
Yr2 Trading a/c	2,000	Yr3 Trading a/c	2,000
Yr3 Trading a/c	3,000		

Dr   Trading a/c   **Cr**

Dr		Cr	
Opening stock	2,000		
		Closing stock	3,000

Year 4

Dr   Stock account   **Cr**

Dr		Cr	
Yr1 Trading a/c	1,000	Yr2 Trading a/c	1,000
Yr2 Trading a/c	2,000	Yr3 Trading a/c	2,000
Yr3 Trading a/c	3,000		

At the end of Year 4 the stock account is closed by crediting £3,000 to the account and debiting the Year 4 trading account with £3,000.

Dr   Stock account   **Cr**

Dr		Cr	
Yr1 Trading a/c	1,000	Yr2 Trading a/c	1,000
Yr2 Trading a/c	2,000	Yr3 Trading a/c	2,000
Yr3 Trading a/c	3,000	Yr4 Trading a/c	3,000

At the end of Year 4 stock is valued and entered in the stock account as an asset.

Dr   Stock account   **Cr**

Dr		Cr	
Yr1 Trading a/c	1,000	Yr 2 Trading a/c	1,000
Yr2 Trading a/c	2,000	Yr3 Treading a/c	2,000
Yr3 Trading a/c	3,000	Yr4 Trading a/c	3,000
Yr4 Trading a/c	4,000		

Stock is an asset so a debit entry is needed. The account is still open at the end of the year so the balance is shown on the balance sheet as a current asset.
The stock account and the trading account now look like this:

Dr   Stock account   **Cr**

Dr		Cr	
Yr1 Trading a/c	1,000	Yr2 Trading a/c	1,000
Yr2 Trading a/c	2,000	Yr3 Trading a/c	2,000
Yr3 Trading a/c	3,000	Yr4 Trading a/c	3,000
Yr 4 Trading a/c	4,000		

Dr   Trading account   **Cr**

Dr		Cr	
Opening stock	3,000		
		Closing stock	4,000

Phew!

This looks rather complicated.

Use a couple of sheets of paper and examine each year column one at a time, by covering the other columns over with the spare paper, and talk yourself through it slowly and carefully.

You can do it!

One final point.

Many years ago it was common practice to present trading accounts as shown in the four examples above. Opening stock was shown as a debit and closing stock was shown as a credit.

This practice has now disappeared and the closing stock is deducted from the debit side of the trading account – it does give the same result arithmetically.

WORKED EXAMPLE

The following trading account has been prepared for Lhasa Trefta for the year ended 30 September 20*3:

	£		£
Opening stock as at 1 October 20*2	3,490	Sales	140,720
Purchases	73,400	Closing stock as at	
		30 September 20*3	3,760
Gross profit	67,590		
	144,480		144,480

Required Prepare the trading account using a layout that shows cost of goods sold.

Answer

Lhasa Trefta
Trading account for the year ended 30 September 20*3

	£		£
Stock as at 1 October 20*2	3,490	Sales	140,720
Purchases	73,400		
	76,890		
Less Stock as at 30 September 20*3	3,760		
Cost of sales	73,130		
Gross profit	67,590		
	140,720		140,720

WORKED EXAMPLE

The following information is available at 30 April 20*3 for Tuan:

stock as at 1 May 20*2 £1,760; stock as at 30 April 20*3 £1,870; purchases for the year ended 30 April 20*3 £24,680; sales for year ended 30 April 20*3 £56,770.

Required (a) Prepare a trading account for the year ended 30 April 20*3 showing clearly the cost of goods sold.
(b) Prepare the stock account as it would appear in the general ledger at 30 April 20*3.

Answer

(a)
Tuan
Trading account for the year ended 30 April 20*3

	£		£
Stock as at 1 May 20*2	1,760	Sales	56,770
Purchases	24,680		
	26,440		
Stock as at 30 April 20*3	1,870		
Cost of sales	24,570		
Gross profit	32,200		
	56,770		56,770

(b)

Dr			Stock account		Cr
30 April 20*2	Trading account	1,760	30 April 20*3	Trading account	1,760
30 April 20*3	Trading account	1,870			

Note the debit entry in the stock account; the corresponding credit entry should be in the trading account but this has been replaced by a negative debit which is arithmetically the same.

QUESTION 3

Tom Jackson provides the following information relating to his business for the year ended 28 February 20*3:

stock as at 1 March 20*2 £2,351; stock as at 28 February 20*3 £3,722; purchases £52,765; sales £87,503.

Required (a) Prepare a trading account for the year ended 28 February 20*3 showing clearly the cost of goods sold.
(b) Prepare the stock account as it would appear in the general ledger as at 28 February 20*3.

QUESTION 4

Sanaa Malik provides the following information relating to her business for the year ended 31 August 20*3:

stock as at 1 September 20*2 £13,579; stock as at 31 August 20*3 £14,217; purchases £126,993; sales £203,741.

Required (a) Prepare a trading account for the year ended 31 August 20*3 showing clearly the cost of goods sold.
(b) Prepare the stock account as it would appear in the general ledger as at 31 August 20*3.

QUESTION 5

Cary Thims provides the following information for her business for the year ended 31 March 20*3:

stock as at 1 April 20*2 £1,768; stock as at 31 March 20*3 £1,439; purchases £23,771; sales £56,880; returns inward £239.

Required Prepare a trading account for the year ended 31 March 20*3 showing clearly the cost of goods sold.

QUESTION 6

Tom O'Leary provides the following information for his business for the year ended 30 November 20*3:

stock as at 1 December 20*2 £8,663; stock as at 30 November 20*3 £6,711; purchases £106,734; sales £214,775; returns outward £231.

Required Prepare a trading account for the year ended 30 November 20*3.

STOCK VALUATION

At the end of the financial year a trader will physically count the items that are in stock in his/her business. He/she will make a list of all the items. Each category of stock has then to be valued.

The over-riding principle used in the valuation of stock is that it is always valued at the lower of cost price or net realisable value. This is an application of the principle of **prudence**.

- If closing stock is overvalued, then gross profit is overvalued.
- If gross profit is overvalued, then net profit is overvalued.
- If closing stock is undervalued, then gross profit is undervalued.
- If gross profit is undervalued, then net profit is undervalued.

We can check this with a simple example:

The following is the trading account of Fergie.

- Closing stock should be valued at £15.
- Sales amount to £50.

Stock overvalued	£	Accurate stock value	£	Stock undervalued	£
Opening stock	10	Opening stock	10	Opening stock	10
Purchases	25	Purchases	25	Purchases	25
	35		35		35
Less Closing stock	20	*Less* Closing stock	15	*Less* Closing stock	8
Cost of sales	15	Cost of sales	20	Cost of sales	27
Gross profit	35	Gross profit	30	Gross profit	23
	50		50		50

Highest stock valuation gives highest gross profit. Lowest stock valuation gives lowest gross profit.

The use of net realisable value causes problems for many students.

Realisable value is selling price.

Net realisable value is selling price less any expenses incurred by the business to get the stock into a saleable condition.

Realisable value is selling price – easy!

Net realisable value is realisable value net of (less) any expenses incurred in making the stock ready for sale – easy!

TRUE OR FALSE?

In a recent examination it was reported that over 95% of students were unable to calculate correctly the net realisable value of goods.

True!

WORKED EXAMPLE

The following information is available regarding the stock held by Tina at 28 February 20*3:

Product	Cost price £	Selling price £
Arkers	12	31
Bodins	23	22
Clarts	8	14
Domps	42	40
Eldivs	17	15

Required State the value of each unit of stock held by Tina.

Answer
Arkers	£12
Bodins	£22
Clarts	£8
Domps	£40
Eldivs	£15

WORKED EXAMPLE

The following information is available regarding stock held by John at 31 August 20*3:

Components	Units in stock	Cost price £	Selling price £
PX/117	21	16	20
QR/2138	13	41	50
T/1798C	8	18	15
S/5319	32	10	20

Required Calculate the total value of the stocks of components held at 31 August 20*3.

Answer

Total value of stock of components = £1,309.

Workings	£
PX/117 at cost	*336*
QR/2183 at cost	*533*
T/1798C at realisable value (selling price)	*120*
S/5319 at cost	*320*

QUESTION 7

Thomas Timms sells furniture. He is uncertain how to value three items of stock:

Article	Cost £	Selling price £	Notes
Table	145	278	
Chair	54	75	The chair is damaged; before it can be sold it will have to be repaired at a cost of £25.
Bed	170	345	The mattress is dirty and will have to be cleaned at a cost of £32 before it can be sold.

Required Calculate the value to be placed on each of the three items of stock.

QUESTION 8

Kerry Picker sells electrical goods. She is uncertain how to value the following three items of damaged stock:

Article	Cost £	Selling price £	Notes
Toaster	12	18	The toaster is damaged; before it can be sold it will have to be repaired at a cost of £8.
Fryer	30	50	The fryer needs a new plug and flex costing £4 before it can be sold.
Microwave	140	225	Repairs costing £46 and a government test costing £24 need to be carried out before the appliance can be sold.

Required Calculate the value to be placed on each of the three items of stock.

Chapter summary

- At the end of each financial year the nominal accounts in the general ledger are closed by transferring the balances to either the trading account or the profit and loss account.
- Accounts that are not closed are shown on the balance sheet.
- The trading account is closed by transferring the gross profit to the profit and loss account.
- The profit and loss account is closed by transferring the net profit or loss to the capital account.
- Stock is valued at the lower of cost or net realisable value.
- Net realisable value is the selling price of the items in stock less any costs that might be incurred in making the items ready for sale.

Self-test questions

- Name three checks that are used throughout the year to verify the accuracy of parts of the double-entry system.
- A trial balance balances; is this proof that it is error-free?
- Name the type of accounts that are closed down at the end of the financial year.
- In which ledger would you expect to find the trading account of a business?
- In which ledger would you expect to find the profit and loss account of a business?
- Why do some traders keep a private ledger?
- What entries are required to close the following accounts?

Account	Debit	Credit
Rent payable		
Discount received		
Purchases		

- Insurance; returns outward; carriage inward; Orton, a debtor; wages. Identify the account that would not be closed at the end of a financial year.

Appleby, a creditor; bank; advertising; capital; vehicles. Identify the account that would be closed at the end of a financial year.
- Explain what is meant by the word 'draft' in 'draft profit and loss account'.
- What is the overriding principle used in the valuation of stock?
- The application of this principle is an example of the .... concept. Fill the space.
- If closing stock is overvalued, gross profit will be .... Fill the space.
- Explain how closing stock is dealt with in the 'final accounts'.

TEST QUESTIONS

QUESTION 9

Bob Banger sells second-hand cars. He has yet to value the vehicles listed below.

Make	Cost £	Selling price £	Notes
Ford	1,200	1,500	Needs a new engine costing £320 before it can be sold.
Citröen	450	600	Before it can be sold it needs two new wings costing £100; spraying the wings will cost £60.
Skoda	560	600	Needs a new tyre costing £24 before it can be sold.

Required Calculate the value placed on each of the three cars in stock.

QUESTION 10

Shirley Burton has a clothes shop. Three items remaining in stock have yet to be valued.

Article	Cost £	Selling price £	Notes
Jeans	24	52	Faulty zip will cost £8 to repair before jeans can be sold.
Gent's suit	64	134	Trousers stolen. Replacement pair will cost £32 before suit can be sold.
Sweater	24	36	Hole in sleeve. Repairs will cost £14 before sweater can be sold.

Required Calculate the value placed on each of the three items of stock.

QUESTION 11

Tammy Mount supplies the following incomplete trial balance and four ledger accounts for her first year of trading:

Draft trial balance as at 31 March 20*3

	Dr £	Cr £
Capital		13,920
Sales		102,786
Purchases	41,903	
Returns inwards	460	
Returns outwards		
Wages	25,600	
Rates		
Telephone		
Fixtures and fittings at cost	12,500	
Vehicle at cost	17,300	
Debtors	3,791	
Creditors		4,286
Bank balance	1,248	
Drawings		

Dr	Returns outwards account		Cr
		Purchases returns day book	80
		Purchases returns day book	25
		Purchases returns day book	105

Dr	Rates account		Cr
Bank	625		
Bank	625		

Dr	Telephone account		Cr
Bank	212		
Bank	216		
Bank	248		
Bank	174		

Dr	Drawings account		Cr
Bank	4,075		
Bank	4,075		
Bank	4,075		
Bank	4,075		

Additional information

After completing the trial balance the following account was opened:

Dr	Stock account		Cr
31 March	Trading a/c	3,240	

Required (a) Complete the trial balance as at 31 March 20*3.
(b) Close the detailed accounts as necessary.
(c) Prepare a trading and profit and loss account for the year ended 31 March 20*3.
(d) Prepare a balance sheet as at 31 March 20*3.

QUESTION 12

Willie Gill provides the following draft trial balance and four detailed ledger accounts:

Draft trial balance as at 30 September 20*3

	Dr £	Cr £
Capital		
Equipment at cost	20,000	
Van at cost	12,000	
Sales		97,612
Debtors	4,992	
Purchases	38,614	
Stock		
Creditors		3,171
Returns inwards		
Carriage inwards	930	
Drawings	17,500	
Rent and rates	4,612	
Heat and lighting		
Wages	29,360	
Bank	1,280	
Cash in hand	70	

Dr	Capital account		Cr
		Balance b/d	35,957

Dr	Returns inwards account		Cr
Sales returns day book 136			
Sales returns day book 276			

Dr	Heat and lighting account		Cr
Bank	1,230		
Bank	819		
Bank	716		
Bank	755		

Dr	Stock account		Cr
1 Oct 20*2 Trading a/c	3,450		

Additional information

Stock was valued at £3,760 as at 30 September 20*3.

Required (a) Complete the trial balance as at 30 September 20*3.

(b) Complete the stock account, showing any transfers to the final accounts.

(c) Close the detailed ledger accounts as necessary.

(d) Prepare a trading and profit and loss account for the year ended 30 September 20*3.

(e) Write up the capital account as it would appear in the general ledger on 30 September 20*3.

(f) Prepare a balance sheet as at 30 September 20*3.

QUESTION 13

Chetan Nath provides the following draft trial balance as at 31 August 20*3. He also provides four detailed ledger accounts.

Draft trial balance as at 31 August 20*3

	Dr £	Cr £
Sales		172,460
Purchases	81,236	
Stock		
Carriage inwards	1,810	
Carriage outwards		
Drawings	23,100	
Equipment at cost	24,000	
Premises at cost	60,000	
Rent payable		
Rates	1,580	
Wages	32,460	
Advertising		
Debtors	8,491	
Creditors		3,984
Bank balance	8,701	
Capital		83,072

Dr	Carriage outwards account		Cr
Bank	934		
Cash	127		
Bank	406		
Cash	175		

Dr	Rent payable account		Cr
Bank	1,500		
Bank	1,500		
Bank	1,500		
Bank	1,500		

Dr	Advertising account		Cr
Cash	76		
Bank	211		
Cash	99		
Bank	2,489		

Dr	Stock account		Cr
1 Sept 20*2 Trading a/c	7,621		

Dr	Capital account		Cr
		Balance b/d	83,072

Additional information

Stock was valued at £8,470 as at 31 August 20*3.

Required (a) Complete the trial balance as at 31 August 20*3.

(b) Complete the stock account, showing any transfers to the final accounts.

(c) Close the detailed ledger accounts as necessary.

(d) Prepare a trading and profit and loss account for the year ended 31 August 20*3.
(e) Write up the capital account as it would appear in the general ledger on 31 August 20*3.
(f) Prepare a balance sheet as at 31 August 20*3.

QUESTION 14

Dave provides the following draft trial balance. He also provides six ledger accounts.

Draft trial balance as at 30 April 20*3

	Dr £	Cr £
Capital		
Vehicles at cost	8,000	
Machinery at cost	15,000	
Premises at cost	45,000	
Purchases		
Sales		188,461
Stock		
Returns inwards	499	
Carriage inwards	213	
Returns outwards		177
Carriage outwards	1,471	
Rent and rates	3,926	
Insurance	4,109	
Debtors	12,430	
Creditors		7,621
Drawings	29,150	
Heat and light	4,288	
Wages	36,490	
Bank balance	1,284	
Cash in hand	126	

Dr	Purchases account		Cr
Purchases day book	17,496		
Purchases day book	23,810		
Purchases day book	12,567		
Purchases day book	19,093		

Dr	Returns outwards account		Cr
		PRDB	84
		PRDB	12
		PRDB	81

Dr	Carriage outwards		Cr
Bank	432		
Bank	618		
Cash	75		
Bank	346		

Dr	Vehicles at cost account		Cr
Balance b/d	2,000		
Bank	6,000		

Dr	Capital account		Cr
		Balance b/d	47,979

Dr	Stock account		Cr
1 May 20*2 Trading a/c	9,286		

Additional information
Stock was valued at £10,140 as at 30 April 20*3.

Required (a) Complete the trial balance as at 30 April 20*3.
(b) Complete the stock account, showing any transfers to the final accounts.
(c) Close the detailed ledger accounts as necessary.
(d) Prepare a trading and profit and loss account for the year ended 30 April 20*3.
(e) Write up the capital account as it would appear in the general ledger on 30 April 20*3.
(f) Prepare a balance sheet as at 30 April 20*3.

CHAPTER
EIGHTEEN

Depreciation of Fixed Assets

A fixed asset is an item that has been purchased by a business in order to generate profits for the business.

Fixed assets will be used by the business for more than one financial year. They will yield benefits to the business over a prolonged period of time.

A business purchases resources to be used in the generation of profits.

Some of the resources are used up in one time period. Other resources will be used over a number of time periods.

- **Goods purchased for resale** will be used in one time period.
- **Petrol** purchased for a delivery vehicle will be used in one time period.
- The **work provided by staff** is used in one time period.

Each of the expenses described here can be classified as **revenue expenditure**. The benefits derived from revenue expenditure will be earned in the year and the expense is entered in the profit and loss account for the year in question.

> **Depreciation** is the apportioning of the cost of an asset over its useful economic life.

- **Premises** will, generally, be used for more than one time period.
- A **delivery van** will, generally, be used for more than one time period.
- **Machinery** will, generally, be used for more than one time period.

Expenditure on these items is classified as **capital expenditure**.

Since the benefits derived from capital expenditure will continue to be earned over a number of years, it seems sensible to charge part of the cost of the fixed assets over those years.

> **Finite life:** a limited life span.
> **Infinite life:** an unlimited life span.

All fixed assets (except land) have a finite life.

The Companies Act 1985 says that all assets with a finite life should be depreciated, so the only asset that should not be depreciated is land because land has an infinite life.

- A machine will eventually cease to produce the goods for which it was purchased.
- A delivery vehicle will eventually cease to be useful for the delivery of goods.

The total cost of a fixed asset is never charged to the profit and loss account for the year in which it was purchased. The cost is spread over all the years that it is used in order to reflect in the profit and loss account the cost of using the asset.

> Fixed assets are recorded in **real accounts** in the general ledger.
> Revenues and expenses are recorded in **nominal accounts**.

FRS 15 – tangible fixed assets states that depreciation 'should be allocated ... over [the fixed asset's] useful economic life'.

Specification coverage:
AQA 12.2; OCR 5.1.4.

By the end of this chapter you should be able to:

- define 'depreciation'
- calculate depreciation using the straight-line method
- calculate depreciation using the reducing balance method
- calculate the profit or loss on the disposal of a fixed asset.

It also identifies the causes of depreciation as:

- physical deterioration due to use or the passing of time
- economic or technological obsolescence.

When a fixed asset is purchased and later sold, the amount that is not recovered is called depreciation.

WORKED EXAMPLE

Donna purchased a fixed asset for £20,000. She sold it three years later for £2,000.

Required Calculate the cost of using the asset (the amount of depreciation) for the three years.

Answer
The cost of using the fixed asset (ie the depreciation) is £18,000 (£20,000 − £2,000).

This means that the actual depreciation can only be calculated when the fixed asset is no longer being used.

The annual depreciation charge is therefore an **estimate**, based on experience.

If we know the cost and can make an estimate of how long the fixed asset will be useful and how much it might be worth at the end of its life, we can calculate the amount of depreciation that will take place over the fixed asset's lifetime.

We need to apportion this lifetime cost into each of the years that the fixed asset was used.

There are many methods of dividing the lifetime depreciation charge. We shall consider three methods:

- straight-line method (also known as equal instalment method)
- reducing balance method
- revaluation method.

THE STRAIGHT-LINE METHOD

This requires that the same amount is charged annually to the profit and loss account over the lifetime of the fixed asset.

FORMULA

The formula is:

Cost of fixed asset − any residual value

To calculate depreciation using the straight-line method it is therefore necessary to consider:

- the **cost** of the fixed asset
- the **estimated life** of the fixed asset
- the **estimated residual value** or **scrap value**.

If we know the life of an asset we can easily calculate the annual rate of depreciation.

- If an asset has an expected life of 10 years, the annual rate of depreciation would be 10% (100% divided by 10 years).
- If an asset has an expected life of 50 years, the annual rate of depreciation would be 2% (100% divided by 50 years).
- If an asset has an expected life of 2 years, the annual rate of depreciation would be 50% (100% divided by 2 years).

WORKED EXAMPLE

A computer is purchased for £2,300. Its useful life is expected to be two years, after which time it will be replaced. It is expected that it will have a trade-in value of £100.

Required Calculate the annual depreciation charge using the straight-line method.

Answer

Annual depreciation charge = £1,100.

Workings

Formula: $\dfrac{\text{Cost of computer £2,200} - \text{residual value £100}}{}$

WORKED EXAMPLE

A machine is purchased for £17,500. It has an expected life of 10 years, after which it will be scrapped. Its estimated scrap value is thought to be £250.

Required Calculate the annual depreciation charge using the straight-line method.

Answer

£1,725.

Workings

Formula: $\dfrac{\text{Cost of machine} - \text{scrap value}}{}$ $\dfrac{£17,500 - £250}{10}$

We need to record depreciation in the ledger.

In which ledger will we find the account for depreciation?

- Is depreciation a credit customer? No.
- Is depreciation a credit supplier? No.
- The account is found in the **general** ledger.

> **A provision** is an amount set aside out of profits for a known expense the amount of which cannot be calculated with substantial accuracy.

I know that my car is depreciating (a known expense) but I cannot tell you exactly the amount of annual depreciation. I will only be able to give you an accurate figure in two or three years' time when I change my car.

> **Net book value** is the cost of the asset shown in the general ledger (and therefore the balance sheet) less the total depreciation charged to date.

We have just seen how to calculate depreciation. How is the charge entered in the double-entry system?

Debit: profit and loss account   Credit: provision for depreciation account

WORKED EXAMPLE

Tanya purchases a delivery van for £18,000 on 1 January 20*1. She will use the van for four years, after which she estimates she will be able to sell it for £6,000.

Tanya's financial year-end is 31 December.

Required Prepare:
- (a) delivery van account
- (b) provision for depreciation account
- (c) profit and loss account extracts to record the necessary entries
- (d) balance sheet extracts for the four years.

Answer

Dr		Delivery van account		Cr
1 Jan 20*1	Bank	18,000		

Dr		Provision for depreciation on delivery van account				Cr
31 Dec 20*1	Balance c/d	3,000	31 Dec 20*1	Profit and loss account	3,000	
		3,000			3,000	
			1 Jan 20*2	Balance b/d	3,000	
31 Dec 20*2	Balance c/d	6,000	31 Dec 20*2	Profit and loss account	3,000	
		6,000			6,000	
			1 Jan 20*3	Balance b/d	6,000	
31 Dec 20*3	Balance c/d	9,000	31 Dec 20*3	Profit and loss account	3,000	
		9,000			9,000	
			1 Jan 20*4	Balance b/d	9,000	
31 Dec 20*4	Balance c/d	12,000	31 Dec 20*4	Profit and loss account	3,000	
		12,000			12,000	
			1 Jan 20*5	Balance b/d	12,000	

Profit and loss account extract for the year ended 31 December 20*1
Provision for depreciation of
  delivery van 3,000

Profit and loss account extract for the year ended 31 December 20*2
Provision for depreciation of
  delivery van 3,000

Profit and loss account extract for the year ended 31 December 20*3
Provision for depreciation of
  delivery van 3,000

Profit and loss account extract for the year ended 31 Decmber 20*4
Provision for depreciation of
  delivery van 3,000

WORKED EXAMPLE *continued*

Balance sheet extract as at 31 December 20*1

Fixed asset

Delivery van at cost	18,000
Less Depreciation to date	3,000
	15,000

Balance sheet extract as at 31 December 20*2

Fixed asset

Delivery van at cost	18,000
Less Depreciation to date	6,000
	12,000

Balance sheet extract as at 31 December 20*3

Fixed asset

Delivery van at cost	18,000
Less Depreciation to date	9,000
	9,000

Balance sheet extract as at 31 December 20*4

Fixed asset

Delivery van at cost	18,000
Less Depreciation to date	12,000
	6,000

Note:
- the double entries – debit profit and loss account; credit provision account
- the equal instalments in each year's profit and loss account
- the delivery van is entered in the balance sheet at cost
- the accumulated (total) depreciation is taken from the fixed asset in the balance sheet
- the total shown at the end of each year in the balance sheet for the delivery van is the net book value (NBV).

THE REDUCING BALANCE METHOD

A fixed percentage is applied to the cost of the fixed asset in the first year of ownership. The same percentage is applied in subsequent years to the net book value of the asset.

WORKED EXAMPLE

A vehicle was purchased for £18,000 on 1 January 20*1.

Depreciation is to be provided at the rate of 40% per annum, using the reducing balance method.

Required Calculate the annual charge for depreciation in years 20*1, 20*2 and 20*3.

Answer

Year 20*1 £7,200	***Workings*** *£18,000 × 40%.*
Year 20*2 £4,320	*(£18,000 − £7,200) × 40%*
Year 20*3 £2,592	*(£18,000 − £7,200 − £4,320) × 40%*

How is this method entered into the double-entry system? In the same way that we entered the straight-line method.

Debit: profit and loss account   Credit: provision for depreciation account

The provision for depreciation account will look very similar no matter which method is used; only the annual charge debited to the profit and loss account will change.

WORKED EXAMPLE

Dev Trater purchased a machine on 1 January 20*1 for £64,000.

Depreciation is to be charged at 20% per annum, using the reducing balance method.

Dev's financial year-end is 31 December.

Required Prepare:
- (a) machinery account
- (b) provision for depreciation of machinery account
- (c) profit and loss account extract to record the necessary entries
- (d) balance sheet extracts for the three years.

Dr		Machinery account		Cr
1 January 20*1	Bank	64,000		

Dr		Provision for depreciation of machinery account			Cr
31 Dec 20*1	Balance c/d	12,800	31 Dec 20*1	Profit and loss account	12,800
		12,800			12,800
			1 Jan 20*2	Balance b/d	12,800
31 Dec 20*2	Balance c/d	23,040	31 Dec 20*2	Profit and loss account	10,240
		23,040			23,040
			1 Jan 20*3	Balance b/d	23,040
31 Dec 20*3	Balance c/d	31,232	31 Dec 20*3	Profit and loss account	8,192
		31,232			31,232
			1 Jan 20*4	Balance b/d	31,232

Profit and loss account extract for the year ended 31 December 20*1
Provision for depreciation of machinery   12,800

Profit and loss account extract for the year ended 31 December 20*2
Provision for depreciation of machinery   10,240

Profit and loss account extract for the year ended 31 December 20*3
Provision for depreciation of machinery   8,192

Balance sheet extract as at 31 December 20*1
Fixed assets
Machinery at cost   64,000
Less Depreciation to date   12,800
                                 51,200

WORKED EXAMPLE *continued*

> **Balance sheet extract as at 31 December 20*2**
>
> **Fixed assets**
> Machinery at cost   64,000
> *Less* Depreciation to date   <u>23,040</u>
>   40,960

> **Balance sheet as at 31 December 20*3**
>
> **Fixed assets**
> Machinery at cost   64,000
> *Less* Depreciation to date   <u>31,232</u>
>   32,768

REVALUATION METHOD

This is the final method considered and is used where the asset is made up of lots of small items.

An example could be the small tools that are used on a regular basis in a large garage or in an engineering works. Clearly, it would be inappropriate to use either of the previous two methods of depreciation on a spanner that cost £2.50 or a pair of wire cutters costing £4.75.

Can you imagine the amount of time that would be wasted if each small tool was to be entered in the general ledger and depreciated separately at the end of each year?

These items are small and may seem insignificant, but they are fixed assets because they are used for more than one time period.

In order to calculate depreciation in such cases, the following calculation is necessary:

- opening value of items
- plus purchases during the year
- less value of items at end of the year
- depreciation for the year.

When a method of calculating deprecition has been decided upon, it should be used consistently so that different years' results can be compared.

WORKED EXAMPLE

The Redfor engineering works has valued small tools on 1 January 20*3 at £2,190. During the year, small tools were purchased for £930. At 31 December 20*3 small tools were valued at £2,400.

Required Calculate the depreciation of small tools for the year ended 31 December 20*3.

Answer

	£
Opening value of small tools	2,190
Plus Purchases during year	<u>930</u>
	3,120
Less Value at end of year	2,400
Depreciation for the year	<u>720</u>

The depreciation would be shown in the manufacturing account (see Chapter 23) since the tools will be used in the factory.

The value at the end of the year (£2,400) is shown as a fixed asset on the balance sheet as at 31 December 20*3.

QUESTION 1

John Frost started in business on 1 January 20*2. He purchased a delivery vehicle £28,000 on that day. He expects to keep the vehicle for four years and hopes to sell the vehicle then for £8,000. John will depreciate his vehicle using the straight-line method.

Required (a) Prepare the delivery vehicles account.
(b) Prepare the provision for depreciation of vehicles account for the years ended 31 December 20*2 and 31 December 20*3.

QUESTION 2

Agnes Trotter started in business on 1 March 20*2. She purchased office machinery £12,000 on that day. She expects the machinery to last 10 years by which time she expects it will have a scrap value of £100. Agnes will depreciate her office equipment using the straight-line method.

Required (a) Prepare the office equipment account.
(b) Prepare the provision for depreciation of office equipment account for the years ended 28 February 20*3 and 29 February 20*4.

QUESTION 3

Shajal Patel started in business on 1 April 20*1. Her financial year-end is 31 March. She made the following purchases of machinery:

■ 1 April 20*1: a machine costing £13,000;
■ 1 April 20*2: two machines costing £8,000 each;
■ 1 October 20*2: a machine costing £10,000.

None of the machines is expected to have any value at the end of its useful life.

Shajal charges depreciation at 10% per annum using the straight-line method, calculated on a monthly basis.

Required (a) Prepare the machinery account.
(b) Prepare the provision for depreciation of machinery account.
(c) Prepare balance sheet extracts as at 31 March 20*2 and 31 March 20*3.

QUESTION 4

Tony Prem started in business on 1 September 20*1. His financial year-end is 31 August. He made the following purchases of machinery:

■ 1 September 20*1: two machines costing £14,000 each;
■ 1 April 20*2: one machine costing £12,000;
■ 1 September 20*2: one machine costing £16,000.

None of the machines is expected to have any value at the end of its useful life.

Tony charges depreciation at 25% using the straight-line method, calculated on a monthly basis.

Required (a) Prepare the machinery account.
(b) Prepare the provision for depreciation of machinery account.
(c) Prepare balance sheet extracts as at 31 August 20*2 and 31 August 20*3.

THE SALE OR DISPOSAL OF FIXED ASSETS

You will notice that the word 'expected' has been used quite freely in the examples used above.

The owner of a business tries to guess for how many years a fixed asset will be used. The owner will try to guess how much cash will be received when the asset is sold when it is no longer of any use.

When an asset is sold it is highly unlikely that the sum received will be the same as the net book value.

When assets are sold it is likely that a profit or loss based on the net book value will arise.

WORKED EXAMPLE

A machine which cost £32,000 five years ago has been sold for £14,000.

The total depreciation to date was £15,000.

Required Calculate the profit or loss arising from the disposal of the machine.

Answer

	£	
Machine at cost	32,000	The cost of the machine
Depreciation to date	15,000	less depreciation to date
Net book value	17,000	gives the value recorded in the ledger
Sale proceeds	14,000	the cash received from the sale
Loss on disposal	3,000	is less than the value shown in the ledger, hence the loss on disposal.

WORKED EXAMPLE

A machine costing £18,000 10 years ago has been sold for £1,500. The aggregate (total) depreciation to date was £17,000.

Required Calculate the profit or loss on disposal.

Answer

	£	
Machine at cost	18,000	The cost of the machine
Depreciation to date	17,000	less depreciation to date
Net book value	1,000	gives the value recorded in the ledger
Sale proceeds	1,500	the cash received from the sale
Profit on disposal	500	is more than the value shown in the ledger, hence the profit on disposal.

⊙ EXAMINATION TIP

If an examination question asks for a calculation you may use this method or you may choose to show a disposal account. However, if a question asks for a disposal account you must show your answer in account format.

If a disposal account is required, this procedure should be followed:

- Open a disposal account.
- Debit the disposal account with the cost of the asset.   Credit the asset account.
- Debit the provision for depreciation account.   Credit disposal account.
- Debit cash with cash received for sale.   Credit disposal account.
- Debit disposal account profit on disposal   OR   Credit disposal account with loss.

WORKED EXAMPLE

Marjorie Dawes provides the following information from her general ledger:

Dr	Machinery Cr account		Dr	Provision for depreciation of machinery account	Cr
31 Mar 20*3 Balance b/d 66,000			31 Mar 20*3 Balance b/d 43,000		

Earlier this year Marjorie sold a machine for £3,000 cash. She has entered the cash received in the cash book but has made no other entries in the ledger.

The machine had cost £18,000 some years ago. The aggregate depreciation relating to the machine amounted to £16,500.

Required The machinery disposal account to record the sale of the machine.

Answer

Dr	Disposal of machinery account			Cr
Machinery	18,000	Provision for depreciation of machinery	16,500	
Profit and loss account (profit)	1,500	Cash	3,000	
	19,500		19,500	

Other entries would be:

- Credit machinery account £18,000. Debit provision for depreciation £16,500.
- Credit profit and loss account £1,500. Debit cash book £3,000.

QUESTION 5

The following information is available as at 30 September 20*3:

- Vehicles account £120,000.
- Provision for depreciation of vehicles account £73,000.
- In July 20*3 a vehicle that had cost £21,000 was sold for £800.
- The aggregate depreciation relating to the vehicle amounted to £19,000.
- Depreciation is provided at 25% per annum using the straight line method.

Required (a) Prepare a disposal of vehicles account to record the sale of the vehicle.
(b) Prepare a balance sheet extract showing the entry for vehicles as at 30 September 20*3.

QUESTION 6

The following information is available as at 30 June 20*3:

- Premises account £278,000.
- Provision for depreciation of premises account £88,960.
- During February 20*3 part of the premises that had cost £56,000 was sold for £68,000. The aggregate depreciation relating to the premises that had been sold amounted to £6,720.
- Depreciation is provided at 1% per annum using the straight line method.

Required (a) Prepare a disposal of premises account to record the sale of premises.
(b) Prepare a balance sheet extract showing the entry for premises as at 30 June 20*3.

Sometimes when an asset is replaced the 'old' asset is traded in and an allowance is made by the supplier of the 'new' asset.

I recently purchased a new car for £14,000. The garage took my 'old' car in part exchange. It made an allowance on my 'old' car of £6,500. I paid £7,500 cash for the new car.

The garage actually bought my old car from me for £6,500. This together with my payment of £7,500, made up the total purchase price.

WORKED EXAMPLE

Doris Eden purchased a delivery van DQ03 WDA costing £19,000.

The new van replaced vehicle B19 JJH which cost £11,500. The aggregate depreciation to date amounted to £9,000.

The garage gave an allowance of £2,750 on B19 JJH. The balance was paid by cheque.

Required Prepare the necessary ledger accounts to record the purchase of the new van.

Answer

Dr	Van B19 JJH account		Cr	Dr	Provision for Depreciation on van B19 JJH account			Cr
Balance b/d	11,500	Disposal 11,500			Disposal	9,000	Balance b/d	9,000

Dr	Dispoal B19 JJH account		Cr	Dr	Van DQ03 WDA account			Cr
Van	11,500	Depreciation	9,000		Disposal	2,750		
Profit and loss		Van DQ03 WDA			Bank	16,250		
Account	250		2,750					
	11,750		11,750					

Note

The procedure is very similar to that used when a fixed asset is purchased for cash only.

The only difference is that the new asset is debited with any allowance being made by the supplier, and the disposal account is credited with the allowance.

THE CONNECTION BETWEEN CASH AND DEPRECIATION

There is no direct connection between providing depreciation on fixed assets in the profit and loss account and providing cash to replace the asset when it is no longer of use.

A collector does not visit the business every Friday night asking for cash to pay for the use of each asset being used!

Depreciation is a **non-cash expense**.

Cash flows out of a business when the asset is purchased; the annual depreciation charge is that cost being spread over the life-time of the asset.

A second-hand car was purchased for £2,750 in January 20*1 for cash. It is kept for four years.

■ The cash outflow took place in January 20*1.
■ No further cash outflows have taken place (apart from the usual running costs).
■ But the car will depreciate each year.

In the case of a business there is an indirect influence that depreciation has on cash-flows.

Depreciation is debited to the profit and loss account. This non-cash expense reduces profits for each year of ownership. The reduction in profit may cause the owner of the business to withdraw less money from the business for personal use, thus conserving more cash within the business.

EXAMPLE

- Tom's business earns around £45,000 profit each year.
- His drawings average £25,000 per year.
- Tom purchases a new machine costing £80,000. The machine is expected to be used for four years before it needs to be replaced.

When depreciation on the new machine (using the straight-line method) is included in the final accounts, annual profits are reduced to £25,000.

Tom may well reduce his cash drawings in recognition of the business's reduced profitability.

Chapter summary

- Depreciation is provided on all fixed assets except land.
- Depreciation represents the use of the fixed asset during each year of ownership.
- The accruals concept is being applied when depreciation is charged to the profit and loss account.
- The two main methods of calculating the annual charge for depreciation are the straight-line method and the reducing balance method. Whichever method is used by a business, the provision for depreciation account in the general ledger will look similar; the only difference will be the annual charge.

Self-test questions

- Define 'depreciation'.
- What is a provision?
- Fill the following gaps:
  - Fixed assets are shown on the .... side of real accounts in the general ledger.
  - All assets with a .... life should be depreciated.
  - Only the asset of .... has an infinite life.
- Name two method of calculating annual depreciation.
- Which account is debited and which account is credited with the annual charge for depreciation?
- What is meant by the term 'aggregate depreciation'?
- What is meant by the term 'net book value'?
- What is the abbreviated form of net book value?
- An asset with a net book value of £4,000 is sold for £3,800. Calculate the profit or loss on disposal.

TEST QUESTIONS

QUESTION 7

A machine is purchased for £20,000. It has an expected life of 10 years and an expected scrap value of £1,000.

Required Calculate the annual depreciation charge using the straight-line method.

QUESTION 8

A machine is purchased for £40,000. It has an expected life of eight years and an expected trade-in value of £6,000.

Required Calculate the annual depreciation charge using the straight-line method.

QUESTION 9

A vehicle is purchased for £30,000. Depreciation is to be provided at 40% per annum, using the reducing balance method.

Required Calculate the annual depreciation charge for the first three years of ownership.

QUESTION 10

A vehicle is purchased for £70,000. Depreciation is to be provided at 30% per annum, using the reducing balance method.

Required Calculate the annual depreciation charge for the first three years of ownership.

QUESTION 11

Equipment is purchased on 1 January 20*2 at a cost of £60,000. It has an expected life of 10 years after which it will have no scrap value.

Required Prepare the provision for depreciaton of equipment account for the two years ended 31 December 20*2 and 31 December 20*3.

QUESTION 12

Equipment is purchased on 1 August 20*1 at a cost of £50,000. It has an expected life of four years after which it will have a scrap value of £2,000.

Required Prepare the provision for depreciation of equipment account for the two years ended 31 July 20*2 and 31 July 20*3.

QUESTION 13

A lorry costing £140,000 was purchased on 1 March 20*1. It is depreciated at 60% per annum, using the reducing balance method.

Required Prepare the provision for depreciation of lorry account for the three years ended 28 February 20*2, 28 February 20*3 and 29 February 20*4.

QUESTION 14

A lorry costing £112,000 was purchased on 1 April 20*1. It is depreciated at 35% per annum, using the reducing balance method.

Required Prepare the provision for depreciation of lorry account for the three years ended 31 March 20*2, 31 March 20*3 and 31 March 20*4.

QUESTION 15

A machine that cost £45,000 on 1 January 20*1 had an expected life of 10 years. It has been depreciated using the straight-line method. It was sold for £31,000 on 31 December 20*3.

Required Calculate the profit or loss on disposal of the machine.

QUESTION 16

A machine that cost £20,000 on 1 January 20*2 had an expected life of four years. It has been depreciated using the straight-line method.

It was sold for £5,200 on 31 December 20*3.

Required Calculate the profit or loss on disposal of the machine.

QUESTION 17

When a machine was purchased on 1 October 20*1 for £19,000 it was thought that it would be used for six years and then sold for scrap at a value of £1,000.

The machine was sold for £13,250 on 30 September 20*3 after only two years' use.

Required Prepare a disposal account for the machine.

QUESTION 18

A vehicle was purchased on 1 June 20*1 for £50,000 when it was thought that it would be used for six years and then sold for scrap at a value of £2,000.

The machine was sold for £16,500 on 31 May 20*5 after only four years' use.

Required Prepare a disposal account for the vehicle.

QUESTION 19

A vehicle was purchased for £26,000. It has been depreciated at 40% per annum, using the reducing balance method. It was sold after two years of use for £9,500.

Required Prepare a disposal account for the vehicle.

QUESTION 20

Equipment costing £30,000 has been depreciated at 50% per annum, using the reducing balance method. It was sold after three years of use for £3,700.

Required Prepare a disposal account for the equipment.

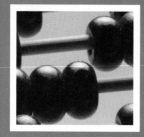

CHAPTER
NINETEEN

Bad Debts and Provision for Doubtful Debts

In the business world of today, a large proportion of all business is conducted on credit.

A business that deals with credit customers always runs the risk that some of those customers may not honour their debt.

Specification coverage:
AQA 12.2;
OCR 5.1.5.

BAD DEBTS

A bad debt occurs when a debtor cannot pay the amount that is owed.

If it is known that a debtor will not or cannot pay his debt, we cannot leave the debit balance in his account.

If we did:

- the total amount of debtors would be overstated
- the current assets would be overstated
- the total assets would be overstated
- capital would be overstated.

Once we are certain that a debtor is unable to pay, the debt must be written off.

This is done by:

debiting a **bad debts account** in the general ledger and

crediting the **debtor** in the sales ledger

By the end of this chapter you should be able to:
- account for bad debts
- make provision for doubtful debts.

WORKED EXAMPLE

The following accounts appear in Noel Neil's sales ledger:

Dr	Mike	Cr	Dr	Cindy	Cr
Balance b/d	143		Balance b/d	619	

Dr	Rett	Cr	Dr	Sandy	Cr
Balance b/d	51		Balance b/d	430	

Dr	Deck	Cr	Dr	Tina	Cr
Balance b/d	628		Balance b/d	92	

WORKED EXAMPLE *continued*

It has been revealed that Mike and Tina are unable to pay their debts and Noel has decided to write them off at the year ended 31 December 20*3.

Required Show the necessary entries to record the transactions.

Answer

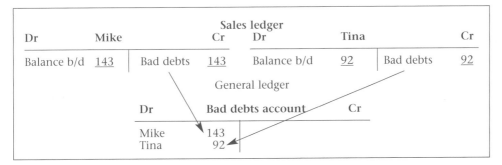

Any entries in the double-entry system must first be entered in a book of prime entry. We ought to have used the journal to record the transfer of each debtor to the bad debts account before recording the entries in the general ledger.

The journal entries would show:

	Dr	Cr
Bad debts account	143	
Mike		143
Writing off Mike's debt (irrecoverable) to the bad debts account		
Bad debts account	92	
Tina		92
Writing off Tina's debt (irrecoverable) to the bad debts account		

At the end of the financial year the bad debts account is totalled and closed by transferring the amount to the profit and loss account as a revenue expense.

Dr	Bad debts account		Cr
Mike	143	Profit and loss account	235
Tina	92		
	235		235

Noel Neil
Profit and loss account extract for the year ended 31 December 20*3

Bad debts	235

PROVISION FOR DOUBTFUL DEBTS

This is sometimes called a provision for bad debts. Debtors who will definitely not pay their debts are transferred to a bad debts account.

As well as actual bad debts, there is always the risk that other debtors *may not* pay. Those who might not pay are called **doubtful debtors**.

An estimate of amounts owed by those credit customers who might be unable to pay their debt is made.

We have already stated that a prudent business man or woman will not anticipate possible profits but will make provision for likely losses.

It therefore seems to be sensible to make provision for debtors where there is a strong possibility that they will not be able to settle their debt. Remember the definition of a provision: 'an amount set aside out of profits for a known expense the amount of which is uncertain'.

When we provide for doubtful debts we know that some debtors may not pay but we are not sure who they will be, therefore we do not know the exact amount of the provision expense.

How do we calculate the amount to be provided?

We can:

■ examine the sales ledger and try to identify the debtors who are most likely to default on payment
■ take a percentage of total debtors based on experience of bad debts written off in previous years
■ prepare an age profile of debtors and base the provision on the age of each outstanding amount.

WORKED EXAMPLE

Digby has estimated that each year around 2% of his debtors fail to pay.

At 31 October 20*3 he has debtors amounting to £31,900.

He wishes to make provision for doubtful debts at the rate of 2%.

Required (a) Calculate the amount of provision for doubtful debts at 31 October 20*3.

(b) Prepare a balance sheet extract as at that date, showing the details.

Answer
The provision for doubtful debts is £638 (£31,900 × 2%).

Balance sheet extract as at 31 October 20*3		
	£	£
Current assets		
Debtors	31,900	
Less Provision for doubtful debts	638	31,262

WORKED EXAMPLE

Deirdre provided the following age profile of her debtors at 31 May 20*3.

The percentage of debtors proving to be bad has been gained from over 20 years' experience in her business.

Time outstanding £	0–1 month £	1–3 months £	3–6 months £	6 months– 1 year £	over 1 year £
Amounts owed	120,000	3,000	400	300	1,100
Provision for doubtful debts	1%	3%	5%	20%	50%

WORKED EXAMPLE *continued*

Required (a) Calculate the amount of provision for doubtful debts at 31 May 20*3.
(b) Prepare a balance sheet extract as at that date showing the details.

Answer

The provision for doubtful debts is £840.

		£
£120,000 × 1%	=	1,200
3,000 × 3%	=	90
400 × 5%	=	20
300 × 20%	=	60
1,100 × 50%	=	550
		1,920

Balance sheet extract as at 31 May 20*3

	£	£
Current assets		
Debtors	124,800	
Less Provision for doubtful debts	1,920	122,880

Note

It was doubtful whether Digby would receive £31,900 from his debtors. From experience, he feels that £31,262 will be a more accurate figure. The creation of the provision has allowed him to be prudent.

It was also doubtful whether Deirdre would receive £124,800 from her debtors. She feels that £122,880 is a more accurate figure. She has been prudent in creating a provision for doubtful debts.

In which ledger would the provision for doubtful debts be found?
Is it a person? No.

So it would be found in the general ledger.

Once a provision for doubtful debts account has been opened in the general ledger, it stays open from one financial year to the next.
Adjustments will be made each year to the balance by either debiting or crediting the profit and loss account with the adjustments.

WORKED EXAMPLE

Lew maintains a provision for doubtful debts account at 2% of debtors outstanding at the financial year-end on 30 June each year.

Debtors outstanding at 30 June 20*2: £36,700.

Required (a) Prepare a provision for doubtful debts account at 30 June 20*2.
(b) Prepare a profit and loss account extract for the year ended 30 June 20*2, showing relevant details.
(c) Prepare a balance sheet extract as at 30 June 20*2.

WORKED EXAMPLE *continued*

Answer

Dr	Provision for doubtful debts account	Cr
	30 June 20*2 Profit and loss account	734

Lew
Profit and loss account extract for the year ended 30 June 20*2

	£
Provision for doubtful debts	734

Balance sheet extract as at 30 June 20*2

	£	£
Current assets		
Debtors	36,700	
Less Provision for doubtful debts	734	35,966

WORKED EXAMPLE

At the financial year-end 30 June 20*3 Lew had outstanding debtors amounting to £41,300. He continues to maintain his provision for doubtful debts account at 2% per annum based on the debtors outstanding at his year-end.

Required (a) Prepare a provision for doubtful debts account at 30 June 20*3.
(b) Prepare a profit and loss extract for the year ended 30 June 20*3, showing relevant details.
(c) Prepare a balance sheet extract as at 30 June 20*3.

Answer

Dr		Provision for doubtful debts account		Cr
30 June 20*2 Balance c/d	734	30 June 20*2 Profit and loss account	734	
		1 July 20*2 Balance b/d	734	
30 June 20*3 Balance c/d	826	30 June 20*3 Profit and loss account	92	
	826		826	
		1 July 20*3 Balance b/d	826	

Lew
Profit and loss account extract for the year ended 30 June 20*3

	£
Provision for doubtful debts	92

WORKED EXAMPLE *continued*

> ### Balance sheet extract as at 30 June 20*3
>
> | | £ | £ |
> |---|---|---|
> | **Current assets** | | |
> | Debtors | 41,300 | |
> | *Less* Provision for doubtful debts | 826 | 40,474 |

Note

The amount entered on the profit and loss account is only the increase in the provision account. It is the amount needed to 'top up' the account to the required level.

QUESTION 1

Darryl has discovered that the three debtors shown below are unable to settle their debts. He has therefore decided to write them off as bad debts in the year ended 31 December 20*3.

	£
Biff	451
Treados Ltd	159
Victor	52

Required Prepare the bad debts account for the year ended 31 December 20*3.

QUESTION 2

Umberto has discovered that the debtors listed are unable to clear their debts. He has decided to write them off as bad debts in the year ended 30 September 20*3.

	£
Ghuster plc	1,436
Jamie	39
Sally	392

Required Prepare the bad debts account for the year ended 30 September 20*3.

QUESTION 3

Umair wishes to maintain a provision for doubtful debts in his general ledger.

	Year 1 £	Year 2 £	Year 3 £
Provision for doubtful debts	400	420	500

Required Prepare the provision for doubtful debts account for each year.

QUESTION 4

Sheila wishes to maintain a provision for doubtful debts in her ledger

Year ended 31 December	20*1 £	20*2 £	20*3 £
Provision for doubtful debts	610	660	740

Required Prepare the provision for doubtful debts account for each year.

QUESTION 5

Robin has his financial year-end on 31 January. He provides the following information:

	£
Debtors 31 January 20*1	12,700
Debtors 31 January 20*2	14,500
Debtors 31 January 20*3	16,000

- £700 is to be written off as a bad debt in the year ended 31 January 20*1
- £200 is to be written off as a bad debt in the year ended 31 January 20*3
- Robin wishes to make provision for doubtful debts of 2½% of debtors outstanding at each year-end.

Required Prepare for each year:
        (a) a bad debts account
        (b) a provision for doubtful debts account
        (c) an extract from the profit and loss account
        (d) an extract from the balance sheet.

QUESTION 6

Mee has her financial year-end on 31 August. She provides the following information:

	£
Debtors 31 August 20*1	42,000
Debtors 31 August 20*2	45,000
Debtors 31 August 20*3	46,000

In each year there have been a number of bad debts which have yet to be written off.

Year ended 31 August	20*1	20*2	20*3
	£	£	£
Total bad debts to be written off	437	521	739

Mee wishes to make provision for doubtful debts of 5% of debtors outstanding at each year-end. (Work to nearest whole number.)

Required Prepare for each year:
        (a) a bad debts account
        (b) a provision for doubtful debts account
        (c) an extract from the profit and loss account
        (d) an extract from the balance sheet.

In each example and question used there has been an increase in the provision for doubtful debts.

A decrease in the provision now needs to be considered.

WORKED EXAMPLE

Bernie maintains a provision for doubtful debts account.

His provisions for the last three years are listed:

Year ended 30 April	20*1	20*2	20*3
	£	£	£
Provision for doubtful debts	250	340	270

WORKED EXAMPLE *continued*

Required Prepare for each of the three years:
(a) a provision for doubtful debts account
(b) a profit and loss account extract showing the adjustment to the provision account.

Answer

Dr			Provision for doubtful debts account		Cr
30 April 20*1	Balance c/d	250	30 April 20*1 Profit and loss account	250	
			1 May 20*1 Balance b/d	*250	
30 April 20*2	Balance c/d	340	30 April 20*2 Profit and loss account	90	
		340		340	
30 April 20*3	P&L account	70	1 May 20*2 Balance b/d	*340	
30 April 20*3	Balance c/d	270			
		340		340	
			1 May 20*3	*270	

Note

* The balance brought down is always equal to the amount of provision needed.

Bernie
Profit and loss account extract for the year ended 30 April 20*1

Provision for doubtful debts   250

Bernie
Profit and loss account extract for the year ended 30 April 20*2

Provision for doubtful debts   90

Bernie
Profit and loss account extract for the year ended 30 April 20*3

                                Overprovision for doubtful debts   70

WORKED EXAMPLE

Mary Green makes a provision for doubtful debts based on 1% of debtors outstanding at her financial year-end.

The following table shows the entries in her final accounts for each of the first five years in business:

WORKED EXAMPLE *continued*

Answer

End of year	Debtors outstanding £	Provision £	Profit and loss account entry £	Balance sheet detail £	£
1	10,000	100	100 expense	10,000 100	9,900
2	12,000	120	20 expense	12,000 120	11,880
3	16,000	160	40 expense	16,000 160	15,840
4	14,000	140	20 'income'	14,000 140	13,860
5	18,000	180	40 expense	18,000 180	17,820

QUESTION 7

Try to fill the spaces for the next four years:

End of year	Debtors outstanding £	Provision £	Profit and loss account entry £	Balance sheet detail £	£
6	23,000				
7	27,000				
8	25,000				
9	26,000				

To summarise:

- The amount needed to increase the provision for doubtful debts is entered as an expense on the profit and loss account.
- The amount needed to decrease the provision for doubtful debts is entered as an 'income' on the profit and loss account.

RECOVERY OF BAD DEBTS

Sometimes a debtor, whose debt has been written off as a bad debt in an earlier year, may subsequently be able to settle his previously outstanding debt.

The simple treatment is:

Debit cash book   Credit bad debt recovery account

Then at the financial year-end:

Debit bad debt recovery account   Credit profit and loss account.

If an examination question does not require ledger accounts, the result of the transactions above can be recorded in the final accounts as:

- an increase in profit and
- an increase in cash.

Howard owed Bill £237 five years ago. Bill wrote Howard off as a bad debt.

Dr	Howard	Cr	Dr	Bad debts account	Cr
Balance b/d 237	Bad debts 237		Howard 237	Profit and Loss account 237	

Howard has set up in business again and is now able to pay the £237 that was previously written off.

Howard should be reinstated as a debtor as he is about to pay the debt. This fact should be recorded in Bill's books of account.

This is important to Howard since he may require credit facilities from Bill in the future and the fact that he has repaid his debt may be taken into consideration by Bill.

Dr	Howard	Cr	Dr	Bad debt recovered account	Cr
Bad debt recovered 237				Howard 237	

Howard has now been reinstated.

Howard is then credited with the payment made to Bill:

Dr	Howard	Cr	Dr	Cash book	Cr
Bad debt recovered 237	Cash 237			Howard 237	

Chapter summary

- Debtors who will definitely not pay their debts are written off to the profit and loss account.
- A provision for doubtful debts is created to take account of credit customers who may not pay their debts. Any increase in the provision is debited to the profit and loss account for the year and any decrease in the provision is credited to the profit and loss account.
- Bad debts recovered are credited to the profit and loss account and debited to the cash book.

Self-test questions

- Define 'debtors'.
- Fill the gaps with the words 'debited' or 'credited':
  - When a bad debt is written off the debtor's account is ......Cr...... and the bad debts account is ....Dr......... .
  - When the provision for doubtful debts is increased the provision account is ....Cr.......... and the profit and loss account is ..Dr........... .
  - When a bad debt is recovered the debtor's account is ....; the bad debts recovered account is ....; when the money is received the debtor is .... and the cash book is ....
- In which ledger would you find the bad debts account? Gen
- Name the three ways that a trader may use to calculate the amount needed for the provision for doubtful debts.
- The creation of a provision for doubtful debts is a use of which concept? Prudence
- In which ledger would you find the provision for doubtful debts account?

QUESTION 8

A business has made a gross profit of £126,734 and a net profit of £64,211.

Debtors amount to £32,967 before bad debts of £467 have been written off.

A provision for doubtful debts of 4% is required.

Required Select the correct answer:

The provision for doubtful debts is calculated as 4% of

A £32,500   B £32,967   C £64,211   D £126,734

QUESTION 9

Pat provides the following information from his sales ledger:

Dr	Defius Ltd	Cr		Dr	Ralph	Cr
Balance b/d	154			Balance b/d	345	

Dr	Gordon	Cr		Dr	Iain	Cr
Balance b/d	87			Balance b/d	620	

All the debtors are bad and need to be written off.

Required Prepare the bad debts account for Pat.

QUESTION 10

Doug informs you that there is no possibility of recovering any cash from the following outstanding debts:

	£
Trish	435
Glaster Ltd	455
Rotrest Ltd	113
Chiter and sons	712

Required Prepare the bad debts account to record writing off the debts.

QUESTION 11

At 31 March 20*3 Morgan has debtors amounting to £40,000. She wishes to make a provision for doubtful debts of 2½%.

Required (a) Calculate the provision for doubtful debts.
         (b) Prepare a balance sheet extract to show how the provision is treated.

QUESTION 12

At 30 June 20*3 Kingsley has debtors amounting to £68,000. He wishes to make a provision for doubtful debts of 5%.

Required Calculate the provision for doubtful debts.

QUESTION 13

Willie uses an age profile of debtors to calculate his provision for doubtful debts.

He provides the following information for the year ended 31 May 20*3, on which to base the calculation.

Time outstanding	0–1 month £	1–3 months £	3–6 months £	6 months– 1 year £	Over 1 year £
Amount owing	23,400	12,900	1,270	730	640
Provision for doubtful debts	1%	2%	3%	5%	20%

Required (a) Calculate the provision for doubtful debts.
(b) Prepare a balance sheet extract showing how the provision is treated.

QUESTION 14

Hayton uses an age profile of debtors to calculate his provision for doubtful debts.

He provides the following information for the year ended 31 October 20*3, on which to base the calculation.

Time outstanding	0–1 month £	1–3 months £	3–6 months £	6 months– 1 year £	Over 1 year £
Amount owing	63,400	32,900	4,500	5,700	450
Provision for doubtful debts	1%	3%	5%	20%	50%

Required (a) Calculate the provision for doubtful debts.
(b) Prepare a balance sheet extract showing how the provision is treated.

QUESTION 15

Trudy McDuff maintains a provision for doubtful debts equal to 2½% of outstanding debtors at the end of each financial year. The following information is available:

	£
Total debtors at 1 May 20*2	34,000
Total debtors at 30 April 20*3	44,000
The following bad debts have been written off during the year:	
30 June 20*2 P Snow	45
31 October 20*2 J Gatwood	239
31 January 20*3 F Golightly	213
31 March 20*3 D Mark	651

Required (a) Prepare the necessary general ledger accounts to record the entries; show clearly any amounts to be entered in the profit and loss account.
(b) Prepare a balance sheet extract showing debtors and the provision for doubtful debts.

QUESTION 16

Maureen Gill maintains a provision for doubtful debts equal to 5% of outstanding debtors at the end of each financial year. The following information is available:

	£
Total debtors 1 January 20*3	64,000
Total debtors 31 December 20*3	83,500
Bad debts not yet written off at 31 December 20*3:	
Stephens	1,670
Greatrix	453
Shawcross	2,352
Treew Ltd	25

Required (a) Prepare the necessary general ledger accounts to record the entries; show clearly the amounts to be entered in the profit and loss account.
(b) Prepare a balance sheet extract showing debtors and the provision for doubtful debts.

QUESTION 17

During the year a trader receives £288 from Geot Ltd. This amount had been written off as a bad debt some years previously.

Required Prepare the three accounts necessary to record the recovery of the bad debt.

QUESTION 18

Jessie receives £761 from Prodo Ltd. Jessie had written the amount off as a bad debt some years ago.

Required Prepare the accounts necessary to record the recovery of the bad debt.

QUESTION 19

Glad Thomson provides the following information for the year ended 31 October 20*3. She maintains a provision for doubtful debts of 5% based on outstanding debtors at the end of each financial year.

	£
Total debtors 31 October 20*2	35,000
Total debtors 31 October 20*3	41,606
Bad debts not yet written off at 31 October 20*3:	
Thaker	216
Simms	97
Hurd	184
Fletcher	109

During the year £246 was received from Broadbent. This amount had been written off as a bad debt three years ago.

Required Prepare:
(a) bad debts account
(b) provision for doubtful debts account
(c) Broadbent's account
(d) bad debt recovery account
(e) profit and loss account extract for the year ended 31 October 20*3.

QUESTION 20

Ryder provides the following information for the year ended 30 April 20*3.

He maintains a provision for doubtful debts based on 2½% of debtors outstanding at his financial year-end.

	£
Total debtors 1 May 20*2	25,200
Total debtors 30 April 20*3	24,952
Bad debts not yet written off at 30 April 20*3:	
Carson	129
Greer	184
Michael	203
Robinson	36

During the year £197 was received from Tickell. This amount had been written off as a bad debt in 20*0.

Required Prepare:
(a) bad debts account
(b) provision for doubtful debts account
(c) Tickell's account
(d) bad debt recovery account
(e) profit and loss account extract for the year ended 30 April 20*3.

CHAPTER
TWENTY

The Vertical Presentation of Final Accounts

We have been preparing our trading and profit and loss accounts in ledger form because they are accounts, as their headings indicate.

Since the Companies Act 1985, limited companies have been required to publish their accounts in prescribed formats.

This means that the accounts published by different limited companies accounts can be more easily compared.

Before the Act became law, a company could produce its published accounts in a way of its own choosing, provided that all legal requirements were observed.

(The final accounts produced for use within the company can be produced in any form, but clearly the internal accounts will closely adhere to the format required by law in order to facilitate the production of the final accounts required for publication.)

Since the 1980s, sole traders' final accounts have also tended to follow the layouts prescribed for limited companies, although there is no legal requirement for them to do so.

The layout for the final accounts is known as the 'vertical layout'. All the information is shown in what looks like a long list of information.

I can hear you complain that you have just mastered the layout for trading accounts and profit and loss accounts! Don't worry too much; you will find the 'new' layout quite easy.

Trust me – I am an accounting teacher!

We will now use the vertical format for the trading account.

WORKED EXAMPLE

Tim Howitt prepared the following trading account for the year ended 31 March 20*3:

	£		£
Stock as at 1 April 20*2	3,400	Sales	63,780
Purchases	27,670		
	31,070		
Stock as at 31 March 20*3	2,940		
Cost of sales	28,130		
Gross profit	35,650		
	63,780		63,780

Required Prepare the trading account for the year ended 31 March 20*3, using a vertical layout.

WORKED EXAMPLE *continued*

Answer

	£		£
Stock as at 1 April 20*2	3,400	Sales	63,780
Purchases	27,670		
	31,070		
Stock as at 31 March 20*3	2,940		
Cost of sales	28,130		
Gross profit	35,650		
	63,780		63,780

Tim Howitt
Trading account for the year ended 31 March 20*3

	£		£
Sales			63,780
Less Cost of sales			
Stock as at 1 April 20*2	3,400		
Purchases	27,670		
	31,070		
Stock as at 31 March 20*3	2,940		28,130
Gross profit			35,650

Can you see what has happened?

We have set the cost of sales calculation back from the main column then

we have taken the total of the cost of sales figure from the sales.

The result – gross profit.

Try this example:

WORKED EXAMPLE

Carmen Engoing
Trading account for the year ended 31 July 20*3

		£		£
Stock as at 1 August 20*2		910	Sales	31,806
Purchases	14,628		*Less* Returns	256
Carriage inwards	372	15,000		
		15,910		
Stock as at 31 July 20*3		1,030		
Cost of sales		14,880		
Gross profit		16,670		
		31,550		31,550

Required Prepare the trading account for the year ended 31 July 20*3, using a vertical format.

WORKED EXAMPLE *continued*

Answer

Carmen Engoing
Trading account for the year ended 31 July 20*3.

	£	£	£
Sales			31,806
Less Returns inwards			256
			31,550
Less Cost of sales			
Stock as at 1 August 20*2		910	
Purchases	14,628		
Carriage inwards	372	15,000	
		15,910	
Stock as at 31 July 20*3		1,030	14,880
Gross profit			16,670

Note the two columns set back. This allows us to see clearly:

- the full cost of purchases
- the cost of sales.

QUESTION 1

Sven Thoms gives you the following trading account:

Sven Thoms
Trading account for the year ended 30 September 20*3

	£	£		£
Stock as at 1 October 20*2		1,456	Sales	51,239
Purchases	29,675			
Less Returns outwards	197	29,478		
		30,934		
Stock as at 30 September 20*3		1,503		
Cost of sales		29,431		
Gross profit		21,808		
		51,239		51,239

Required Redraft the trading account using a vertical layout.

QUESTION 2

The following trading account has been produced for Marjorie Street:

Marjorie Street
Trading account for the year ended 28 February 20*3

	£	£		£
Stock as at 1 March 20*2		4,519	Sales	64,976
Purchases	24,767		*Less* Returns	452
Less Returns	983			
	23,784			
Carriage inwards	1,459	25,243		
		29,762		
Stock as at 28 February 20*3		3,865		
Cost of sales		25,897		
Gross profit		38,627		
		64,524		64,524

Required Prepare the trading account, using a vertical layout.

QUESTION 3

The following information is given for Greta Freer:

stock as at 1 February 20*2 £456; stock as at 31 January 20*3 £488; purchases £24,761; sales £56,999; returns outward £642.

Required Prepare a trading account for the year ended 31 January 20*3, using a vertical layout.

QUESTION 4

The following information is given for Hari Mistry:

stock as at 1 May 20*2 £4,578; stock as at 30 April 20*3 £4,670; purchases £56,831; sales £102,675; returns inwards £1,321; returns outwards £789.

Required Prepare a trading account for the year ended 30 April 20*3, using a vertical layout.

QUESTION 5

The following information relates to Alec McDuff:

stock as at 1 January 20*3 £938; stock as at 31 December 20*3 £1006; purchases £20,098; sales £63,971; returns inwards £773; returns outwards £629; carriage inwards £438.

Required Prepare a trading account for the year ended 31 December 20*3, using a vertical layout.

QUESTION 6

The following information relates to Glenda Sewell:

stock as at 1 May 20*2 £145; stock as at 30 April 20*3 £267; purchases £24,672; sales £54,601; returns inwards £151; returns outwards £105; carriage inwards £277; carriage outwards £410.

Required Prepare a trading account for the year ended 30 April 20*3, using a vertical layout.

When we use a vertical layout for the trading account we must be consistent so we must also use a vertical layout for the profit and loss account.

After preparing the trading account vertically, this should cause few problems.

We simply list the revenue expenditure incurred by the business; total these expenses and deduct the total from the gross profit.

Nothing could be easier! Well, some things are easier, but the layout should prove to be fairly straightforward.

WORKED EXAMPLE

Becky Harrison has made a gross profit of £131,897; she has incurred the following business expenses during the financial year ended 30 November 20*3:

wages £34,650; rent and rates £1,860; insurance £345; motor expenses £7,549; advertising £757; general expenses £5,348.

Required Prepare the profit and loss account for the year ended 30 November 20*3, using a vertical layout.

WORKED EXAMPLE *continued*

Answer

Becky Harrison
Profit and loss account for the year ended 30 November 20*3

	£	£
Gross profit		131,897
Less Expenses		
Wages	34,650	
Rent and rates	1,860	
Insurance	345	
Motor expenses	7,549	
Advertising	757	
General expenses	5,348	50,509
Net profit		81,388

So you can see that the profit and loss account consists of a list of expenses that reduce the gross profit, thus revealing the net profit.

WORKED EXAMPLE

Fret Bjork supplies the following information relating to his business:

stock as at 1 January 20*3 £1,348; stock as at 31 December 20*3 £1,070; purchases £49,627; sales £98,768; wages £16,072; rent and rates £2,480; advertising and insurance £2,367; heat and light £3,481; motor expenses £9,788; general expenses £4,603; depreciation on fixed assets £1,000.

Required Prepare a trading and profit and loss account for the year ended 31 December 20*3, using a vertical layout.

Answer

Fret Bjork
Trading and profit and loss account for the year ended 31 December 20*3.

	£	£
Sales		98,768
Less Cost of sales		
Stock as at 1 January 20*3	1,348	
Purchases	49,627	
	50,975	
Stock as at 31 December 20*3	1,070	49,905
Gross profit		48,863
Less Expenses		
Wages	16,072	
Rent and rates	2,480	
Advertising and insurance	2,367	
Heat and light	3,481	
Motor expenses	9,788	
General expenses	4,603	
Depreciation on fixed assets	1,000	39,791
Net profit		9,072

Note

- Only one heading is necessary for both the trading account and the profit and loss accounts.
- It is important that you use the descriptions for gross and net profits.

QUESTION 7

Clyde Buno supplies the following information for his business:

stock as at 1 January 20*3 £1,996; stock as at 31 December 20*3 £2,352; purchases £14,674; sales £23,567; wages £2,391; motor expenses £1,743; rent £700; insurance £980; general expenses £793.

Required Prepare a trading and profit and loss account for the year ended 31 December 20*3, using a vertical presentation.

QUESTION 8

The following information relates to the business of Dixie Reid:

stock as at 1 September 20*2 £345; stock as at 31 August 20*3 £326; purchases £23,863; sales £63,001; returns inwards £433; rent £6,000; light and heating expenses £1,488; insurance £1,350; wages £6,534; general expenses £312.

Required Prepare a trading and profit and loss account for the year ended 31 August 20*3, using a vertical presentation.

QUESTION 9

Raagi Hosah supplies the following information, which relates to his business:

stock as at 1 April 20*2 £1,342; stock as at 31 March 20*3 £2,753; purchases £45,773; sales £80,705; returns outwards £1,189; rent £3,500; motor expenses £3,679; wages £16,875; insurance £2,050; general expenses £4,992.

Required Prepare a trading and profit and loss account for the year ended 31 March 20*3, using a vertical presentation.

QUESTION 10

Brenda Robinson supplies the following information which relates to her business:

stock as at 1 August 20*2 £2,597; stock as at 31 July 20*3 £3,004; purchases £97,610; sales £184,773; returns inwards £562; returns outwards £1,277; wages £32,665; motor expenses £9,775; lighting and heating expenses £2,884; rent £1,500; insurance £2,940.

Required Prepare a trading and profit and loss account for the year ended 31 July 20*3, using a vertical presentation.

QUESTION 11

The following information relates to the business of David Mark:

stock as at 1 February 20*2 £4,455; stock as at 31 January 20*3 £2,774; purchases £54,892; sales £107 500; returns inwards £491; returns outwards £1,309; carriage inwards £277; wages 36,873; rent and rates £3,784; heating and lighting expenses £5,785; motor expenses £10,648; general expenses £2,888.

Required Prepare a trading and profit and loss account for the year ended 31 January 20*3, using a vertical layout.

QUESTION 12

The following information relates to the business of Gary Jones:

stock as at 1 July 20*2 £1,640; stock as at 30 June 20*3 £1,522; purchases £41,904; sales £98,662; returns inwards £287; returns outwards £245; carriage inwards £277; carriage outwards £782; wages £27,867; rent and rates £4,561; motor expenses £7,546; insurance £880; heating and lighting expenses £3,688; general expenses £2,731.

Required Prepare a trading and profit and loss account for the year ended 30 June 20*3, using a vertical layout.

If we prepare a trading and profit and loss account using a vertical layout we should prepare the balance sheet in the same way.

Once again, you may find this is rather tricky at first but once you have completed a few you should not find the layout too difficult.

> **Net current assets** is another term for **working capital**. It is calculated by deducting current liabilities from current assets. If current liabilities are greater than current assets then working capital would be negative; negative working capital is also described as *net current liabilities*.

WORKED EXAMPLE

Here is the summarised balance sheet as at 31 December 20*3 for Alec Graves:

	£		£
Fixed assets	75,000	Capital	48,000
Current assets	16,000	Long-term liability	30,000
		Current liabilities	13,000
	91,000		91,000

Firstly we move the current liabilities over to the left side of the balance sheet.

We deduct them from the current assets.

	£			£
Fixed assets		75,000	Capital	48,000
Current assets	16,000		Long-term liability	30,000
Less Current liabilities	13,000	3,000		
		78,000		78,000

As you can see, this does not affect the balance sheet arithmetically – it still balances.

Secondly, we move the long-term liability across to the left. To maintain the arithmetic, this too is deducted from the 'asset side'.

	£			£
Fixed assets		75,000	Capital	48,000
Current assets	16,000			
Less Current liabilities	13,000	3,000		
		78,000		
Less Long-term liability		30,000		
		48,000		48,000

Finally, we move the capital figure over also . . .

So our completed summarised balance sheet would look like this:

Alec Graves
Summarised balance sheet as at 31 December 20*3

	£	£
Fixed assets		75,000
Current assets	16,000	
Less Current liabilities	13,000	3,000
		78,000
Less Long-term liabilities		30,000
		48,000
Capital		48,000

WORKED EXAMPLE

Bernie Cohen provides you with the following balance sheet as at 31 December 20*3 for his business:

	£	£		£
Fixed assets			**Capital**	93,669
Premises at cost		120,000	*Add* Profit	34,784
Vehicles at cost		48,500		128,453
Office equipment at cost		22,500	*Less* Drawings	21,500
		191,000		106,953
Current assets				
Stock	12,670		**Long-term liability**	100,000
Trade debtors	9,067			
Bank balance	1,653	23,390	**Current liabilities**	
			Trade creditors	7,437
		214,390		214,390

Required Prepare the balance sheet as at 31 December 20*3, using a vertical layout.

Answer

Bernie Cohen
Balance sheet as at 31 December 20*3

	£	£
Fixed assets		
Premises at cost		120,000
Vehicles at cost		48,500
Office equipment at cost		22,500
		191,000
Current assets		
Stock	12,670	
Trade debtors	9,067	
Bank balance	1,653	
	23,390	
Less **Current liabilities**		
Trade creditors	7,437	
Net current assets		15,953
		206,953
Less **Long-term liability**		100,000
		106,953
Capital as at 1 January 20*3		93,669
Add Profit		34,784
		128,453
Less Drawings		21,500
		106,953

Chapter summary

- Most sets of final accounts produced today use a vertical layout. This emphasises cost of sales, net current assets and total assets.
- Although this does not conform to double-entry principles it is widely used because the vast majority of people who use final accounts are not well versed in the double-entry system.

QUESTION 13

The following trial balance has been extracted from the books of Ted Croft:

Trial balance as at 30 September 20*3

	£	£
Capital		70,482
Drawings	15,000	
Bank balance	1,021	
Cash in hand	75	
Debtors	6,523	
Creditors		3,750
Stock as at 1 October 20*2	6,754	
Delivery van at cost	23,000	
Office equipment at cost	13,700	
Purchases	34,976	
Sales		79,261
Motor expenses	5,674	
Telephone	973	
Rent	4,500	
Wages	32,710	
Insurance	1,856	
General expenses	6,731	
	153,493	153,493

Stock as at 30 September 20*3 was valued at £5,872.

Required (a) Prepare a trading and profit and loss account for the year ended 30 September 20*3, using a vertical presentation.
(b) Prepare a balance sheet as at 30 September 20*3, using a vertical presentation.

QUESTION 14

The following trial balance has been extracted from the books of Lara Molt:

Trial balance as at 30 April 20*3

	£	£
Sales		198,764
Purchases	88,761	
Stock as at 1 May 20*2	1,885	
Returns inwards	367	
Returns outwards		419
Wages	45,710	
Motor expenses	7,118	
Rent and rates	6,337	
General expenses	6,972	
Vehicles	34,900	
Equipment	12,450	
Debtors	12,656	
Creditors		8,431
Bank balance	457	
Capital		36,999
Drawings	27,000	
	244,613	244,613

Stock as at 30 April 20*3 was valued at £2,341.

Required Prepare a trading and profit and loss account for the year ended 30 April 20*3 and a balance sheet as at that date. Use a vertical presentation.

QUESTION 15

The following trial balance has been extracted from the books of Rajan Randev:

Trial balance as at 31 March 20*3

	£	£
Purchases	67,813	
Sales		141,809
Stock as at 1 April 20*2	2,570	
Returns inwards	1,834	
Returns outwards		458
Carriage inwards	1,003	
Carriage outwards	751	
Wages	34,671	
Rates and insurance	1,962	
Motor expenses	9,701	
Heating and lighting expenses	3,559	
General expenses	7,682	
Fixtures and fittings	3,800	
Delivery vehicle	8,450	
Debtors	4,634	
Creditors		8,463
Bank balance	2,579	
Cash in hand	89	
Drawings	16,750	
Capital		17,118
	167,848	167,848

Stock as at 31 March 20*3 was valued at £3,339.

Required (a) Prepare a trading and profit and loss account for the year ended 31 March 20*3, using a vertical presentation.
(b) Prepare a balance sheet as at 31 March 20*3, using a vertical presentation.

QUESTION 16

The following trial balance has been extracted from the books of Bob Ratchet:

Trial balance as at 31 August 20*3

	£	£
Capital		93,440
Sales		152,775
Purchases	130,950	
Stock as at 1 September 20*2	11,349	
Returns inwards	1,254	
Returns outwards		752
Carriage inwards	350	
Carriage outwards	88	
Wages	3,492	
Debtors	17,460	
Creditors		13,968
Premises at cost	62,000	
Van at cost	8,000	
Rent	1,310	
Bank balance (overdrawn)		1,570
General expenses	5,150	
Drawings	18,500	
Insurance	1,345	
Bank charges	35	
Heating and lighting expenses	1,222	
	262,505	262,505

Stock as at 31 August 20*3 was valued at £10,588.

Required Prepare a trading and profit and loss account for the year ended 31 August 20*3 and a balance sheet as at that date. Use a vertical presentation.

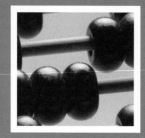

CHAPTER
TWENTY ONE

The Final Accounts Revisited

In previous chapters, we have seen, in detail, how financial transactions are dealt with through the double-entry book-keeping system. We have also seen the checks that are undertaken to ensure that errors do not lie undiscovered until the year-end when they might prove extremely difficult to locate and then correct.

We have also seen how to deal with adjustments to the accounts, such as accruals, pre-payments and provisions. Until now we have considered and dealt with each type of adjustment in isolation. However, in the real world it is likely that many of adjustments would be necessary at the end of every financial year in most businesses. For this reason we need to be able to incorporate these into one set of final accounts.

You have seen and worked through examples for each of the possible adjustments required. Now is the time for you to practise applying your knowledge in more complex situations.

Remember, if you get into difficulty with these questions, the odd-numbered questions have the answers detailed in the back of the book. But only look if you really are struggling!

Specification coverage:
AQA 12.2;
OCR 5.1.5.

By the end of this chapter you should be able to:
■ prepare a set of final accounts, taking into account
  ■ goods for own use
  ■ accrued expenses and incomes
  ■ pre-paid expenses and incomes
  ■ provision for depreciation
  ■ provision for doubtful debts
  ■ bad debts recovered.

QUESTION 1

The following trial balance has been extracted from the books of Hanif Mohammed:

Trial balance as at 28 February 20*3

	Dr £	Cr £
Stock as at 1 March 20*2	8,963	
Purchases	56,817	
Sales		123,601
Wages	39,113	
Rent	2,000	
Lighting and heating expenses	8,617	
General expenses	2,834	
Motor expenses	4,619	
Capital		139,181
Drawings	13,500	
Premises at cost	100,000	
Equipment at cost	16,000	
Delivery van at cost	8,000	
Debtors	8,607	
Bank balance	1,281	
Cash in hand	45	
Creditors		7,614
	270,396	270,396

Additional information at 28 February 20*3
■ stock was valued at £7,432.
■ Rent owing £200.

Required Prepare:
(a) a trading and profit and loss account for the year ended 28 February 20*3
(b) a balance sheet as at 28 February 20*3.

QUESTION 2

Siobhan Murgatroyd has extracted the following trial balance from her books of account:

Trial balance as at 31 July 20*3

	Dr £	Cr £
Stock as at 1 August 20*2	840	
Purchases	34,872	
Sales		97,121
Wages	41,483	
Rent and rates	6,490	
Insurances	1,840	
Motor expenses	4,238	
Advertising	2,761	
General expenses	11,218	
Equipment at cost	14,260	
Delivery vehicle at cost	32,700	
Debtors	8,641	
Bank balance	2,884	
Cash in hand	236	
Capital		72,718
Drawings	16,340	
Creditors		8,964
	178,803	178,803

Additional information at 31 July 20*3
- Stock was valued at £1,166.
- Insurance paid in advance amounted to £315.

Required Prepare:
      (a) a trading and profit and loss account for the year ended 31 July 20*3
      (b) a balance sheet as at 31 July 20*3.

QUESTION 3

Hibo Ahmed has provided the following trial balance extracted from her books of account:

Trial balance as at 31 May 20*3

	Dr £	Cr £
Stock as at 1 June 20*2	12,461	
Purchases	132,778	
Sales		206,981
Wages	46,337	
Rent payable	6,000	
Insurances	2,387	
Motor expenses	8,123	
Advertising	2,164	
General expenses	8,837	
Office equipment at cost	32,716	
Delivery vehicle at cost	23,500	
Debtors	5,871	
Cash in hand	236	
Capital		100,969
Drawings	38,500	
Creditors		7,162
Bank overdraft		4,798
	319,910	319,910

Additional information at 31 May 20*3
- Stock was valued at £13,106.
- Wages owing £814.
- Insurance paid in advance £628.

Required Prepare:
      (a) a trading and profit and loss account for the year ended 31 May 20*3
      (b) a balance sheet as at 31 May 20*3.

QUESTION 4

Helen Duff provides the following information:

Trial balance as at 31 December 20*3

	Dr £	Cr £
Stock as at 1 January 20*3	8,119	
Purchases	98,437	
Sales		196,347
Wages	56,320	
Rent and rates	4,760	
Advertising and insurances	5,982	
Motor expenses	15,135	
Office equipment at cost	27,300	
Delivery vehicle at cost	40,000	
Provision for depreciation		
Office equipment		5,460
Delivery vehicle		10,000
Debtors	15,781	
Bank balance	3,202	
Cash in hand	126	
Capital		68,039
Drawings	19,400	
Creditors		14,716
	294,562	294,562

Additional information at 31 December 20*3

- Stock was valued at £9,003.
- Helen provides depreciation on office equipment at 10% per annum, using the straight line method; she provides depreciation on her delivery vehicle at 25% per annum, using the straight-line method.

Required Prepare:
(a) a trading and profit and loss account for the year ended 31 December 20*3
(b) a balance sheet as at 31 December 20*3.

QUESTION 5

Lynn Parker provides the following information:

Trial balance as at 31 October 20*3

	Dr £	Cr £
Stock as at 1 November 20*3	2,468	
Purchases	64,128	
Sales		192,587
Returns inwards	1,111	
Returns outwards		382
Wages	67,491	
Rent and rates	5,400	
Advertising and insurances	3,780	
Lighting and heating expenses	6,437	
Motor expenses	18,542	
Office equipment at cost	17,400	
Delivery vehicles at cost	46,000	
Provision for depreciation		
Office equipment		8,874
Delivery vehicles		29,440
Debtors	14,673	
Bank overdraft		4,372
Cash in hand	430	
Capital		27,706
Drawings	21,300	
Creditors		5,799
	269,160	269,160

- Stock was valued at £3,199.
- Lynn provides depreciation on all assets, using the reducing balance method.
- The annual charges are:
  - office equipment 20% (round up)
  - delivery vehicles 40%

Required Prepare:
   (a) a trading and profit and loss account for the year ended 31 October 20*3
   (b) a balance sheet as at 31 October 20*3.

QUESTION 6

David Lycett provides the following information:

Trial balance as at 31 January 20*3

	Dr £	Cr £
Stock as at 1 February 20*2	4,967	
Purchases	87,328	
Sales		212,439
Returns inwards	726	
Returns outwards		460
Carriage inwards	642	
Carriage outwards	1,723	
Insurance	2,140	
Wages	72,048	
Motor expenses	8,461	
Lighting and heating expenses	3,487	
Telephone	1,348	
Office equipment at cost	16,500	
Vehicles at cost	30,000	
Provision for depreciation		
Office equipment		9,900
Vehicles		19,710
Debtors	18,461	
Bank balance	8,237	
Cash in hand	252	
Capital		25,992
Drawings	28,500	
Creditors		16,319
	284,820	284,820

- Stock was valued at £5,141.
- Wages owing £312.
- Lighting and heating expenses paid in advance £248.
- Depreciation on office equipment is calculated using the straight-line method at 10% per annum.
- Depreciation on vehicles is calculated using the reducing balance method at 30% per annum.

Required Prepare:
   (a) a trading and profit and loss account for the year ended 31 January 20*3
   (b) a balance sheet as at 31 January 20*3.

QUESTION 7

Gladys Jones provides the following information:

Trial balance as at 31 August 20*3

	Dr £	Cr £
Stock as at 1 September 20*2	18,461	
Purchases	115,268	
Sales		296,431
Returns inwards	816	
Returns outwards		203
Carriage inwards	348	
Insurance	2,400	
Wages	105,892	
Motor expenses	8,420	
Lighting and heating expenses	2,436	
Telephone	1,348	
General expenses	7,421	
Provision for doubtful debts		280
Discount allowed	436	
Premises at cost	120,000	
Office equipment at cost	15,000	
Vehicles at cost	50,000	
Provision for depreciation		
Premises		52,800
Office equipment		6,000
Vehicles		39,200
Debtors	15,200	
Bank	6,132	
Cash	228	
Capital		104,958
Drawings	42,750	
Creditors		12,684
	512,556	512,556

Additional information at 31 August 20*3

- Stock was valued at £16,984.
- Insurance paid in advance £180.
- Telephone bill outstanding £351.
- Provision for doubtful debts to be maintained at 2% of debtors outstanding at the year-end.
- Depreciation is to be provided on fixed assets at the following rates:
  - Premises 2% per annum (straight-line)
  - Office equipment 10% per annum (straight-line)
  - Vehicles 40% per annum (reducing balance).

Required   Prepare:
(a) a trading and profit and loss account for the year ended 31 August 20*3
(b) a balance sheet as at 31 August 20*3.

QUESTION 8

Tom Green provides the following information:

Trial balance as at 30 April 20*3

	Dr £	Cr £
Stock as at 1 May 20*2	819	
Purchases	32,461	
Sales		84,261
Returns inwards	138	
Returns outwards		261
Carriage inwards	412	
Discount received		151
Rent payable	8,300	
Wages	16,272	
Motor expenses	3,420	
Insurance	1,746	
Bad debts	211	
Bad debts recovered		74
General expenses	11,412	
Provision for doubtful debts		361
Office equipment at cost	24,500	
Motor vehicles at cost	20,000	
Provision for depreciation		
Office equipment		14,700
Motor vehicles		6,000
Debtors	8,100	
Cash	347	
Capital		33,377
Drawings	17,000	
Creditors		3,472
Bank overdraft		2,481
	145,138	145,138

Additional information at 30 April 20*3
- Stock was valued at £612.
- Motor expenses accrued amounted to £182.
- Insurance pre-paid £132.
- Provision for doubtful debts is maintained at 5% of year-end debtors.
- Depreciation is provided at 10% on office equipment using the straight-line method and at 30% on motor vehicles using the reducing balance method.

Required Prepare:
(a) a trading and profit and loss account for the year ended 30 April 20*3
(b) a balance sheet as at 30 April 20*3.

QUESTION 9

Isadorah Boom provides the following information:

Trial balance as at 31 August 20*3

	Dr £	Cr £
Stock as at 1 September 20*2	6,483	
Purchases	48,972	
Sales		97,481
Returns inwards	127	
Returns outwards		197
Carriage inwards	348	
Carriage outwards	812	
Bad debts	711	
Bad debts recovered		137
Wages	18,461	
Rent payable	6,500	
Lighting and heating expenses	3,481	
Telephone	1,856	
General expenses	15,860	
Provision for doubtful debts		276
Discount received		432
Machinery at cost	60,000	
Equipment at cost	36,000	
Debtors	6,400	
Creditors		2,968
Drawings	13,500	
Bank overdraft		2,487
Cash in hand	136	
Provision for depreciation		
Machinery		36,000
Equipment		31,500
Capital		48,169
	219,647	219,647

Additional information at 31 August 20*3
- Stock was valued at £6,543.
- Wages owing amounted to £380.
- Rent paid in advance £500.
- Provision for doubtful debts is to be maintained at 5% of debtors outstanding at the year-end.
- Depreciation is to be provided on fixed assets at the following rates:
  - machinery at 10% per annum using the straight-line method and
  - equipment at 50% per annum using the reducing balance method.

Required Prepare:
    (a) a trading and profit and loss account for the year ended 31 August 20*3
    (b) a balance sheet as at 31 August 20*3.

QUESTION 10

The following information is provided for Cindy Ash:

Trial balance as at 30 November 20*3

	Dr £	Cr £
Stock as at 1 December 20*2	11,461	
Purchases	72,384	
Sales		156,382
Returns inwards	817	
Returns outwards		388
Carriage inwards	278	
Carriage outwards	241	
Discounts allowed	159	
Motor expenses	4,817	
Wages	26,481	
Rent	4,500	
Bad debts	211	
Bad debts recovered		179
Provision for doubtful debts		450
General expenses	7,919	
Telephone	812	
Lighting and heating expenses	1,487	
Office equipment at cost	48,700	
Motor van at cost	16,000	
Provision for depreciation		
Office equipment		17,045
Motor van		3,200
Debtors	6,780	
Bank balance	4,831	
Cash in hand	199	
Capital		51,053
Drawings	28,100	
Creditors		7,480
	236,177	236,177

Additional information at 30 November 20*3

- Stock was valued at £10,177.
- Motor expenses owing amounted to £130.
- Lighting and heating expenses had been pre-paid £102.
- Cindy had withdrawn goods from the business for her private use £1,200.
- Provision for doubtful debts is to be maintained at 10% of debtors outstanding at the year-end.
- Depreciation is to be provided for on fixed assets at the following rates:
  - Office equipment at 5% per annum using the straight-line method
  - Motor van at 20% per annum using the reducing balance method.

Required Prepare:
(a) a trading and profit and loss account for the year ended 30 November 20*3
(b) a balance sheet as at 30 November 20*3.

QUESTION 11

Jack Simms provides the following information:

Trial balance as at 30 September 20*3

	Dr £	Cr £
Stock as at 1 October 20*2	26,381	
Purchases	197,384	
Sales		313,461
Returns inwards	813	
Returns outwards		212
Carriage inwards	277	
Carriage outwards	1,732	
Rates	4,780	
General expenses	8,274	
Wages	59,334	
Motor expenses	13,981	
Bad debts	3,140	
Bad debts recovered		497
Provision for doubtful debts		622
Discounts allowed	814	
Discounts received		1,346
Commission receivable		4,712
Premises at cost	200,000	
Equipment at cost	100,000	
Vehicles at cost	84,000	
Provision for depreciation		
Premises		86,000
Equipment		50,000
Vehicles		53,760
Debtors	28,000	
Bank balance	4,986	
Cash in hand	512	
Capital		91,289
Drawings	32,488	
Creditors		16,497
Long-term loan		150,000
Loan interest	1,500	
	768,396	768,396

Additional information at 30 September 20*3
- Stock was valued at £27,492.
- Wages owing amounted to £853.
- Rates paid in advance £1,270.
- Jack had withdrawn goods from the business for personal use amounting to £2,500.
- Commission receivable outstanding amounted to £180; this will be paid to Jack in December.
- Provision for doubtful debts is to be maintained at 2½% of debtors outstanding at the year-end.
- Depreciation is to be provided for on fixed assets at the following rates:
  - Premises: 1% per annum using the straight-line method
  - Equipment: 10% per annum using the straight-line method
  - Vehicles: 40% using the reducing balance method.

Required Prepare:
(a) a trading and profit and loss account for the year ended 30 September 20*3
(b) a balance sheet as at 30 September 20*3.

QUESTION 12

Annie Lim provides the following information:

Trial balance as at 30 June 20*3

	Dr £	Cr £
Stock as at 1 July 20*2	7,481	
Purchases	99,246	
Sales		214,683
Returns inwards	187	
Returns outwards		211
Carriage inwards	1,287	
Carriage outwards	462	
Rates	3,618	
Insurances	2,700	
Wages	81,342	
Discounts allowed	624	
Discounts received		1,438
Commission received		2,500
Rent received		4,250
Motor expenses	8,134	
Bad debts	1,400	
Bad debts recovered		120
Premises at cost	250,000	
Office equipment at cost	68,000	
Vehicles at cost	32,000	
Provision for depreciation		
Premises		150,000
Office equipment		27,200
Vehicles		11,520
Debtors	18,300	
Creditors		6,422
Bank overdraft		7,968
Cash in hand	714	
Capital		164,857
Drawings	16,500	
Provision for doubtful debts		826
	591,995	591,995

Additional information at 30 June 20*3

- Stock was valued at £9,284.
- Annie has taken goods from the business £1,750 for her personal use.
- Insurance pre-paid £350.
- Motor expenses owing £299.
- Commission receivable owing to Annie £500.
- Rent receivable paid in advance £600.
- A provision for doubtful debts is to be maintained at 5% of debtors outstanding at the year-end.
- Depreciation is to be provided for on fixed assets at the following rates:
  - Premises: 2% per annum using the straight-line method
  - Office equipment: 10% per anum using the straight-line method
  - Vehicles: 20% per annum using the reducing balance method.

Required Prepare:
(a) a trading and profit and loss account for the year ended 30 June 20*3
(b) a balance sheet as at 30 June 20*3.

Accounting Concepts

Over the years, accounting has evolved rules that all accountants use when preparing the final accounts of a business.

These rules are referred to as **accounting concepts** or **accounting principles**. Some of these principles are enshrined in law and in standards (FRSs and SSAPs) laid down by the major accounting bodies. For the moment, we will discuss the broad principles and will look at the legal and professional aspects in Book 2.

The application of these rules by all accountants means that the users of the accounts can rely on the information they contain safe in the knowledge that a set of accounts prepared for a butcher, baker and candlestick maker or accounts in Penrith, Penzance or Perth have been prepared using the same ground rules.

The concepts are a popular topic for questions in examinations as they underpin all of the work done by accountants.

1. THE GOING CONCERN CONCEPT

Says that, unless we have knowledge to the contrary, we assume that the business will continue to trade in its present form for the foreseeable future.

This means that we value all business assets at cost, not at what they would fetch if sold. If the business is going to continue, the assets will not be sold, so sale value is irrelevant.

WORKED EXAMPLE

- Land and buildings cost £100,000.
- Machinery cost £42,000.

- Vehicles cost £86,000.
- Warehouse costs £75,000.

They could be sold for £220,000.
They have a current scrap value of £3,000
They could be sold for £55,000
It has a current market value of £310,000

Required Identify the value of each asset to be shown on the balance sheet.

Answer

The assets should be shown on the balance sheet as follows:

Land and buildings at cost: £100,000
Machinery at cost: £42,000
Vehicles at cost: £86,000
Warehouse at cost: £75,000

2. THE ACCRUALS CONCEPT

As accountants, we are concerned with the value of resources used by the business and the benefits derived from the use of those resources by the business in any one financial year. The value of the resources used in any time period may be different from the price paid to acquire the resources.

WORKED EXAMPLE

Juanita has a financial year-end on 31 December 20*3.

The following amounts have been paid during the year ended 31 December 20*3:

	£
Wages	48,000
Rent	5,500
Rates	1,800
Insurance	2,100
Motor expenses	14,300

Wages due to workers for work completed in the week 24–31 December 20*3 but unpaid amount to £970.

Rent for December 20*3, £500, was paid on 19 January 20*4.

Rates have been paid for the period ending 31 March 20*4. £450 relates to 1 January–31 March 20*4.

Insurance includes a premium £300 for the period 1 January–29 February 20*4.

Motor expenses do not include £236 paid on 27 January 20*4 for a vehicle service completed on 15 December 20*3.

Required Calculate the amounts to be included in the profit and loss account for the year ended 31 December 20*3 for Juanita in respect of wages, rent, rates, insurance and motor expenses.

Answer

Wages   £48,970:
Juanita has used £48,970 worth of the skills and expertise of her workers during the year, even though she has paid them only £48,000.

Rent   £6,000:
Juanita has had the use of premises worth £6,000 to her; even though she had paid only £5,500.

Rates   £1,350:
Juanita has used local authority facilities valued at £1,350 for the year. She has also paid £450 for the use of facilities in the following year – we are not, at the moment, interested in the figures relating to next year.

Insurance   £1,800:
The payment of £2,100 includes £300 for insurance cover next year. This means that only £1,800 refers to this year.

Motor expenses   £14,536:
*The service was completed in the year ended 31 December 20*3 even though it was not paid for until the following year.*

Title is the legal term for ownership. For example, 'title deeds' to premises shows that the holder of the deeds is the owner of the premises.

3. PRUDENCE

This requires that revenues and profits are only included in the accounts when they are realised or their realisation is reasonably certain. We have already used the concept of prudence when we were valuing stock. If stock is overvalued at the year-end, gross profit will be overstated and net profit will also be overstated. This is why we value stock at the lower of cost or net realisable value.

However, the concept of prudence allows provision to be made for all known expenses or losses when they become known. For example, if damages were awarded against the business in a court case, the business could make a provision on the estimated amount that it might have to pay out in compensation.

4. THE REALISATION CONCEPT

This states that profits are normally recognised when the title to the goods passes to the customer, not necessarily when money changes hands. This concept is an extension of the accruals concept.

EXAMPLE

Fiona is an engineer, she is fairly certain that, in July, Jack will sign a contract to purchase lathes valued at £18,000.

The £18,000 should not be included in Fiona's accounts until the title to the lathes has passed to Jack.

5. THE CONCEPT OF CONSISTENCY

This requires that once a method of treating information has been established, the method should continue to be used in subsequent years' accounts.

The application of this concept was seen in Chapter 18 when methods of providing for depreciation of fixed assets were considered.

If information is treated differently each year then inter-year results cannot be compared and trends cannot be determined.

6. THE (BUSINESS) ENTITY CONCEPT

This states that only the expenses and revenues relating to the business are recorded in the business books of account. Transactions involving the private affairs of the owner are not part of the business and should not be included in the business books.

The owner's private electricity bills or private grocery bills should not be included as business expenditure.

If the business cheque book is used to pay the proprietor's private mortgage payments, the amount should be included in the drawings account.

7. THE CONCEPT OF MATERIALITY

If the inclusion or exclusion of information in a financial statement would mislead the users of that statement, then the information is material.

The concept recognises that some types of expenditure are less important in a business context than others. So, absolute precision in the recording of these transactions is not absolutely essential.

To spend much time in deciding how to treat a transaction of little consequence in the final accounts is detrimental to the wellbeing of the business – it would be a waste of time and resources.

We have already seen that capital expenditure is spending on fixed assets or their improvement. Revenue expenditure is spending on the normal running costs of a business. Fixed assets are used in a business for more than one time period. If we apply the accruals concept we should spread the cost of a fixed asset over the years it is used to generate the product and hence the profits.

A business purchases a ruler. The ruler costs 45p. It estimated that the ruler should last for three years. Technically, the ruler is a fixed asset and should therefore be classified as capital expenditure. To do this would be rather silly for such a trivial amount. The 45p would be treated as revenue expenditure and would be debited to either general expenses or office expenses. This treatment is not going to have a significant impact on profits or the valuation of net assets on the balance sheet – the absolute accuracy of its treatment is not material.

8. DUAL ASPECT

There are two aspects to accounting and they are always equal to each other. The assets of a business are always equal to the liabilities of the business. This means that every financial transaction has a double impact on the financial records of the business. Every debit has a corresponding credit. Every credit has a corresponding debit.

The dual aspect concept has already been encountered earlier in the double-entry system and also as the accounting equation.

9. OBJECTIVITY

As accountants we should view the business and its transactions in a dispassionate way. The accounts should not be prepared with any personal bias. To avoid this bias figures should, where possible, be backed by source documents.

George owns a 1937 vintage delivery van that cost £8,000 a number of years ago. He could sell it for £23,000 today but he said recently 'I love that van and I would not sell it if you offered me £100,000'.

The balance sheet value that George should use is £8,000 for two reasons: the £23,000 is based on a non-going concern basis and the £100,000 is a very subjective valuation on his part.

ACCOUNTING BASES

These are methods that have been developed in order to apply accounting concepts and principles to particular accounting transactions. With the publication of statements of standard accounting practice (SSAPs) and financial reporting standards (FRSs) the number of alternatives bases has been reduced. Examples of accounting bases would include the necessity to provide for depreciation over the useful economic life of fixed assets; the acceptable methods of valuing stocks and work in progress.

ACCOUNTING POLICIES

Accounting policies are the 'most appropriate to its [the business] circumstances for the purpose of giving a true and fair view'.

The policies should be 'consistent with accounting standards but should be appropriate to the particular industry in which the business operates'.

This means that the policies should be:

- relevant
- reliable

- comparable and
- understandable.

The policies with regard to depreciation would involve the choice of method that is most appropriate to the particular business and the field that it operates in (i.e. straight-line; reducing balance; depletion etc).

The choice of which method of stock valuation a business should use is also selection of an accounting policy.

Chapter summary

- Accounting concepts and principles are the basic rules of accounting.
- They should be applied to recording all transactions and the preparation of all accounting statements.

TEST QUESTIONS

QUESTION 1

Complete the following statements:
- Stocks being valued at the lower of cost or net realisable value is an example of using the .... concept.
- The petrol in the tank of the delivery van, worth £8.50, has not been recorded in the business balance sheet. This is an example of using the concept of ....
- The owner is using 10% depreciation on all fixed assets in the business because fixed assets have always been depreciated using this percentage. This is an example of the concept of ....

QUESTION 2

Outline one reason why accountants apply accounting concepts when preparing end-of-year financial statements.

QUESTION 3

The owner of a business is planning to include his financial manager as an asset in the end-of-year balance sheet at a value to the business of £200,000. However, the personnel manager feels that this is too high a value and says that the financial manager should be included at £50,000 since this is his annual salary.

QUESTION 4

The business has just purchased a specialised piece of computerised manufacturing machinery for £240,000. It will be used for three years. It would certainly have no re-sale value because of its specialised nature.

How should the machinery be valued?

- Cost: £240,000
- Re-sale value: £0
- Average value: £80,000.

Give reasons for your answer.

QUESTION 5

Rent received for the year is £3,500. The tenant should have paid £4,000.

The amount to be included in the profit and loss account is .... This is an example of using the .... concept.

QUESTION 6

Select the accounting concept to be used in the following circumstances:

(a) Wages outstanding at the end of the financial year: £362.
- ▨ accruals
- ▨ materiality
- ▨ consistency
- ▨ going concern

(b) A fixed asset costs £10,000. It is expected to have a life of ten years with no residual value. Depreciation is to be charged at £1,000 per annum.
- ▨ accruals
- ▨ materiality
- ▨ business entity
- ▨ prudence

(c) A customer is expected to place a substantial order worth £8,800 next month.
- ▨ accruals
- ▨ consistency
- ▨ business entity
- ▨ going concern

(d) A regular customer who owes £2,720 has just gone into liquidation.
- ▨ accruals
- ▨ materiality
- ▨ business entity
- ▨ prudence

(e) Audrey puts some of her home telephone bill on the business profit and loss account as she regularly uses her home telephone to ring clients.
- ▨ accruals
- ▨ materiality
- ▨ business entity
- ▨ money measurement

QUESTION 7

Accounting policies should be relevant, ..., comparable and understandable. Fill the gap.

QUESTION 8

Select the accounting concept to be used in the following circumstances:

(a) Jim feels that the old 'Olivetti' typewriter valued at cost £47 on the balance sheet could fetch £350 at auction.
- ▨ entity
- ▨ realisation
- ▨ objectivity
- ▨ money measurement

(b) A new 'Sellotape' dispenser has been purchased. It will be used for at least five years. The purchase price of £8.99 has been included in stationery.
- ▨ accruals
- ▨ going concern
- ▨ entity
- ▨ materiality

(c) It has been estimated that the factory cat has saved the business hundreds of pounds by catching mice that previously had caused much damage. The owner of the business wishes to put the cat on the balance sheet at a value of £200 despite the fact that it was purchased for only £3.50.
- ▨ accruals
- ▨ materiality
- ▨ going concern
- ▨ prudence

(d) Tom is to put the family holiday on the profit and loss account because he needs the relaxation to help him cope with the rigours of business.
- ▨ accruals
- ▨ going concern
- ▨ entity
- ▨ money measurement

(e) Frank believes that about 2% of debts outstanding at the year-end are doubtful. He intends to create a provision for doubtful debts of 2%.
- ▨ accruals
- ▨ money measurement
- ▨ entity
- ▨ prudence

Manufacturing Accounts

So far we have prepared the accounts of traders – businessmen and women who have bought finished goods and sold them on to the final customer. Most of the businesses that you come into contact with in everyday life fall into the category of trading organisations.

QUESTION

Identify three businesses that you use that are trading organisations.

Your answer will probably have included Kentucky Fried Chicken, McDonald's, Topshop, Virgin Megastores etc. The common factor here is that all these businesses buy their products from a manufacturer and sell them on. McDonald's do not make the buns or burgers; Topshop do not make the clothes that they sell to you. Virgin do not make the DVDs, CDs, videos etc.

We have already produced many trading and profit and loss accounts. Now, we need to prepare the final accounts of businesses that make goods that are sold by retailers. The business organisations that make the products prepare manufacturing accounts as part of their final accounts.

A manufacturing account shows the costs of running and maintaining the factory in which the final product is made.

A manufacturing business will also trade by selling its finished product to wholesalers or retailers – so it will prepare a trading account as well as a manufacturing account. A manufacturing business will need to have an administration section too – so it will prepare a profit and loss account as well as a manufacturing account and a trading account.

Specification coverage:
AQA 12.4;
OCR 5.3.1.

By the end of this chapter you should be able to:
- prepare the final accounts of a manufacturing business
- calculate provision for unrealised profit
- show relevant entries in a profit and loss account
- show the treatment of the provision of unrealised profit in a balance sheet.

Manufacturing account	Factory Account
↓	
Trading account	Warehouse Account
↓	
Profit and loss account	Administration (Office Account)
↓	
Balance sheet	Statement of affairs

> **Direct costs** are defined by the Chartered Institute of Management Accountants (CIMA) as 'expenditure which can be economically identified with a specific saleable cost unit'.

Examples of direct costs include purchases of direct materials and direct labour charges. The purchase of wood and varnish to make your table and the wages of the person who assembled the parts of the table are direct costs.

> **Indirect costs** are factory expenses that are not directly identifiable with the final product.

Examples of indirect costs include factory rent and rates and depreciation of factory machinery.

> **Royalties** are payments made to the inventor of a product or a process or an idea. It is often a percentage of the revenue earned by the user.

A manufacturing account is split into two main sections: prime costs and overheads.

The **prime cost section** shows all the direct expenses incurred in production. The expenses can be *directly* and clearly traced to the particular product being produced. For example, in every pair of jeans that you buy you can see the denim used, the studs, the thread and the zip. You also know that someone has stitched the pieces together – they have worked *directly* on the jeans, so their wages are a direct cost. The other main direct cost is the payment of royalties.

WORKED EXAMPLE

Hinge & Co are manufacturers of woollen sweaters.

Place a tick beside the expenses that would be used to prepare the prime cost section of the manufacturing account of Hinge & Co.

- sales staff wages
- purchases of wool
- office heating and lighting expenses
- wool dyes
- managers' salary
- rent of canteen
- knitting machine operatives' wages.

Answer

You should have ticked purchases of wool; wool dyes; and knitting machine operatives' wages. All of these expenses can be easily traced to the final product.

The prime cost section of a manufacturing account would contain all the **resources** used in the manufacturing process:

- purchases of raw materials
- direct wages
- royalties
- any other direct costs.

The raw materials used in the manufacturing process are not necessarily the raw materials purchased and so we have to make an adjustment to the raw material purchase figure in order to find how many of the raw material purchases were actually used during the year (remember the calculation to determine how much bread I had eaten while on my diet?).

WORKED EXAMPLE

Ralph Shoemaker makes footwear. The following information relates to the year ended 31 March 20*3:

stock of leather as at 1 April 20*2 £4,790; purchases of leather during the year £50,790; stock of leather as at 31 March 20*3 £3,640.

Required Calculate the value of leather used to produce shoes during the year ended 31 March 20*3.

Answer

	£
Stock as at 1 April 20*2	4,790
Purchases of leather	50,790
	55,580
Stock as at 31 March 20*3	3,640
Leather used	51,940

WORKED EXAMPLE

V. Alve manufactures radios from components bought from around the world. The following information relates to the year ended 31 August 20*3:

stock of components as at 1 September 20*2 £8,790; stock of components as at 31 August 20*3 £10,460; purchases of components during the year £112,900; wages of assembly workers £372,610.

Required Calculate the value of components used by Alve during the year ended 31 August 20*3.

Answer

	£
Stock of components as at 1 September 20*2	8,790
Purchases of leather	112,900
	121,690
Stock of components as at 31 August 20*3	10,460
Components used	111,230

If you are unsure about this calculation, talk yourself through it. Ralph had £4,790 stock of leather at the start of the year; he purchased a further £50,790 of leather so he could have used £55,580 worth of leather during the year. However, he didn't use it all; he had £3,640 left so he must have used £51,940 worth.

Talk yourself through the calculation for Alve's components.

The prime cost section can now be prepared.

WORKED EXAMPLE

Trevor Roberts makes cakes for sale to hotels and restaurants. He provides you with the following information for the year ended 30 April 20*3:

stock of materials as at 1 May 20*2 £376; stock of materials as at 30 April 20*3 £297; purchases of materials during the year £58,748; direct wages £27,380; other wages £16,492.

Prepare a statement showing the prime costs for the year ended 30 April 20*3.

Answer

Statement showing prime costs for the year ended 30 April 20*3.

	£
Stock of raw materials as at 1 May 20*2	376
Purchases of raw materials	58,748
	59,124
Stock of raw materials as at 30 April 20*3	297
Cost of raw materials used	58,827
Direct wages	27,380
Prime cost	86,207

Note

Only the direct wages have been included. Prime cost lists only the resources directly used in the production of the cakes, i.e. the flour, butter, sugar etc, plus the wages of the people who actually work directly on producing the cakes – the people who mix the ingredients, bake the cakes and decorate them.

Office workers' wages or cleaners' wages are not included; these people do not work in the factory.

WORKED EXAMPLE

Eliza Doolot produces DVD players from components purchased from the Far East. Her workers assemble the components using a Japanese design for which she pays royalties.

She provides the following information for the year ended 30 September 20*3:

manufacturing royalties £7,500; purchases of components £457,300; stock of components as at 1 October 20*2 £17,450; stock of components as at 30 September 20*3 £26,100; direct wages £317,520; other direct costs £26,720.

Required Prepare the prime cost section of the manufacturing account for the year ended 30 September 20*3 for Eliza Doolott.

WORKED EXAMPLE *continued*

Answer

Eliza Doolott
Prime cost section of manufacturing account for the year ended 30 September 20*3

	£
Stock of components as at 1 October 20*2	17,450
Purchases of components	457,300
	474,750
Stock of components as at 30 September 20*3	26,110
Cost of components used	448,640
Direct wages	317,520
Royalties	7,500
Other direct costs	26,720
Prime cost	800,380

Overheads are described by CIMA as 'expenditure on labour, materials or services which cannot be economically identified with a specific saleable cost'.

Factory overheads are the expenses incurred in running the factory that cannot be easily traced to the product.

QUESTION 1

Moin Syyed owns a manufacturing business. He provides the following information for the year ended 28 February 20*3:

	£
Stocks of raw materials as at 1 March 20*2	23,658
Stocks of raw materials as at 28 February 20*3	18,439
Purchases of raw materials	156,364
Direct wages	236,451
Indirect wages	74,590
Royalties	35,000
Office salaries	86,418

Required Prepare the prime cost section of Moin's manufacturing account.

WORKED EXAMPLE

The following list has been prepared by Brenda Beech, a manufacturer of garden furniture:

Purchases of timber	Depreciation of power saws, planes etc.
Rent of workshop	Wages of assembly workers
Office manager's wages	Screws and nails
Delivery van expenses	Brenda's drawings
Wood glue	Factory power

Required Place alongside each of the expenses 'PC' for prime cost or 'OH' for overhead.

WORKED EXAMPLE *continued*

Answer

Purchases of timber, screws and nails, wood glue and wages of assembly workers can all be identified as prime costs. Rent of workshop, depreciation of power saws, planes etc and factory power are all overheads.

Office manager's wages would appear in the profit and loss account, as would delivery van expenses. Brenda's drawings would be deducted from her capital on the balance sheet.

Let us put the two sections together. Initially, you might find it helpful to label the items 'PC' (prime cost) or 'OH' (overhead).

WORKED EXAMPLE

The factory manager of Fawcett products has supplied the following information for the year ended 30 November 20*3:

	£
Stock of raw materials as at 1 December 20*2	90,000
Stock of raw materials as at 30 November 20*3	80,000
Purchases of raw materials	390,000
Manufacturing wages	212,000
Manufacturing royalties	15,000
Supervisor's wages	27,000
Factory rent	120,000
Factory insurance	30,000
Depreciation of machinery	17,500

Required Prepare the manufacturing account for the year ended 30 November 20*3 for Fawcett Products.

Answer

Fawcett Products
Manufacturing account for the year ended 30 November 20*3

	£	£
Stock of raw materials as at 1 December 20*2		90,000
Purchases of raw materials		390,000
		480,000
Stock of raw materials as at 30 November 20*3		80,000
Cost of raw materials used		400,000
Manufacturing wages		212,000
Royalties		15,000
Prime cost		627,000
Factory overheads		
Supervisor's wages	27,000	
Factory rent	120,000	
Factory insurance	30,000	
Depreciation – machinery	17,500	194,500
Cost of manufacture		821,500

Note

- The most common mistake that examination candidates make when preparing a manufacturing account is to deduct the total overheads from the prime cost. Remember, we are calculating the total cost of manufacturing the product.
- Always label the prime cost and the cost of manufacture – examiners often give a mark for those labels.

In an earlier chapter we saw that carriage inwards was included on the trading account. Carriage inwards always makes purchases more expensive. A manufacturing business is no exception.

Carriage inwards is added to the purchases (of raw materials) in the manufacturing account.

WORKED EXAMPLE

The following balances have been extracted as at 31 December 20*3 from the books of Atul Patel, a manufacturer of kitchen furniture:

	£(000)
Purchases of raw materials	2,470
Manufacturing wages	1,380
Manufacturing royalties	37
Supervisory wages	87
Carriage inwards	3
Factory rent	60
Factory power	30
Other factory overheads	27
Depreciation of machinery	42
Depreciation of office equipment	13
Stock of raw materials as at 1 January 20*3	99
Stock of raw materials as at 31 December 20*3	111

Required Prepare the manufacturing account for the year ended 31 December 20*3, showing prime cost and cost of manufacture.

Answer

Atul Patel
Manufacturing account for the year ended 31 December 20*3

	£(000)	£(000)
Stock of raw materials as at 1 January 20*3		99
Purchases of raw materials	2,470	
Carriage inwards	3	2,473
		2,572
Stock of raw materials as at 31 December 20*3		111
Cost of raw materials used		2,461
Manufacturing wages		1,380
Royalties		37
Prime cost		3,878
Factory overheads		
Supervisory wages	87	
Factory rent	60	
Factory power	30	
Other factory overheads	27	
Depreciation – machinery	42	246
Cost of manufacture		4,124

Note

Office equipment is not used in the factory – it is an office expense and so should be entered in the profit and loss account. Machinery is always used in the factory, hence its inclusion in the manufacturing account.

STOCK

In any manufacturing business there are always three kinds of stock:

- stocks of **raw materials** – as yet, these stocks are in the works in the condition in which they were bought; they have not entered the manufacturing process. Examples of stocks of raw materials from previous questions would include stocks of flour, butter, leather, DVD components, wood, etc.
- stocks of **work in progress** – these are partly finished goods; goods that are still undergoing part of the manufacturing process – cakes waiting to be decorated; partly finished shoes, DVD players short of a few components, kitchen furniture without doors and handles etc.
- stocks of **finished goods** – goods that have completed the journey through the manufacturing process and are simply waiting to be sold.

Each type of stock appears in a different part of the final accounts. They appear in chronological order in the revenue accounts (i.e. the manufacturing, trading and profit and loss accounts).

Stock is a current asset and is shown in the balance sheet. In the case of a manufacturing business, the three types of stock held have to be identified in the balance sheet.

We have just seen how to treat stocks of raw materials.

You have already worked with stocks of finished goods – in the trading account – a business usually trades with finished goods.

Work in progress still has to go through the remainder of the manufacturing process before it becomes a finished product so it should appear in the manufacturing account.

Work in progress appears after the cost of manufacture has been calculated.

The treatment is the same as for all types of stock. We add the value of work in progress at the start of the period and deduct the value of work in progress at the end of the period.

There are two ways of doing this. Both are acceptable – each will be rewarded with the same number of marks in an examination.

Choose one method and always use it. In the examples shown we will use Method 1 (it is usually considered to be easier).

WORKED EXAMPLE

Bert Loggs is a manufacturer. He provides the following information for the year ended 31 July 20*3:

	£
Cost of manufacture	217,432
Work in progress as at 1 August 20*2	4,698
Work in progress as at 31 July 20*3	6,481

Required Calculate total production costs for the year ended 31 July 20*3 for Bert.

Method 1	£	Method 2	£	£
Cost of manufacture	217,432	Cost of manufacture		217,432
Add Work in progress as at 1 August 20*3	4,698	Work in progress as at 1 August 20*2	4,698	
Subtotal	222,130	*Less* Work in progress as at 31 July 20*3	3,481	1,217
Less Work in progress as at 31 July 20*3	3,481			
Total production cost	218,649	Total production cost		218,649

Answer

You can see that both methods give exactly the same total production costs.

WORKED EXAMPLE

Laura Shaw is a manufacturer. She provides the following information for the year ended 28 February 20*3:

	£
Stocks	
Raw materials as at 1 March 20*2	16,500
Work in progress as at 1 March 20*2	18,200
Finished goods as at 1 March 20*2	20,600
Purchases of raw materials	237,300
Manufacturing wages	458,900
Office salaries	186,200
Factory supervisor's wages	17,800
Carriage inwards	1,500
Rent and rates	
Factory	14,900
Office	7,200
Depreciation	
Machinery	90,000
Office equipment	21,000
Royalties	7,500
Other indirect expenses	
Factory	32,600
Office	28,400
Sales	1,000,000
Stocks	
Raw materials as at 28 Feb 20*3	16,000
Work in progress as at 28 Feb 20*3	19,400
Finished goods as at 28 Feb 20*3	21,350

Required (a) Prepare the manufacturing account for the year ended 28 February 20*3.

(b) Prepare a balance sheet extract as at 28 February 20*3 showing how stocks would appear.

Answer

(a)
Laura Shaw
Manufacturing account for the year ended 28 February 20*3

	£	£
Stock of raw materials as at 1 March 20*2		16,500
Purchases of raw materials	237,300	
Carriage inwards	1,500	238,800
		255,300
Stock of raw materials as at 28 Feb 20*3		16,000
		239,300
Manufacturing wages		458,900
Royalties		7,500
Prime cost		705,700
Factory overheads		
Supervisor's wages	17,800	
Rent and rates	14,900	
Other indirect expenses	32,600	
Depreciation – machinery	90,000	155,300
Manufacturing cost		861,000
Add Work in progress as at 1 March 20*2		18,200
		879,200
Less Work in progress as at 28 February 20*3		19,400
Total production cost		859,800

WORKED EXAMPLE *continued*

(b)	Balance sheet extract as at 28 February 20*3	
Current assets	**£**	
Stocks – Raw materials	16,000	
Work in progress	19,400	
Finished goods	<u>21,350</u>	56,750

WORKED EXAMPLE

Mike Tong is a manufacturer who has produced the following information for the year ended 31 May 20*3:

	£
Sales	2,913,502
Stocks as at 1 June 20*2	
Raw materials	49,780
Work in progress	23,640
Finished goods	40,210
Purchases of raw materials	846,289
Direct wages	750,199
Supervisors' wages	68,720
Indirect wages	187,442
Royalties	19,000
Carriage inwards	4,612
Carriage outwards	5,218
Rent and rates – factory	48,700
– office	21,300
Insurance – factory	19,170
– office	10,830
Heat and light – factory	4,260
– office	1,830
Factory power	17,282
Other production expenses	5,671
Depreciation – factory equipment	48,000
– office equipment	12,000
Stocks as at 31 May 20*3	
Raw materials	48,340
Work in progress	20,119
Finished goods	38,461

Required (a) Prepare the manufacturing account for the year ended 31 May 20*3.

(b) Prepare the trading account for the year ended 31 May 20*3.

WORKED EXAMPLE *continued*

Answer

(a)

Mike Tong
Manufacturing account for the year ended 31 May 20*3

	£	£
Stock of raw materials as at 1 June 20*2		49,780
Purchases of raw materials	846,289	
Carriage inwards	4,612	850,901
		900,681
Stock of raw materials as at 31 May 20*3		48,340
		852,341
Direct wages		750,199
Royalties		19,000
Prime cost		1,621,540
Factory overheads:		
Indirect wages	187,442	
Supervisors' wages	68,720	
Rent and rates	48,700	
Insurance	19,170	
Heat and light	4,260	
Power	17,282	
Other indirect expenses	5,671	
Depreciation	48,000	399,245
		2,020,785
Add Work in progress as at 1 June 20*2		23,640
		2,044,425
Less Work in progress as at 31 May 20*3		20,119
Total production cost		2,024,306

(b)

Trading account for the year ended 31 May 20*3

	£
Stock as at 1 June 20*2	40,210
Production cost of goods completed	2,024,306
	2,064,516
Stock as at 31 May 20*3	38,461
	2,026,055
Gross profit on trading	887,447
Sales	2,913,502

QUESTION 2

Fritz Zeller provides the following information:

Stocks	1 January 20*3	31 December 20*3
	£	£
Raw materials	23,500	24,700
Work in progress	17,800	16,300
Finished goods	16,300	17,250

	£
Purchases of raw materials	212,650
Wages: direct labour	143,680
indirect labour	67,340
sales staff	78,290
Factory overheads	56,700
Depreciation: factory machinery	23,000
office equipment	8,000
delivery vehicles	26,000
Sales	£1,448,560

Required Prepare:
(a) a manufacturing account for the year ended 31 December 20*3
(b) a trading account for the year ended 31 December 20*3.

QUESTION 3

Jane Doyle provides the following information:

Stocks	1 August 20*2	31 July 20*3
	£	£
Raw materials	17,650	23,510
Work in progress	8,570	7,340
Finished goods	10,760	10,740

	£
Purchases of raw materials	203,510
Wages: direct labour	123,930
indirect labour	58,900
sales staff	67,500
office staff	37,320
Rent and rates: factory	37,800
office and showrooms	18,450
Factory power	38,900
Lighting and heating expenses: factory	9,450
office and showrooms	6,210
Insurances: factory	14,620
offices and showrooms	5,990
Depreciation: machinery	87,000
office equipment	13,450
delivery vehicles	9,800
Carriage: inwards	1,350
outwards	870
Sales	£987,430

Required Prepare:
(a) a manufacturing account for the year ended 31 July 20*3
(b) a trading account for the year ended 31 July 20*3

Sometimes the managers of a business will wish to gauge how efficiently their factory is operating. They compare the price that the goods manufactured cost to produce with the cost or purchasing the same amount of goods from an 'outside' supplier. If it would be cheaper to purchase the goods externally then it may be in the best interest of the business to cease manufacturing and purchase the goods. (But see sections on marginal costing and social accounting later.)

MANUFACTURING PROFIT

When the managers of a business transfer the total production cost to the trading account, gross profit is found by deducting the cost of sales (COGS) from sales revenue. This method does have a flaw – there is no indication of how profitable the factory is.

Gross profit is derived in two ways:

■ by manufacturing efficiently
■ by selling the goods at a price that is higher than the production cost.

We can determine the factory manufacturing profit by finding the difference between the cost of production and the cost of purchasing the goods externally.

Let us look at the manufacturing accounts of Laura Shaw and Mike Tong produced earlier.

WORKED EXAMPLE

The same number of goods made in Laura's factory could be purchased by Laura's buying department for £900,000.

Required Prepare:
  (a) a summarised manufacturing account for the year ended 28 February 20*3 showing the manufacturing profit
  (b) a trading account for the year ended 28 February 20*3.

Answer

(a) **Summarised manufacturing account for the year ended 28 February 20*3**

	£
Prime cost	705,700
Overheads	155,300
	861,000
Add Work in progress as at 1 March 20*2	18,200
	879,200
Less Work in progress as at 28 February 20*3	19,400
Total production cost	859,800
Manufacturing profit	40,200
Transfer price to trading account	900,000

(b) **Trading account for the year ended 28 February 20*3**

	£
Stock of finished goods	20,600
Transfer price of manufactured goods	900,000
	920,600
Stock of finished goods on 28 February 20*3	21,350
	899,250
Gross profit on trading	100,750
Sales	1,000,000
Gross profit from manufacturing	40,200
Gross profit on trading	100,750
Total Gross Profit	140,950

WORKED EXAMPLE

Mike Tong's buying department could purchase for £2.5m the same number of goods made in his factory.

Required   A summarised manufacturing account for the year ended 30 May 20*3 and a trading account for the year ended 31 May 20*3.

Answer

Manufacturing account for the year ended 31 May 20*3

	£
Prime cost	1,621,540
Overheads	399,245
	2,020,785
Work in progress as at 1 June 20*2	23,640
	2,044,425
Work in progress as at 31 May 20*3	20,119
Total production cost	2,024,306
Factory profit	475,694
Transfer price to trading account	2,500,000

Trading account for the year ended 31 May 20*3

	£
Stock of finished goods as at 1 June 20*2	40,210
Transfer price of manufactured goods	2,500,000
	2,540,210
Stock of finished goods as at 31 May 20*3	38,461
Cost of goods sold	2,501,749
Gross profit on trading	411,753
Sales	2,913,502
Gross profit on manufacturing	475,694
Gross profit on trading	411,753
Total gross profit	887,447

It is usual in examination questions to add a percentage to the total production costs in order to arrive at the transfer price.

WORKED EXAMPLE

Olga Stravinska is a manufacturer. The following information relates to her business as at 31 October 20*3:

total production costs £348,700; stock of finished goods as at 1 November 20*2 £37,498; stock of finished goods as at 31 October 20*3 £39,613; sales £598,136.

Olga transfers goods from her factory to the trading account at cost plus 20%.

Required   An extract from the manufacturing account and trading account for the year ended 31 October 20*3 showing the manufacturing profit and the transfer price of the goods manufactured.

WORKED EXAMPLE *continued*

Answer

Manufacturing account extract for the year ended 31 October 20*3

	£
Total production costs	348,700
Factory profit	69,740 (£348,700 × 20%)
Transfer price	418,440

Trading account for the year ended 31 October 20*3

	£
Stock of finished goods as at 1 November 20*2	37,498
Transfer price of manufactured goods	418,440
	455,938
Stock of finished goods as at 31 October 20*3	39,613
Cost of goods sold	416,325
Gross profit on trading	181,811
Sales	598,136
Gross profit from manufacturing	69,740
Gross profit on trading	181,811
Total gross profit	251,551

QUESTION 4

Tabitha Todd supplies the following information for her manufacturing business for the year ended 31 March 20*3:

	£
Total production costs	456,000
Transfer price to trading account	520,900
Sales	873,500
Stocks of finished goods as at 1 April 20*2	34,600
Stocks of finished goods as at 31 March 20*3	36,200

Required Prepare:
  (a) a extract from the manufacturing account for the year ended 31 March 20*3 showing factory profit and the amount to be transferred to the trading account
  (b) a trading account for the year ended 31 March 20*3
  (c) an extract from the profit and loss account for the year ended 31 March 20*3 showing clearly the total gross profit earned by Tabitha's business.

QUESTION 5

Harry Parker supplies the following information for his manufacturing business for the year ended 31 October 20*3:

	£
Total production cost	1,326,900
Transfer price to trading account	2,100,000
Sales	3,210,600
Stocks of finished goods as at 1 November 20*2	186,000
Stocks of finished goods as at 31 October 20*3	191,450

Required Prepare:
   (a) an extract from the manufacturing account for the year ended 31 October 20*3 showing factory profit and the amount to be transferred to the trading account
   (b) a trading account for the year ended 31 October 20*3
   (c) an extract from the profit and loss account for the year ended 31 October 20*3 showing clearly the total gross profit earned by Harry's business.

QUESTION 6

Harpreet Nahal supplies the following information for her manufacturing business for the year ended 31 May 20*3:

	£
Total production cost	842,000
Sales	1,347,500
Stocks of finished goods as at 1 June 20*2	62,000
Stocks of finished goods as at 31 May 20*3	57,000

Finished goods are transferred from the manufacturing account to the trading account at cost plus 25%.

Required Prepare:
   (a) an extract from the manufacturing account for the year ended 31 May 20*3 showing factory profit and the amount to be transferred to the trading account
   (b) a trading account for the year ended 31 May 20*3
   (c) an extract from the profit and loss account for the year ended 31 May 20*3 showing clearly the total gross profit earned by Harpreet's business.

QUESTION 7

Hilary Nike supplies the following information for her manufacturing business for the year ended 31 March 20*3:

	£
Total production cost	943,750
Sales	1,448,560
Stocks of finished goods as at 1 April 20*2	85,820
Stocks of finished goods as at 31 March 20*3	87,360

Finished goods are transferred from the manufacturing account to the trading account at cost plus 40%.

Required Prepare:
   (a) an extract from the manufacturing account for the year ended 31 March 20*3 showing factory profit and the amount to be transferred to the trading account
   (b) a trading account for the year ended 31 March 20*3
   (c) an extract from the profit and loss account for the year ended 31 March 20*3 showing clearly the total gross profit earned by Hilary's business.

QUESTION 8

Zack Hill provides the following information for his manufacturing business for the year ended 31 December 20*3:

	£
Total production cost	1,342,700
Sales	3,420,000
Stocks of finished goods as at 1 January 20*3	98,400
Stocks of finished goods as at 31 December 20*3	102,600

Finished goods are transferred from the manufacturing account to the trading account at cost plus 50%.

Required Prepare:
   (a) an extract from the manufacturing account for the year ended 31 December 20*3 showing factory profit and the amount to be transferred to be transferred to the trading account

(b) a trading account for the year ended 31 December 20*3

(c) an extract from the profit and loss account for the year ended 31 December 20*3 showing clearly the total gross profit earned by Hilary's business.

PROVISION FOR UNREALISED PROFITS

We have seen in an earlier chapter the over-riding principle that governs all stock valuations is that all stocks should be valued at the lower of cost or net realisable value (because it is prudent). This does not pose a problem with raw materials or work in progress. However, it can cause a problem with finished goods.

Finished goods are stored in a warehouse ready for sale or ready to be despatched to a customer. There will, in all probability, be some of these finished goods left unsold, i.e. in stock at the end of the financial year. How should these stocks be valued?

There is no problem if the finished goods are passed to the warehouse at their cost price. Like raw materials and work in progress, the finished goods would be valued at cost.

A problem does arise when stock is passed from the factory at cost price plus a profit margin.

We have already stated that stock should be valued at cost (if cost is less than net realisable value), not at cost and some factory profit.

If stock is valued at cost plus some factory profit we need to shed the factory profit because it has not yet been earned – we need to find the cost price of the goods.

WORKED EXAMPLE

Martin Godin manufactures printed circuits. He passes the goods from his factory at cost plus 25%. At his financial year-end his stock of finished goods is valued at £250,000.

Required Calculate the cost price of Martin's closing stock to be entered in the business balance sheet.

Answer
The cost price of the closing stock of finished goods is £200,000

So

$$\frac{100}{125} \text{ of £250,000} \quad + \quad \frac{25}{125} \text{ of £250,000} \quad = \quad £250,000$$

£200,000 + £50,000 = £250,000

WORKED EXAMPLE

Siobhan O'Riley manufactures generators. The finished generators are transferred to the trading account at cost plus 10%. At her financial year-end Siobhan's stock of finished goods is valued at £385,000.

Required Calculate the cost price of Siobhan's closing stock of finished goods as it would be shown in her balance sheet drawn up at the end of the year.

Answer
The closing stock of finished generators should be valued at £350,000.

10% 10% 10% 10% 10% / 10% 10% 10% 10% 10% + 10% = 110% of cost	=	£385,000

10% 10% 10% 10% 10% / 10% 10% 10% 10% 10% + 10%	=	£385,000

So

$$\frac{100}{110} \text{ of £385,000} \quad + \quad \frac{10}{110} \text{ of £385,000} \quad = \quad £385,000$$

$$£350,000 \quad + \quad £35,000 \quad = \quad £385,000$$

QUESTION 9

Value of finished goods £	Transfer price to trading account Cost plus
4,080	50%
1,080	12.5%
1,450	30%
900	20%
10,500	75%

Required Calculate:
(a) the cost price of the following stocks of finished goods
(b) identify the element of profit added to the cost price of the stock.

Both methods used to calculate the cost price or the profit element are quite tricky, so it is worth practising them.

This is a popular examination topic and many examination candidates find it difficult.

If the value of stock is increased by the profit element then the gross profit and hence net profit will also be increased by the same amount.

The closing stock of finished goods has yet to be sold so we are anticipating the earning of profit that as yet has not been realised.

The concept of prudence tells us that we should not do this. We need to remove the profit element from our final accounts. We do this by creating a provision for unrealised profit.

We saw earlier how to deal with provisions for depreciation, provision for doubtful debts and provisions for discounts.

We need to make a provision for the profits as yet unrealised.

All provision accounts look similar:

Dr		Provision for ?!???!!! account		Cr
		Start of year Balance b/d		2,000
End of yearBalance c/d	2,150	End of year Profit and loss account		150
	2,150			2,150
		Start of year Balance b/d		2,150

The '?!???!!!' could say 'depreciation', 'doubtful debts', 'discounts' or 'unrealised profits'.

The balance is shown in the balance sheet (the sheet for balances) as a deduction from the closing stock of finished goods, while the profit and loss account amount is shown as a deduction from the gross profit on manufacturing in the profit and loss account.

WORKED EXAMPLE

Paquito plc transfers manufactured goods to its trading account at cost plus 30%. The balance brought down in the provision for unrealised profits account as at 1 April 20*2 is £1,300. Stock of finished goods is valued at £6,500 on 31 March 20*3.

Required Prepare a provision for unrealised profit account showing clearly the amount to be transferred to the profit and loss account.

Answer

Dr	Provision for unrealised profit account		Cr	
		1 Apl Balance b/d	1,300	
31 Mar Balance c/d	1,500	31 Mar P & L a/c	200	missing figure to be deducted from GP on manufacture in P&L a/c
	1,500		1,500	
		1 Apl Balance b/d	1,500	£6,500 × 30% ÷ 130%

WORKED EXAMPLE

Snodgrass & Co transfers manufactured goods to the trading account at cost plus 25%. The balance on the provision for unrealised profit account at 1 August 20*2 was £3,700. At 31 July 20*3 the stock of finished goods was £20,000.

Required Prepare a provision for unrealised profit account at 31 July 20*3 showing clearly the amount to be transferred to the P & L account.

Answer

Dr	Provision for unrealised profit account		Cr	
		1 Aug Balance b/d	3,700	
31 Jul Balance c/d	4,000	31 Jul P & L a/c	300	missing figure to be deducted from GP on manufacture in the P&La/c
	4,000		4,000	
		1 Aug Balance b/d	4,000	£20,000 × 25% ÷ 125%

Frequently in examination questions the whole of the provision account has to be prepared (including the calculation of the opening balance). If you can calculate the closing balance in the questions above, the opening balance should pose no problem.

WORKED EXAMPLE

Seline Smith marks up the goods manufactured in her factory by 35% to transfer them to the trading account. Her stock of finished goods on 1 March 20*2 was £9,450; her stock of finished goods one year later on 28 February 20*3 was £9,720.

Required Prepare a provision for unrealised profit for the year ended 28 February 20*3.

Answer

Dr Provision for unrealised profit account Cr		
28 Feb Balance c/d	2,520	1 Mar Balance b/d	2,450	£9,450 × 35% ÷ 135%
		28 Feb P & L a/c	70	missing P&L a/c figure
	2,520		2,520	
		1 Mar Balance b/d	2,520	£9,720 × 35% ÷ 135%

WORKED EXAMPLE

Bertram Stink manufactures washing machines. They are transferred to the trading account at cost plus 60%. The stock of finished washing machines as at 1 June 20*2 was £57,600; as at 31 May 20*3 it was £60,160.

Required Prepare a provision for unrealised profit showing the amount to be transferred to the P & L account for the year ended 31 May 20*3.

Answer

Dr Provision for unrealised profit account Cr		
31 May Balance c/d	22,560	1 Jun Balance b/d	21,600	£57,600 × 60% ÷ 160%
		31 May P & L a/c	960	missing figure
	22,560		22,560	
		1 Jun Balance b/d	22,560	£60,160 × 60% ÷ 160%

Like all provision accounts, it is possible that the provision at the end of the financial year could be less than the provision brought down at the start of the financial year. In such cases the amount transferred to the P & L account would be added to the gross profit on manufacture shown in the P & L account.

WORKED EXAMPLE

Seok Chin manufactures woks. The finished woks are transferred to her trading account at cost price plus 50%. The stock of finished woks at 1 November 20*2 was £4,500. The stock of finished woks at 31 October 20*3 was £3,900.

Required Prepare a provision for unrealised profit showing clearly the amount to be transferred to the profit and loss account for the year ended 31 October 20*3.

Answer

Dr	Provision for unrealised profit account			Cr
Missing figure added to GP 31 Oct P & L a/c	200	1 Nov Balance b/d	1,500	£4,500 × 50% ÷ 150%
31 Oct Balance c/d	1,300			
	1,500		1,500	
		1 Nov Balance b/d	1,300	£3,900 × 50% ÷ 150%

QUESTION 10

Denis Walters is a manufacturer. He transfers goods to his trading account at cost plus 30%. He provided the following information:

	£
Stocks of finished goods as at 1 February 20*2	6,136
Stocks of finished goods as at 31 January 20*3	6,513

Required Prepare a provision for unrealised profit account for the year ended 31 January 20*3

QUESTION 11

Doug Down is a manufacturer. He transfers goods to his trading account at cost plus 40%. He provides the following information:

	£
Stocks of finished goods as at 1 September 20*2	12,054
Stocks of finished goods as at 31 August 20*3	13,356

Required Prepare a provision for unrealised profit account for the year ended 31 August 20*3.

QUESTION 12

Joyce Black is a manufacturer. She transfers goods to her trading account at cost plus 60%. She provides the following information:

	£
Stocks of finished goods as at 1 July 20*2	16,192
Stocks of finished goods as at 30 June 20*3	16,416

Required Prepare a provision for unrealised profit account for the year ended 30 June 20*3.

Finally, let us see how the relevant figures are dealt with in the profit and loss account.

WORKED EXAMPLE

Martin Simpson manufactures lawnmowers. He transfers finished goods from the factory to his trading account at cost plus 30%. He provides the following information for the financial year ended 30 September 20*3:

	£
Total production at cost price	76,500
Stock of finished goods as at 1 October 20*2	6,045
Stock of finished goods as at 30 September 20*3	6,864
Sales for the year ended 30 September 20*3	210,000

Required (a) Calculate the transfer price of goods manufactured for inclusion in the trading account.
(b) Prepare a trading account for the year ended 30 September 20*3.
(c) Prepare a provision for unrealised profit account for the year.
(d) Prepare an extract from the profit and loss account for the year ended 30 September 20*3 showing total gross profit and the treatment of the provision for unrealised profit;
(e) Prepare a balance sheet extract as at 30 September 20*3 to show how stocks of finished goods are treated.

Answer

(a) Transfer price is £99,450. Production cost £76,500 plus
£22,950 (£76,500 × 30%)

(b)

Trading account for the year ended 30 September 20*3		
	£	
Stock as at 1 October 20*2	6,045	
Production cost of goods completed	99,450	(£76,500 × 130%)
	105,495	
Stock as at 30 September 20*3	6,864	
Cost of sales	98,631	
Gross profit on trading	111,369	
Sales	210,000	

(c)

Dr Provision for unrealised profit account Cr			
30 Sep Balance c/d	1,584	1 Oct Balance b/d 1,395	£6,045 × 30% ÷ 130%
	1,584	30 Sep P & L a/c 189	missing figure
		1,584	
		1 Oct Balance b/d 1,584	£6,864 × 30% ÷ 130%

(d)

Profit and loss account extract for the year ended 30 September 20*3		
	£	£
Gross profit on manufacturing (from part (a))	22,950	
Less Provision for unrealised profit	189	22,761
Gross profit on trading		111,369
		134,130

WORKED EXAMPLE *continued*

(e)

Balance sheet extract as at 30 September 20*3		
Current assets		
	£	£
Stocks of finished goods	6,864	
Less Provision for unrealised profit	1,584	5,280

WORKED EXAMPLE

Ian Rawstron manufactures bedroom furniture. He transfers finished goods from his factory to his trading account at cost plus 70%. He provides the following information for the year ended 31 December 20*3:

	£
Sales for the year ended 31 December 20*3	974,000
Total production at cost price	476,400
Stock of finished goods as at 1 January 20*3	10,540
Stock of finished goods as at 31 December 20*3	15,980

Required (a) Calculate the transfer price of goods manufactured for inclusion in the trading account.
(b) Prepare a trading account for the year ended 31 December 20*3.
(c) Prepare a provision for unrealised profit account for the year.
(d) Prepare an extract from the profit and loss account for the year ended 31 December 20*3 showing total gross profit and the treatment of the provision for unrealised profit;
(e) Prepare a balance sheet extract as at 31 December 20*3 to show how finished goods are treated.

Answer
(a) Transfer price £809,880. Production cost £476,400 plus
£333,480 (£476,400 × 70%)

(b)

Trading account for the year ended 31 December 20*3	
	£
Stock as at 1 January 20*3	10,540
Production cost of goods completed	809,880
	820,420
Stock as at 31 December 20*3	15,980
Cost of sales	804,440
Gross profit	169,560
Sales	974,000

(c)

Dr	Provision for unrealised profit account			Cr	
		1 Jan Balance b/d	4,340	£10,540 × 70% ÷ 170%	
31 Dec Balance c/d	6,580	31 Dec P & L a/c	2,240		
	6,580		6,580		
		1 Jan Balance b/d	6,580	£15,980 × 70% ÷ 170%	

(d)

Profit and loss account extract for the year ended 31 December 20*3		
	£	£
Gross profit on manufacturing	333,480	
Less Provision for unrealised gross profit	2,240	331,240
Gross profit on trading		169,560
		500,800

(e)

Balance sheet extract as at 31 December 20*3		
Current assets		
	£	£
Stocks of finished goods	15,980	
Less Provision for unrealised profit	6,580	9,400

Chapter summary

- Businesses that produce goods prepare a manufacturing account as part of their final accounts.
- A manufacturing account lists all the costs involved in running a factory.
- Goods are often transferred from the manufacturing account to the trading account inclusive of a factory profit.
- A provision account must be opened to eradicate the unrealised profit from the accounts.

Self-test questions

- Name two businesses that prepare a manufacturing account.
- Identify two costs that would be included in the calculation of prime cost.
- Identify two costs that would be included as factory overheads.
- Name the three types of stock generally held by a manufacturing business.
- Define the term 'direct costs'.
- Give an example of a direct cost for a car manufacturer.
- Define 'indirect costs'.
- Give an example of an indirect cost for a manufacturer of trainers.
- Why might a manufacturing business transfer goods to the trading account at a price exceeding total production cost?
- Why is there a need to provide for unrealised profit?
- Name the two types of gross profit usually earned in a manufacturing business.

■ From which type of stock is the provision for unrealised profit deducted in the balance sheet of a manufacturing business?

TEST QUESTIONS

QUESTION 13

The following information is provided for the year ended 30 November 20*3:

	£
Stocks of raw materials as at 1 December 20*2	7,968
Stocks of finished goods as at 1 December 20*2	7,670
Stocks of raw materials as at 30 November 20*3	8,429
Stocks of finished goods as at 30 November 20*3	7,950
Purchases of raw materials	102,177
Sales of finished goods	212,540
Wages – direct labour	82,440
indirect labour	45,670
Manufacturing royalties	1,200

Required Select the appropriate information and prepare the prime cost section of a manufacturing account for the year ended 30 November 20*3.

QUESTION 14

The following information is provided for the year ended 30 April 20*3:

	£
Stocks of raw materials as at 1 May 20*2	16,480
Stocks of work in progress as at 1 May 20*2	13,276
Stocks of raw materials as at 30 April 20*3	15,981
Stocks of work in progress as at 30 April 20*3	14,538
Purchases of raw materials	232,741
Purchases of delivery vehicles	135,000
Carriage inwards	2,478
Carriage outwards	3,560
Wages – direct labour	168,430
indirect labour	87,549
Manufacturing royalties	15,000

Required Select the appropriate information and prepare the prime cost section of a manufacturing account for the year ended 30 April 20*3.

QUESTION 15

The following information relates to the Trogle manufacturing company for the year ended 30 June 20*3:

	£
Stocks as at 1 July 20*2 – raw materials	17,480
work in progress	8,977
finished goods	12,548
Stocks as at 30 June 20*3 – raw materials	18,597
work in progress	10,431
finished goods	13,547
Purchases of raw materials	234,772
Purchases of office equipment	17,400
Wages – direct labour	419,828
indirect labour	21,720
Rent – factory	9,500
offices	12,000
Insurances – factory	8,390
offices	3,510
Factory power	17,460
Depreciation – factory machinery	45,000
office equipment	11,200
Manufacturing royalties	12,500

Additional information as at 30 June 20*3

Factory insurance paid in advance amounted to £360; an outstanding amount for factory power remained unpaid £940.

Required Select the appropriate information and prepare a manufacturing account for the year ended 30 June 20*3.

QUESTION 16

The following information is given for the Duthie Manufacturing company for the year ended 31 December 20*3:

	£
Stocks as at 1 January 20*3 – raw materials	23,841
work in progress	12,402
finished goods	14,539
Stocks as at 31 December 20*3 – raw materials	19,781
work in progress	14,701
finished goods	15,439
Purchases of raw materials	312,741
Wages – direct labour	212,441
indirect wages	126,481
Manufacturing royalties	32,500
Carriage inwards	2,481
Carriage outwards	3,146
Returns inwards	2,548
Returns outwards	1,718
Rent of factory	18,000
Factory insurance	12,461
Factory power	34,772
Factory machinery at cost	500,000

Additional information at 31 December 20*3

Factory rent owing amounted to £2,000; insurance paid in advance £380; depreciation on factory machinery is to be provided for at 10% per annum on cost.

Required Prepare a manufacturing account for the year ended 31 December 20*3.

QUESTION 17

Dreght and Sons own a manufacturing business. Goods are transferred from the manufacturing account to the trading account at cost plus 30%.

The following information is available for the year ended 31 March 20*3:

	£
Stocks as at 1 April 20*2 – raw materials	8,162
work in progress	6,183
finished goods	7,451
Stocks as at 31 March 20*3 – raw materials	7,466
work in progress	5,774
finished goods	8,549
Purchases of raw materials	112,431
Sales	873,442
Carriage inwards	798
Carriage outwards	1,328
Wages – direct labour	189,410
indirect labour	64,822
Factory power	17,231
General factory overheads	21,461
Depreciation of factory machinery	28,000

Additional information at 31 March 20*3

An outstanding amount for factory power £230 remained unpaid; general factory overheads £488 had been paid in advance.

Required Prepare:
(a) a manufacturing account for the year ended 31 March 20*3 and
(b) a trading account for the year ended 31 March 20*3.

QUESTION 18

Jasdeep Gahir owns a manufacturing business. Goods are transferred from the manufacturing account to the trading account at cost plus 20%. She provides the following information for the year ended 30 September 20*3:

	£
Stocks as at 1 October 20*2 – raw materials	17,489
work in progress	11,023
finished goods	88,149
Stocks as at 30 September 20*3 – raw materials	21,603
work in progress	9,621
finished goods	99,341
Purchases of raw materials	237,780
Sales	2,177,085
Carriage inwards	1,248
Carriage outwards	2,971
Returns inwards	653
Returns outwards	861
Wages – direct labour	372,005
indirect labour	83,750
Manufacturing royalties	120,000
Factory power	27,473
Factory rent and rates	19,716
Factory insurances	7,483
Factory machinery at cost	316,000

Additional information at 30 September 20*3

Indirect wages accrued and unpaid amounted to £1,250; factory insurances paid in advance amounted to £272; depreciation is to be provided for at 10% per annum on cost.

Required Prepare:
(a) a manufacturing account for the year ended 30 September 20*3
(b) a trading account for the year ended 30 September 20*3.

QUESTION 19

Rod Bowler provides the following information for the year ended 28 February 20*3:

	At 1 March 20*2 £	28 February 20*3 £
Stocks of finished goods	27,300	32,500

Stocks have been valued at cost plus 30%.

Required Prepare a provision for unrealised profit account for the year ended 28 February 20*3.

QUESTION 20

Nancy Chou provides the following information for the year ended 31 January 20*3:

	At 1 February 20*2 £	31 January 20*3 £
Stocks of finished goods	38,251	42,543

Stocks have been valued at cost plus 45%.

Required Prepare a provision for unrealised profit account for the year ended 31 January 20*3.

QUESTION 21

Pusmeena Turner provides the following information for the year ended 30 November 20*3:

	At 1 December 20*2 £	At 30 November 20*3 £
Stocks of finished goods	80,500	89,250

Stocks have been valued at cost plus 75%.

Required Prepare a provision for unrealised profit account for the year ended 30 November 20*3.

QUESTION 22

Jon Fret provides the following information for the year ended 31 May 20*3:

	At 1 June 20*2 £	At 31 May 20*3 £
Stocks of finished goods	42,550	32,200

Stocks have been valued at cost plus 15%.

Required Prepare a provision for unrealised profit account for the year ended 31 May 20*3.

QUESTION 23

Sandra Gavington provides the following information for her manufacturing business for the year ended 31 December 20*3. She transfers goods from the manufacturing account to the trading account at cost price plus 20%.

	£
Stocks as at 1 January 20*3 – raw materials	7,966
work in progress	6,200
finished goods	14,880
Stocks as at 31 December 20*3 – raw materials	8,618
work in progress	8,000
finished goods	16,440
Purchases of raw materials	214,283
Sales	900,000
Wages – direct labour	125,750
indirect labour	63,489
Manufacturing royalties	19,500
Factory power	18,240
Factory insurances	7,960
General factory overheads	23,470
Factory machinery at cost	800,000

Additional information at 31 December 20*3

Direct labour wages accrued and unpaid amount to £2,500; factory insurance paid in advance £740; depreciation is to be provided on factory machinery at 10% per annum on cost.

Required Prepare:
(a) a manufacturing account for the year ended 31 December 20*3
(b) a trading account for the year ended 31 December 20*3
(c) a provision for unrealised profit account for the year ended 31 December 20*3
(d) an extract from the profit and loss account for the year ended 31 December 20*3 showing the total gross profit and the treatment of the provision for unrealised profit
(e) an extract from the balance sheet as at 31 December 20*3 showing how all stocks are treated.

QUESTION 24

James Johns provides the following information for his manufacturing business for the year ended 31 August 20*3. He transfers goods from the manufacturing account to the trading account at cost price plus 25%.

	£
Stocks as at 1 September 20*2 – raw materials	27,932
work in progress	13,420
finished goods	22,500
Stocks as at 31 August 20*3 – raw materials	26,880
work in progress	11,601
finished goods	25,500
Purchases of raw materials	211,499
Sales	1,780,976
Returns inwards	976
Returns outwards	138
Manufacturing royalties	24,000
Wages – direct labour	477,816
indirect labour	112,420
Factory power	21,961
Factory insurance	9,750
General factory overheads	48,361
Factory machinery at cost	750,000

Additional information at 31 August 20*3

Amount accrued and unpaid for royalties £1,000; indirect wages accrued and unpaid £830; factory insurances paid in advance amounted to £370; depreciation is to be provided on factory machinery at 10% per annum on cost.

Required Prepare:
  (a) a manufacturing account for the year ended 31 August 20*3
  (b) a trading account for the year ended 31 August 20*3
  (c) a provision for unrealised profit for the year ended 31 August 20*3
  (d) an extract from the profit and loss account for the year ended 31 August 20*3 showing total gross profit and the treatment of the provision for unrealised profit
  (e) an extract from the balance sheet as at 31 August 20*3 showing how all stocks are treated.

TWENTY FOUR

The Final Accounts of Limited Companies

The main disadvantages of being in business as a sole trader are:

- that liability is not limited to the amount of money invested by the owner. This means that if the business fails and creditors cannot be paid from the proceeds raised from the sale of business assets then the proprietor must provide further finance from his or her private assets. This could mean that the business failure could result in a sole trader losing both his or her business assets and some, if not all, of his or her personal assets;
- that generally the amount of money that one person can afford to invest in a business is comparatively small.

Limited liability companies came into existence because of the need for businesses to raise capital and at the same time to give the investors a degree of security. They appeared when businesses found the need to raise large amounts of capital.

A person who invests capital in a limited company is a **shareholder.** Shareholders are the owners of a limited company. They own shares in the company. (Shareholders are sometimes known as members.)

Nominal value is the face value or par value of a share, for example the nominal value of ordinary shares in Matalan plc is 10p while the nominal value of ordinary shares in Whitbread plc is 50p.

Shares are the equal parts into which a company's capital is divided.

Liquidation is the term used when a limited company is unable to discharge its liabilities.

Limited liability means that the liability of shareholders for the debts of a limited company of which they are members is limited to the amount they have agreed to subscribe.

The capital of a limited company is divided into shares. Shares can have a nominal value of 5p each, 10p each, 50p, £1 each – in fact, any amount!

To become a shareholder, a person must buy at least one share.

If a company goes into liquidation, each shareholder could lose his or her shares but he or she cannot be asked to contribute further finance to cover the company's debts.

If, however, shareholders have only partially paid for the shares, they can be required to pay the balance outstanding.

Specification coverage:
AQA 12.5 and 12.6.

By the end of this chapter you should be able to:
- understand the concept of limited liability
- prepare a profit and loss appropriation account for a limited company
- prepare a balance sheet for a limited company
- distinguish between authorised and issued share capital
- recognise the difference between ordinary and preference shares
- make transfers to reserves
- make the necessary adjustments to record
  - share premium
  - revaluation of fixed assets
  - the issue of shares
  - dividends.

Limited companies are treated as separate legal entities. This means that in the eyes of the law a limited company is a 'person' who can sue others (including its shareholders) just like you can or I can. It also means that we can sue a limited company if we so desire.

There are two kinds of limited company:

- Private limited companies:
  - there are far more private limited companies than public limited companies
  - private limited companies cannot offer shares to the general public
  - they cannot be listed on the stock market
  - they are often run by a family or a group of friends. The name of a private limited company must end with 'Limited' or 'Ltd'.

- Public limited companies' share capital must be more than £50,000:
  - they must produce more detailed final accounts than private limited companies
  - they can raise capital from the general public
  - they generally find it easier to raise finance than a private limited company – since members are likely to view them as less risky than private limited companies – this might also result in a lower rate of interest being charged by lenders of finance
  - companies that issue their shares through the stock market are referred to as quoted or listed companies
  - the name of a public limited company must end with 'plc'.

> **Directors** are the people who are responsible for the day-to-day running of the business. They are appointed by the shareholders at general meetings of the company. They report on their stewardship of the business each year at the company's Annual General Meeting.

ADVANTAGES OF LIMITED LIABILITY STATUS

- Limited liability status for shareholders.
- Larger amounts of capital can be raised by directors for use within the company.

DISADVANTAGES OF LIMITED LIABILITY STATUS

- Annual accounts must be audited.
- Directors must complete an annual return and file their accounts with the Registrar of Companies.
- The filed accounts may be inspected by the public.
- Companies are subjected to more 'red tape' than sole traders.
- Copies of the company's annual audited accounts must be sent to each shareholder and debenture holder.

All of these disadvantages involve extra expenditure.

THE PROFIT AND LOSS APPROPRIATION ACCOUNT OF A LIMITED COMPANY

> **Dividends** are the rewards paid to shareholders out of profits of a limited company.

The dividends are paid to individual shareholders in proportion to the size of their holding of shares. Dividends are usually paid annually but there may be an interim dividend paid based on the half-year profits of the business.

As far as we are concerned, the accounts of both private limited companies and public limited companies are treated in the same manner.

The final accounts of all businesses are similar. In the case of a sole trader who manufactures goods, the following final accounts would be prepared:

Profit would then be transferred to the capital section of the balance sheet.

Note

Since directors are employees of a company overseeing the day-to-day running of the business, payments to them are a profit and loss account expense.

In the case of a limited company we need to insert another account in order to show what has happened to the business profits. We need to prepare a profit and loss appropriation account. (sometimes shortened to simply the 'appropriation account').

The diagram would show:

Who is entitled to the profits of a limited company?

Since a company is a legal entity (a 'person' in its own right), it is subject to taxation just like everyone else.

Companies do not pay income tax; they pay corporation tax. The amount of taxation to be levied on a company's profits will be given in an examination question. The tax charged will reduce profits. The adjusted sub-total is shown in the profit and loss appropriation account as profit after tax.

WORKED EXAMPLE

Nota Ltd has made a net profit of £287,300 for the year ended 31 March 20*3. Corporation tax due on the profit amounts to £71,400.

Required Calculate the profit after tax for the year ended 31 March 20*3 for Nota Ltd.

Answer

Nota Ltd
Profit and loss appropriation account for the year ended 31 March 20*3

	£
Net profit	287,300
Corporation tax	71,400
Profit after tax	215,900

Very straightforward – but do identify each figure used.

The corporation tax is due – it will actually be paid to the tax authorities some months later and it needs to be shown as a creditor in the balance sheet.

Who else, apart from the Inland Revenue, is entitled to the profit?

Interim dividends are dividends that are paid during the financial year. They are based on half-yearly profits.

Proposed dividends. The amount of profit that the directors feel that they can pay to the shareholders based on the end of year's results.

When directors have prepared the final accounts of the company they can determine how much of the profits they can afford to pay to the shareholders. Since the directors work for the shareholders they can only recommend how much they think should be paid as dividends. This amount has to be agreed by the shareholders at the annual general meeting before it can be paid.

If the shareholders agree the dividend it will be paid by the company some months later. Until it is paid, it is shown on the balance sheet as a creditor.

So under the heading

Creditors: amounts falling due in less than one year

we will find amounts owed to the Inland Revenue and amounts owed for final dividends.

The owners are entitled to a share of the profits.

The shareholders are entitled to dividends based on the number of shares they each own. The total amount of dividend is deducted from the profit after tax. Any remaining profit is retained within the company to provide for expansion or the replacement of assets.

WORKED EXAMPLE

Mutar Ltd has made a profit of £482,460 for the year ended 31 August 20*3. Corporation tax due on the profits is £96,000. The directors have paid an interim dividend on ordinary shares of £48,000 and they propose a final dividend on ordinary shares of £120,000.

Required Prepare:
- (a) the profit and loss appropriation account for the year ended 31 August 20*3
- (b) an extract from the balance sheet as at 31 August 20*3 showing any entries under the heading 'Creditors: amounts falling due in less than one year'.

Answer

Mutar Ltd
Profit and loss appropriation account for the year ended 31 August 20*3

		£
Net profit		482,460
Corporation tax due		96,000
Profit after tax		386,460
Interim ordinary dividend paid	48,000	
Ordinary proposed dividend	120,000	168,000
Retained profit for the year		218,460

Balance sheet extract as at 31 August 20*3

	£
Creditors : amounts falling due in less than one year	
Corporation tax due	96,000
Proposed ordinary dividend	120,000

QUESTION 1

The following information relating to GraZeb Ltd for the year ended 31 March 20*3 is given:

	£
Net profit	347,320
Corporation tax due	117,450
Directors' fees paid	234,700
Interim ordinary dividend paid	34,500
Final proposed dividend on ordinary shares	112,600.

Required Prepare a profit and loss appropriation account for the year ended 31 March 20*3.

QUESTION 2

The following information relating to Rutor Ltd for the year ended 31 December 20*3 is given:

	£
Net profit for the year	246,821
Interim ordinary dividend paid	42,000
Final proposed dividend on ordinary shares	87,000
Directors' fees paid	126,750
Corporation tax due	74,350

Required Prepare a profit and loss appropriation account for the year ended 31 December 20*3.

Before proceeding any further we need to consider the construction of the balance sheet of a limited company.

The balance sheet of Tom Crabb, a sole trader, might look like this:

Tom Crabb
Balance sheet as at 31 December 20*3

	£	£
Fixed assets		
Premises at cost		70,000
Machinery at cost		20,000
Vehicles at cost		15,000
		105,000
Current assets		
Stock	12,000	
Debtors	8,000	
Bank balance	1,000	
	21,000	
Current liabilities		
Creditors	6,000	15,000
		120,000
Capital as at 1 January 20*3		108,000
Add Profit		28,000
		136,000
Less Drawings		16,000
Total		120,000

If we draw up the balance sheet of a limited company, Tom Crabb Ltd, it might look like this:

	£	£
Fixed assets		
Premises		70,000
Machinery at cost		20,000
Vehicles at cost		15,000
		105,000
Current assets		
Stock	12,000	
Debtors	8,000	
Bank balance	1,000	
	21,000	
Creditors: amounts falling due in less than one year		
Creditors	6,000	15,000
		120,000
Capital		120,000

So you can see that the two are almost identical except for the renaming of the current liabilities. In limited companies accounts these are headed 'Creditors: amounts falling due in less than one year'. There is also a difference in the capital section.

> **Incorporation** is the act of forming a registered limited company.

When a limited company is incorporated it raises capital so that it can purchase the fixed assets necessary to enable it to conduct its business. It raises capital through the issue of shares. In the balance sheet this total is called the share capital.

There are two main types of shares issued by a limited company:

PREFERENCE SHARES

Preference shareholders receive a fixed dividend which is expressed as a percentage of the nominal value of the share, e.g. 7% preference share of £1 each; 8% preference shares of 50p each. This dividend can only be paid if the company earns sufficient profits but preference shareholders do receive their dividend before the ordinary shareholders receive theirs. In the event of a company going into liquidation the preference shareholders are entitled to receive the nominal value of their shares before the ordinary shareholders are repaid. (Hence their name – they receive preferential treatment in the winding-up of a limited company.) Since the holders' are entitled to receive the nominal value of their shares before ordinary shareholders in the event of a liquidation, preference shares are a less risky form of investment.

Preference shares may be

- **cumulative** – if a dividend is not paid in one year, the dividend accumulates until such time as the arrears are able to be paid. These arrears must be paid before ordinary shareholders receive anything (most preference shares are of this type)
- **non-cumulative** – if a dividend is not paid in any one year, that year's dividend is lost.
- **redeemable** – the company may buy these preference shares back at a stipulated time in the future.

ORDINARY SHARES

These are the most common type of share.

The ordinary shareholders are the owners of a company and as such have voting rights. This means that they have control of the company. They appoint and dismiss directors. They also decide whether the dividend proposed by the directors is appropriate (they may reduce the dividend but they cannot increase it). All the profits remaining after preference dividends belong to the ordinary shareholders – although only the part of the profits not retained to expand or replace fixed assets will be paid to them as dividend. Ordinary dividends vary with levels of profits. So you can deduce from this that dividends could be zero with no upper limit.

Note

All dividend payments require:

- sufficient profits being available
- sufficient cash being available to actually pay the dividend.

A memorandum of association is a document filed with the Registrar of Companies before a limited company can become incorporated. It defines the external relationship of the company to the outside world.

The details filed include:

- the company's name, address and registered office
- share capital
- the company's objectives.

Articles of association: The document contains the rules that govern the internal Organisation of a limited company. It must be filed with the Registrar of Companies together with the memorandum of association.

It shows the company's rules with regard to:

- organisation and control
- voting right
- conduct of directors' meetings
- conduct of shareholders' annual general meeting
- directors' powers
- rights attached to the different classes to shares.

You will encounter a number of headings that relate to a company's share capital.

Authorised share capital (also known as 'registered share capital' or 'nominal share capital') sets the maximum number of each type of share that a company can issue to its shareholders. It is stated in the company's memorandum and articles of association.

> **Issued share capital** shows the actual number of each type of share that the company has issued to its shareholders. It cannot exceed the authorised share capital.

> **Paid-up capital** is the amount of share capital that has been paid by the shareholders.

EXAMPLE

A balance sheet drawn up immediately after incorporation but prior to any trading activities might have looked like this:

Reginald Satu Ltd
Balance sheet as at 30 November 20*3

	£	£
Fixed assets		
Premises at cost		400,000
Machinery at cost		120,000
Vehicles at cost		80,000
		600,000
Current assets		
Stock	30,000	
Bank	70,000	100,000
		700,000
Authorised share capital		
750,000 Ordinary Shares of £1 each		750,000
1,000,000 6% preference shares of 50p each		500,000
Issued share capital		
500,000 Ordinary shares of £1 each		500,000
400,000 6% Preference shares of 50p each		200,000
		700,000

QUESTION 3

The following information is given for Arbres Ltd as at 30 April 20*3:

authorised share capital 500,000 ordinary shares of 50 pence each; issued share capital 300,000 ordinary shares 50 pence paid; machinery at cost £80,000; vehicle at cost £40,000; stock £25,000; trade debtors £15,000; bank balance £1,000; trade creditors £11,000.

Required Prepare a balance sheet as at 30 April 20*3.

QUESTION 4

The following information is given for Helaminge Ltd as at 30 September 20*3:

authorised and issued share capital 800,000 ordinary shares of 25 pence each; premises at cost £80,000; machinery at cost £60,000; vehicle at cost £30,000; stock £20,000; trade debtors £12,000; bank balance £6,000; trade creditors £8,000.

Required Prepare a balance sheet as at 30 September 20*3.

The profit generated by the business of a sole trader belongs to the trader. It is credited to his or her capital account.

The profits that are removed from the business as drawings are deducted from the capital.

The remainder of the profit is 'ploughed back' and may be used to purchase assets.

The same is true of a limited company. Some profits will leave the business as dividends. The remainder is 'ploughed back' and may be used to purchase assets.

Consider this illustration:

Daphne Baird is a sole trader	D. Baird Ltd is a private limited company
Her capital account has a balance of £50,000	The authorised share capital consists of 50,000 £1 ordinary shares
The business makes a net profit of £35,000	The business makes a net profit of £35,000
Her drawings amount to £17,000	The directors recommend a dividend of £17,000
The capital section of her balance sheet would look like this:	The capital section of the company balance sheet would look like this:

Extract from the balance sheet of Daphne Baird

	£
Capital	50,000
Add Profit	35,000
	85,000
Less Drawings	17,000
	68,000

Extract from the balance sheet of D. Baird Ltd

	£
Capital and reserves	
50,000 Ord. Shares of £1 each	50,000
Retained profit	18,000
(£35,000 less £17,000 paid out as dividends)	
	68,000

Not so different!

> **Profit and loss account** is the name given to a revenue reserve to which the profits of a limited company for each year is credited. It is also known as retained profits or retained earnings.

> **General reserve** is a revenue reserve appropriated from trading profits to strengthen the financial position of a limited company.

Note

The retained profits in the balance sheet of the company cannot be credited to each individual shareholder. In a large public limited company there could be hundreds of thousands of shareholders. The retained profits are shown as one figure – it still belongs to the shareholders and they will receive it if the company is ever wound up. Retained profits (also known as retained earnings or more usually profit and loss account) are a reserve.

WORKED EXAMPLE

The following trial balance has been extracted from the books of Clangitt Co. Ltd as at 31 July 20*3:

	£	£	
Retained profit for the year		42,000	
Fixed assets at cost	180,000		
Current assets	20,000		
Trade creditors		8,000	
Issued share capital – 50,000 ordinary shares of £1 each		50,000	
Profit and loss account (retained earnings)		100,000	profits retained from previous years
	200,000	200,000	

WORKED EXAMPLE *continued*

Required Prepare a summarised balance sheet as at 31 July 20*3 for Clangitt Ltd.

Answer

Clangitt Ltd
Balance sheet as at 31 July 20*3

	£	£
Fixed assets at cost		180,000
Current assets	20,000	
Creditors: amounts falling due in less than one year	8,000	12,000
		192,000
Capital and reserves		
Ordinary shares of £1 each		50,000
Profit and loss account (retained earnings)		142,000
		192,000

○ EXAMINATION TIP

A common mistake made by examination candidates is to say that reserves are money set aside: they are not. There is one reserve shown in the above balance sheet – the profit and loss account.

Note that it is not a current asset – it is not cash.

Share capital and reserves show how much the company is worth. They show how the assets have been financed – do you remember the accounting equation?

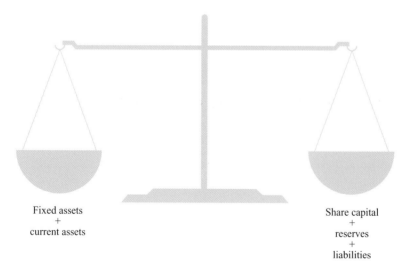

Fixed assets	Share capital
+	+
current assets	reserves
	+
	liabilities

Reserves are profits. Retained profits are a major source of finance for all successful companies.

WORKED EXAMPLE

The following balance sheet as at 31 January 20*3 for Vorg Ltd is given.

This year's profits have not yet been incorporated into the balance sheet.

The net profit for the year is £25,000.

This has been retained in the business and has been used to purchase additional fixed assets.

£5,000 is to be transferred to a general reserve.

	£	£
Fixed assets at cost		100,000
Current assets	50,000	
Creditors: amounts falling due in less than one year	30,000	20,000
		120,000
Share capital and reserves		
Ordinary shares of £1 each		80,000
Profit and loss account		40,000
		120,000

Required A balance sheet as at 31 January after making necessary adjustments.

Answer

Vorg Ltd
Balance sheet as at 31 January 20*3

	£	£
Fixed assets at cost (£100,000 + £25,000)		125,000
Current assets	50,000	
Creditors: amounts falling due in less than one year	30,000	20,000
		145,000
Share capital and reserves		
Ordinary shares of £1 each		80,000
General reserve		5,000
Profit and loss account (£40,000 + £20,000)		60,000
		145,000

Any transfer to general reserve must be shown as an appropriation of profits.

WORKED EXAMPLE

The following information is given for Bowman Ltd for the year ended 31 October 20*3:

	£
Net profit for year	210,000
Corporation tax due	65,000
Interim ordinary dividend paid	36,000
Proposed final ordinary dividend	48,000
Transfer to general reserve	15,000

Required Prepare a profit and loss appropriation account for the year ended 31 October 20*3.

Answer

Bowman Ltd
Profit and loss appropriation account for the year ended 31 October 20*3

	£	£
Net profit for year		210,000
Less Corporation tax		65,000
Profit for year after taxation		145,000
Less Transfer to general reserve	15,000	
dividends:		
interim ordinary dividend paid	36,000	
proposed ordinary dividend	48,000	99,000
Retained profit for year		46,000

The balance sheet would show increases in both revenue reserves:

- general reserve would increase by £15,000
- profit and loss account would increase by £46,000.

SHAREHOLDER'S FUNDS

These are made up of:

- share capital of the company and
- all reserves.

All reserves belong to the ordinary shareholders of a company – reserves are part of the shareholders' funds.

Reserves fall into two main categories:

- **revenue reserves** – these reserves arise from the normal trading activities of the business; they are created at the discretion of the directors of a company. They are profits that have been withheld from dividend distribution in order to strengthen the financial position of the company. If the directors wish to use them they are available for distribution to the shareholders in the form of cash dividends.
  The two revenue reserves most commonly encountered are the:
  - general reserve
  - profit and loss account.

- **capital reserves** are amounts set aside out of profits but are not provisions. They arise from capital transactions and adjustments to the capital structure of the company. They are not available for transfer to the profit and loss appropriation account so they are not available for cash dividend purposes.
  Capital reserves include:
  - share premium accounts
  - revaluation reserve.

Share premium account is credited when a company issues shares at a price that is greater than the nominal value of the shares.

WORKED EXAMPLE

- 5,000 ordinary shares of £1 each are issued by Boom Ltd at £1.50 each
- 2 million ordinary shares of 50p each are issued by Gatwood plc at 80p each
- 90,000 ordinary shares of 10p are issued by Jibe Ltd at 40p each
- 2,500 ordinary shares of £5 each are issued by Gerrat plc at £8 each
- 1 million ordinary shares of 5p each are issued by Ken Platt plc at 35p each.

Required Calculate the amounts to be credited to
  (a) the ordinary share capital account
  (b) the share premium account.

Also indicate the total amount of finance raised by the share issue.

Answer

	Ordinary Share Capital Account £	Share Premium Account £	Finance Raised £
Boom Ltd	5,000	2,500	7,500
Gatwood plc	1,000,000	600,000	1,600,000
Jibe Ltd	9,000	27,000	36,000
Gerrat plc	12,500	7,500	20,000
Ken Platt plc	50,000	300,000	350,000

A share premium account only arises when a company issues shares.

O EXAMINATION TIP

Always be precise in written questions.

'A share premium account is opened when shares are sold at a price above their par value' is imprecise and would not gain marks.

If you sell some shares through a stockbroker at a higher price than you paid for them this will not give rise to a share premium. This is a private transaction and is not recorded in the company's books of account.

The company will record the change of ownership in its register of shareholdings otherwise you would continue to receive copies of the annual report and any dividends that the company might pay out in the future.

How does the issue of shares affect the balance sheet of the company?

In some of the examples and questions that follow the company bank balance is shown separately from other current assets so that any effect that occurs because of cash transactions can be clearly seen.

WORKED EXAMPLE

The summarised balance sheet as at 31 December 20*2 of Swelt plc is as follows:

	£	£
Fixed assets at cost		400,000
Current assets	74,000	
Bank balance	6,000	
	80,000	
Creditors: amounts falling due in less than one year	30,000	50,000
		450,000
Share capital and reserves		
Ordinary shares of £1 each		350,000
Profit and loss account		100,000
		450,000

On 31 January 20*3 the company issues a further 200,000 ordinary shares of £1 each at a price of £1.30 each.

Required Prepare a summarised balance sheet as at 31 January 20*3 for Swelt plc as it would appear immediately after the share issue.

Answer

Swelt plc summarised balance sheet as at 31 January 20*3

	£	£
Fixed assets at cost		400,000
Current assets	74,000	
Bank balance (6,000 + 260,000)	266,000	
	340,000	
Creditors: amounts falling due in less than one year	30,000	310,000
		710,000
Share capital and reserves		
Ordinary shares of £1 each (350,000 + 200,000)		550,000
Share premium account		60,000
Profit and loss account		100,000
		710,000

WORKED EXAMPLE

The summarised balance sheet as at 31 October 20*3 for Capdo Ltd is as follows:

	£	£
Fixed assets at cost		17,000
Current assets	10,000	
Bank balance	2,000	
	12,000	
Creditors: amounts falling due in less than one year	10,000	2,000
		19,000
Share capital and reserves		
Ordinary shares of 10p each		10,000
Profit and loss account		9,000
		19,000

On 1 November 20*3 Capdo Ltd issued a further 200,000 ordinary shares of 10p each at a premium of 40p each.

Required Prepare a summarised balance sheet as at 1 November 20*3 for Capdo Ltd after the share issue.

Answer

Capdo Ltd
Summarised balance sheet as at 1 November 20*3

	£	£
Fixed assets at cost		17,000
Current assets	10,000	
Bank balance *(2,000 + 100,000)*	102,000	
	112,000	
Creditors: amounts falling due in less than one year	10,000	102,000
		119,000
Share capital and reserves		
Ordinary shares of 10p each *(£10,000 + £20,000)*		30,000
Share premium account *(200,000 × 40p)*		80,000
Profit and loss account		9,000
		119,000

QUESTION 5

The summarised balance sheet of Duvase Ltd as at 30 November 20*3 is shown:

	£	£
Fixed assets at cost		120,000
Current assets	22,000	
Bank balance	15,000	
	37,000	
Creditors: amounts falling due in less than one year	8,000	29,000
		149,000
Share capital and reserves		
Ordinary shares of £1 each		100,000
Profit and loss account		49,000
		149,000

On 1 December 20*3 Duvase Ltd issued a further 200,000 ordinary shares at a price of £1.60 per share.

Required Prepare a summarised balance sheet as at 1 December 20*3 as it would appear after the share issue has been completed.

QUESTION 6

The summarised balance sheet of D. Lilly Ltd as at 31 March 20*3 is shown:

	£	£
Fixed assets at cost		500,000
Current assets	125,000	
Bank balance	8,000	
	133,000	
Creditors: amounts falling due in less than one year	96,000	37,000
		537,000
Share capital and reserves		
Ordinary shares of 50 pence each		450,000
Profit and loss account		87,000
		537,000

On 1 April 20*3 D. Lilly Ltd issued a further 400,000 ordinary shares at a price of 80 pence per share.

Immediately after the share issue the company purchased additional fixed assets of £300,000, paying by cheque.

Required Prepare the balance sheet as at 1 April 20*3, immediately after the share issue and the purchase of the additional fixed assets.

Up to now we have always shown assets at cost on balance sheets.

QUESTION

Which concepts are being applied when assets are being valued at cost?

Answer
- The going concern concept.
- Objectivity.

REVALUATION RESERVES

Many limited companies revalue some of their fixed assets to reflect an increase in the value of those assets and to ensure that the balance sheet reflects the permanent change in the value of the assets and therefore the capital structure of the business (remember the accounting equation?).

Generally, the only assets to be revalued upwards are land and buildings.

Why do companies revalue their assets while sole traders do not?

If the company's assets do not reflect a current market value the company could be subject to a hostile takeover bid by a predatory rival company.

The increase in the value of the fixed assets is matched with an increase in reserves. The revaluation reserve is a capital reserve and is not therefore available for dividend purposes.

This reserve is a 'profit' due to inflation that will not be realised as cash until the asset is sold.

The creation of a revaluation reserve clearly illustrates the earlier point about reserves not being cash put aside for use in the future. All that has happened is that the top part of the balance sheet has been increased by the fixed asset being revalued and the bottom part has been increased by the same amount.

EXAMPLE

I purchased my house a number of years ago for £30,000. I confidently know that I can sell it now for over £100,000. This increase in value cannot be used to buy a new car or to pay for a meal for my family. It is not cash – it is an unrealised profit.

Reserves are not piles of cash waiting to be spent! If only they were!

In the examples that follow, some businesses are private limited companies and others are public limited companies. Treat both types in the same way. Any differences in presentation will be indicated later.

Also notice the par value of the shares. The value ranges from 1 penny to £1. The par value can be any amount; it will not affect your working of a question. It may affect the ability of the company to raise future finance.

WORKED EXAMPLE

The summarised balance sheet of Dox plc as at 30 June 20*3 shows:

	£	£
Fixed assets at cost		400,000
Less Aggregate depreciation		50,000
		350,000
Current assets	99,000	
Bank balance	1,000	
	100,000	
Creditors: amounts due in less than one year	40,000	60,000
		410,000
Share capital and reserves		
Ordinary shares of 25 pence each		400,000
Profit and loss account		10,000
		410,000

The fixed assets are revalued at £600,000 on 1 July 20*3.

Required Prepare the balance sheet of Dox plc as at 1 July 20*3 after the assets have been revalued.

Answer

Dox plc
Balance sheet as at 1 July 20*3

	£	£
Fixed assets at valuation		600,000
Current assets	99,000	
Bank balance	1,000	
	100,000	
Creditors: amounts falling due in less than one year	40,000	60,000
		660,000
Share capital and reserves		
Ordinary shares of 25 pence each		400,000
Revaluation reserve		250,000
Profit and loss account		10,000
		660,000

WORKED EXAMPLE *continued*

Workings

Dr	Fixed assets account	Cr	Dr	Provision for depreciation of fixed assets account	Cr
Bal b/d	400,000				
Revn Res	200,000		Revn Res 50,000	Bal b/d 50,000	

Dr	Revaluation reserve	Cr
	Fixed assets 200,000	
	Depr of fixed assets 50,000	

Note
- The fixed assets are 'at valuation'.
- There has been no change in the bank balance.
- The reserve must be called revaluation reserve.

QUESTION 7

The summarised balance sheet of Ousby Ltd as at 31 October 20*3 is given:

	£	£
Fixed assets at cost		250,000
Current assets	40,000	
Bank balance	8,000	
	48,000	
Creditors: amounts falling due within one year	36,000	12,000
		262,000
Share capital and reserves		
Ordinary shares of 10 pence each		200,000
Profit and loss account		62,000
		262,000

The fixed assets were revalued at £400,000 on 1 November 20*3.

Required Prepare the balance sheet as at 1 November 20*3, after the assets were revalued.

QUESTION 8

The summarised balance sheet of Graf Ltd as at 28 February 20*3 is given:

	£	£
Fixed assets at cost		75,000
Current assets	12,000	
Bank balance	2,000	
	14,000	
Creditors: amounts falling due within one year	9,000	5,000
		80,000
Share capital and reserves		
Ordinary shares of 1 penny each		60,000
Profit and loss account		20,000
		80,000

The fixed assets were revalued at £200,000 on 1 March 20*3.

Required Prepare the balance sheet as at 1 March 20*3, after the assets were revalued.

DEBENTURES

Many limited companies raise additional capital by issuing debentures. Debentures are long-term loans to the company. A debenture is the legal document issued by the company that is managing the debt. Debentures are generally secured against the company's assets. The security may be fixed, that is it relates to a specific asset or group of assets, or it may be a floating charge where no specific assets are identified. If the company were to be wound up, the debenture holders would be in a safer position than either the preference shareholders or the ordinary shareholders because of this security. Debentures are usually for a fixed time period and are redeemable by the company at the end of that period.

Like all forms of borrowing, the debt has to be serviced and the interest due will usually be paid half-yearly. The interest that the company pays to the holders of the debentures, like all interest payable, is a charge against the profits and appears as an expense on the profit and loss account.

Note

Debenture interest is not an appropriation of profits. It must be paid whether the company is profitable or not.

An issue of debentures will have the following effect on a balance sheet:

Increase bank balance   Increase creditors: amounts due in more than one year.

OR

Decrease bank overdraft   Increase creditors: amounts due in more than one year.

Debentures are not part of the share capital. Debenture holders are not shareholders.

We show debentures on the balance sheet under the heading 'Creditors: amounts falling due after more than one year'.

The amount is deducted from the total assets less current liabilities.

Here is an example of how debentures should be treated in a balance sheet.

EXAMPLE

Studret plc
Summarised balance sheet as at 30 September 20*3

	£	£
Fixed assets at cost		750,000
Current assets	150,000	
Creditors: amounts falling due within one year	60,000	90,000
Total assets less current liabilities		840,000
Creditors: amounts falling due after more than one year		
7% Debentures (2035)		200,000
		640,000
Share capital and reserves		640,000

Debentures should be shown in the balance sheet with all their details, e.g. '7% debentures (2035)'. This means that the interest to be paid by the company to the lenders is 7% per annum. The date shown means that the company will redeem the debentures in the year 2035.

Let us put the parts of the final accounts together.

Here are two examples showing the layout:

WORKED EXAMPLE

The following information relates to Becktom plc (all necessary adjustments, transfer and provisions have already been made):

	£
Fixed assets at valuation	590,000
Current assets	283,000
Creditors: amounts falling due within one year	170,000
6% debentures (2012)	90,000
Net profit for the year	207,300
Corporation tax due	73,300
Transfer to general reserve	25,000
Interim dividend paid	
– ordinary shares	8,000
– preference shares	3,000
Proposed dividends	
– ordinary shares	17,000
– preference shares	3,000
Share premium account	20,000
Revaluation reserve	80,000
General reserve	75,000
Profit and loss account	138,000
Authorised share capital	
Ordinary shares of £1 each	500,000
7% preference shares of £1 each	250,000
Issued share capital	
Ordinary shares of £1 each	200,000
7% preference shares	100,000

Required (a) Prepare the profit and loss appropriation account for the year ended 31 March 20*3.

(b) Prepare the balance sheet as at 31 March 20*3.

Answer

(a)

Becktom plc
Profit and loss appropriation account for the year ended 31 March 20*3

	£	£	£
Net profit			207,300
Corporation tax			73,300
			134,000
Transfer to general reserve			25,000
			109,000
Dividends: interim paid			
Ordinary shares	8,000		
Preference shares	3,000	11,000	
Dividends: proposed			
Ordinary shares	17,000		
Preference shares	3,000	20,000	31,000
Retained profits for the year			78,000

WORKED EXAMPLE *continued*

(b)

Balance sheet as at 31 March 20*3

	£	£
Fixed assets at valuation		590,000
Current assets	283,000	
Creditors: amounts falling due within one year	170,000	113,000
		703,000
Creditors: amounts falling due after more than one year		
6% debentures (2012)		90,000
		613,000
Authorised share capital		
Ordinary shares of £1		500,000
6% preference shares of £1 each		250,000
Share capital and reserves		
Ordinary shares of £1 each		200,000
6% preference shares of £1 each		100,000
Share premium account		20,000
Revaluation reserve		80,000
General reserve		75,000
Profit and loss account		138,000
		613,000

WORKED EXAMPLE

Kneal plc provides the following trial balance as at 31 December 20*3 which has been prepared **after** completion of the profit and loss account for the year ended 31 December 20*3:

	£	£
Profit before tax for the year ended 31 December 20*3		499,000
Profit and loss account (retained profits) balance at 1 January 20*3		301,700
General reserve		25,000
Revaluation reserve		85,000
Share premium account		125,000
7% preference shares of £1 each		200,000
Ordinary shares of £1 each		250,000
Patents	75,000	
Land and buildings at valuation	1,000,000	
Vehicles	130,000	
Investments 4¼% Treasury stock (2032)	150,000	
Stock	142,000	
Trade debtors	85,000	
Trade creditors		18,000
Interim dividend paid 3 August 20*3		
Ordinary shares	28,000	
Preference shares	7,000	
Debenture interest owing		3,300
6% Debentures (2020)		110,000
	1,617,000	1,617,000

The following information is also available:

The directors recommend:

1 transfer to general reserve £50,000
2 a final dividend on ordinary shares of £42,000 be provided
3 a final dividend on preference shares of £7,000 be provided
4 a provision for corporation tax £154,000 be made.

Required (a) Prepare the profit and loss appropriation account for the year
               ended 31 December 20*3 for Kneal plc.
          (b) Prepare a balance sheet as at 31 December 20*3.

Answer

Kneal plc
Profit and loss appropriation account for the year ended 31 December 20*3

	£	£	£
Profit before tax			499,000
Corporation tax			154,000
Profit after tax			345,000
Transfer to general reserve			50,000
			295,000
Dividends paid			
Ordinary share		28,000	
Preference shares		7,000	
Dividend proposed			
Ordinary shares		42,000	
Preference shares		7,000	84,000
Retained profit for the year			211,000

Balance sheet as at 31 December 20*3

	£	£	£
Intangible assets			
Patents			75,000
Tangible fixed assets			
Land and buildings at valuation			1,000,000
Vehicles			130,000
Investments			
4¼% Treasury stock (2032)			150,000
			1,355,000
Current assets			
Stock		142,000	
Trade debtors		85,000	
		227,000	
Creditors: amounts falling due in less than one year			
Trade creditors	18,000		
Corporation tax due	154,000		
Proposed preference dividend	7,000		
Proposed ordinary dividend	42,000		
Debenture interest due	3,300	224,300	2,700
			1,357,700

Creditors: amounts falling due after more than one year	£
6% debenture (2020)	110,000
	1,247,700
Capital and reserves	
Ordinary shares of £1 each	250,000
7% preference shares of £1 each	200,000
Share premium account	125,000
Revaluation reserve	85,000
General reserve	75,000
Profit and loss account	512,700
	1,247,700

Points to note:
Three types of fixed assets have been identified: intangible, tangible and investments.
Capital reserves are shown before revenue reserves.

DIFFERENT TYPES OF FIXED ASSETS

In the balance sheet of a limited company, we need to distinguish between the different types of fixed assets.

1. **Intangible** assets – these are non-physical assets, i.e. assets that cannot be seen or touched. Example include patents and brand names, e.g. the brand name 'Coca Cola' or 'Oxo' etc, would come under this heading.
2. **Tangible** assets – these are physical assets, i.e. those that can be seen and touched, e.g. delivery vehicles, premises etc.
3. **Investments** – if investments are to be kept for a number of years, they are treated as fixed assets. However, if the intention is to sell the investments within the current year, they would be classified as current assets.

The aggregate depreciation on fixed assets should be shown in the balance sheet of a limited company along with any revaluations of fixed assets that have taken place during the year.

The accounts that limited companies produce are used by the managers of that company for decision-making purposes. If the accounts used by the managers were published in this very useful form, rivals might gain access to much information that could undermine the company.

Although legally a limited company must send its shareholders and lenders a set of accounts, the law protects the company by allowing it to publish an 'abridged' version.

At this stage of your studies you will not be asked to prepare a set of final accounts for publication.

The final accounts of limited companies for publication will dealt with in Book 2 and may be examined in your A Level year examinations.

Some time after the final accounts are prepared and checked for their truthfulness and accuracy, the 'abridged' version is sent to the shareholders and other interested parties.

The published accounts are accompanied by:

■ a director's report
■ an auditor's report.

DIRECTOR'S REPORT

This is rather like a school or college report in that it outlines the progress of the company over the past year and also it looks towards performance in the future.

It is a legal requirement that the directors do report to the shareholders (Companies Act 1985) and the report must contain the following:

- a review of performance during the year
- the position of the company at the end of the year
- the main activities of the company during the year plus any major changes in activities that may have taken place during the year
- important changes to fixed assets that have taken place during the year
- particulars of important events affecting the company since the financial year end
- an indication of any likely future developments in the business of the company
- an indication of research and development undertaken by the company
- amounts of recommended dividends and transfers to reserves
- names of people who were or are directors during the year
- the number of shares and debentures in the company held by directors
- any charitable donations or donations to political parties if these donations exceed £200
- information regarding the health, safety and welfare of e mployees while at work
- if the company employs more than 250 people, a statement on the policy regarding the employment of disabled people.

AUDITOR'S REPORT

This is a report addressed to the shareholders, not to the directors.

The auditors must ensure that:

- the company keeps proper books of account
- proper records are kept
- the final accounts are in agreement with the records kept.

The auditors must report on whether, in their opinion:

- the balance sheet and profit and loss account have been prepared in accordance with the requirements of the Companies Act
- the balance sheet give a 'true and fair view' of the company's affairs at the end of the financial year
- the profit and loss account gives a 'true and fair view' of the profit or loss for the financial year.

Chapter summary

- A limited company has a legal status separate from that of its shareholders.
- Liability of the members is limited to the amount they have paid or have agreed to pay for their shares.
- Public limited companies may issue shares to the general public but private limited companies cannot.
- Finance is raised by selling shares to preference shareholders and ordinary shareholders; further finance may be raised by issuing debenture stock.
- Reserves are past profits ploughed back into the company.
- Revenue reserves are past profits earned through normal activities of the company.
- Capital reserves are past profits derived through 'non-normal' activities.

Self-test questions

- Explain what is meant by 'limited liability'.
- Does a sole trader have limited liability?
- Does a shareholder in a limited company have limited liability?
- Define what is meant by the 'par value' of a share.
- The owners of a limited company are its directors. True or false?
- The owners of a limited company are its shareholders. True or false?
- .... are the rewards given to shareholders of a limited company. Debenture holders earn ....

- How are current liabilities described in the balance sheet of a limited company?
- A limited company must be profitable and also have .... in order to pay dividends to shareholders.
- Explain the difference between authorised share capital and issued share capital.
- Reserves are cash put aside for future use. True or false?
- Identify the two components of shareholders' funds.
- Identify the two types of reserves.
- Explain what is meant by the term 'share premium account'.
- Identify two reports that must be sent to shareholders along with the final accounts of a limited company.

TEST QUESTIONS

QUESTION 9

Douglas Ltd supplies the following information after the first year of trading:

Trial balance as at 28 February 20*3

	Dr £	Cr £
Net profit for year		312,000
Fixed assets at cost	300,000	
Current assets	150,000	
Interim dividend paid	40,000	
Ordinary shares of £1 each		178,000
	490,000	490,000

Additional information
The directors wish to transfer £50,000 to general reserve and recommend a final dividend of £60,000; they wish to provide for corporation tax due £82,000.

Required Prepare:
(a) a profit and loss appropriation account for the year ended 28 February 20*3
(b) a balance sheet as at 28 February 20*3.

QUESTION 10

Donald Ltd provides the following information after the first year of trading:

Trial balance as at 31 August 20*3

	Dr £	Cr £
Fixed assets at cost	200,000	
Current assets	150,000	
Ordinary shares of 50 pence each		100,000
Net profit for year		276,000
Interim dividend paid	26,000	
	376,000	376,000

Additional information
The directors wish to transfer £40,000 to general reserve and recommend a final dividend of £50,000; they wish to provide for corporation tax due £65,000.

Required Prepare:
(a) a profit and loss appropriation account for the year ended 31 August 20*3
(b) a balance sheet as at 31 August 20*3.

QUESTION 11

Hox Ltd provides the following summarised balance sheet as at 31 May 20*3:

	£	£
Fixed assets at cost		180,000
Current assets	23,000	
Bank balance	18,000	
	41,000	
Creditors: amounts falling due in less than one year	40,000	1,000
		181,000
Share capital and reserves		
Ordinary shares of 25 pence each		70,000
General reserve		30,000
Profit and loss account		81,000
		181,000

The fixed assets were revalued at £300,000 on 1 June 20*3.

Required Prepare a summarised balance sheet as at 1 June 20*3, after revaluing the fixed assets.

QUESTION 12

Wong Ltd provides the following summarised balance sheet as at 31 December 20*3:

	£	£
Fixed assets at cost		30,000
Current assets	46,000	
Bank balance	2,000	
	44,000	
Creditors: amounts falling due within one year	24,000	20,000
		50,000
Share capital and reserves		
Ordinary shares of 10 pence each		40,000
Profit and loss account		10,000
		50,000

The fixed assets were revalued on 1 January 20*4 at £210,000.

Required Prepare a summarised balance sheet as at 1 January 20*4, after revaluing the fixed assets.

QUESTION 13

The summarised balance sheet of Norest Ltd as at 31 January 20*3 is given:

	£	£
Fixed assets at cost		60,000
Current assets	15,000	
Bank balance	1,000	
	16,000	
Creditors: amounts falling due in less than one year	9,000	7,000
		67,000
Share capital and reserves		
Ordinary shares of 5 pence each		50,000
Profit and loss account		17,000
		67,000

On 1 February 20*3 Norest Ltd issued a further 100,000 ordinary shares at a price of 30 pence per share.

Required Prepare a summarised balance sheet as at 1 February 20*3, after the new shares were issued.

QUESTION 14

The summarised balance sheet of Trosh Ltd as at 31 October 20*3 is given:

	£	£	£
Fixed assets at cost			360,000
Current assets		27,000	
Creditors: amounts falling due in less than one year			
Trade creditors	12,000		
Bank overdraft	6,000	18,000	9,000
			369,000
Share capital and reserves			
Ordinary shares of £1 each			300,000
General reserve			50,000
Profit and loss account			19,000
			369,000

On 1 November Trosh Ltd issued a further 200,000 ordinary shares at a price of £1.75 each.

Required Prepare a summarised balance sheet as at 1 November 20*3, after the new shares were issued.

QUESTION 15

The summarised balance sheet of Smith-Patel Ltd as at 31 March 20*3 is given:

	£	£
Fixed assets at cost		500,000
Current assets	100,000	
Bank balance	20,000	
	120,000	
Creditors: amounts falling due in less than one year	70,000	50,000
		550,000
Share capital and reserves		
Ordinary shares of £1 each		400,000
Profit and loss account		150,000
		550,000

On 1 April 20*3 Smith-Patel Ltd issued a further 200,000 £1 ordinary shares at £1.50. On the same date the company revalued the fixed assets at £750,000.

Required A summarised balance sheet as at 1 April 20*3, after the revaluation of fixed assets and the share issue.

QUESTION 16

The summarised balance sheet of Wiley-Fox Ltd as at 30 November 20*3 is given:

	£	£	£
Fixed assets at cost			150,000
Less aggregate depreciation			35,000
			115,000
Current assets		16,000	
Creditors: amounts falling due in less than one year			
Trade creditors	10,000		
Bank overdraft	2,000	12,000	4,000
			119,000
Share capital and reserves			
Ordinary shares of 25 pence			80,000
Profit and loss account			39,000
			119,000

On 1 December 20*3 Wiley-Fox Ltd issued a further 100,000 ordinary shares at 40 pence per share. On the same date the company revalued the fixed assets at £150,000.

Required A summarised balance sheet as at 1 December 20*3, after the revaluation of fixed assets and the share issue.

QUESTION 17

The following trial balance has been extracted from the books of Stephanie Hood Ltd. on 30 April 20*3:

	Dr £	Cr £
Net profit for the year		267,432
Issued share capital share capital		
Ordinary shares of £1 each		400,000
6% preference shares of £1 each		100,000
General reserve		70,000
Profit and loss account		80,000
Fixed assets at cost	950,000	
Provision for depreciation of fixed assets		230,000
Stock as at 30 April 20*3	143,461	
Trade debtors	21,380	
Trade creditors		17,211
Bank balance	34,802	
Interim dividends paid		
ordinary shares	12,000	
preference shares	3,000	
	1,164,643	1,164,643

Additional information

The directors recommend:
1. a transfer to general reserve £50,000
2. a final ordinary dividend of £26,000 be provided
3. a final preference dividend be provided
4. provision for corporation tax £58,196 be made.

Required Prepare:
(a) a profit and loss appropriation account for the year ended 30 April 20*3
(b) a summarised balance sheet as at 30 April 20*3.

QUESTION 18

Pling Ltd has an authorised capital of 500,000 ordinary shares of £1 each and 250,000

10% preference shares of £1 each. The following trial balance has been extracted from the books of account at 30 September 20*3:

	Dr £	Cr £
Issued capital		
100,000 ordinary shares of £1 each		100,000
30,000 10% preference shares of £1 each		30,000
Buildings at cost	350,000	
Office equipment at cost	30,000	
Delivery vehicles at cost	60,000	
Provision for depreciation		
buildings		180,000
office equipment		15,000
delivery vehicles		36,000
Trade debtors	16,840	
Trade creditors		6,970
Stock as at 1 October 20*2	14,710	
Purchases	183,940	
Sales		412,480
Motor expenses	12,470	
Rent and rates	10,100	
Wages	57,200	
General expenses	18,520	
Profit and loss account		27,000
General reserve		10,000
Bank balance	41,220	
Provision for doubtful debts		550
Interim dividends paid		
ordinary shares	20,000	
preference shares	3,000	
	818,000	818,000

Additional information at 30 September 20*3
- Stock was valued at £16,320.
- Wages accrued and unpaid amounted to £1,550.
- Rates paid in advance amounted to £600.
- Provision for doubtful debts is to be maintained at 5% of debts outstanding at the year-end.
- The directors recommend:
  1. a transfer to general reserve £20,000
  2. a final dividend on ordinary shares of £25,000 be provided
  3. a final preference dividend be provided
  4. provision for corporation tax £28,420 be made.

Required Prepare:
(a) a trading and profit and loss account for the year ended 30 September 20*3
(b) a balance sheet as at 30 September 20*3.

CHAPTER
TWENTY FIVE

Cash-flow Statements

The **trading and profit and loss accounts** of a business concentrate on the determination of profits or losses, since profits should ensure the long-term survival of the business.

The **balance sheet** concentrates on the state of affairs of the business at one moment in time.

Cash-flow statements concentrate on cash. Cash-flow statements reveal information that is not disclosed overtly in the trading and profit and loss account and balance sheet.

These three statements taken together show summaries of most of the financial information required by the users of accounting information. The cash-flow statement takes information from a variety of sources to show an overall picture of the monies flowing into and out of the business during the financial year.

The statement concentrates on liquidity and may help to explain why, for example, a business may need a bank overdraft in a year when profits were buoyant.

FRS1 is intended to ensure that businesses report their cash generation and cash absorption in a way that makes the statements comparable with other businesses.

The statement provides 'information that assists in the assessment of . . . liquidity, solvency and financial adaptability'. It is intended to show information that is not available from examining the profit and loss account and balance sheet. It is intended to fill in gaps in the available published information. The opening balance sheet of a company shows the state of affairs of the company on the first day of the financial year. The closing balance sheet shows the position on the last day of the financial year. What has gone on during the year?

The profit and loss account bridges the gap from one important perspective: profits.

The cash-flow statement bridges the gap from the equally important perspective of cash.

This concentration on liquidity is very important, since the inability to generate cash resources is the biggest single reason for many businesses going into liquidation.

All but the smallest companies are required to produce the statement.

Even though small companies and sole traders do not have to produce a cash-flow statement, they may find that it is a useful addition to their year-end accounting information.

> **Specification coverage:**
> AQA 11.3.
>
> **By the end of this chapter you should be able to:**
> - list the main elements in a cash-flow statement
> - identify the cash flows that are included under each heading
> - comment on the purposes of producing cash-flow statements.

Cash flows arise through monies being received by a business and monies being paid by it through financial transactions.

Cash is cash in hand, balances at banks (or other financial institutions), bank overdrafts and any other deposits that are repayable to the business on demand.

Changes in cash held by a business over the period of a year are not the same as the profits generated by the business over the year.

A business could have a positive bank balance at the start of a year, make a profit over the year and yet end the year with a bank overdraft.

A business could improve its bank balance over the course of a year yet have incurred a loss.

HOW CAN THIS BE SO?

WORKED EXAMPLE

The following transactions have been undertaken by a business:

	PROFIT	CASH
Purchases of goods for resale for cash	no effect	reduce £200
Purchase of goods for resale on credit £300	no effect	no effect
Sale of goods (which cost £150) for cash for £400	£250	increase £400
Sale of goods (which cost £250) on credit £600	£350	no effect
Depreciation of fixed assets £2,500	reduce £2,500	no effect
Increase in provision for doubtful debts by £67	reduce £67	
Purchase of new delivery van for £23,500 cash		reduce £23,500
Sale of old computer NBV £150 for £60 cash		
Sale of office equipment NBV £450 for £460 cash		
Injection of £5,000 cash by proprietor		
Cash drawings £1,067 by proprietor		

Required Indicate the effects each transaction will have on profits and cash.

Answer

In the case of both sets of purchases of goods for resale, purchases in the trading account increases but so does closing stock, so there is no overall change in the cost of sales and so there can be no change in gross profit (or net profit).

Depreciation does reduce profits since it is a profit and loss expense, but there is no cash flow involved in providing for depreciation.

The increase in the provision for doubtful debts will reduce profits because it is an entry in the profit and loss account, thus reducing profits by £67, but it is simply a debit entry in the profit and loss account and a credit entry in the provision for doubtful debts account. It is a 'book entry' and no cash changes hands.

The purchase of a new delivery van is an example of capital expenditure and so no entry appears on the profit and loss account (at the year end, depreciation will be charged to the profit and loss account).

The sale of the computer brings £60 cash into the business. The loss on the sale is a book transfer from the disposal account to the debit of the profit and loss account. So profits will be reduced by £90.

Similarly, with the office equipment, the profit on disposal is purely a transfer of figures from one account to another (disposal account to profit and loss account). Profits will increase by £10. However, the movement of cash is £460.

£5,000 cash paid into the business clearly involves a movement of cash from the proprietor's private resources to the business bank account. However, this transaction involves a capital receipt for the business and should not be recorded in the profit and loss account.

Similarly, drawings of £1,067 will reduce cash but will not affect profits.

Some examples of transactions that will reduce cash balances in a business but that would not affect profits:

SOLE TRADER	LIMITED COMPANY
Drawings	
	Dividends
Capital expenditure	Capital expenditure
Withdrawals of capital	
Repayments of loans	Repayment of loans
	Repayment of debentures
	Payment of taxation

Some examples of transactions that would increase the cash balances but that would not affect profits:

SOLE TRADER	LIMITED COMPANY
Capital introduced	
	Issue of shares and/or debentures
Sale of fixed assets	Sale of fixed assets
	Tax refunds

Some examples of transactions that would reduce profits (or increase losses) in a business but that would not affect cash:

SOLE TRADER	LIMITED COMPANY
Increase in provision for depreciation	Increase in provision for depreciation
Increase in provision for doubtful debts	Increase in provision for doubtful debts
Loss on sale of fixed assets	Loss on sale of fixed assets

Some examples of transactions that would increase profits (or decrease losses) in business but that would not affect cash:

SOLE TRADER	LIMITED COMPANY
Decrease in provision for depreciation	Decrease in provision for depreciation
Decrease in provision for doubtful debts	Decrease in provision for doubtful debts
Profit on sale of fixed assets	Profit on sale of fixed assets

It is most important that you understand the clear distinction between cash flows and profits. The distinction is often asked for in examination questions.

FRS1 makes cash-flow statements a mandatory requirement for most limited companies. The cash-flow statement should be included with the published profit and loss accounts and balance sheet.

A published cash-flow statement for a limited company should list cash flows for the financial year under the following headings (FRS1):

- operating activities
- returns on investments and servicing of finance
- taxation
- capital expenditure and financial investment
- *acquisitions and disposals (this section is related to cash-flow statements for group accounts)*
- equity dividends paid
- management of liquid resources
- financing.

Note
- The statement deals with cash inflows and cash outflows. Indeed, FRS1 states that 'transactions that do not result in cash … should not be reported …'.
- The headings used when preparing a cash-flow statement should be presented in the order shown above.

THE HEADINGS EXPLAINED

- **Operating activities** – shows the cash effects of transactions relating to the normal trading activities of the business.
  The calculation is shown in detail in the 'reconciliation of operating profit to net cash flow from operating activities'.

- **Returns on investments and servicing of finance** – shows inflows from interest and dividends received by the business and outflows of cash in the form of interest paid and dividends on non-equity shares (i.e. dividends paid during the year to preference shareholders).

- **Taxation** – cash flows under this heading are payments to and from the tax authorities. Taxes refunded to the business are treated as inflows while payments paid by the business to the Inland Revenue are outflows of cash.

- **Capital expenditure and financial investment.** Cash outflows relate to the purchase of fixed assets and investments that are not included in the management of liquid resources. Cash inflows result from sales or disposals of fixed assets.

- **Acquisitions and disposals.** *Deals with cash-flow statements for group accounts and is outside the scope of AS or A level specifications.*

- **Equity dividends** paid refers to dividends paid by the company to ordinary shareholders.

- **Management of liquid resources** – liquid resources are assets held for less than one year. They are usually term deposits and government securities.
  Cash inflows would result from the sale of such assets. Cash outflows result from the purchase of such investments.

- **Financing** – cash inflows would include receipts from a share issue, a debenture issue or any other long-term borrowing. Cash outflows would include repayments of long-term loans and payments to purchase back the company's own shares.

You need to learn these headings.

○ EXAMINATION TIP

You may find this mnemonic useful:

ORTCEMF.

Some students have learned:

'Oprah Returns Tax Cos 'Er Man is Fine'.

Not exactly English that Shakespeare would have condoned, or English that will score four Quality of Language marks! But if it helps you to remember the headings …

FRS1 requires that two reconciliation statements are produced:

- a reconciliation between operating profits and net cash flow from operating activities
- a reconciliation between the movement in cash during the year and the movement in net debt.

These statements are not part of the cash-flow statment and should be shown separately.

A reconciliation is the bringing together of two apparently differing items.

In an earlier chapter we used a reconciliation statement to bring together the balance shown in the cash book bank column so that it agreed with the balance shown in the bank statement produced by the business's bankers.

RECONCILIATION OF OPERATING PROFIT TO NET CASH FLOW FROM OPERATING ACTIVITIES

This is technical jargon saying 'let us bring together the profit shown in the profit and loss account and the cash generated by the business' because the two are unlikely to be the same even though they are derived from the same books of account.

The operating profits are adjusted to take into account movements in:

■ stocks
■ debtors
■ creditors and

non-cash items like:

■ depreciation charges for the year
■ profits or losses on the sales of fixed assets.

WORKED EXAMPLE

Ghina Ltd provides the following information for the year ended 30 June 20*3:

	£
Operating profit for the year	187,612
Depreciation of fixed assets for the year	34,000
Profit on sale of delivery vehicle	350
Loss on sale of office equipment	100
Increase in stocks during the year	2,432
Increase in debtors during the year	1,759
Increase in creditors during the year	872

Required Prepare a reconciliation of operating profit to net cash flow from operating activities.

Answer

Reconciliation of operating profit to net cash flow from operating activities

	£
Operating profit	187,612
Depreciation charges for year	34,000
Profit on sale of tangible fixed assets	(350)
Loss on sale of tangible fixed assets	100
Increase in stocks	(2,432)
Increase in debtors	(1,759)
Increase in creditors	872
Net cash inflow from operating activities	218,043

WORKED EXAMPLE *continued*

Note

- Depreciation reduces profits but not cash......................added to profit to arrive at cash.
- Profit on sale increases profits but not cash...........deducted from profit to arrive at cash.
- Loss on sale reduces profits but not cash......................added to profit to arrive at cash.
- Increase in stock ....deducted from profit to arrive at cash.
- Increase in debtors....................................deducted from profit to arrive at cash.
- Increase in creditors...added to profit to arrive at cash.

This tells us that that the business generated £30,431 more cash than the profits revealed.

QUESTION 1

Waystrell Ltd provides the following information for the year ended 28 February 20*3:

operating profit £167,549; depreciation charges for the year £26,000; loss on sale of fixed assets £2,350; increase in stock £280; decrease in debtors £760; increase in creditors £180.

Required Prepare a reconciliation of operating profit to net cash flow from operating activities.

QUESTION 2

Wallace Ltd provides the following information for the year ended 31 December 20*3:

operating profit £67,800; depreciation charges for the year £15,500; profit on the sale of fixed assets £3,460; decrease in stock £1,670; increase in debtors £360; increase in creditors £1,450.

Required Prepare a reconciliation of operating profit to net cash flow from operating activities.

Net debt is borrowings (debentures, loans, overdrafts) less cash and liquid resources. If cash and other liquid resources are greater than the borrowings of the company the excess is referred to as **net funds.**

WORKED EXAMPLE

The following information relates to Moytle Ltd:

	As at 30 November 20*1 £	As at 30 November 20*2 £	As at 30 November 20*3 £
Bank balance	1,250	–	2,350
Bank overdraft		2,500	
Cash in hand	1,000	750	2,100
6% debentures	100,000	120,000	150,000

Required Calculate the amount of net debt for each of the three years.

Answer

	20*1 £	20*2 £	20*3 £
Net debt	97,750	121,750	145,550
Workings	*100,000*	*122,500*	*150,000*
	(2,250)	*(750)*	*(4,450)*

RECONCILIATION OF THE MOVEMENT IN CASH TO MOVEMENT IN NET DEBT

This statement provides the reader with information that enables an assessment of liquidity and solvency to be made.

WORKED EXAMPLE

The following extracts are from the balance sheets of Wellie Ltd:

	As at 31 July 20*2 £	As at 31 July 20*3 £
Bank overdraft	50,000	40,000
Cash in hand	2,000	3,500
7% debentures	150,000	120,000
Increase in cash from cash-flow statement		11,500

Required Prepare a reconciliation of net cash to movement in net debt.

Answer

	£	
Increase in cash during period	11,500	
Cash used to redeem debentures	30,000	
Change in net debt	41,500	
Net debt at 1 August 20*2	198,000	(£150,000 + £50,000 − £2,000)
Net debt at 31 July 20*3	156,500	(£120,000 + £40,000 − £3,500)

At advanced subsidiary (AS) level you will not be asked to prepare cash-flow statements but you do need to be able to tell an examiner what are the main elements that make up the statement.

Do remember that cash-flow statements are historic documents; that is, they relate to a past time period.

Do not confuse a cash-flow statement with a cash-flow **forecast** which should more properly be known as a cash budget. Cash-flow statements do not try to determine future cash flows. Detailed knowledge of specific sources of cash receipts and the uses of cash outflows made may have some use in the assessment of future inflows and outflows of cash.

WHY MIGHT BUSINESSES PREPARE A CASH-FLOW STATEMENT?

- It may be a statutory requirement.
- Together with the profit and loss account and balance sheet, it helps to give a fuller picture of the activities of the business.
- The statement is one of the 'bridges between balance sheet dates'.
- Cash flows are an objective measure.

WHAT ARE THE USES OF A CASH-FLOW STATEMENT?

- It shows how a business has generated cash inflows.
- It shows how a business has used cash resources during the year.
- Because a standard format is used, significant components of cash flows can be identified.
- Because a standard format is used, inter-business comparisons can be made.

- It highlights liquidity which is of great interest to creditors, shareholders, workers, etc. because liquidity problems often cause business failure.
- The statement explains why profits and losses are different from changes in cash and cash equivalents.
- The statement shows changes in assets and liabilities.
- It shows movements in share capital and debentures.
- The statement shows sources of internal financing and the extent to which the business has relied on external financing.

Chapter summary

- The amount of profit generated by a business over a financial period is not generally equal to the amount of cash generated by a business over the same period.
- Cash inflows represent money that has been received into a business; cash outflows represent moneys spent by the business.
- The difference between cash inflows and cash outflows during a financial period will result in an increase or decrease in cash over the same period.

Self-test questions

- Explain why cash and profits are not necessarily equal.
- Identify the cash flows in the following transactions:
  - sold £50 goods on credit to Tom
  - sold £35 goods on credit to Harriet
  - purchased goods for resale on credit from Yasmin £54
  - purchased goods for resale for cash from Jock £39
  - paid rent £290 by cheque
  - paid rates £116 using cash
  - sold car net book value £230 to Angie for £200 cash
  - sold van net book value £560 to Den for £575; he will pay next month.
- Explain two circumstances that could result in a business making a profit while experiencing a fall in cash resources.
- Explain two circumstances that could result in a business making a loss while experiencing an increase in cash resources.
- List the standard headings used in FRS 1 on cash flow statements.

TEST QUESTIONS

QUESTION 3

Which of the following items would appear under the heading 'Operating activities'?:

- increase in creditors
- debenture interest paid
- tax refund
- decrease in stock
- issue of preference shares.

QUESTION 4

Which of the following items would appear under the heading 'Equity dividends paid'?:

- debenture interest paid
- interim dividend on ordinary shares
- interim dividend on preference shares
- final proposed dividend on ordinary shares
- final proposed dividend on preference shares.

QUESTION 5

Which of the following items would appear under the heading 'Capital expenditure and financial investment'?:

- payment to acquire the trade name 'Thoodles'
- receipt from sale of patent
- receipt from sale of excess machinery
- payment to acquire a new computerised accounting system
- receipts from sale of stock.

QUESTION 6

Which of the following items would appear under the heading 'Financing'?:

- receipts from issue of ordinary shares
- receipts from share premium on issue of ordinary shares
- receipts from issue of preference shares
- receipts from share premium on issue of preference shares
- receipts from issue of debentures
- repayment of debentures.

TWENTY SIX

Accounting Ratios

Accounting is a medium of communication. Financial statements are prepared to convey information.

The statements that we have prepared up to now have contained much information but, as yet, we have been unable to make judgements as to whether performance has been good, bad or indifferent.

In order to make judgements, we need to make comparisons between similar organisations.

QUESTION

A business has made £230,000 profit for the year ended 31 December 20*3.

Is this a good profit?

You would need to have more information before you could give an intelligent answer.

If the profit for the year was generated by BP plc, what is your verdict?

If the profit for the year has been generated by Sandra, my wife, selling cosmetics to her friends, what would your reaction be?

Even if we can make comparisons, we still may not be able to make a judgement on whether or not the business is performing well or badly.

Mark Allen owns and runs a general store in Ousby, a small village in the north of England. His profits for the year ended 31 March 20*3 are £17,500.

Marllen plc is a large supermarket chain that has 72 stores throughout the country. Its profits for the same financial year were £132,000,000. Which business has been run most efficiently during the year?

On the basis of the information given, it is very difficult to say. The only thing we can say with any certainty is that the overall business profits were greater in the case of Marllen plc. But you would, generally, expect a business with 72 outlets to have a larger profit than a small village store.

How can we overcome the problems of comparing businesses of differing sizes, operating in different locations etc?

We do not compare raw data, that is the actual results as they appear in the final accounts. We convert the data to a common base.

Consider Pat in Class 4B. She scores 12 out of 20 in this week's history test. Danny, her friend, is in Class 4D and scores 23 out of 50 in a similar history test. Clearly, Danny has scored a higher mark in the weekly test. But who has done better?

I think that you know the answer. By converting both results to the same base, out of 100 (converting them both into a percentage), we can make a very easy comparison.

Pat scores 60% and Danny scores 46%.

AQA 13.1.

By the end of this chapter you should be able to:
- define and calculate basic profitability and liquidity ratios
- explain the significance of the ratios
- comment on the performance of businesses
- make year-on-year comparisons
- make comparisons with other businesses
- explain the limitations of using ratio analysis.

The use of percentages is one of the approaches we use when comparing the results of one business with another; or if we are comparing the results of one business in two different time periods.

Who would be interested in the results of a business? Many groups of people. They might include:

- bank managers
- creditors
- Customs and Excise
- debtors
- employees
- press
- students.

What are these people and any other users of accounting information interested in? They are interested, in the main, in the survival of the business. Survival depends on the businesses ability to

- generate profits – its profitability
- generate positive cash flows – its liquidity.

QUESTION

Why is it necessary for a business to be profitable? Why is it necessary for a business to have a positive cash flow?

Answer
A business needs to be profitable to ensure its long-term survival. In the short run a business can make a loss but losses cannot be sustained over long periods of time.
A business needs a positive cash flow in order to meet its everyday commitments, ie in order to pay wages and creditors

> **Ratio** is the term applied to a variety of calculations used to compare the results of a business over time or to compare the results of two or more businesses in the same business sector.

How do the users of accounting information assess whether or not the profitability and/or liquidity of a business are acceptable?
They use precisely the same techniques that you would use in deciding whether the rate of pay in your part-time job was acceptable.

- You *compare* your earning with what you earned last year.
- You *compare* your earnings with those earned by your friends and relatives.
- You *compare* your earnings with the average earnings in the sector in which you work.
- You may even *compare* your earnings with what you thought you might earn and what you think you might spend your earnings on.

Performance evaluation is about **making comparisons**.
Ratio analysis and interpretation of ratios is about **making comparisons**.

When trying to evaluate the performance of a business, the users of accounting information go through the same processes that you would go through when considering your weekly wages slip.

The users will:

- *compare* the performance of the business with its performance in earlier years
- *compare* the performance of the business with that of similar businesses
- *compare* the performance of the business with the sector as a whole.

Some users, e.g. managers of the business and bank managers, may also *compare* actual performance with the performance that has been predicted in any budgets drawn up for the business.

Comparing the results of a business with its previous results is fairly straightforward.

Comparing the results of a business with the results achieved in the whole sector in which the business operates also is reasonably straightforward.

However, **inter-firm** comparisons are difficult in that a true 'like with like' comparison is impossible.

Why?

Because all businesses are different. Each business has:

■ a different level of turnover
■ a different sales mix
■ a different location
■ a different set of employees
■ a different set of managers ...

the list of differences can go on and on.

Some textbooks sub-divide ratios into:

■ profitability ratios
■ financial ratios
■ utilisation of resources ratios
■ investment ratios.

Also, in some cases, into:

■ primary
■ secondary
■ tertiary.

Although these are important categories, examination questions will not generally ask you for such a classification.

Important note

You should learn the formula used for each calculation.

I can hear you say 'I can't learn things – I have a poor memory'.
This is just not true.

When Atomic Kitten's latest CD hits the record shops, you are word perfect within a couple of hours of hearing it.

You **can** learn things and you **must** learn the basic ratios if you are to gain a good result in your examination.

The following set of final accounts for Fradtly plc will be used to calculate and explain each ratio:

Fradtly plc
Trading and profit and loss account for the year ended 31 October 20*3

	£(000)	£(000)
Sales		25,200
Less Cost of sales		
Stock as at 1 November 20*2	1,730	
Purchases	8,900	
	10,630	
Less Stock as at 31 October 20*3	1,600	9,030
Gross profit		16,170
Less Expenses		
Distribution expenses	7,752	
Administration costs	4,316	12,068
Operating profit on ordinary activities		4,102
Interest payable		210
Operating profit on ordinary activities before taxation		3,892
Taxation		960
Profit on ordinary activities after taxation		2,932
Interim preference dividend paid	35	
Interim ordinary dividend paid	360	
Proposed final preference dividend	35	
Proposed final ordinary dividend	520	950
Retained profit for the year		1,982

	£000	£000	£000
Fixed assets			
Freehold land and buildings			5,400
Plant and machinery			4,500
Vehicles			1,800
Office equipment			200
			11,900
Current assets			
Stock		1,600	
Trade debtors		2,320	
Bank		40	
		3,960	
Creditors: amounts falling due in less than one year			
Trade creditors	965		
Taxation	960		
Proposed dividends	555	2,480	
Net current assets			1,480
			11,380
Creditors: amounts falling due after more than one year			1,400
Net assets			9,980
Capital and reserves			
Ordinary shares of 50 pence each			2,500
7% preference shares of £1 each			1,000
Share premium account			900
Profit and loss account			5,580
			9,980

All sales and purchases are on credit.

THE RATIOS

RETURN ON CAPITAL EMPLOYED (ROCE) (PROFITABILITY IN RELATION TO CAPITAL EMPLOYED)

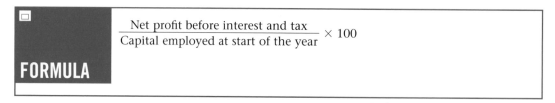

$$\frac{\text{Net profit before interest and tax}}{\text{Capital employed at start of the year}} \times 100$$

FORMULA

Return on capital employed $= \dfrac{4,102}{9,398} \times 100 = 43.65\%$

This ratio measures the return (profit earned) in relation to the total amount of money invested in the business by all the providers of long-term finance.

Net profit is taken before interest and tax since neither interest nor tax are common elements in the final accounts of some businesses with whom we may wish to compare our ratios.

Long-term finance is provided by lenders and all shareholders. In the case of Fradtly plc, long-term finance amounts to £11,380,000 (£9,980,000 plus £1,400,000) but we need to deduct this year's retained profit of £1,982,000.

The return on capital employed should be compared to the return from similar businesses and may also be compared to the return that could be obtained from risk-free investments.

The ratio tells us that for every £1 invested in the business the company earns a return of just over 43 pence.

This ratio is sometimes calculated for different parts of a business. If a department or a branch has a return that is below the average for the business as a whole or is deemed by managers to be unacceptable then remedial measures should be taken.

GROSS PROFIT MARGIN

FORMULA

$$\frac{\text{Gross profit}}{\text{Sales}} \times 100$$

$$\text{Gross profit margin} = \frac{16,170}{25,200} \times 100 = 64.17\%$$

This shows that for every £1 of sales, Fradtly plc earns just over 64 pence. Each £1 of sales earns 64.17 pence towards covering company overheads.

The gross profit margin will be affected by both the cost price of purchases and the selling price charged by the business.

To improve the gross profit margin, a business could buy goods for resale more cheaply while maintaining its selling price. Alternatively, the business could buy at the price presently being charged and put up the selling price if its customers will accept the increase without reducing quantity demanded.

GROSS PROFIT MARK-UP.

FORMULA

$$\frac{\text{Gross profits}}{\text{Cost of sales}} \times 100$$

$$\text{Mark-up} = \frac{16,170}{9,030} \times 100 = 179.07\%$$

This tells us that every £1 of purchases made by Fradtly plc is sold for just over £2.79. Every £1 of purchases earns £1.79 towards covering the company overheads.

Mark-up and margin are different perspectives on the same data. So improvements to mark-up would be achieved by using the same policies with regard to purchase and selling price strategies as those outlined in improving margin.

NET PROFIT MARGIN (NET PROFIT IN RELATION TO TURNOVER)

FORMULA

$$\frac{\text{Net profit before interest and taxation}}{\text{Sales}} \times 100$$

$$\text{Net profit margin} = \frac{4,102}{25,200} \times 100 = 16.28\%$$

Each £1 of sales that Fradtly plc makes earns just over 16 pence. This will pay corporation tax and provide dividends and any profits to be ploughed back for expansion or purchase of further assets.

Probably the greatest impact on this ratio is the level of gross profit earned. If gross profit margins improve, one would expect the net profit margin to improve too. However, this will depend on the behaviour patterns of the overhead costs. (See types of costs in the next chapter.)

OVERHEADS IN RELATION TO TURNOVER

Overheads are another way of describing expenses incurred by a business.

FORMULA

$$\frac{\text{Overheads}}{\text{Sales}} \times 100$$

Overheads in relation to turnover $= \dfrac{12{,}068}{25{,}200} \times 100 = 47.89\%$

This ratio tells us that out of every £1 of sales, almost 48 pence goes to paying Fradtly's expenses (wages, rent, rates etc).

This ratio will be adversely affected by changes in the expenses incurred by the business, e.g. a wage rise; an increase in rent paid; an increase in business rates etc.

The ratio would improve should any of the expenses incurred fall or if any resources were used more efficiently.

Note

Remember that

$$\text{gross profit} - \text{expenses} = \text{net profit}$$

So

$$\text{gross profit margin} - \text{overheads in relation to turnover} = \text{net profit margin}$$

Let us check the calculation that we have done

$$64.17\% - 47.89\% = 16.28\%$$

Yes!

RATE OF STOCK TURNOVER (STOCK TURN OR STOCK TURNOVER)

FORMULA

$$\frac{\text{Cost of sales}}{\text{Average stock held}}$$

Rate of stock turnover $= \dfrac{9{,}030}{1{,}665^*} = 5.42$ *times* (Note that this is not a %.)

*(1,730 opening stock + 1,600 closing stock = 3,330 divided by 2)

This shows that on average Fradtly sells its stocks 5.42 times per year.

If we divide a year by 5.42 it will tell us how long, on average, Fradtly plc keeps stock. So ...

Fradtly keeps stocks on average for about 67 days: $\dfrac{365}{5.42}$ days $= 67.34$

or for about nine and a half weeks $\qquad \dfrac{52 \text{ weeks}}{5.42} = 9.59$

or for about two and a quarter months $\qquad \dfrac{12 \text{ months}}{5.42} = 2.21$

We cannot really say whether these figures are good or bad. We can only comment if we know the type of business that the figures relate to. If Fradtly plc deals with perishable goods (fruit, flowers etc) it would seem that to hold stocks for over two months is a little excessive!

This calculation gives the average time taken for stock to be sold. The result may conceal very slow-moving stocks.

If the business is selling a variety of different products it may be beneficial to calculate the rate of stock turnover for each different category of stock. It can then be seen which type of stock is selling slowly and which products are being sold more quickly.

There is an element of profit wrapped up in each 'bundle' of stock; there is also cash tied up in it. The more quickly stock is being turned round, the more quickly the profits are earned and the more often cash is released for use within the business.

QUESTION 1

The information given relates to the business of Sean Brady:

Summarised trading and profit and loss account for the year ended 30 November 20*3

	£	£
Sales		213,000
Less Cost of sales		
Stock as at 1 December 20*2	22,000	
Purchases	142,000	
	164,000	
Stock as at 30 November 20*3	18,000	146,000
Gross profit		57,000
Expenses		39,000
Net profit		18,000

Required Calculate:
  (a) gross profit margin
  (b) net profit margin
  (c) overheads in relation to turnover
  (d) rate of stock turnover.

QUESTION 2

The following information relates to the business of May Styles:

Summarised trading and profit and loss account for the year ended 28 February 20*3

	£	£
Sales		313,500
Less Cost of sales		
Stock as at 1 March 20*2	39,000	
Purchases	167,000	
	206,000	
Stock as at 28 February 20*3	41,000	165,000
Gross profit		148,500
Expenses		88,500
Net profit		60,000

Required Calculate:
  (a) mark-up
  (b) net profit margin
  (c) overheads in relation to turnover
  (d) rate of stock turnover.

TURNOVER IN RELATION TO FIXED ASSETS.

FORMULA

$$\frac{\text{Sales}}{\text{Fixed assets}}$$

Turnover in relation to fixed assets $= \dfrac{25,200}{11,900} = 2.12 \; times$

This ratio gives an indication of how efficiently the company is using its fixed assets. Like all ratios, they are a historic measure and will be used to predict or measure future use of fixed assets.

NET CURRENT ASSET RATIO (CURRENT RATIO OR WORKING CAPITAL RATIO)

$$\frac{\text{Current assets}}{\text{Current liabilities}}$$

FORMULA

This ratio is a 'true' ratio in that it is always expressed as 'something' to one e.g. 2.4:1, 1.65:1 etc.

Current ratio $= \dfrac{3,960}{2,480} = 1.597$ expressed as 1.6 : 1

This means that for each £1 owed, the company can cover this with current assets 1.6 times.

There is no ideal current ratio. Different businesses work very effectively with very low ratios; others have what could be considered very high ratios, so do avoid stating categorically that this ratio should be 2:1. Many examination candidates quote this – it will not gain a mark for you.

It can be said that a high current ratio is wasteful of resources. Current assets do not generally yield a return, unlike fixed assets, so the reduction of a high current ratio could release resources that might be more efficiently converted into fixed assets that could be used to earn greater profits.

LIQUID CAPITAL RATIO (ACID TEST RATIO OR QUICK ASSET RATIO)

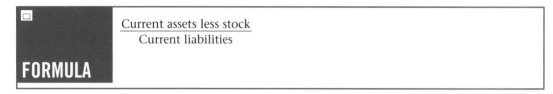

$$\frac{\text{Current assets less stock}}{\text{Current liabilities}}$$

FORMULA

Liquid ratio $= \dfrac{2,360}{2,480} = 0.95$ expressed as 0.95 : 1

This means that for every £1 owed, Fradtly plc can only raise 95 pence by way of liquid assets. Stocks are ignored because they are the least liquid form of current asset; that is, they are the least easily converted into cash resources.

DEBTORS' COLLECTION PERIOD

$$\text{Debtors} \times 365$$

FORMULA

Debtors' collection period $= \underline{2,320 \times 365} = 34$ days (33.60 but always round up)

This means that on average debtors are taking 34 days before settling their debts. Because the result of this calculation is an average figure, it could conceal a number of debts that have been outstanding for some time.

The compilation of an age profile of debtors on a regular basis would reveal debtors whose debts were outstanding for an unacceptable length of time.

A high average debtor collection period could indicate a number of 'older' debts. Old debts are more likely to become bad debts. This means that in reality the current asset figure shown in the balance sheet might be lower than the figure indicated.

CREDITORS' PAYMENT PERIOD

$$\frac{\text{Creditors} \times 365}{}$$

FORMULA

Creditors' payment period = $\underline{965 \times 365}$ = 40 days (39.58 but rounded up).

This tells us how much time Fradtly is taking to pay its creditors.
This is a valuable source of finance for any business. So the longer that can be taken before making a payment, the better. However, care must be taken not to upset suppliers in this respect.

It is worth noting that Fradtly plc are, on average, settling their debts in 40 days while their debtors are taking, on average, 34 days to pay. This is a good situation for any business to be in as it aids liquidity.

O EXAMINATION TIP

Do calculations to two decimal places or to the number of decimal places given in the data for comparative purposes.

QUESTION 3

The information is given for the business of Agnes Tutin:

Summarised balance sheet as at 30 September 20*3

	£	£
Fixed assets		170,000
Current assets		
Stock	23,500	
Trade debtors	13,500	
Bank balance	13,000	
	50,000	
Current liabilities		
Trade creditors	10,000	40,000
		210,000
Capital		210,000

Additional information

Purchases all on credit £160,000; sales all on credit £350,000.

Required Calculate:
(a) turnover in relation to fixed assets
(b) net current asset ratio
(c) liquid capital ratio
(d) debtors' collection period
(e) creditors' payment period.

QUESTION 4

The information is given for Trefor Johns:

Summarised balance sheet as at 31 January 20*3

	£	£	£
Fixed assets			450,000
Current assets			
Stock		34,000	
Trade debtors		26,500	
		60,500	
Current liabilities			
Trade creditors	19,460		
Bank overdraft	11,540	31,000	29,500
			479,500
Capital			479,500

Additional information

Purchases all on credit £291,900; sales all on credit £450,500.

Required Calculate:
- (a) turnover in relation to fixed assets
- (b) net current asset ratio
- (c) liquid capital ratio
- (d) debtors' collection period
- (e) creditors' payment period.

Many students are quite good at calculating the ratios and so score good marks. However, they are less confident in analysing the results of their calculations.

Examiners and teachers alike expect students to reach earth-trembling conclusions from their calculations and analysis. Try not to be daunted by this prospect. We can only analyse at a very basic level. Even the city fund managers are not very good at analysing the results of major businesses; otherwise scores of pension funds and other investment portfolios would not be in such a mess at the moment!

Let us consider how to tackle the written sections of a question. The presenter of a popular quiz programme on television coined the saying 'Say what you see'. Remember the saying when you are making observations and comments.

The pattern to follow is:

- state the formula
- do the calculation
- state whether the ratio shows an improvement or a worsening of performance
- quantify the change identified
- suggest reasons for any changes.

The five headings should be considered when comparing different businesses; and when trying to identify the trends that have occurred within a single business.

WORKED EXAMPLE

The following information is given for Breen Ltd:

Trading and profit and loss account for the year ended 31 December 20*3

	£	£
Sales (all on credit)		500,000
Less Cost of sales		
Stock as at 1 January 20*3	18,000	
Purchases	184,000	
	202,000	
Stock as at 31 December 20*3	22,000	180,000
Gross profit		320,000
Expenses		156,000
Net profit for year		164,000

Balance sheet as at 31 December 20*3

	£	£
Fixed assets		300,000
Current assets		
Stock	22,000	
Trade debtors	23,000	
Bank balance	11,000	
	56,000	
Creditors: amount falling due in less than one year		
Trade creditors	20,000	36,000
		336,000
Share capital and reserves		
Ordinary shares of £1 each		100,000
Profit and loss account		236,000
		336,000

Additional information

The following ratios were calculated for the year ended 31 December 20*2:

- gross profit margin — 60%
- mark-up — 150%
- net profit margin — 29.23%
- return on capital employed — 92.68%
- overheads in relation to turnover — 30.77%
- rate of stock turnover — 8 times
- turnover in relation to fixed assets — 1.54 times
- net current assets ratio — 2.6:1
- liquid capital ratio — 1.47:1
- debtors' collection period — 22 days
- creditors' payment period — 35 days

Required (a) Calculate the ratios shown above for the year ended 31 December 20*3.
(b) Comment on the ratios for the two years.

Answer

Note
In each case the formula should be stated.

Ratios should be calculated to two decimal places since two decimal places have been used for the previous year's results.

	31 December 20*2	31 December 20*3
gross profit margin	60%	64%
mark-up	150%	177.78%
net profit margin	29.23%	32.8%
return on capital employed	92.68%	95.35%
overheads in relation to turnover	30.77%	31.2%
rate of stock turnover	8 times	9 times
turnover in relation to fixed assets	1.54 times	1.67 times
net current assets ratio	2.6:1	2.8:1
liquid capital ratio	1.47:1	1.7:1
debtors' collection period	22 days	17 days
creditors' payment period	35 days	40 days

Let us follow the pattern. Have the ratios improved or worsened? How much of an improvement or deterioration?

There has been an improvement in the **gross margin**; it has gone up from 60% to 64%. This means that in 20*2 every £1 of sales yielded 60p gross profit; in 20*3 every £1 of sales yielded 64p gross profit.

Possible reasons for the improvement?

The improvement could be due to Breen Ltd increasing the selling price of its products with cost of sales remaining the same (or even going down); or selling price remaining the same as in the previous year but Breen Ltd's buyers purchasing the goods to be sold at a cheaper price.

Since the **mark-up** and **margin** are very closely related, the comments are identical.

Net profit margin has also improved. It has increased from 29.23% to 32.8%. After expenses, every £1 of sales now gives the business 32.8p net profit; in the previous year, each £1 of sales gave 29.23p net profit. This is due to the increase in the gross profit.

The proportion of **expenses** taken from each £1 of sales has increased from 30.77p to 31.2p, so the position has worsened. Although this is a very small amount, the ratio should be monitored to ensure that the position does not deteriorate further. The reason for the increase could be certain overheads increasing without a corresponding increase in productivity.

The **return on capital employed** has improved from 92.68% to 95.35%. This means that every £1 invested in the business in 20*3 gave a return of 95.35p. This is because of the improved profits. (In certain circumstances the increase could be because of a decrease in capital employed. We have no indication that this is the case and we can only 'say what we see'!)

The **rate of stock turnover** has improved. It has risen from 8 times per year to 9 times per year. Breen is selling 'bundles' of stock in 41 days (365 ÷ 9); in the previous year, stock was sold on average every 46 days (365 ÷ 8).

This will have improved cash flows and the magnitude of the profits (it will not change either of the margins).

Turnover in relation to fixed assets has improved. Each £1 invested in fixed assets produced £1.67 sales in 20*3 compared with £1.54 in the previous year. This could be because of an increase in sales or better use of existing fixed assets. Care should be taken in trying to 'guess' reasons for this improvement. In some circumstances the ratio will improve simply because fixed assets depreciate.

For example, sales £100, fixed assets £50 = 2 times

One year later fixed assets are less efficient ... so produce less ... have depreciated ...

For example, sales £90, fixed assets £40 = 2.25 times

Sales have gone down – machines are older but the ratio has improved!

Notice that we are still following the pattern.

- Has the ratio improved or worsened?
- Quantify the change.
- Give reasons for any change.

Net current asset ratio has improved. It has increased from 2.6:1 to 2.8:1. This could be because of increases in any of the current assets or a reduction in short-term creditors. We have not been given the details for 20*2 so we can't say what we see! We could perhaps comment on the fact that for every £1 owed Breen now has £2.80 covering liabilities. Is this excessive? Could some current assets be converted into fixed assets in order to increase earning power?

Liquid capital ratio has improved. It has risen from 1.5:1 to 1.7:1. For every £1 owed Breen has current assets (not including stock) of £1.70; in the previous year, for every £1 owed Breen had £1.50. Is the proportion of resources held as liquid assets too high? Could some of those liquid assets be converted into fixed assets and improve earning power? The proportion of stock held as current assets remains static at £1.10 for every £1 owed.

The **debtors' collection period** has improved. It has fallen from an average of 22 days to an average of 17 days. Is this average masking some debts that are outstanding for much longer? Is this too short a time? Has too much pressure been put on debtors to pay up quickly? If too much pressure is put on credit customers they may desert Breen and use a supplier with a much more relaxed credit management policy.

Creditors' payment period has improved. Breen is now settling its debts on average in 40 days; in the previous year, they settled in 35 days. Care must be taken to ensure that suppliers are not alienated by not paying them within the agreed terms.

It is generally worth comparing the **debtors' collection period** with the creditors' payment period. Consider this situation: you owe your brother £10 and your sister owes you £12. Which situation would you prefer:

You pay your brother on Monday ... your sister pays you Friday?

Or

Your sister pays you on Monday ... you pay your brother Friday?

The same principle applies in business. The debtors' collection period should be shorter than the creditors' payment period.

THE LIMITATIONS OF USING RATIO ANALYSIS FOR ASSESSING THE PERFORMANCE OF A BUSINESS

- Ratio analysis uses historic information, that is, the results are based on events that have already taken place.
- The merit of using historic cost is that it is objective. However, its use does throw doubt on results compared over a long time period. In Dickens' time an annual average salary was £20 so presumably one could buy a house for less than £100. Salaries and house prices have risen substantially since those days. In the case of sole traders and partnerships, assets are valued at cost. Will the use of historic cost invalidate some ratios if the assets are valued at 1970s prices?
- The emphasis on past results provides indications for future results but nothing is guaranteed. A football team may win the Premiership. This does not mean that it will necessarily win it for the next five or ten years.
- The bases of the ratios, that is the published accounts, just give an overview of the whole business. One department or product may yield a return on capital employed of 45% while another yields 2% yet overall the business may be earning an acceptable 20%.

- The ratios only consider the monetary aspects of the business. They do not record management and/or staff strengths and weaknesses.
- The final accounts are prepared on a particular day. This could mean that a balance sheet may well be unrepresentative of the normal position of the business.
- The external environment facing the business is constantly changing. Some changes may take a considerable time to impact on the business. An increase in the price of raw materials may only be incorporated into costing calculations in a few months' time.
- Different organisations have different structures; different methods of financing their operations; different expense and revenue patterns; and they may use different accounting bases. No matter how similar businesses may appear to outsiders, they are all different and so inter-firm comparison can prove to be misleading

Despite all the limitations of using ratios it is the most widely recognised tool for comparing, analysing and evaluating the results.

Chapter summary

- Ratio analysis is a valuable way of analysing the performance of a business.
- To be of any value, ratios must be compared with either previous years' performance or those of other businesses to determine trends.
- Ratios are used to compare the performance of businesses in the same industry.
- Ratios are used to make judgements about the likely future performance of a business.
- Although it is very difficult to compare 'like with like', it is the best measure that is available.
- Remember:
  - show the formula
  - do the calculation
  - state 'better' or 'worse'
  - quantify
  - give likely reasons for change.

Self-test questions

- Why do we use ratios rather than actual results to evaluate business performance?
- 'A profit of £87,000 is very good.' Comment on this statement.
- Identify three groups of people who might use ratios.
- Gross profit ÷ sales is a .... ratio. Fill the gap.
- Current assets : current liabilities is a .... ratio. Fill the gap.
- What does ROCE stand for?
- Give alternative names for the following ratios:
  - net profit in relation to turnover
  - overheads in relation to turnover
  - profitability in relation to capital employed
  - net current asset ratio
  - liquid capital ratio
  - working capital ratio
  - acid test ratio.
- Identify two weaknesses in using ratios to evaluate the performance of a business.

TEST QUESTIONS

QUESTION 5

The following information is given for Sadie Lolly for the year ended 31 August 20*3:

	£
Sales (all on credit)	145,000
Stock as at 1 September 20*2	23,000
Stock as at 31 August 20*3	27,000
Purchases (all on credit)	110,000
Gross profit	39,000
Expenses	25,000
Net profit	14,000
Fixed assets	92,000
Trade debtors	18,000
Bank balance	5,000
Trade creditors	12,500
Drawings	23,000
Capital as at 1 September 20*2	138,500

Required Calculate the following ratios, showing the models or formulae used:
- (a) gross profit margin
- (b) net profit margin
- (c) overheads in relation to turnover ratio
- (d) return on capital employed
- (e) rate of stock turnover
- (f) turnover in relation to fixed assets
- (g) net current asset ratio
- (h) liquid capital ratio
- (i) debtors' collection period
- (j) creditors' payment period.

QUESTION 6

The following information is given for Hemal Limbachia for the year ended 31 December 20*3:

	£
Sales (80% credit sales)	250,000
Stock as at 1 January 20*3	11,000
Purchases (all on credit)	141,000
Gross profit	139,000
Expenses	78,000
Fixed assets	120,000
Trade debtors	15,000
Bank balance	8,000
Trade creditors	20,000
Drawings	30,000
Capital as at 1 January 20*3	127,000

Required Calculate the following ratios, showing the formulae used:
- (a) mark-up
- (b) net profit margin
- (c) overheads in relation to turnover ratio
- (d) rate of stock turnover
- (e) turnover in relation to fixed assets
- (f) net current asset ratio
- (g) liquid capital ratio
- (h) debtors' collection period
- (i) creditors' payment period.

QUESTION 7

The following information is given for Zena Paul:

Trading account for the year ended 30 November 20*3

	£	£
Sales		234,000
Less Cost of sales		
Stock as at 1 December 20*2	14,000	
Purchases	98,000	
	112,000	
Stock as at 30 November 20*3	16,000	96,000
Gross profit		138,000

Balance sheet as at 30 November 20*3

	£	£
Fixed assets		300,000
Current assets		
Stock	16,000	
Trade debtors	19,000	
Bank balance	3,000	
	38,000	
Current liabilities		
Trade creditors	15,000	23,000
		323,000
Capital		264,000
Add Profit		86,000
		350,000
Less Drawings		27,000
		323,000

Additional information
- All purchases and sales are on credit.
- The net profit margin for the year ended 30 November 20*2 was 29.48%.
- The net current asset ratio at 30 November 20*2 was 2.78:1.

Required Calculate the following ratios, showing the formulae used:
- (a) gross profit margin
- (b) net profit margin
- (c) overheads in relation to turnover ratio
- (d) return on capital employed
- (e) rate of stock turnover
- (f) turnover in relation to fixed asset ratio
- (g) net current asset ratio
- (h) liquid capital ratio
- (i) debtors' collection period
- (j) creditors' payment period.

Comment on the results revealed by the net profit margin and net current asset ratio.

QUESTION 8

The following information is given for Chris Tynan:

Trading account for the year ended 31 March 20*3

	£	£
Sales		560,000
Less Cost of sales		
Stock as at 1 April 20*2	45,000	
Purchases	368,000	
	413,000	
Stock as at 31 March 20*3	43,000	370,000
Gross profit		190,000

Balance sheet as at 31 March 20*3

	£	£	£
Fixed assets			312,000
Current assets			
Stock		43,000	
Trade debtors		36,000	
		79,000	
Current liabilities			
Trade creditors	42,000		
Bank overdraft	21,000	63,000	16,000
			328,000
Capital			309,000
Add Profit			61,000
			370,000
Less Drawings			42,000
			328,000

Additional information
- All purchases and sales were on credit.
- The gross profit margin for the year ended 31 March 20*2 was 35.62%.
- The liquid asset ratio at 31 March 20*2 was 0.63:1.
- The debtors' collection period at 31 March 20*2 was 21 days.

Required Calculate the following ratios, showing the formulae used:
  (a) gross profit margin
  (b) net profit margin
  (c) overheads in relation to turnover ratio
  (d) return on capital employed
  (e) turnover in relation to fixed assets ratio
  (f) net current asset ratio
  (g) liquid capital ratio
  (h) debtors' collection period
  (i) creditors' payment period.

Comment on the results revealed by the gross margin; the liquid capial ratio; and the debtors' collection period.

QUESTION 9

The following information is given for the business of Selena Chulk:

Trading account for the year ended 31 July 20*3

	£	£
Sales		758,000
Less Cost of sales		
Stock as at 1 August 20*2	65,400	
Purchases	452,000	
	517,400	
Stock as at 31 July 20*3	64,600	452,800
Gross profit		305,200

Balance sheet as at 31 August 20*3

	£	£
Fixed assets		450,000
Current assets		
Stock	64,600	
Trade debtors	37,000	
Bank balance	4,400	
	106,000	
Current liabilities		
Trade creditors	56,000	50,000
		500,000
Capital		451,000
Profit		103,000
		554,000
Less Drawings		54,000
		500,000

Additional information

- 80% of total sales were on credit.
- 75% of total purchases were on credit.
- The gross margin for the year ended 31 August 20*2 was 48 63%.
- The net margin for the year ended 31 August 20*2 was 14 .77%.
- The rate of stock turnover for the year ended 31 August 20*2 was 10.4 times.
- The debtors' collection period at 31 August 20*2 was 22 days.
- The creditors' payment period at 31 August 20*2 was 45 days.

Required Calculate the following ratios, showing the formulae used:
(a) gross margin
(b) net profit margin
(c) overheads in relation to turnover ratio
(d) return on capital employed
(e) rate of stock turnover
(f) turnover in relation to fixed assets ratio
(g) net current assets ratio
(h) liquid capital ratio
(i) debtors' collection period
(j) creditors' payment period.

Comment on the results revealed by the gross margin; the net margin; the rate of stock turnover; the debtors' collection period; and the creditors' payment period.

QUESTION 10

The following information is given for two businesses in the same industry for the year ended 30 June 20*3:

	Jim Flack £	Josie Chan £
Sales	230,000	896,000
Stock as at 1 July 20*2	12,400	32,000
Stock as at 30 June 20*3	11,600	30,000
Purchases	58,600	515,000
Overhead expenses	84,600	126,000
Fixed assets	200,000	450,000
Trade debtors	14,000	80,000
Trade creditors	16,000	47,000
Bank balance	2,400	4,000
Capital as at 1 July 20*2	142,000	332,000
Drawings	16,000	68,000

All purchases and sales were on credit.

Required (a) Prepare a summarised trading and profit and loss account for the year ended 30 June 20*3 for each business.
(b) Prepare a summarised balance sheet as at 30 June 20*3 for each business.
(c) Calculate the following ratios for each business, stating the formulae used:
- gross profit margin
- net profit margin
- return on capital employed
- overheads in relation to turnover ratio
- rate of stock turnover
- turnover in relation to fixed assets
- net current asset ratio
- liquid capital ratio
- debtors' collection period
- creditors' payment period.
(d) Compare the performance of each business.

TWENTY SEVEN

Classification of Costs

We said in an earlier chapter that financial accounts were produced to fulfil two basic needs:

■ **Stewardship** function
Financial accounts are prepared to reassure the providers of finance that the resources that they have provided are safe and that they are being used wisely. If the providers feel that their investment is unsafe or being used frivously then they may decide to withdraw the finance that they have provided, with obvious consequences for the business.

■ **Management** function
Financial accounts are used by the managers of a business to:
　▪ plan future actions and activities of the business
　▪ organise the sections of the business into a coherent whole and
　▪ control the activities of the business.

THE BRANCHES OF ACCOUNTING INFORMATION

In small businesses, all aspects of the business are most probably dealt with by the owner.

In large businesses, the accounting function will most probably be divided into:

FINANCIAL ACCOUNTING

The accounts deal with:

■ largely historic information and its presentation to the external users of the final accounts
■ analysis for historic performance evaluation
■ recording all the financial transactions that have taken place
■ classifying all the financial transactions that have taken place into major headings
■ summarising all the financial transactions that have taken place into the final accounts, ensuring that the final accounts show a true and fair view of the state of affairs of the business
■ the application of the many regulations laid down in the Companies Acts, Financial Reporting Standards and Statements of Standard Accounting Practice.

MANAGEMENT ACCOUNTING

This deals with:

■ the comparison of the results shown by the final financial accounts with the forecast results as predicted in budgets. By doing this, managers may be able to control costs in the future
■ the determination of selling price by reference to information supplied by the financial accountant and the cost accountant
■ the use of budgets to prepare future plans
■ the use of budgets to compare the plans with actual outcomes and determine where any variations occur and the cause of these differences
■ the use of budgets to co-ordinate the various sections/departments/branches so that a unified approach and results will be obtained
■ the making of decisions regarding future investment in the business.

Specification coverage:
AQA 13.2.

By the end of this chapter you should be able to:
■ explain the terms
　▪ direct costs
　▪ indirect costs
　▪ variable costs
　▪ semi-variable costs
　▪ fixed costs.

COST ACCOUNTING

Cost accountants gather information about the costs of running the business. They will provide this information to the management accountant in order that rational decisions may be made. Information supplied by cost accountants must be submitted to management regularly in order that speedy corrective measures may be taken.

Indeed the two branches of accounting are generally merged into a cost and management accounting department supervised by the cost and management accountant.

> A **direct cost** as defined by CIMA is 'expenditure which can be economically identified with a specific saleable cost unit'.

In order that information gathered by cost accountants for use by management accountants is useful, it is necessary to classify the costs incurred. It may be useful in a manufacturing business to classify costs into

Direct costs

Direct costs will vary (change) in direct proportion to the number of units of the product (or service) produced, so that if 1.5 metres of cotton is used to produce one shirt then 15 metres will be used to manufacture 10 shirts, 45 metres of material will be used to manufacture 30 shirts etc. If seven shirts can be produced by using one hour of labour, then 14 shirts will be produced by using two hours of labour; 56 shirts will be produced by using eight hours of labour etc.

Direct materials can be identified easily as being used in a specific product. Direct material costs are involved in the acquisition of materials that can be identified clearly as being part of the finished product.

Direct labour are workers whose work can be identified clearly with converting raw materials or components into the final product. It could include machine operators, assembly workers and packers.

Direct labour costs are directly attributable to a unit of production. They form part of the prime cost in a manufacturing account. They can be traced easily to the final product.

Other direct expenses may include manufacturing royalties. These are paid when the product made by the business uses a pattern or process that has been invented by another person or business.

If direct expenses were drawn on a graph they would look like this:

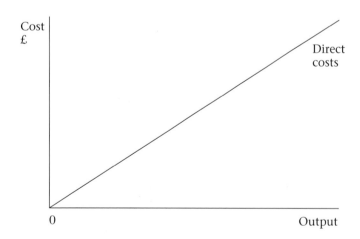

> **Variable costs** always change in direct proportion to a change in the level of activity undertaken by the business.

Direct costs are always variable costs.

> **Indirect costs** are costs which cannot be identified directly to the end product. They are also known as overheads.

Indirect costs

Indirect costs can be categorised as:

- **Manufacturing overheads** – these include indirect expenses which are not directly identifiable with the final product. Examples might include factory rent and rates; depreciation of factory machinery; factory power; factory lighting and heating expenses etc.
- **Indirect labour costs** are the costs involved in employing staff whose work cannot be directly identified with the final product. Examples might include wages paid to maintenance engineers; wages of supervisory staff etc.
- **Indirect material costs** are costs incurred in acquiring materials which cannot be directly identified with the final product. Examples might include factory cleaning materials; machinery lubricating oil etc.
- **Selling and distribution expenses** are not directly identifiable with the final product but are necessary in order to sell and distribute the final product to customers. These expenses might include advertising expenses; marketing expenses; delivery costs; costs for maintenance of showrooms; sales staff salaries etc.
- **Administration overheads** cannot be directly identified with the final product but again are necessary in order to run the business. These expenses might include office rent and rates; office lighting and heating expenses; telephone charges; stationery; depreciation of office equipment etc.

The division of cost into direct and indirect costs helps when identifying the various parts that constitute the full cost of sales.

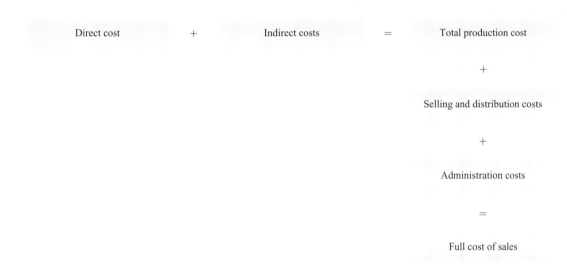

Direct cost	+	Indirect costs	=	Total production cost
				+
				Selling and distribution costs
				+
				Administration costs
				=
				Full cost of sales

> **Fixed costs** are costs that do not change with levels of business activity.

Fixed costs are also known as period costs since they are time based. That is, they tend to remain the same over a period of time. Examples might include supervisors' wages; rent and rates etc.

Warning

Do not say that fixed costs do not change – they might over time: supervisors might be awarded an increase in pay; the landlord might increase the rent; the local authority might increase the business rates.

If fixed costs were drawn on a graph, they would look like this:

Semi-variable costs cannot be classified as either fixed costs or variable costs because they contain an element of both. (These costs are also known as semi-fixed costs.)

An example of a semi-variable cost is the charge for electricity. Part of the total invoice is a fixed cost which must be paid even if no electricity is used; while the other part is based on the number of units of electricity used by the business. If semi-variable costs were drawn on a graph, they would look like this:

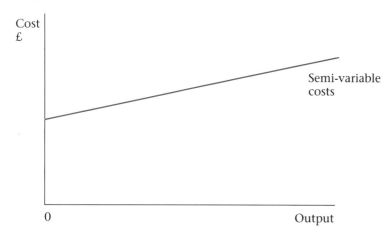

Chapter summary

- Direct costs can be easily identified with the end product.
- Indirect costs cannot be easily identified with the end product.
- Variable costs change with levels of business activity.
- Fixed costs do not change with levels of business activity.
- Semi-variable costs are partly fixed costs and partly variable costs.

Self-test questions

- State the difference between a direct cost and an indirect cost.
- Give an example of a direct cost for a manufacturer of clothing.
- Give an example of an indirect cost for a furniture manufacturer.
- State the difference between a fixed cost and a variable cost.
- Give an example of a fixed cost for a haulage contractor.
- Give an example of a variable cost for a builder.
- Define the term 'period cost'.
- Give an example of a period cost for a supermarket.

- Define the term 'semi-variable cost'.
- Give an example of a semi-variable cost for a bank.

TEST QUESTIONS

QUESTION 1

Greensward Ltd manufactures lawnmowers. It has the following costs:

- sales staff salaries
- purchases of cutter blades
- wages of assembly workers
- rent of factory
- rates for offices
- royalties paid to Swedish designer of lawnmower
- purchases of materials for construction of grass box
- depreciation of factory machinery
- advertising expenses
- chief executive's salary.

Required Classify the costs into:
  (a) direct production costs
  (b) factory overhead expenses
  (c) administrative overhead costs
  (d) selling and distribution overhead costs.

QUESTION 2

Woodvedge Ltd manufactures pottery. It has the following costs:

- factory rent
- clay
- office rates
- delivery vehicle service costs
- glaze for pottery
- pottery painters' wages
- factory supervisors' wages
- factory power
- delivery drivers' wages
- heat and light for offices.

Required Classify the costs into:
  (a) direct production costs
  (b) factory overhead expenses
  (c) administrative overhead expenses
  (d) selling and distribution overhead costs.

QUESTION 3

The following costs are incurred by a garage:

(a) spares for car repairs
(b) electricity
(c) accountant's wages.

Required Sketch graphs to show the cost patterns for each.

QUESTION 4

The following costs are incurred by a manufacturer of jeans:

(a) purchases of denim
(b) factory power
(c) supervisors' wages
(d) wages of sewing machine operatives.

Required Sketch graphs to show the cost patterns for each.

QUESTION 5

The following information relates to a chair manufacturer:

Number of chairs produced per week	Variable costs £	Fixed costs £	Total costs £
100	1,700	*	1,930
110	1,870	230	*
120	*	*	*
130	*	230	*
140	*	*	*

Required Fill the gaps in the table.

QUESTION 6

The following information relates to a manufacturer of televisions:

Number of televisions produced per week	Variable costs £	Fixed costs £	Total costs £
350	39,200	*	46,200
400	44,800	*	*
450	*	*	*
600	*	*	74,200
750	*	*	*

Required Fill the gaps in the table.

QUESTION 7

- A delivery van travels 15,000 miles per year.
- The road fund tax costs £280 per annum.
- The comprehensive insurance for the van costs £340 per annum.
- The van will travel 3 miles on a litre of fuel, and the fuel costs 85 pence per litre.

Required Calculate:
      (a) the total cost of using the van per year
      (b) the variable cost per mile
      (c) the fixed cost per mile
      (d) the total cost per mile.

QUESTION 8

The following information is given for the weekly production of 4600 'plikes':

	£
Direct materials	15,000
Machine operatives' wages	23,000
Manufacturing royalties	1,000
Supervisors' wages	1,800
Factory light and heat	2,400
Factory power	1,600
Factory rent and rates	750
Factory insurance	450

Calculate:
        (a) prime cost of weekly production
        (b) total manufacturing cost of weekly production
        (c) prime cost per unit of production
        (d) total manufacturing cost per unit.

QUESTION 9

The following information is given for the production of component TG/32 used in the production of vacuum cleaners:

Levels of output	1,000 units £	2,000 units £	3,000 units £
Direct materials costs	4,000	8,000	12,000
Direct labour costs	6,000	12,000	18,000
Production overheads	10,000	12,000	14,000
Other overheads	7,000	7,000	7,000
Total costs	27,000	39,000	51,000

(a) Classify the costs into fixed; variable; and semi-variable costs.
        (b) Calculate the total cost for the production of 5,000 units of component TG/32.

QUESTION 10

The following information is given for the production of 'vigols':

Levels of output	100 units £	150 units £	200 units £
Direct materials	350	525	700
Direct wages	700	1,050	1,400
Production overheads	6,750	6,875	7,000
Other overheads	2,000	2,000	2,000
Total costs	9,800	10,400	11,100

(a) Classify the costs into fixed, variable and semi-variable costs.
        (b) Calculate the total cost for the production of 300 units of 'vigols'.

CHAPTER
TWENTY EIGHT

An Introduction to Marginal Costing

Specification coverage:
AQA 13.2.

Marginal costing is defined by CIMA as 'the cost of one unit of a product or service which would be avoided if that unit were not produced or provided'.

Marginal costing is a decision-making technique used by management accountants. It is based on the extra costs incurred and the extra revenue generated by the production and sale of an additional unit.

Marginal costing requires that a clear distinction can be made between variable costs and fixed costs.

No attempt is made to apportion fixed costs to a product.

Total variable cost of sales = variable production cost

+

variable selling and distribution cost

+

variable administration cost

The term **'variable cost'** when used in a marginal cost statement or a marginal cost calculation is total variable cost of sales.

We have already seen, in the previous chapter, that the total cost of a product is made up of variable costs plus fixed costs.

We have also seen that fixed costs or period costs are not affected by changes in the numbers of units produced.

Therefore, if the number of units produced is increased then only the variable cost part of total cost would increase.

By the end of this chapter you should be able to:
- explain the terms 'marginal costing' and 'contribution'
- explain the uses of break-even analysis
- calculate break-even point by formula
- determine break-even point by use of a graph
- explain the limitations of break-even analysis.

WORKED EXAMPLE

The cost of producing 1,000 units of 'sqwort' is made up as follows:

	£	
Variable costs	1,000	(£1 per unit)
Fixed costs	500	
Total production cost	1,500	

Required Calculate the total cost of producing 1,100 and 1,500 units of 'sqwort'.

Answer

Production level	1,100 units	1,500 units
	£	£
Variable costs	1,100	1,500
Fixed costs	500	500
Total production cost	1,600	2,000

Note
The fixed costs remain unchanged whether 1,000, 1,100 or 1,500 sqworts are produced.

Contribution is the difference between selling price and total variable cost. It should be called 'contribution towards fixed costs and profits'.

Contribution is available to pay the fixed costs of the business. Once fixed costs have been covered, contribution becomes profit.

MARGINAL COST STATEMENTS

Marginal cost statements offer an alternative layout to the traditional trading and profit and loss account.

Marginal cost statements emphasise fixed and variable costs separately and so emphasise the components of total fixed costs incurred by the business.

WORKED EXAMPLE

Rault Ltd is a manufacturing business. The following information relates to the year ended 30 April 20*3:

	£
Direct materials	120,000
Direct wages	360,000
Fixed factory overhead expenses	110,000
Fixed selling and distribution overhead expenses	80,000
Fixed administration overhead expenses	90,000
Fixed total sales revenue	850,000

Required Prepare a marginal costing statement for the year ended 30 April 20*3.

WORKED EXAMPLE *continued*

Answer

Rault Ltd
Marginal costing statement for the year ended 30 April 20*3.

	£	£
Sales		850,000
Less **Variable costs**		
Direct materials	120,000	
Direct wages	360,000	480,000
Total contribution		370,000
Less **Fixed costs**		
Factory overheads	110,000	
Selling and distribution overheads	80,000	
Administration overheads	90,000	280,000
Net profit		90,000

QUESTION 1

Akhtar Ltd is a manufacturing business. The following information is available for the year ended 30 June 20*3:

	£
Direct material costs	130,000
Direct labour costs	120,000
Fixed factory overhead expenses	60,000
Fixed selling and distribution overhead expenses	70,000
Fixed administration overhead expenses	80,000
Total sales revenue	600,000

Required Prepare a marginal costing statement for the year ended 30 June 20*3.

QUESTION 2

O'Leary Ltd is a manufacturing business. The following information is available for the year ended 31 August 20*3:

	£
Direct material costs	300,000
Direct labour costs	580,000
Fixed factory overhead expenses	120,000
Fixed selling and distribution overhead expenses	60,000
Fixed administration overhead expenses	150,000
Total sales revenue	1,500,000

Required Prepare a marginal costing statement for the year ended 31 August 20*3.

QUESTION 3

Guillaume supplies the following information that relates to the year ended 31 August 20*3 for his manufacturing business:

Selling price	£90 per unit
Variable cost of sales	£43 per unit
Total fixed costs	£16,000

Guillaume produced and sold 7,000 units.

Required Prepare a marginal costing statement for the year ended 31 August 20*3.

QUESTION 4

Tamsin supplies the following information relating to the year ended 31 December 20*3 for her manufacturing business:

Selling price	£100 per unit
Direct material costs	£23 per unit
Direct labour costs	£38 per unit
Total fixed factory overhead expenses	£32,000
Total fixed selling and distribution overhead expenses	£27,000
Total fixed administration overhead expenses	£49,000

Tamsin produced and sold 2,450 units.

Required Prepare a marginal costing statement for the year ended 31 December 20*3.

Marginal costing may be used in a variety of situations to determine what course of action a business should take.

We shall consider how to establish the break-even point for a product and leave the other uses until Book 2.

> **Break-even analysis** calculates the level of output and/or sales revenue at which a product makes neither a profit nor a loss.

> **Break-even point** indicates the lowest level of sales or units sold at which total revenue received for a product is equal to the total costs of producing that product.

> **Margin of safety** is the difference between the actual sales achieved (or forecast as achievable) and the break-even level of sales. It indicates how far the sales of a product can fall before it moves out of profit and into a loss-making situation.

CALCULATING BREAK-EVEN POINT

The break-even point for a product can be established using the following techniques.

THE UNIT CONTRIBUTION METHOD

This is the simplest method to use and should always be used unless an examination question stipulates another method.

We have already said that contribution should be called

'contribution towards fixed costs and profits'.

If we can calculate contribution per unit, it should then be quite simple to determine how many of those units must be sold to cover the total fixed costs incurred.

WORKED EXAMPLE

The following information relates to the production and sales of 'grests', a product made by Salim Ltd:

	£
Direct material costs	14 per unit
Direct labour costs	32 per unit
Total fixed costs	74,000
Selling price	83 per unit

WORKED EXAMPLE *continued*

Required Calculate the break-even point in units for 'grests'.

Answer

$$\text{Contribution} = \text{Selling price per unit} - \text{variable costs per unit}$$

$$\text{Contribution} = 83 - (14 + 32)$$

$$\text{Contribution} = £37$$

If each 'grest' sold pays for its own variable costs, it only leaves the fixed costs to be covered.

One grest sold will contribute £37 towards the total fixed costs;

two grests sold will contribute £74 towards the total fixed costs;

three grests sold will contribute £111 towards the total fixed costs;

How many grests sold will contribute £74,000 towards total fixed costs?

$$\text{Break-even} = \frac{\text{Total fixed costs}}{\text{Contribution per unit}} = \frac{£74,000}{£37} = 2,000 \text{ grests}$$

THE FORMULA METHOD

Break-even point formula

$$\text{Break-even} = \frac{\text{Total fixed costs}}{\text{Contribution per unit}}$$

Sometimes the information is not given in precisely the way that we would like. We may need to get it into a form that suits us.

WORKED EXAMPLE

The following information relates to the production and sales of 2,450 'hupers':

	£
Total direct labour costs	41,650
Total direct material costs	56,350
Total fixed costs	54,000
Total sales revenue	183,750

Required (a) Calculate the number of 'hupers' that need to be sold in order to break even.
(b) Calculate the margin of safety.

Answer

The information given is total costs and total revenues.

The break-even point formula uses total fixed costs but uses contribution per unit. It is therefore necessary to calculate the contribution per unit before using the formula.

WORKED EXAMPLE *continued*

	£	
Direct labour cost per unit	= 17	£41,650/2,450
Direct material costs per unit	= 23	£56,350/2,450
Total variable costs per unit	= 40	
Sales revenue per unit	= 75	£183,750/2,450
Contribution per unit	= 35	£75 − £40

$$\text{Break-even point} = \frac{\text{Total fixed costs}}{\text{Contribution per unit}} = \frac{£54,000}{£35} = 1,543 \text{ hupers}$$

The margin of safety = achievable sales − break-even sales level

$$= 2,450 - 1,543$$

$$= 907 \text{ hupers}$$

Note

The exact answer is 1542.857 hupers, but we always **round up** since it is usually impossible to sell a part of the unit that is the subject of the question.

WORKED EXAMPLE

The following information is given for the production and sales of 1,500 'dorcs':

	£
Direct labour costs per unit	13.00
Direct material costs per unit	8.00
Fixed costs per unit	7.50
Selling price per unit	40.00

Required (a) Calculate the number of 'dorcs' to be sold in order to break even.
(b) Calculate the margin of safety.

Answer

The formula to be used requires that we use *total* fixed costs but contribution *per unit*.

Total fixed costs = £11,250 *£7.50 × 1,500*

Contribution per unit = Selling price per unit − variable costs per unit

$$= £40 - £13 \text{ plus } £8$$

$$= £19$$

$$\text{Break-even} = \frac{\text{Total fixed costs}}{\text{Contribution per unit}} = \frac{£11,250}{£19} = 593 \text{ dorcs (actually 592.105 but rounded up)}$$

Margin of safety = achievable sales − break even level of sales

$$= 1,500 - 593$$

$$= 907 \text{ dorcs}$$

If we required the total sales revenue generated at the break-even point, we have to multiply the break-even volume by the selling price charged for each unit.

The total sales revenue required in order for 'hupers' to break even was £115,725 (1,543 × £75).

The total sales revenue required in order for 'dorcs' to break even was £23,720 (593 × £40).

> ● **EXAMINATION TIP**
>
> If your answer gives a break-even point that is very low, check that you have used total fixed costs, not fixed costs per unit.

QUESTION 5

The following information is given for Bernard:

	£
Selling price per unit	50.00
Variable cost per unit	23.00
Total fixed cost	50,000

Required Calculate the break-even point in units and in total sales revenue.

QUESTION 6

The following information is given for Donna:

	£
Selling price per unit	66.00
Variable cost per unit	47.00
Total fixed cost	43,000

Required Calculate the break-even point in units and in total sales revenue.

QUESTION 7

The following information relates to the production and sales of 2,000 units of 'relur':

	£
Total direct labour costs	72,000
Total direct material costs	40,000
Total fixed costs	35,000
Total sales revenue	160,000

Required (a) Calculate the break-even point for 'relur' in units and total sales revenue.
(b) Calculate the margin of safety.

QUESTION 8

The following information relates to the production and sale of 3,750 units of 'licnep':

	£
Total direct labour costs	33,750
Total direct material costs	11,250
Total fixed costs	63,750
Total sales revenue	142,500

Required (a) Calculate the break-even point for 'licnep' in units and in total sales revenue.
(b) Calculate the margin of safety.

QUESTION 9

The following information is given for production and sales of 3,400 units of 'kuilp':

	£
Direct material costs per unit	13
Direct labour costs costs per unit	12
Fixed costs per unit	6
Selling price per unit	48

Required (a) Calculate the break-even point for 'kuilp' in units and in total sales revenue.

(b) Calculate the margin of safety.

QUESTION 10

The following information is given for production and sales of 9,000 units of 'doth':

	£
Direct material costs per unit	3
Direct labour costs per unit	14
Fixed costs per unit	9
Selling price per unit	50

Required (a) Calculate the break-even point for 'doth' in units and in total sales revenue.

(b) Calculate the margin of safety.

Break-even analysis can be used to determine the level of production and sales revenue that would be required to achieve a particular level of profits.

This information is useful to management when planning the future activities of the business.

Target profit point formula

$$\text{Units to be sold to reach target} = \frac{\text{Fixed costs} + \text{profit\_required}}{}$$

WORKED EXAMPLE

Tanzeel requires a profit of £80,000. He supplies the following information:

	£
Selling price per unit	56.00
Variable costs per unit	32.00
Total fixed costs	60,000

Required Calculate the number of units that must be sold in order to achieve a profit of £80,000.

Answer

$$\text{Level of sales required} = \frac{\text{Total fixed costs} + \text{target profits}}{}$$

$$= £60,000 + £80,000$$

$$= \frac{£140,000}{£24}$$

$$= 5,834 \text{ rounded up (actual answer 5,833.33)}.$$

QUESTION 11

Darren produces and sells 'tunfo'. He requires a profit of £35,000.

He supplies the following information which is based on production and sales of 4,000 units:

	£
Direct labour costs per unit	23.00
Direct material costs per units	16.00
Fixed costs per unit	10.00
Selling price per unit	80.00

Required Calculate the number of units to be sold and the total sales revenue necessary for Darren to achieve his desired profit level of £35,000.

QUESTION 12

Tara produces and sells 'klim'. She requires a profit of £56,000.

She supplies the following information which is based on production and sales of 5,000 units:

	£
Direct labour costs per unit	49.00
Direct material costs per unit	28.00
Fixed costs per unit	12.00
Selling price per unit	110.00

Required Calculate the number of units to be sold and the total revenue necessary for Tara to achieve her desired profit of £56,000.

The major drawback with the method of determining break-even outlined above is that it will only work for a single product. Obviously, different products have different cost patterns and therefore different contributions to different fixed costs.

In order to overcome this problem the following method can be used. However, the method about to be described will not calculate the number of units to be sold in order to break even.

THE CONTRIBUTION/SALES METHOD (SOMETIMES REFERRED TO AS THE PROFIT/VOLUME METHOD)

This method can be used in marginal costing where the variable cost per unit and the selling price per unit are not available or would be extremely difficult to determine.

The method expresses contribution as a percentage of sales.

$$\text{Formula} = \frac{\text{Contribution}}{\text{Sales}} \times 100 = \text{contribution/sales ratio, also known as profit/volume}$$
$$(\text{P/v) ratio.}$$

Provided that the selling price per unit and the marginal costs per unit do not change, then the contribution/sales ratio will remain fixed.

A simple illustration demonstrates this fact:

	1 unit £	2 units £	3 units £	10 units £	1000 units £
Sales £4 per unit	4	8	12	40	4,000
Marginal cost £3 per unit	3	6	9	30	3,000
Contribution	1	2	3	10	1,000

$\dfrac{\text{Contribution}}{\text{Sales}} \times 100$ $\quad \dfrac{1}{4} \times 100 \quad \dfrac{2}{8} \times 100 \quad \dfrac{3}{12} \times 100 \dots\dots\dots$ all equal 25%.

We can use the information to calculate the break-even point and the total sales revenue needed to achieve a particular level of profits.

WORKED EXAMPLE

The following information is given for Rodit Ltd:

Marginal costing statement for the year ended 31 May 20*3	
	£
Sales	200,000
Less Variable costs	110,000
Contribution	90,000
Fixed costs	40,000
Net profit	50,000

Required Calculate the contribution/sales ratio and hence the break-even point for Rodit Ltd.

Answer

$$\text{Contribution/sales ratio} = \frac{90,000}{200,000} \times 100 = 45\%$$

$$\text{Break-even point} = \frac{\text{Fixed costs}}{\text{Contribution/sales ratio}}$$

$$= \frac{£40,000}{45\%}$$

$$= £88,889 \text{ sales revenue.}$$

Note
This method gives the level of sales revenue at which the business would break even.

WORKED EXAMPLE

The following information relates to Greta Ltd:

Marginal costing statement for the year ended 30 November 20*3	
	£
Sales	400,000
Less Variable costs	190,000
Contribution	210,000
Fixed costs	140,000
Net profit	70,000

Required Calculate the sales revenue necessary to give Greta Ltd a profit of £90,000.

Answer

$$\text{Contribution/sales ratio} = \frac{210,000}{400,000} \times 100 = 52.5\%.$$

WORKED EXAMPLE *continued*

Sales volume required to produce £90,000 profit = $\dfrac{\text{Fixed costs} + £90{,}000}{}$.

Sales volume required = $\dfrac{140{,}000 + 90{,}000}{} = \dfrac{230{,}000}{52.5\%}$

= £438,096.

So sales would have to increase by £38,096.

QUESTION 13

The following information is given for Dasty Ltd:

Marginal costing statement for the year ended 28 February 20*3

	£
Sales	560,000
Less Variable costs	200,000
Contribution	360,000
Fixed costs	150,000
Net profit	210,000

The managers of Dasty Ltd wish to increase profits to £250,000.

Required Calculate the total sales revenue required to give a profit of £250,000.

QUESTION 14

The following marginal costing statement is given for Thomas Ltd:

	£
Sales	430,000
Less Variable costs	280,000
Contribution	150,000
Fixed costs	120,000
Net profit	30,000

The managers of Thomas Ltd wish to increase profits to £50,000.

Required Calculate the total sales revenue necessary to give a profit of £50,000.

THE GRAPHICAL METHOD OF DETERMINING THE BREAK-EVEN POINT

- Only use the graphical method of finding the break-even point for a product when it is asked for in a question.
- When drawing the graph, work methodically.
- Build up the graph in stages.
- Often there will be marks scored at each stage of the construction, so work carefully.
- The accuracy of your graph and the results you can read from it will depend on the amount of care you take.

Plot is to draw the information on the graph.

Lines drawn on a graph are generally referred to as **curves**, even though they may be straight!

WORKED EXAMPLE

The following information is given for the production of 100,000 coffee tables:

		£
Selling price per table		25
Costs per unit	Wood	4
	Direct wages	7
	Variable manufacturing overhead	3
	Fixed manufacturing overhead	4
	Variable sales overhead	1
	Fixed sales overhead	2

Required Prepare a break-even graph for coffee tables, showing the break-even point and the margin of safety.

Answer

Stage 1
The horizontal axis of your graph is used to show the sales output in units.

The vertical axis of your graph is used to show costs and revenues.

Where the two axes meet is called the origin and denotes zero for both axes. It should be marked 0.

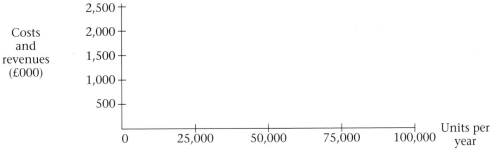

It is important to remember that the data must be scaled evenly otherwise the graph that you draw will be distorted and will give incorrect results.

O EXAMINATION TIP

Graphs are a visual aid. They must be accurate and easily read.

Make your graph as large as the graph paper will allow.

Stage 2
Always give your graph a heading.

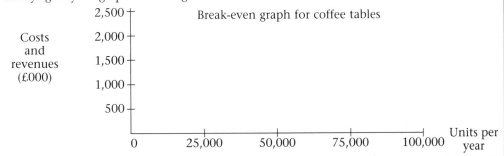

Stage 3

Draw in the fixed costs.

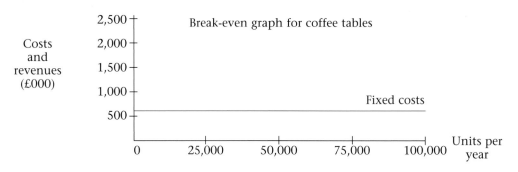

Stage 4

In order to plot the variable costs, a few calculations need to be done.

The variable costs are £15 per table.

(Wood costs + direct wages + variable manufacturing overheads + variable sales overhead.)

Sales output	0 £	10,000 £	60,000 £
Variable costs (£15 per unit)	0	150,000	900,000
Fixed costs	600,000	600,000	600,000
Total costs	600,000	750,000	1,500,000

We now indicate with an x the point that indicates 0 on the horizontal axis and 600,000 on the vertical axis.

We then put an x on the point that indicates 10,000 on the horizontal axis and 750,000 on the vertical axis.

We then put an x on the point that indicates 60,000 on the horizontal axis and 1,500,000 on the vertical axis.

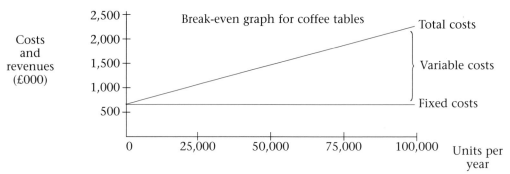

We now have in place the total cost curve.

Remember to mark each curve after you have finished drawing it

WORKED EXAMPLE *continued*

Stage 5
Draw in the sales revenue curve.

The complete graph should look like this:

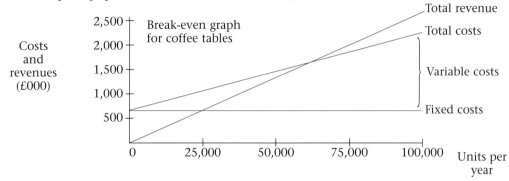

Stage 6
Mark on your graph the break-even point and indicate the margin of safety.

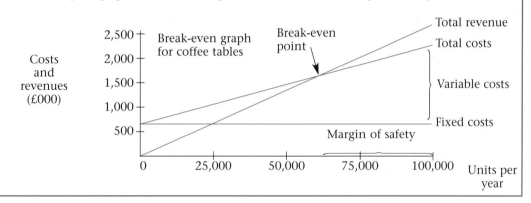

QUESTION 14

The following information is given for 5,000 sales of Product A:

	£
Variable cost per unit	20
Fixed costs per unit	8
Selling price per unit	40

Required (a) Prepare a break-even graph.
(b) Indicate the break-even point.
(c) Identify the margin of safety.

QUESTION 15

The following information is given for 1,000 sales of product B:

	£
Variable costs per unit	35
Fixed costs per unit	10
Selling price per unit	50

Required (a) Prepare a break-even chart.
(b) Indicate the break-even point.
(c) Identify the margin of safety.

QUESTION 16

The following unit costs and revenues are given for production and sales of 5,000 'Tertos':

	£
Direct materials	1.70
Direct labour	3.50
Royalties	1.30
Fixed factory overheads	2.40
Selling price	10.00

Required (a) Prepare a break-even chart.
          (b) Indicate the break-even point.
          (c) Identify the margin of safety.

QUESTION 17

The following unit costs and revenues are given for the production and sales of 4,000 units of 'frootos':

	£
Direct materials	3.10
Direct labour	6.00
Fixed factory overheads	4.35
Selling price	12.00

Required (a) Prepare a break-even graph.
          (b) Indicate the break-even point.
          (c) Identify the margin of safety.

LIMITATIONS OF BREAK-EVEN CHARTS

- There is an assumption that all data behaves in a linear manner:
  - fixed costs are assumed to remain fixed regardless of circumstances
  - selling price is assumed to remain constant in all circumstances.
- The break-even chart assumes that the only factor affecting costs and revenues is sales volume. Costs and revenues may be affected by:
  - increases in output
  - changes in economic climate
  - changes in technology etc.
- It is assumed that the cost mix remains constant, but business change their capital–labour mix over time or as circumstances may dictate.
- There is an assumption that all production is sold.
- The charts generally only apply to one product.

Chapter summary

- 'Marginal' means 'extra'. Marginal costs are the extra costs incurred when an extra product is produced. Marginal revenue is the extra revenue earned by the sale of one extra unit of production.
- Contribution towards fixed costs and profit is the difference between selling price and variable costs.
- The break-even point is the lowest level of sales or units sold at which total revenue received by a business is equal to the total costs of the business.
- Margin of safety is the difference between the actual sales achieved or forecast as achievable and the break-even level of sales.
- Target profit point is found by adding the target profit to the fixed costs and dividing by the contribution per unit.
- Graphs are a useful way of showing the break-even point but they are time-consuming to prepare.

Self-test questions

- Define 'marginal cost'.
- Define 'marginal revenue'.
- Marginal cost = variable costs + fixed costs. True or false?
- Marginal cost = variable costs − fixed costs. True or false?
- Marginal cost = variable costs. True or false?
- Marginal cost = fixed costs. True or false?
- Total revenue produced through the sales of 300 units is £6,300; total revenue for 301 units is £6,321. Calculate marginal revenue.
- Total costs £34,723; total revenue £34,723 is the .... point. Fill the gap.
- Break-even point is 2,300 units; actual sales are 3,000 units. The margin of safety is ..... .
- Name two limitations of using a break-even chart.

TWENTY NINE

Budgeting and Budgetary Control

A budget is a short-term financial plan. It is defined by CIMA as 'a plan expressed in money'.

We have already said that accounting fulfils two purposes:

■ the stewardship function
■ the management function.

The management function can be broken down into:

■ planning
■ co-ordinating
■ communicating
■ decision-making
■ controlling.

Budgets help to achieve all five of these functions.

■ The budgets produced by a business are 'plans expressed in money'. The budgets show what management hopes to achieve in a future time period in terms of overall plans as well as departmental plans.
■ The individual budgets are intertwined with each other – they depend on each other and influence each other. There is a need to ensure that the individual budgets are not contradictory or in conflict.
■ Because of the inter-dependency and the co-ordination of the budgets, managers must communicate with each other when preparing budgets – they must also communicate the plans to staff below and management above.
■ The nature of forecasting means that decisions have to be made. If profits are to increase then decisions must be made regarding sales; production levels etc.
■ Budgets will be compared with actual results. Remedial action can then be taken when actual results are worse than budgeted results. In cases where actual results are better than those budgeted, examples of good practice may be identified and copied elsewhere in the organisation.

By the end of this chapter you should be able to:
■ understand the need for budgeting
■ explain the benefits of budgetary control
■ explain the limitations of budgetary control
■ prepare budgets for
  ■ cash
  ■ purchases
  ■ sales
  ■ production
  ■ debtors
  ■ creditors
■ show how these budgets relate to the master budget.

BENEFITS OF BUDGETING

The benefits of budgeting are:

■ The preparation of individual budgets means that planning must take place.
■ These plans need to be prepared in a co-ordinated way and this requires communication throughout all levels of the business.
■ The budgeting process defines areas of responsibility and targets to be achieved by different personnel.
■ Budgets can act as a motivating influence at all levels – this is generally only true when all staff are involved in the preparation of budgets. If budgets are imposed on staff they might have a de-motivating effect on morale.
■ Budgets are a major part of the overall strategic plan of the business and as such individual departmental and personal goals are more likely to be an integral part of the 'bigger picture'.
■ Budgets generally lead to a more efficient use of resources at the disposal of the business – leading to a better control of costs.

LIMITATIONS OF BUDGETING

- Budgets are only as good as the data being used – if data is inaccurate the budget will be of little use. Should one departmental budget be over-optimistic or pessimistic this will have a 'knock-on effect' on other associated budgets.
- Budgets might become an over-riding goal – this could lead to a misuse of resources or incorrect decisions being made.
- Budgets might act as a demotivator if they are imposed rather than negotiated.
- Budgets might be based on plans that can be achieved easily – so making departments/managers appear to be more efficient than they really are. There is also a possibility that this could also lead to complacency and/or under-performance.
- Budgets might lead to departmental rivalry.

THE SALES BUDGET

The sales budget is generally the first budget to be prepared since most businesses are sales led. It shows predicted sales and the revenues that are expected to be generated for the budget period.

Once the sales budget has been drawn up the other budgets can be prepared using the information from the sales budget. If the sales budget is inaccurate, these inaccuracies will filter through and make the other budgets inaccurate too.

The budget will be based on sales forecasts for the budgeted period.

Sales forecasts are very difficult to prepare because there are so many variables that are out of the control of the managers preparing the budget.

These variables could include:

- actions of customers – customers changing to or from other suppliers
- actions of competitors – competitors increasing or decreasing their price
- the state of the economy – the economy in a state of 'boom or bust'
- governmental action – changes in the levels of taxation; changes in government spending; imposition of sanctions etc.

WORKED EXAMPLE

Mentoff Ltd produces one type of machine: the ZT/103. The expected sales for machine ZT/103 for the three months ending 31 October 20*3 are:

	August	September	October
Budgeted sales	10	12	13
Expected selling price per machine	£2,100	£2,100	£2,150

Required Prepare the sales budget for the three months ending 31 October 20*3.

Answer

	August	September	October
Budgeted sales	£21,000	£25,200	£27,950

THE PRODUCTION BUDGET

A production budget is prepared to determine whether the required future levels of production necessary to satisfy the anticipated the level of predicted sales are attainable. It decides on the quantities of finished goods that must be produced to meet expected sales plus any increase in stock levels that might be required.

WORKED EXAMPLE

Mentoff Ltd is expected to have an opening stock of five ZT/103 machines on 1 August 20*3. It requires a closing stock of six machines at 31 October 20*3.

Required   Prepare a production budget (based on the budgeted sales used in the previous example). Mentoff Ltd requires an even production flow throughout the year.

Answer

The total production is found by using the following calculation:

Budgeted sales	35 (10 + 12 +13)
Plus Budgeted closing stock	6
Total production needed to meet budgeted sales and closing stock	41
Less Budgeted opening stock	5
Budgeted production	36

Note
The calculation has been used to determine the budgeted production for a period of three months. The same calculation could be used to determine the budgeted production for a month, six months, a year etc.

EXAMPLE

An even production flow means that Mentoff Ltd will have to produce 12 units per month. The production budget will look like this:

	August	September	October
Budgeted sales	10	12	13
Plus Budgeted closing stock	7	7	6
Total production needed...	17	19	19
Less Budgeted opening stock	5	7	7
Budgeted production	12	12	12

THE PURCHASES BUDGET

A purchases budget is required to determine the quantities of purchases required either for resale or for use in a production process. The calculation to be used is similar to that used in compiling a production budget.

WORKED EXAMPLE

Danst Ltd has the following budgeting sales of 'limts':

	February	March	April
Budgeted sales	120	140	160

The opening stock on 1 February is expected to be 26 units of 'limts' and the closing stock on 30 April is expected to be 41 units of 'limts'.

Required Calculate the number of 'limts' to be purchased over the three months ending 30 April.

Answer

Budgeted sales	420 (120 + 140 + 160)
Plus Budgeted closing stock	41
Total purchases needed to meet budgeted sales and closing stock	461
Less Budgeted opening stock	26
Budgeted purchases of goods for resale	435

435 units have to be purchased during February, March and April. If an even amount of purchases were required throughout the year, then 145 units (435 divided by 3) would be purchased each month and the budget would look like this:

If we put in the figures that we know ...

	February	March	April
Budgeted sales	120	140	160
Plus Budgeted closing stock	___	___	41
Total purchases needed			201
Less Budgeted opening stock	26	___	___
Budgeted purchases of goods for resale	145	145	145

We can now fill in the blanks (we hope) by working backwards:

	February	March	April
Budgeted sales	120	140	160
Plus Budgeted closing stock	*51*	*56*	41
Total needed	*171*	*196*	201
Less Budgeted opening stock	26	*51*	*56*
Budgeted purchases of goods for resale	145	145	145

It is not usually necessary to have an equal flow of purchases each month.

However, it might be necessary to have a specified number of units in stock at the start of each month.

The calculation for this type of budget is the same as that just used.

WORKED EXAMPLE

Batt & Co supply the following budgeted sales figures:

	July	August	September	October
Budgeted sales	40	72	92	100

It is policy to maintain stocks at a level of 25 % of the following month's budgeted sales.

Required Prepare a purchases budget for the three months ending 30 September.

Answer

We know that the opening stock in July should be 10 (25% of 40)

in August it should be 18 (25% of 72)

in September it should be 23 (25% of 92).

We also know that the budgeted closing stock at the end of September should be 25 (25% of 100).

First, we put in the figures that we know:

	July	August	September
Budgeted sales	40	72	92
Plus Budgeted closing stock	18	23	25
Total purchases needed . . .			
Less Budgeted opening stock	10	18	23
Budgeted purchases of goods for resale			

We can fill in the blanks:

	July	August	September
Budgeted sales	40	72	92
Plus Budgeted closing stock	18	23	25
Total purchases needed . . .	58	95	117
Less Budgeted opening stock	10	18	23
Budgeted purchases of goods for resale	48	77	94

QUESTION 1

Toni is to start business on 1 May selling food-mixers; she believes that she will sell 300 mixers in May and she expects that her monthly sales will increase by 20% on the previous month's budgeted sales until the end of the year.

Stocks are to be maintained at 10% of the following month's budgeted sales.

(Note that a 20% increase in sales in July would result in August sales of 518.4 food-mixers. Impossible to sell 0.4 of a mixer! So sales for August will be predicted at 519 mixers.

Likewise, stocks held at 31 July could not be 51.84 or 51.9 mixers – we have to keep whole mixers in stock! Closing stock at 31 July is therefore 52 mixers.)

Required Prepare a purchases budget for the three months ending 31 July.

QUESTION 2

Lawrence sells calculators. His budgeted sales for January are expected to be 200 calculators. He expects sales to increase by 10% on the previous month's sales until the end of April.

Stocks are to be maintained at 50% of the following month's budgeted sales.

Required Prepare a purchases budget for the three months ending 31 March.

THE DEBTORS' BUDGET

Debtors' budget forecasts the amount owed to a business by credit customers at the end of each month.

The debtors' budget is linked to the production budget; to the sales budget; and to the cash budget. It will also take into account the length of credit period that is allowed on outstanding customers' balances.

WORKED EXAMPLE

The managers of Mayne Ltd provide the following budgeted information for the three months ending 31 March:

		£
1 January amounts owed by debtors		30,000
Budgeted credit sales for	January	40,000
	February	50,000
	March	60,000
Cash sales for	January	12,000
	February	10,000
	March	14,000

All credit customers are expected to settle their debts in the month following the sale of goods. They are allowed and will take 5% cash discount.

Required Prepare a debtors' budget for the three months ending 31 March.

Answer

	January	February	March
Balance brought forward	30,000	40,000	50,000
Credit sales	40,000	50,000	60,000
	70,000	90,000	110,000
Cash received from debtors	28,500	38,000	47,500
Discount allowed	1,500	2,000	2,500
Balance carried forward	40,000	50,000	60,000

Note
Cash sales have not been included. Cash customers do not have an account in the sales ledger. Cash customers are never debtors.

WORKED EXAMPLE

The managers of Hoof Ltd provide the following budgeted information for the three months ending 30 November:

		£	
Budgeted credit sales	July	33,000	
	August	27,000	
31 August amount by owed by debtors		38,000	(debtors from July £11,000, debtors from August £27,000)
Budgeted credit sales	September	30,000	
	October	39,000	
	November	36,000	

Two-thirds of credit customers are expected to settle their debts in the month following receipt of the goods; the remainder will settle two months after receipt.

Required Prepare a debtors' budget for the three months ending 30 November.

Answer

	September £		October £		November £	
Balance brought forward	38,000		39,000		49,000	
Credit sales	30,000		39,000		36,000	
	68,000		78,000		85,000	
Cash received	18,000	(Aug)	20,000	(Sept)	26,000	(Oct)
Cash received	11,000	(Jul)	9,000	(Aug)	10,000	(Sept)
Balance carried forward	39,000		49,000		49,000	

QUESTION 3

The budgeted sales for Cerne Ltd are as follows:

	February £	March £	April £	May £
Budgeted sales	60,000	70,000	80,000	90,000

20% of all budgeted sales are expected to be for cash.

Debtors are allowed and will take one month's credit.

Required Prepare a debtors' budget for the three months ending 31 May.

QUESTION 4

The following information relates to La Ville Ltd:

	March £	April £	May £	June £
Budgeted sales	30,000	40,000	50,000	60,000

10% of budgeted sales are expected to be cash sales.

Debtors are allowed and will take one month's credit.

Required Prepare a debtors' budget for the three months ending 30 June.

THE CREDITORS' BUDGET

A creditors' budget forecasts the amounts that will be owed to creditors at the end of each month. It is linked to the purchases budget (i.e. purchases of components or raw materials in the case of a manufacturing business or purchases of goods for resale in the case of a retailing business) and to the cash budget.

WORKED EXAMPLE

The managers of Withers Ltd provide the following budgeted information for the three months ending 30 June:

		£
1 April predicted amount owed to creditors		14,000
Budgeted credit purchases for	April	15,000
	May	16,000
	June	17,000
Budgeted cash purchases for	April	2,000
	May	5,000
	June	3,000

Withers Ltd will pay all creditors in the month following purchase. They expect to receive cash discount of 5% on all credit purchases.

Required Prepare a creditors' budget for the three months ending 30 June.

Answer

	April £	May £	June £
Balance brought forward	14,000	15,000	16,000
Credit purchases	15,000	16,000	17,000
	29,000	31,000	33,000
Cash paid to creditors	13,300	14,250	15,200
Discount received	700	750	800
Balance carried forward	15,000	16,000	17,000

WORKED EXAMPLE

The managers of Tayle Ltd provide the following budgeted information for the three months ending 30 September:

		£	
Budgeted credit purchases for	May	30,000	
	June	24,000	
1 July predicted amount owed to creditors		39,000	(creditors from May £15,000, creditors from June £24,000)
Budgeted credit purchases	July	27,000	
	August	32,000	
	September	29,000	

Tayle Ltd will settle 50% of outstanding creditors in the month following purchase of the goods and the remainder will be settled in the following month.

WORKED EXAMPLE *continued*

Required Prepare a creditors' budget for the three months ending 30 September.

Answer

	July	August	September
Balance brought forward	39,000	39,000	45,500
Credit purchases	27,000	32,000	29,000
	66,000	71,000	74,500
Cash paid to creditors	15,000 (May)	12,000 (June)	13,500 (July)
Cash paid to creditors	12,000 (June)	13,500 (July)	16,000 (Aug)
Balance carried forward	39,000	45,500	45,000

QUESTION 5

The following information is available for Bolay Ltd:

	May £	June £	July £	August £
Budgeted purchases	15,000	20,000	25,000	30,000

5% of all purchases are for cash.

Creditors will be paid in the month following the purchase of goods.

Required Prepare a creditors' budget for the three months ending 31 August.

QUESTION 6

The following information is available for Trinity Ltd:

	July £	August £	September £	October £
Budgeted purchases	40,000	30,000	50,000	45,000

90% of all purchases are on credit.

Creditors will be paid in the month following purchase.

Required Prepare a creditors' budget for the three months ending 31 October.

CASH BUDGETS

A cash budget shows estimates of future cash incomes and cash expenditures. It is usually prepared monthly and includes both capital and revenue transactions. It is drawn up to help management be aware of any potential shortages or surpluses of cash resources that could occur; thus allowing management to make any necessary financial arrangements.

The preparation of a cash budget:

■ helps to ensure that there is always sufficient cash available to allow the normal activities of the business to take place
■ will highlight times when the business will have cash surpluses, thus allowing management time to arrange short-term investment of those surpluses in order to gain maximum return
■ will highlight times when the business might have cash deficits, thus allowing management to arrange short-term alternative sources of finance through the arrangement of overdraft facilities or the arrangement of extended periods of credit or the re-structuring of existing longer-term debts.

WORKED EXAMPLE

The following budgeted figures relate to Cropp Ltd for the three months ending 30 September:

	July £	August £	September £
Cash sales	10,000	10,000	12,000
Cash received from debtors	26,000	28,000	27,000
Payments made to creditors	9,000	11,000	12,000
Cash purchases	6,000	6,000	7,000
Payment for rent		21,000	
Payment for rates			1,200
Payment of wages	8,000	8,000	8,000
Payments for other expenses	2,750	3,750	2,800

It is expected that cash in hand at 30 June will be £820.

Required Prepare a cash budget for each of the three months ending 30 September.

Answer

	July £	August £	September £
Receipts			
Cash sales	10,000	10,000	12,000
Cash received from debtors	26,000	28,000	27,000
	36,000	38,000	39,000
Payments			
To creditors	9,000	11,000	12,000
Cash purchase	6,000	6,000	7,000
Rent		21,000	
Rates			1,200
Wages	8,000	8,000	8,000
Other expenses	2,750	3,750	2,800
	25,750	49,750	31,000
Balance brought forward	820	11,070	(680)
Receipts	36,000	38,000	39,000
	36,820	49,070	38,320
Payments	25,750	49,750	31,000
Balance carried forward	11,070	(680)	7,320

The cash budget shows that overdraft facilities must be arranged during August.

There are alternative layouts. The one shown above is the version most frequently used.

Cash budgets are the most popular type of budget examined. It is well worth practising the layout shown.

Note
- Cash budgets include bank transactions. It is therefore possible to have negative balances in a cash budget.
- Only cash and bank items are included.
- The cash budget deals only with transactions involving the movement of cash. It therefore will not include any non-cash expenses such as a provision for depreciation or provision for doubtful debts.
- That some business studies textbooks refer to cash budgets as cash-flow forecasts. Do not confuse cash-flow forecasts with cash-flow statements (FRS1).

WORKED EXAMPLE

Bradley Ltd sells one type of lathe at a price of £6,600 each. 50% is payable in the month of sale and 50% the following month.

The lathes are purchased from a supplier at a cost of £1,500 paid in the month following purchase.

	Dec 20*3	Jan 20*4	Feb 20*4	March 20*4	April 20*4
Budgeted sales (in units)	4	6	3	5	7
Budgeted purchases	6	3	5	7	8
Budgeted operating costs are	£	£	£	£	£
Rent	1,500	1,500	1,500	1,500	1,650
Wages	16,000	19,000	19,000	19,000	19,000
Other expenses	4,700	5,200	5,100	4,800	5,000
Depreciation	2,500	2,500	2,500	2,500	2,500

All operating costs are paid in the month in which they occur.

The balance of cash in hand at 1 January 20*3 is expected to be £1,800.

Required Prepare a cash budget for each of the three months ending 31 March 20*4.

Answer

	January £		February £		March £	
Receipts						
Cash received from debtors	13,200	(Dec)	19,800	(Jan)	9,900	(Feb)
Cash received from debtors	19,800	(Jan)	9,900	(Feb)	16,500	(Mar)
	33,000		29,700		26,400	
Payments						
Payments to creditors	9,000	(Dec)	4,500	(Jan)	7 500	(Feb)
Rent	1,500		1,500		1,500	
Wages	19,000		19,000		19,000	
Other expenses	5,200		5,100		4,800	
	34,700		30,100		32,800	
Balance brought forward	1,800		100		(300)	
Receipts	33,000		29,700		26,400	
	34,800		29,800		26,100	
Payments	34,700		30,100		32,800	
Balance carried forward	100		(300)		(6,700)	

Note
Depreciation has not been included – it is a **non**-cash expense.

QUESTION 7

The following budgeted information relates to Rajpoot Ltd for the three months ending 30 October.

The cash balance at 1 August is expected to be £2,100.

	August £	September £	October £
Cash sales	90,963	106,125	116,230
Payments to creditors	29,650	35,050	38,400
Payments for wages	19,100	28,000	21,500
Rent and rates	2,800	2,800	2,800
Other expenses	5,700	5,500	5,300
Payment for purchase of machine		84,000	
Depreciation on machine		700	700

Required Prepare a cash budget for each of the three months ending 30 October.

QUESTION 8

The following budgeted information relates to Chin Ltd for the three months ending 31 July.

The cash balance at 1 May is expected to be £120.

	May £	June £	July £
Cash sales	6,400	8,000	8,000
Receipts from debtors	36,800	59,200	56,000
Payments to creditors	25,600	28,800	27,200
Cash purchases	3,680	4,320	3,840
Rent	3,200	3,200	3,200
Wages	12,800	12,800	12,800
Other expenses	2,800	5,696	4,960
Purchase of shop fittings	3,000		
Depreciation of shop fittings	250	250	250

Required Prepare a cash budget for each of the three months ending 31 July.

MASTER BUDGET

Just like all the individual ingredients that are put together to make a successful meal, after all the separate budgets are prepared they are drawn together to prepare the master budget.

This provides a summary of all the planned operations of the business for the period covered by the budgets. It is a sum of all the individual budgets prepared by the different parts of the business.

It is made up of:

■ a budgeted manufacturing account (where appropriate)
■ a budgeted trading account
■ a budgeted profit and loss account
■ a budgeted balance sheet.

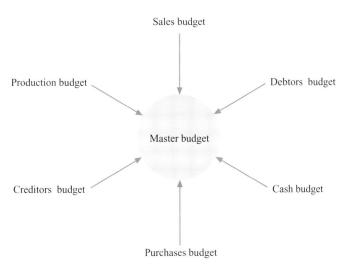

Examination questions do not usually expect candidates to prepare detailed master budgets because of limited time available in the examination.

However, it is possible for an examiner to require candidates to prepare a summarised profit and loss account from a cash budget.

This type of question is designed to test a candidate's ability to:

■ apply the accruals and realisation concepts
■ differentiate between capital and revenue expenditures and incomes
■ distinguish between cash and non-cash expenses.

WORKED EXAMPLE

The following budgeted information is given for Plum Ltd:

Year 20*3	August £	September £	October £	November £
Credit sales	30,000	40,000	35,000	45,000
Credit purchases	15,000	20,000	15,000	25,000
Wages paid	7,500	7,500	7,500	7,500
Other expenses	8,200	8,400	8,100	9,000
Purchase of machine		10,000		
Depreciation of machine		100	100	100

■ Debtors pay one month after goods are sold.
■ Creditors are paid one month after receipt of the goods.
■ All expenses are paid in the month in which they occur.
■ It is expected that cash in hand at 1 September 20*3 will be £1,200.
■ Stock as at 1 September 20*3 £2,000.
■ Stock as at 30 November 20*3 £2,500.

Required (a) Prepare a cash budget for each of the three months ending 30 November 20*3.
(b) Prepare a budgeted trading and profit and loss account for the three months ending 30 November 20*3

Answer

(a) **Cash budget for the three months ending 30 November 20*3**

	September £	October £	November £
Receipts: cash received from debtors	30,000	40,000	35,000
Payments:			
Cash paid to creditors	15,000	20,000	15,000
Wages	7,500	7,500	7,500
Other expenses	8,400	8,100	9,000
Purchase of machine	10,000		
	40,900	35,600	31,500
Balance brought forward	1,200	(9,700)	(5,300)
Receipts	30,000	40,000	35,000
	31,200	30,300	29,700
Payments	40,900	35,600	31,500
Balance carried forward	(9,700)	(5,300)	(1,800)

Remember: depreciation does not involve cash leaving the business.

WORKED EXAMPLE *continued*

(b)   **Budgeted trading and profit and loss account for the three months ending 30 November 20*3**

	£	£
Sales		120,000
Less Cost of sales		
Stock as at 1 September	2,000	
Purchases	60,000	
	62,000	
Stock as at 30 November	2,500	59,500
Gross profit		60,500
Less Expenses		
Wages	22,500	
Other expenses	25,500	
Depreciation of machinery	300	48,300
Net profit		12,200

The sales figure is the total of the budgeted figures for the three months under review – September £40,000; October £35,000 and November £45,000, not the amounts shown in the cash budget. Remember the realisation concept?

The purchases figure is the total of the budgeted figures for the three months under review – September £20,000; October £15,000 and November £25,000, not the amounts shown in the cash budget. Once again, the realisation concept is being used.

Depreciation is included in the budgeted profit and loss account because of the accruals concept – the machine is a resource that has been used to generate the profits, so a charge has to be made.

BUDGETARY CONTROL

Budgetary control delegates financial planning to managers. It evaluates their performance by continuously comparing actual results achieved by their departments against those set in the budget.

> **Variances** arise when there is a difference between actual and budgeted figures.

> Favourable variances increase profits.

> Adverse variances reduce profits.

Responsibility for variances rests with departmental heads.

The process requires that variances are analysed and in the case of adverse variances any necessary remedial action is taken.

The benefits and limitations of budgeting as those outlined at the start of the chapter also apply to budgetary control.

Chapter summary

- Budgets are an important part of the management function.
- They are plans expressed in money.
- Budgets help with planning and control of a business.
- Individual departmental budgets are summarised in the master budget.
- The master budget comprises budgeted trading accounts; budgeted profit and loss accounts; and budgeted balance sheets. (A budgeted manufacturing account is also part of the master budget where appropriate.)
- Cash budgets are the most frequently examined budget.
- Cash budgets are prepared on a cash basis.
- Master budgets are prepared using the accruals basis.

Self-test questions

- Define a 'budget'.
- Identify two functions of budgeting.
- Identify two benefits of budgeting.
- Identify two limitations of budgeting.
- Which budget should usually be prepared first?
- Budgeted sales are 12 units; opening stock 2 units; closing stock 3 units. How many units should be produced?
- Name the budget used to forecast the amounts owed by credit customers at the end of each month.
- Identify one reason why a cash budget might be prepared.
- Explain why depreciation is not included in a cash budget.
- What is meant by the term 'master budget'?
- Name one component of a master budget.
- Explain the term 'variance'.

TEST QUESTIONS

QUESTION 9

The following budgeted information is available for Hunter Ltd:

	January £	February £	March £	April £
Credit sales	21,000	28,000	30,000	31,000
Cash purchases	8,000	12,000	9,000	10,000
Cash expenses	21,000	20,000	22,000	18,000
Cash purchase of office machinery		24,000		
Depreciation of office machinery		200	200	200

It is expected that the cash balance at 1 February will be £3,200.

Debtors are expected to settle their debts one month after sales have taken place.

Required Prepare a cash budget for each of the three months ending 30 April.

QUESTION 10

The following budgeted information is available for Slipper Ltd:

	February £	March £	April £	May £
Sales	40,000	38,000	39,000	41,000
Cash purchases	14,000	12,000	13,000	15,000
Cash expenses	16,000	18,000	17,000	19,000
Cash purchase of machinery		60,000		
Depreciation of machinery		500	500	500

It is expected that the cash balance at 1 March will be £2,900.

Cash sales are expected to be 10% of total sales. Debtors are expected to settle their debts one month after the sales have taken place.

Required Prepare a cash budget for each of the three months ending 31 May.

QUESTION 11

The following budgeted information is given for Singh Ltd:

	March £	April £	May £	June £
Cash sales	50,000	40,000	50,000	56,000
Purchases	20,000	30,000	25,000	35,000
Cash expenses	21,000	16,000	24,000	20,000
Depreciation of fixed assets	1,000	1,000	1,000	1,000

It is expected that the cash balance at 1 April will be £1,500 overdrawn.

5% of purchases are expected to be for cash. Creditors will be paid in the month following purchase.

Required Prepare a cash budget for each of the three months ending 30 June.

QUESTION 12

The following budgeted information is given for O'Casey Ltd:

	April £	May £	June £	July £
Cash sales	40,000	60,000	80,000	30,000
Purchases	20,000	20,000	30,000	30,000
Cash expenses	15,000	10,000	14,000	13,000
Depreciation of fixed assets	1,500	1,500	1,500	1,500

It is expected that the cash balance at 1 May will be £800 overdrawn.

10% of purchases are expected to be for cash. Creditors will be paid in the month following purchase.

Required Prepare a cash budget for each of the three months ending 31 July.

QUESTION 13

The following budgeted information relates to the business of Pierre:

	May £	June £	July £	August £	September £
Sales	64,000	62,000	60,000	65,000	64,000
Purchases	30,000	32,000	38,000	42,000	39,000
Wages	12,500	12,500	13,000	12,500	12,500
Other expenses	8,500	8,700	8,300	8,500	8,500
Cash purchase of shop fittings			14,000		
Depreciation of shop fittings	150	150	150	150	150

It is expected that:

- the cash balance at 1 July will be £350 overdrawn
- 5% of sales will be for cash
- 10% of purchases will be cash purchases
- debtors will be collected one month after sale
- creditors will be paid two months after purchase
- wages and other expenses are paid as incurred.

Required Prepare a cash budget for each of the three months ending 30 September.

QUESTION 14

The following information relates to the business of Marcel:

	June £	July £	August £	September £	October £
Sales	34,000	36,000	35,000	34,000	37,000
Purchases	15,000	16,000	15,000	15,000	16,000
Wages	5,600	5,700	5,600	5,800	5,600
Rent	2,000	2,000	2,000	2,000	2,000
Other expenses	4,800	4,900	4,300	4,000	5,000
Cash purchase of delivery van			17,000		
Depreciation of vehicles	300	300	600	600	600

It is expected that:

- the cash balance at 1 August will be £2,570
- 10% of sales will be cash sales
- 10% of purchases will be for cash
- debtors will be collected two months after sale
- creditors will be paid one month after purchase
- wages, rent and other expenses will be paid as incurred.

Required Prepare a cash budget for each of the three months ending 31 October.

QUESTION 15

Tommy Chan supplies the following budgeted information relating to his business:

	August £	September £	October £	November £	December £
Sales	23,000	24,000	29,000	34,000	43,000
Purchases	12,000	13,000	15,000	24,000	35,000
Wages	4,500	4,500	4,500	6,000	6,500
Rent	400		400		450
Other expenses	1,750	1,850	3,400	1,600	980
Depreciation of office equipment	450	450	450	450	450

It is expected that:

- the cash balance at 1 October will be £670
- 10% of all sales will be on credit

- 10% of purchases will be for cash
- debtors will settle their debts in the month following sale
- creditors will be paid two months after purchase
- wages, rent and other expenses will be paid as incurred
- stock at 1 October is expected to be £7,000; at 31 December it is expected to be £8,000.

Required (a) Prepare a cash budget for each of the three months ending 31 December.
(b) Prepare a budgeted trading and profit and loss account for the three months ending 31 December.

QUESTION 16

Andy Gillespie supplies the following budgeted information relating to his business:

	May £	June £	July £	August £	September £
Sales	34,000	35,000	37,000	40,000	35,000
Sale of old office machine			150		
Profit on sale of machine			50		
Purchases	16,000	16,500	17,000	19,000	15,000
Purchase of new office machine			1,800		
Wages	5,600	5,500	5,600	5,500	5,600
Other expenses	4,570	4,700	3,950	4,780	5,400
Depreciation of office equipment	250	250	265	265	265

It is expected that:

- the cash balance at 1 July will be £580 overdrawn
- 30% of sales will be credit sales
- 20% of purchases will be for cash
- 50% of credit sale customers will pay in the month following sale; the remainder will pay the following month
- creditors will be paid two months after purchase
- wages will be paid in the month after they are incurred
- other expenses will be paid for as incurred
- stock at 1 July is expected to be £2,000; at 30 September it is expected to be £2,400.

Required (a) Prepare a cash budget for each of the three months ending 30 September.
(b) Prepare a trading and profit and loss account for the three months ending 30 September.

CHAPTER THIRTY

Social Accounting

NON-FINANCIAL ASPECTS OF ACCOUNTING

Businesses increasingly need to consider not only the financial aspects of the organistion but also non-financial factors. Traditionally, managers prepare financial statements that concentrate on the monetary aspects of business in order to make decisions. This is a one-dimensional approach. The non-financial aspects are an increasingly important element of the decision-making process for businesses.

Businesses affect all our lives, in one way or another, whether we are directly involved or not. Consumers and society in general are becoming more aware of the environmental damage that is often the by-product of business activity. We are also conscious, more than over before, of the danger of depleting our non-renewable resources at an unsustainable rate.

SOCIAL AWARENESS

As consumers become more aware of environmental implications, producers are under pressure to show that they are accepting their social responsibility and are manufacturing their products with an appreciation of more than just financial factors.

Profitability is not the only concern of business now. There has been a move in recent years to consider the impact that businesses have on our lives. We are consumers, perhaps employees, and we all live in an environment which is influenced in a multitude of ways by the business world.

Businesses may be profitable but what of the 'hidden costs'? In securing the profits, what are the costs inflicted on people outside the organisation as well as those working within it? What are the costs to the immediate environment and the wider world?

SOCIAL COSTS

What are the social costs involved in carrying out business?
Stress in the workforce? Pollution in the workplace, e.g. fumes, dust etc?
Does the business have an effect on the immediate environs of the business, e.g. noise, dirt etc?
Does the business have an environmental impact of global significance, e.g. acid rain?

SOCIAL COSTS AND PROFITABILITY

You may be cynical and say that businesses do not care about these things as long as they make sufficient profit, but these factors do affect profitability.

If the workforce are unhappy about the environment that they work in, they are less likely to work at full capacity and so productivity will suffer. If working conditions are poor there may be high staff turnover/absenteeism. New staff may need to be trained in the ways of the business, thus incurring recruitment and training costs.

If the environment near to the business is poor, perhaps recruitment of new staff will suffer. There might be bad local publicity affecting product sales in the locality. If the problems are not resolved satisfactorily, the publicity may become more widespread, affecting sales even more.

Specification coverage:
AQA 13.5.

By the end of this chapter you should be able to:
- demonstrate an awareness of social factors faced by businesses
- demonstrate an awareness of situations where social factors might compromise profitability.

With larger firms there may well be a more global reaction, as we have seen in the past with the consumer pressure that was brought to bear on the Shell petroleum company when it announced its intention to sink the Brent Spar oil platform in the North Sea.

Businesses cannot afford to ignore the views of their customers. If consumers decide to unite in opposition against a producer/supplier and cease to purchase from the business this will inevitably reduce sales and ultimately profits. No business can afford to ignore this type of action from pressure groups in the long term.

The major problem that a business faces, in evaluating the consequences of following a particular line of action, is that it is very difficult to put a price on many of the factors that we have mentioned. We saw earlier, as accountants, that we do not include in our accounts things that cannot be measured in monetary terms (the money measurement concept).

If a factory closes, we can calculate the savings in variable costs and in the longer term the savings in fixed costs. We can calculate with some degree of accuracy the redundancy payments. How do we measure the distress that a worker experiences at the loss of their employment?

If a business buys a new computer system, the cost is easily calculated. The savings on staff time can be costed but, once again, how can we put a value on the redundant workers' feelings or the frustration felt by employees who find the operation of computer software a nightmare?

If a business opens an out-of-town superstore, how do we value the convenience that many will experience by being able to do all of their shopping in one outing? Balance this against the cost to your grandparents who can now no longer shop at the local corner shop because it had to close down – its prices were much higher than those charged at the superstore and therefore it could no longer compete.

○ EXAMINATION TIP

- Answer the question as set, not the question you wish had been set.
- Read the question carefully.
- If a question asks what the impact would be on the workforce if a rural branch were to be closed, your answer should focus on the impact on the workforce
  - not the environment
  - not the business
  - not the customers
  - not . . .

Chapter summary

This chapter has dealt with an aspect of accounting that is likely to appear as part of a question that tests other parts of the specification. For example, the purchase of a computerised accounting system may be part of a cash budget question but there might also be an ancillary question that requires you to consider the wider issues of this purchase, ie the potential social consequences.

Self-test questions

- Identify a non-financial aspect of running a haulage business.
- Identify the use of a non-renewable resource.
- Identify one financial cost of a business closing a rural branch.
- Identify one financial benefit of closing a rural branch.
- Identify one non-financial cost of closing a rural branch.
- Identify one non-financial benefit of closing a rural branch.

TEST QUESTIONS

QUESTION 1

Clapper and son are installing a computerised accounting system.

Required Identify the benefits and problems that are likely to be encountered by the workforce.

QUESTION 2

Dronson Ltd manufactures 'Brito' toothpaste. A recent article in a tabloid newspaper has said that the use of Brito over long periods of time can cause mouth ulcers.

Required Advise Dronson on the action it should take with regard to Brito toothpaste.

QUESTION 3

Froudly Ltd has always used the local river to cool its machinery. Recently, the local anglers' association has complained to the board of directors that the fish that they catch are much smaller than they used to be. They demand that Froudly Ltd addresses the problem.

Required Advise the board of directors of Froudly Ltd what action it should take.

QUESTION 4

Bonwinder makes double-glazing window units. Orders have dropped over the past two years. The directors have decided to close the factory in West Cumbria, an area of high unemployment.

Required Identify the non-financial implications of the closure of the local branch of a double-glazing manufacturer.

CHAPTER ONE

1. Money owed to Kellogg's; HP debt.
3. Capital £58,000; fixed assets £60,000; current liabilities £4,000; capital £15,000; current assets £15,000.
5. CA; FA; CA; CA; FA; FA.
7. £214,000.
9. **Sandeep**
Balance sheet as at 31 January 20*3

	£
Fixed assets	
Tools at cost	250
Vehicle at cost	8,000
	8,250
Current assets	
Stock of paint	110
	8,360
Capital	4,300
Bank loan	4,000
Current liability:	
Creditor	60
	8,360

11. **Sandra**
Balance Sheet as at 31 March 20*3

	£
Fixed assets	
Premises at cost	40,000
Machinery at cost	10,000
Office equipment (at cost)	4,000
Vehicle at cost	9,000
	63,000
Capital	50,500
Long-term liability:	
Bank loan	18,000
Current liabilities:	
Creditors	500
Stock	4,000
Debtors	1,200
Bank	800
	6,000
	69,000

13. Capital is the amount the business 'owes' the owner.

CHAPTER TWO

1. A balance sheet can be drawn up at any time.
3. Flowers; crisps; vegetables are all drawings.
5. Profit £5,400.
7. Loss £37,300.
9. Loss £18,250.
11. FA 42,000 + CA 17,000 − CL 14,000 → Capital 45,000
FA 56,000 + CA 20,000 − CL 15,000 − LTL 10,000 → Capital 51,000

	£
Increase in capital	6,000
Add Drawings	14,000
	20,000
Less Legacy	12,000
Net profit for year	8,000

CHAPTER THREE

1. Capital; worth.
3. Jeans; sweatshirts; trainers and leather jackets are all purchases.

---

5. **Biddulph**
Trading account for the year ended 31 March 20*3

	£		£
Stock	4,560	Sales	84,350
Purchases	47,800		
	52,360		
Stock	5,050		
Cost of goods sold	47,310		
Gross profit	37,040		
	84,350		84,350

7. **Clary**
Trading account for the year ended 30 April 20*3

	£		£
Stock	340	Sales	52,900
Purchases	23,560		
	23,900		
Stock	530		
Cost of goods sold	23,370		
Gross profit	29,530		
	52,900		52,900

9. **Joe**
Trading account for the year ended 31 December 20*3

	£		£
Stock	238	Sales	54,760
Purchases	34,930		
	35,168		
Stock	432		
Cost of goods sold	34,736		
Gross profit	20,024		
	54,760		54,760

11. **Rob Berry**
Trading account for the year ended 30 November 20*3

	£	£		£
Stock		1,657	Sales	98,651
Purchases	54,672		Returns inwards	421
Returns outwards	803			
		53,869		
		55,526		
Stock		2,004		
Cost of goods sold		53,522		
Gross profit		44,708		
		98,230		98,230

13. Profit and loss account for the year ended 30 June 20*2.
Trading account for the year ended 30 April 20*2.
Balance sheet as at 31 December 20*2.
15. Gross profit £110,000.
17. Returns inwards; carriage inwards; opening stock.
19. Opening stock plus purchases.

21.

	£
Stock as at 1 July 20*2	256
Purchases	71,006
Goods available for sale	71,262

23. Del

Trading account for the year ended 31 January 20*3

	£		£
	970	Sales	56,710
Stock			
Purchases	35,780		
	36,750		
Stock	1,050		
Cost of goods sold	35,700		
Gross profit	21,010		
	56,710		56,710

25. Natalie

Trading account for the year ended 31 January 20*3

	£	£		£
Stock		1,560	Sales	176,040
Purchases	65,090		Returns inwards	360
Carr. inwards	960			
	66,050			
Returns outwards	770			
		65,280		
		66,840		
Stock		1,640		
Cost of goods sold		65,200		
Gross profit		110,480		
		175,680		175,680

27. Mao

Trading account for the year ended 31 December 20*3

	£	£		£
Stock		12,651	Sales	342,960
Purchases	175,873		Returns inwards	4,532
Carr. inwards	733			
	176,606			
Returns outwards	1,364			
		175,242		
		187,893		
Stock		11,537		
Cost of goods sold		176,356		
Gross Profit		162,072		
		338,428		338,428

3. Pierre Roi

Trading account for the year ended 31 December 20*3

	£		£
Stock	613	Sales	25,047
Purchases	14,661		
	15,274		
	770		
Cost of goods sold	14,504		
Gross profit	10,543		
	25,047		25,047

5. Jack

Profit and loss account for the year ended 31 January 20*3

	£		£
Wages	15,437	Gross profit	43,719
Motor expenses	2,864		
Rent and rates	1,442		
Insurance	3,669		
General expenses	8,742		
Net profit	11,565		
	43,719		43,719

7. Terry

Trading and profit and loss account for the year ended 31 May 20*3

	£		£
Stock	1,329	Sales	65,782
Purchases	23,664		
	24,993		
Stock	1,275		
Cost of goods sold	23,718		
Gross profit	42,064		
	65,782		65,782
Wages	12,674	Gross profit	42,064
Motor expenses	6,710		
General expenses	441		
Heat and light	1,375		
Advertising	2,674		
Net profit	18,190		
	42,064		42,064

9. Gwenelle

Trading and profit and loss account for the year ended 30 November 20*3

	£		£
Stock	12,453	Sales	325,007
Purchases	157,994		
	170,447		
Stock	10,661		
Cost of goods sold	159,786		
Gross profit	165,221		
	325,007		325,007

CHAPTER FOUR

1. Your answer could have included payments for rent, business rates, insurance, wages, electricity, gas, advertising, motor expenses, stationery etc.
   Your answers should **not** have included capital expenditure, that is spending on new vehicles, money spent on extending the store and such like.

	£			£
Wages	56,743		Gross profit	165,221
Rates	6,740			
Heat and light	5,441			
Advertising	1,250			
Insurance	6,750			
General expenses	7,531			
Net profit	80,766			
	165,221			165,221

11. Helen
Trading and profit and loss account for the year ended 31 March 20*3

	£	£		£
Stock		1,554	Sales	51,311
Purchases	23,887		Returns inwards	367
Rets outwards	541			
	23,346			
		24,900		
		977		
Stock		23,923		
Cost of goods sold		27,021		
Gross profit		50,944		
				50,944
			Gross profit	27,021
Wages		8,712		
Rates		2,350		
Heat and light		1,458		
Advertising		2,350		
Insurance		2,005		
General expenses		4,637		
Net profit		5,509		
		27,021		27,021

13. Janice
Trading and profit and loss account for the year ended 31 August 20*3

	£	£		£
Stock			Sales	93,673
Purchases	29,041		Rets inwards	276
Carr. inwards	452			
	29,493			
Rets outwards	450			
		29,043		
		29,716		
		891		
Stock		28,825		
Cost of goods sold		64,572		
Gross profit		93,397		
				93,397
			Gross profit	64,572
Carr. outwards		772		
Wages		23,774		
General expenses		5,675		
Motor expenses		2,563		
Rent		3,600		
Rates		895		
Telephone		779		
Advertising		1,250		
Heat and light		2,588		
Net profit		22,676		
		64,572		64,572

15. Catherine
Trading and profit and loss account for the year ended 31 March 20*3

	£	£		£
Stock			Sales	127,773
Purchases	54,772		Rets inwards	321
Carr. inwards	270			
	55,042			
Rets outwards	84			
		54,958		
		56,507		
		1,471		
Stock		55,036		
Cost of goods sold		72,416		
Gross profit		127,452		
				127,452
			Gross profit	72,416
Wages		41,005		
Motor expenses		2,756		
Rent		4,750		
Rates		1,254		
Insurance		2,674		
Advertising		1,547		
Heat and light		2,541		
Telephone		3,428		
General expenses		6,539		
Net profit		5,922		
		72,416		72,416

CHAPTER FIVE
1. Ashley Peacock
Trading and profit and loss account for the year ended 30 June 20*3

	£		£
Stock	7,854	Sales	175,672
Purchases	70,031		
	77,885		
Stock	9,004		
Cost of goods sold	68,881		
Gross profit	106,791		
	175,672		175,672
		Gross profit	106,791
Wages and gen. exp.	38,962		
Repairs and renewals	7,459		
Rent and rates	5,350		
Ins. and advertising	5,312		
Motor expenses	13,674		
Net profit	36,034		
	106,791		106,791

Balance sheet as at 30 June 20*3

	£		£
Fixed assets			
Premises at cost	150,000	Capital	108,044
Machinery at cost	45,000	Add Profit	36,034
Van at cost	17,500		144,078
	212,500	Less Drawings	16,500
			127,578

Current assets

	£	£
Stock	9,004	
Debtors	13,563	
Bank	1,245	23,812

Long-term liability

	£
Loan	100,000

Current liabilities

	£
Creditors	8,734
	236,312
	236,312

3.

Leslie Harris

Trading and profit and loss account for the year ended 31 December 20*3

	£	£		£
			Sales	102,367
Stock		3,691		
Purchases	48,775			
Carr. inwards	693	49,468		
		53,159		
Stock		4,187		
Cost of goods sold		48,972		
Gross profit		53,395	Gross profit	102,367
		102,367		

	£		£
		Gross profit	53,395
Carr. outwards	528		
Wages and salaries	28,570		
Motor expenses	6,371		
Heat and light	2,448		
Advert. and ins.	3,691		
Gen. expenses	7,999		
Net profit	3,788		53,395
	53,395		

Balance sheet as at 31 December 20*3

	£	£		£	£
Fixed assets			**Capital**		58,591
Machinery at cost		85,750	*Add* Profit		3,788
Vehicles at cost		50,000			62,379
		135,750	*Less* Drawings		21,700
Current assets					40,679
Stock	4,187		**Long-term liabilities**		
Debtors	5,367	9,554	Loan		100,000
			Current liabilities		
			Creditors	3,753	
			Bank o/draft	872	4,625
		145,304			145,304

	£	£
Carr. outwards		332
Salaries		28,749
Motor expenses		5,673
Advertising		1,350
Insurances		3,764
Heat and light		2,479
Rates		1,245
General expenses		941
Net profit		7,900
		52,433

	£
Gross profit	52,433
	52,433

Balance sheet as at 31 March 20*3

	£	£		£	£
Fixed assets			**Capital**		98,827
Premises at cost		65,000	*Add* Profit		7,900
Office equipment at cost		18,750			106,727
Motor vehicles at cost		35,000	*Less* Drawings		24,675
		118,750			82,052
Current assets			**Long-term liability**		
Stock	1,007		Loan		40,000
Debtors	4,601	5,608	**Current liabilities**		
			Creditors	1,955	
			Bank overdraft	351	2,306
		124,358			124,358

CHAPTER SIX

1.

Sales	
	1,634
	65

Cash	
1,634	899
	180
	328

Wages	
899	

Drawings	
180	

Motor expenses	
328	

Squash club	
65	

Purchases	
350	

Bank	
671	350
	478
	345

Sales	
	671

Insurance	
478	

Display unit	
15	

Cash	
	15

DVD player	
345	

3.

5.

Dvatesh Narowal

Trading and profit and loss account for the year ended 31 March 20*3

	£	£		£
			Sales	102,453
			Returns inwards	743
Stock		48,661		101,710
Purchases	49,289			
Carr. inwards	1,539			
	50,200			
Returns outwards	911	49,289		
		50,284		
Stock		1,007		
Cost of goods sold		49,277		
Gross profit		52,433		
		101,710		101,710

CHAPTER SEVEN

1.

Returns inwards	
165	

Wages	
421	

Returns outwards	
	43

Andrew	
	460

Kijah	
	593

Zara	
	34

Peter	
	742

3.

PDB

Froot	213
Acme	54
Dixon	730
Gold	107
	1,104

Froot (PL)	
	213

Acme (PL)	
	54

Dixon (PL)	
	730

Purchases	
1,829	

Gold (PL)	
	107

Purchases (GL)	
1,104	

5.

Parker	
439	

Fitton	
29	

Clive	
51	

Gray	
882	

Sales	
	1,401

7.

SDB

Rowan	91
Ash	631
Holly	76
Berry	522
	1,320

Rowan (SL)	
91	

Berry (SL)	
522	

Ash (SL)	
631	

Holly (SL)	
76	

Sales (GL)	
	1,320

9.

Samson (PL)	
23	

Tardy (PL)	
54	

11.

Returns outwards (GL)	
	91

Randall (SL)	
38	

Hamilton (SL)	
15	

Returns inwards (GL)	
156	

Suchard (PL)	
14	

Frame (SL)	
	103

13. 15 June

	Dr	Cr
Delivery van	35,000	
Fogg's Garage		35,000

Delivery van purchased on credit from Fogg's Garage.

15. 6 January

	Dr	Cr
Tippers Ltd	200	
Machinery		200

Sale of machine on credit to Tippers Ltd.

5.

Debit	Credit
Rent	Cash
Purchases	Knight
Cash	Sales
Wages	Bank
Fixed Assets	Bank
Carriage inwards	Cash
Purchases	Cash
Motor expenses	Bank
Drawings	Cash
Fixed assets	Lock
Carriage outwards	Bank

7.

Wages	
349	

Cash	
211	349
	62
	109
	210

Sales	
	211

Telephone	
62	

Purchases	
109	

Drawings	
	210

9.

Sales	
	1,287
	1,473

Cash	
1,287	

Vehicle	
42,500	

W. Rekers	
	42,500

Purchases	
3,538	

Esso	
	3,538

11.

I. Hurry	
1,473	

Cash register	
2,650	

Bank	
	2,650

Sales	
	3,642
	188

Bank	
3,642	166
	320

Wages	
784	

Cash	
	784

Hitters Squash Club	
188	

Telephone	
166	

Purchases	
340	

13.

Dorak Ltd	
24	340

Drawings	
320	

Purchase returns	
	24

Purchases	
457	
265	

Sales	
	759
	395
	511

Cash	
759	457

Noel	
43	265

Bank	
395	421

Daser Ltd	
511	165

17.

Cash book	Cash	Fixed asset
PDB	Purchases	Supplier
Cash book	Cash	Sales
Cash book	Purchases	Cash
Cash book	Bank	Customers
Cash book	Drawings	Cash
Cash book	Insurance	Cash
Journal	Buyers account	Fixed asset
Cash book	Wages	Cash

19. PDB; CB; SRDB; J.

CHAPTER EIGHT

1.
- £48.30
- £152.43
- £117.25
- £34.48
- £69.13
- £640.13
- £7.30
- £1904.30

3.

5. (a)
- £449.23
- £11.52
- £6,345.08
- £1.21
- £57.13

(b)
- £2,567.00
- £65.80
- £36,257.60
- £6.90
- £326.43

7. (a) Purchases day book

	Purchases £	VAT £	Total £
Datf plc	297.05	51.98	349.03
Halifax Fabrics	151.90	26.58	178.48
Fred's Threads	22.47	3.93	26.40
	471.42	82.49	553.91

(b) Purchases returns day book

	Returns £	VAT £	Total £
Datf plc	70.13	12.27	82.40
Fred's Threads	2.35	0.41	2.76
	72.48	12.68	85.16

(c) General ledger

Purchases

471.42	

Purchases ledger

Datf plc

82.40	349.03

VAT

82.49	12.68

Returns outwards

	72.48

Halifax Fabrics

	178.48

Fred's Threads

2.76	26.40

9.

	Trade discount £	Sales day book amount £
Odd	698	2,792
Rowell	189	441
Rick	300	900
Ortar	160	160

11.

	Trade discount £	Purchases £	VAT £	Total £
		Purchases day book amount		
Range	68	272.00	47.60	319.60
Omme	300	900.00	157.50	1,057.50
Ear	210	420.00	73.50	493.50
Root	53	212.00	37.10	249.10
		1,804.00	315.70	2,119.70

13. (a) £264.10 (b) £275.50 (c) £34.20 (d) £1,415.50

15. £1,380.17.

17. C

19. (a) Purchases day book

	Purchases £	VAT £	Total £
Sharan	300.00	49.88	349.88
Frere & Son	1,224.00	208.85	1,432.85
Cuvee	420.00	72.77	492.77
Sagoo	1,530.00	254.36	1,784.36
	3,474.00	585.86	4,059.86

(b) Purchases ledger

Sharan

Cash 334.86	PDB 349.86
Disc. Rec. 15.00	

Cuvee

Cash 488.57	PDB 492.77
Disc. Rec. 4.20	

Frere & Son

Cash 1,402.25	PDB 1,432.85
Disc. Rec. 30.60	

Sagoo

Cash 1,707.86	PDB 1,784.36
Disc. Rec. 76.50	

(c) General ledger

Purchases

3,474	

VAT

585.84	

Cash

334.86
1,402.25
488.57
1,707.86

Discount received

	126.30

21. (a) Purchases returns day book

	Returns £	VAT £	Total £
Boon & Co.	108.48	18.98	127.46
Slump	36.02	6.30	42.32
Rage Ltd	48.03	8.41	56.44
	192.53	33.69	226.22

Sales returns day book

	Returns £	VAT £	Total £
Gosling	25.99	4.55	30.54
Vickers	13.42	2.35	15.77
	39.41	6.90	46.31

(b)
Purchases ledger

Boon & Co.
127.46 |

Sales ledger

Gosling
| 30.54

General ledger

Returns inwards
39.41 |

Rage Ltd
56.44 |

Slump
42.32 |

Vickers
| 15.77

Returns outwards
| 192.53

VAT
6.90 | 33.69

23. (a) **Sales day book**

	Sales £	VAT £	Total £
J. Oliver	385.78	67.51	453.29
F. Wingett	341.34	59.73	401.07
W. Lowther	110.49	19.34	129.83
R. Shears	761.97	133.34	895.31
	1,599.58	279.92	1,879.50

Purchases day book

	Purchases £	VAT £	Total £
J. Knowsley	39.00	6.83	45.83
J. Lewis	38.94	6.82	45.76
L. Franks	29.69	5.19	34.88
L. Pritchard	112.63	19.71	132.34
	220.26	38.55	258.81

Sales returns day book

	Returns £	VAT £	Total £
S. Weller	48.31	8.46	56.77
J. Oliver	18.15	3.18	21.33
	66.46	11.64	78.10

Purchases returns day book

	Returns £	VAT £	Total £
I. Williams	43.62	7.63	51.25
J. Lewis	56.00	9.80	65.80
	99.62	17.43	117.05

(b)
Sales ledger

J. Oliver
453.29 | 21.33

F. Wingett
401.07 |

W. Lowther
129.83 |

R. Shears
895.31 |

S. Weller
| 56.77

Purchases ledger

J. Knowsley
| 45.83

J. Lewis
65.80 | 45.76

L. Pritchard
| 132.34

L. Franks
| 34.88

I. Williams
51.25 |

General ledger

Sales
| 1,599.58

Returns inwards
66.46 |

Purchases
220.26 |

Returns outwards
| 99.62

VAT
38.55 | 279.92
11.64 | 17.43

Rent
100 |

Wages
78 |

Duncan
| 330

CHAPTER NINE

1. £14 Cr; £14 Dr; £80 Dr.

3.

Cash
750		100
		78
		69
		Bal c/d 503
750		750
Bal b/d 503		

Sales
Bal c/d 798		750
		48
798		798
		Bal b/d 798

Purchases
330		69 Bal c/d 399
399		399
Bal b/d 399		

Chas
48 |

Trial balance

	Dr £	Cr £
Sales		798
Cash	503	
Rent	100	
Chas (Debtor)	48	
Wages	78	
Duncan (Creditor)		330
Purchases	399	
	1,128	1,128

5.

Account		Type	Dr/Cr
Motor vehicles	GL	Asset	Debit
Rates	GL	Expense	Debit
Mortgage	GL	Liability	Credit
Carriage inwards	GL	Expense	Debit
Premises	GL	Asset	Debit
Quentin	SL	Asset	Debit
Capital	GL	Liability	Credit
Tara	PL	Liability	Credit
Purchases	GL	Expense	Debit
Insurance	GL	Expense	Debit
Sales	GL	Income/benefit	Credit
Carriage outwards	GL	Expense	Debit

7.

Account	Gross profit	Net profit
Rent	No	Yes
Mortgage	No	No
Insurance	No	Yes
Drawings	No	No
Advertising	No	Yes
Returns outwards	Yes	Yes
Carriage outwards	No	Yes
Purchases	Yes	Yes

9. Trial balance as at 31 August 20*3

	Dr £	Cr £
Capital		45,578
Vehicles at cost	43,500	
Office equipment at cost	17,600	
Debtors	4,656	
Creditors		2,873
Stock as at 1 September 20*2	4,502	
Purchases	56,221	
Sales		132,448
Wages	34,662	
Motor expenses	3,189	
Rent and rates	4,692	
Insurances	1,634	
Advertising	2,654	
General expenses	4,654	
Carriage inwards	543	
Carriage outwards	511	
Returns inwards	1,985	
Returns outwards		588
Bank balance	346	
Cash in hand	138	
	181,487	181,487

11. 1 compensating 2 commission 3 principle 4 omission.

13. (a) Journal

	Dr £	Cr £
Rent	200	
Rates		200
Wages	400	
Suspense		400
Tom	146	
Suspense		146
Insurance	546	
Cash		546

(b) Suspense account

	£		£
Trial balance difference	546	Wages	400
		Tom	146
	546		546

(c) The credit side was the larger side.

15. (a) Journal

	Dr £	Cr £
Suspense	642	
Beatrice		642
Returns inwards	100	
Suspense		100
VAT	1,461	
Suspense		1,461
Sales	1,010	
Suspense		1,010

(b) Suspense account

	£		£
Beatrice	642	Returns inwards	100
Trial balance difference	1,929	VAT	1,461
		Sales	1,010
	2,571		2,571

(c) The credit side was the larger side.

(d)

	£
Gross profit	48,712
Returns inwards	(100)
Sales	(1,010)
Corrected gross profit	47,602

(e)

Net profit	13,467
Returns inwards	(100)
Sales	(1,010)
Corrected net profit	12,357

CHAPTER TEN

1.
- PDB
- PRDB
- CB
- SDB
- CB

3.

(a)

SDB	£
Fallon	217
Slee	52
Earley	770
	1,039

PDB	£
Westby	179
Rawstron	731
Coulson	229
	1,139

(b) **Sales ledger**

	Fallon	
217		

	Slee	
52		

	Earley	
770		

Purchases ledger

	Westby	
		179

	Rawstron	
		731

	Coulson	
		229

General ledger

	Sales	
		1,039

	Purchases	
1,139		

5.

(a)

SDB	£
Davidson	59
Nixon	563
Nismo	518
	1,140

PDB	£
Sellars	911
Garewal	187
Chan	67
	1,165

SRDB	£
Davidson	19

PRDB	£
Sellars	45
Garewal	12
	57

(b) **Sales ledger**

	Davidson	
59		19

	Nixon	
563		

	Nismo	
518		

Purchase ledger

	Sellars	
45		911

	Garewal	
12		187

	Chan	
		67

General ledger

	Sales	
		1,140

	Purchases	
1,165		

	Returns inwards	
19		

	Returns outwards	
		57

7.

(a)

Sales day book	£
Clements	456
Lycett	53
Clements	437
	946

Purchases day book	£
Crosby	598
Cox	674
Patel	771
Frear	50
	2,093

Journal	Dr £	Cr £
Delivery van	23,580	
Austen		23,580

Sales returns day book	
Clements	34

Purchase returns day book	
Crosby	140

(b) **Sales ledger**

	Clements	
456		34
437		

	Lycett	
53		

	Patel	
		771

	Frear	
		50

	Austen	
		23,580

Purchases ledger

	Crosby	
140		598

	Cox	
		674

General ledger

	Sales	
		946

	Returns inwards	
34		

	Returns outwards	
		140

	Van	
23,580		

9.

(a)

Sales day Book	£
Thomas	97
Shah	254
	351

Purchases day Book	£
Tunk	573
Tupp	880
Rult	349
	1,802

Sales returns day book	£
Thomas	108

Purchases returns day book	£
Tupp	97

Journal	Dr £	Cr £
Display units	3,750	
Sheep Ltd		3,750

Cash book

752	
893	
439	
1,065	

(b) Sales ledger

Thomas

97	97

Shah

254	

Purchase ledger

Tupp

108	880

Tunk

573	

Rult

349	

Sheep

	3,750

General ledger

Sales

351	
752	
893	
439	

Purchases

1,802	

Returns inwards

	97

Returns outwards

108	

Display units

3,750	

CHAPTER ELEVEN

1. Cash book

	Cash			
Cling	76		Cleaning	94
Sales	522		Motor expenses	51
Laker	83		Wages	317

3. Cash book

Hanks	138		Insurance	548
Sales	2,693		Wages	752
Kann	198		Drawings	150

5. Cash balance £746 Debit; Bank balance £2,066 Debit.

7. Cash book

	Cash	Bank			Cash	Bank
Sales	349	561		Electricity	163	
Ed	670		C	Bank	500	471
Sales		500		Wages		
Cash			C	Stationery	112	
				Balances c/d	244	590
	1,019	1,061			1,019	1,061
Balances b/d	244	590				

9. Cash book

	Cash	Bank			Cash	Bank
Sales	1,792	1,500		Bank	1,500	
Cash			C	Rent	110	240
Burgess	135			Insurance		
Sales		286	C	Repairs		892
				Balances c/d	317	654
	1,927	1,786			1,927	1,786
Balances b/d	317	654				

Cash book

11.

	Cash	Bank			Cash	Bank
Sales		3,487		Motor expenses		345
Thompson	172			Rates		210
Sales	1,372			Bank	1,000	C
Cash		1,000	C	Motor expenses	48	
				Balance c/d	496	3,932
	1,544	4,487			1,544	4,487
Balance b/d	496	3,932				

13.

	Cash	Bank			Cash	Bank
Sales	2,380			Stationery	120	
Cash		1,950	C	Motor expenses	38	
Sales		2,785		Bank	1,950	C
Bank	2,500		C	Todd		490
				Cash		2,500	C
				Wages	1,988	
				Balances c/d	784	1,745
	4,880	4,735			4,880	4,735
Balances b/d	784	1,745				

CHAPTER TWELVE

1.

Receipts £	Folio	Date	Details	Voucher	Payment £
100	CB	1 July	Cash		
		6 July	Cleaning	1	22
		13 July	Postages	2	15
		22 July	Petrol	3	28
		23 July	Postages	4	11
					76
		23 July	Bal c/d		24
100					100
24		24 July	Bal b/d		
76	CB	24 July	Cash		

3. £96; £82; £69; £78.

5.

Receipts £	Folio	Date	Details	Total £	Travelling expenses £	Postages £	Cleaning £
32		23 Jan	Bal b/d				
168	CB	23 Jan	Cash				
		23 Jan	Trav. exp.	45	45		
		24 Jan	Postages	20		20	
		24 Jan	Cleaning	19			19
		24 Jan	Trav. exp.	30	30		
		26 Jan	Trav. exp.	51	51		
		28 Jan	Postages	8		8	
				173	126	28	19
		28 Jan	Bal c/d	27			
200				200			
27		29 Jan	Bal b/d				
173	CB	29 Jan	Cash				

7.

Receipts	Folio	Date	Details	Total	Motor expenses	Accom	Postages	Cleaning
68		17 July	Bal b/d					
432	CB	17 July	Cash					
		17 July	Mot exps	56	56			
		18 July	Accom	107		107		
		18 July	Postages	30			30	
		21 July	Accom	88		88		
		23 July	Cleaning	19				19
		23 July	Accom	102		102		
		24 July	Postages	15			15	
		25 July	Accom	54		54		
		25 July	Bal c/d	471	56	351	45	19
500				29				
29		26 July	Bal b/d	500				
471	CB	26 July	Cash					

CHAPTER THIRTEEN

1. (a)

Date	Details	Cash	Bank	Sales	VAT		Date	Details	Cash	Bank	Purch	VAT
1 Feb	Bals b/d	217	1,132				1 Feb	Mowlem	126	834	107	19
	Sales	912		776	136		4 Feb	Laker	488	137	415	73
2 Feb	McAllister		138				5 Feb	Purchases	750		522	92
3 Feb	Sales	468		398	70			Purchases				
4 Feb	Tyson		1,172					Bank		2,221		
5 Feb	Cash		750			C		Bals c/d	233	3,192		
		1,597	3,192	1,174	206				1,597	3,192	522	92
6 Feb	Bals b/d	233	2,221									

(b) General ledger

Sales		
		1,174

VAT		
	92	206

Purchases	
522	

3. (a)

Date	Details	Disc.	Cash	Bank	Sales	VAT		Date	Details	Disc.	Cash	Bank	Purch	VAT
1 May	Bals b/d		88	376				2 May	Purchases		308		262	46
2 May	Gholar	30		600				3 May	Purchases		613		522	91
3 May	Sales		845		719	126		6 May	Breem			40		
3 May	Tempest	12		210				7 May	Bank		250	1,516		
4 May	Trevor	8		120			C		Bal c/d		228			
7 May	Sales		466		397	69					1,399	1,556	784	137
	Cash			250			C							
		50	1,399	1,556	1,116	195								
8 May	Bals b/d		228	1,516										

(b) General ledger

Sales		
		1,116

VAT		
	137	195

Purchases	
784	

Disc. allowed	
50	

Purchases ledger

Breem		
Bank	40	40

Sales ledger

Gholar		Tempest		Trevor	
Bank	600	Bank	210	Brink	120
Disc. all.	30	Disc. all.	12	Disc. all.	8

5.

Receipts	Date	Details	Total	VAT	Motor expenses	Postages	Stationery	Cleaning
£			£	£	£	£	£	£
13.28	1 Aug	Bal b/d						
136.72	1 Aug	Cash						
	1 Aug	Postages	20.00			20.00		
	2 Aug	Stationery	17.84	2.66			15.18	
	3 Aug	Cleaning	3.61	0.54				3.07
	4 Aug	Postages	25.00			25.00		
	4 Aug	Petrol	40.00	5.96	34.04			
	5 Aug	Stationery	7.84	1.17			6.67	
	5 Aug	Cleaning	9.16	1.36				7.80
	5 Aug	Petrol	20.00	2.98	17.02			
	5 Aug	Bal c/d	143.45	14.67	51.06	45.00	21.85	10.87
150.00			6.55					
6.55	6 Aug	Bal b/d	150.00					
143.45	6 Aug	Cash						

CHAPTER FOURTEEN

1. Credit bank £200; debit cash £1,730; credit bank £190; credit discount received £10; debit bank £3,430; credit cash £435; debit cash £2,000; credit bank £2,000 contra.

3. Bank reconciliation statement as at 28 July

	£
Balance at bank as per cash book	189
Add Unpresented cheque	312
Balance at bank as per bank statement	501

5. **Bank reconciliation statement as at 29 November**

	£
Balance at bank as per cash book	85
Less Lodgements not yet credited	29
Balance at bank as per bank statement	56

7. **Bank reconciliation statement as at 28 January**

	£
Balance at bank as per cash book	452
Add Unpresented cheques	456
	908
Less Lodgements not yet credited	412
Balance at bank as per bank statement	496

9. (a) Cash book

		Bal c/d	146.44
		Bank chgs	12.52
		Overdraft interest	26.78
		Electricity	246.38
Bal c/d	432.12		432.12
	432.12	Bal b/d	432.12

(b) **Bank reconciliation statement as at 31 January**

	£
Balance at bank as per cash book	(432.12)
Add Unpresented cheques	147.07
	(285.05)
Less Lodgement not yet credited	530.22
Balance at bank as per bank statement	(815.27)

11. (a) Cash book

Bal b/d	180	Error	180
Lodg't	200		
Cr. trans.	165	Bal c/d	365
	545		545
Bal b/d	365		

(b) **Bank reconciliation statement as at 30 April 20*3**

	£
Balance at bank as per cash book	365
Add Unpresented cheques	493
Balance at bank as per bank statement	858

13. (a) Cash book

Cred. trans.	66	Bal b/d	590
		Interest	83
Bal c/d	638	Water	31
	704		704
		Bal b/d	638

(b) **Bank reconciliation statement as at 31 March**

	£
Balance at bank as per cash balance	(638)
Add Unpresented cheques	938
	300
Less Lodgements not yet credited	206
Balance at bank as per bank statement	94

CHAPTER FIFTEEN

1. Purchases ledger; sales ledger; general ledger.

3. **Sales ledger control account for July 20*3**

	£		£
Balances b/d	3,830	Cash	7,200
Sales	9,600	Discount allowed	910
		Returns inwards	340
		Balances c/d	4,980
	13,430		13,430
Balances b/d	4,980		

5. **Purchases ledger control account for April 20*3**

	£		£
Cash	9,300	Balances b/d	2,445
Discount received	700	Purchases	9,200
Returns outwards	150		
Balances c/d	1,495		
	11,645		11,645
		Balances b/d	1,495

7. **Purchases ledger control account for October 20*3**

	£		£
Cash	9,779	Balances b/d	3,741
Discounts received	1,230	Purchases	10,452
Balances c/d	3,184		
	14,193		14,193
		Balances b/d	3,184

9. **Sales ledger control account for December 20*3**

	£		£
Balances b/d	1,006	Cash	4,921
Sales	5,408	Discounts allowed	561
		Balances c/d	932
	6,414		6,414
Balances	932		

11. **Purchases ledger control account for May 20*3**

	£		£
Cash	109,621	Balances b/d	22,556
Discounts received	3,551	Purchases	117,004
Returns outwards	1,572		
Balances c/d	24,816		
	139,560		139,560
		Balances b/d	24,816

Commission receivable   £8,775

3. **Current asset**
Commission receivable owing   £1,775

5. **Ben Trent**
Trading and profit and loss account for the year ended 31 March 20*3

	£		£
Purchases	44,832	Sales	123,563
Stock	8,459		
Cost of goods sold	36,373		
Gross profit	87,190		
	123,563		123,563
Rent	5,600	Gross profit	87,190
Rates	2,340		
Wages	48,766		
Motor expenses	2,357		
General expenses	7,459		
Net profit	20,668		
	87,190		87,190

Balance sheet as at 31 March 20*3

	£	£	£
Fixed assets			
Equipment at cost		8,000	26,061
Van at cost		12,000	20,668
		20,000	46,729
Current assets			14,670
Stock	8,459		32,059
Debtors	8,564		
Bank	1,340		
		18,363	
		38,363	
Capital		8,000	
Add Profit		12,000	
		20,000	
Less Drawings			
Current liabilities			
Creditors	5,430		
Accruals	874		6,304
			38,363

13. **Sales ledger control account for August 20*3**

	£		£
Balances b/d	456	Cash	8,634
Sales	10,674	Discounts allowed	1,329
		Returns inward	566
		Balances c/d	601
	11,130		11,130
Balances b/d	601		

15. **Purchases ledger control account for October 20*3**

	£		£
Balances b/d	37	Balances b/d	3,551
Cash	12,440	Purchases	15,338
Discounts received	1,084		
Returns outwards	32		
Balances c/d	5,450	Balances c/d	154
	19,043		19,043
Balances b/d	154	Balances b/d	5,450

17. (a) **Sales ledger control account for December 20*3**

	£		£
Balances b/d	7,449	Balances b/d	247
Sales	43,650	Cash	39,754
		Discounts allowed	166
		Returns inwards	510
		Transfers to purchases ledger	300
Balances c/d	188	Balances c/d	10,310
	51,287		51,287
Balances b/d	10,310	Balances b/d	188

(b) **Purchases ledger control account for December 20*3**

	£		£
Balances b/d	342	Balances b/d	4,552
Cash	19,003	Purchases	20,005
Discounts received	251		
Returns outwards	543		
Transfers to sales ledger	300		
Balances c/d	4,163	Balances c/d	45
	24,602		24,602
Balances b/d	45	Balances b/d	4,163

CHAPTER SIXTEEN

1.

	Profit and loss entry	Current liability
	£	£
Wages	43,872	872
Motor expenses	9,350	750
Telephone	2,680	280
Advertising	2,360	560
Heating and lighting	2,391	391

7. Toby Moore
Trading and profit and loss account for the year ended 31 July 20*3

	£	£		£
Stock		8,756	Sales	134,908
Purchases	54,731		Returns inwards	453
Returns outwards	612			134,455
		54,119		
		62,875		
Stock		9,315		
Cost of goods sold		53,560		
Gross profit		80,895		
		134,455		
Wages		34,770	Gross profit	80,895
Motor expenses		1,443		
Insurance		822		
General expenses		4,119		
Net profit		39,741		
		80,895		80,895

Balance sheet as at 31 July 20*3

	£	£		£	£
Fixed assets			Capital		76,810
Premises at cost		65,000	Add Profit		39,741
Machinery at cost		16,000			116,551
Vehicles at cost		7,400	Less Drawings		25,000
		88,400			91,551
Current assets					
Stock	9,315		Current liabilities		
Debtors	811		Creditors	2,678	
Cash in hand	282		Bank overdraft	4,637	
Pre-payment	58				7,315
		10,466			
		98,866			98,866

9. Seok Chin
Trading and profit and loss account for the year ended 30 April 20*3

	£	£		£
Stock		23,510	Sales	407,843
Purchases	238,056		Returns inwards	1,453
Returns outwards	573			406,390
		237,483		
		260,993		
Stock		26,449		
Cost of goods sold		234,544		
Gross profit		171,846		
		406,390		
Carriage outwards		1,323	Gross profit	171,846
Rates		1,318		
Wages		75,016		
Motor expenses		32,540		
Telephone		3,760		
General expenses		8,116		
Net profit		49,773		
		171,846		171,846

Balance sheet as at 30 April 20*3

	£	£		£	£
Fixed assets			Capital		72,318
Premises at cost		80,000	Add Profit		49,773
Equipment at cost		23,000			122,091
Vehicles at cost		84,000	Less Drawings		26,500
		187,000			95,591
Current assets			Long-term liability		
Stock	26,449		Bank loan		120,000
Debtors	34,534				
Cash	377		Current liabilities		
Pre-payments	342		Creditors	23,665	
		61,702	Bank overdraft	7,439	
			Accruals	2,007	
					33,111
		248,702			248,702

11. Julie Wreak
Trading and profit and loss account for the year ended 31 May 20*3

	£	£		£
Stock		36,734	Sales	407,563
Purchases	239,075		Returns inwards	1,554
Carriage inwards	347			406,009
		239,422		
Returns outwards		658		
		238,764		
		275,498		
Stock		34,897		
Cost of goods sold		240,601		
Gross profit		165,408		
		406,009		
Carriage outwards		1,453	Gross profit	165,408
Wages		90,580	Rent receivable	3,000
Motor expenses		34,527		
Stationery		3,642		
Rates		2,345		
Insurances		4,111		
Loan interest		3,000		
Net profit		28,750		
		168,408		168,408

Balance sheet as at 31 May 20*3

	£	£		£	£
Fixed assets			Capital		95,894
Premises at cost		240,000	Add Net profit		28,750
Office equipment at cost		17,000			124,644
Lorry at cost		45,000	Less Drawings		34,700
		302,000			89,944
Current assets			Long-term liability		
Stock	34,897		Bank loan		250,000
Debtors	28,976		Current liabilities		
Cash	754		Creditors	18,785	
Pre-payments	1,397		Bank overdraft	2,457	
		66,024	Accruals	6,838	
					28,080
		368,024			368,024

CHAPTER SEVENTEEN

1.

Advertising

120		P & L a/c	1,340
340			
720			
160			
1,340			1,340

Rates

1,400		P & L a/c	2,800
1,400			
2,800			2,800

Motor expenses

2,160		P & L a/c	3,906
814			
932			
3,906			3,906

Rent received

P & L a/c	2,400		2,400
	2,400		2,400

Purchases

9,000		Trading a/c	14,000
2,000			
3,000			
14,000			14,000

Machinery

	14,000	Bal c/d	26,000
	12,000		
	26,000		26,000
Bal b/d	26,000		

Sales

Trading a/c	27,500		27,500
	27,500		27,500

Discount received

P & L a/c	229		121
			72
			36
	229		229

Trading account

Purchases	14,000	Sales	27,500

Profit and loss account

Advertising	1,340	Rent received	2,400
Rates	2,800	Discount rec'd	229
Motor expenses	3,906		

Balance sheet

Fixed assets
Machinery 26,000

3. Tom Jackson

Trading account for the year ended 28 February 20*3

	£		
Stock	2,351	Sales	87,503
Purchases	52,765		
	55,116		
Stock	3,722		
Cost of goods sold	51,394		
Gross profit	36,109		
	87,503		87,503

Stock account

28 Feb 20*2	Trading a/c	2,351	28 Feb 20*3 a/c	2,351
28 Feb 20*3	Trading a/c	3,722		

5. Cary Thums

Trading account for the year ended 31 March 20*3

	£		
Stock	1,768	Sales	56,880
Purchases	23,771	Returns inwards	239
	25,539		
Stock	1,439		
Cost of goods sold	24,100		
Gross profit	32,541		
	56,641		56,641

7.

Table	£145
Chair	£50
Bed	£170

9.

Ford	£1,180
Citroen	£440
Skoda	£560

11.

Trial balance totals £121,202 after inserting credit returns outwards £210; debit rates £1,250; debit telephone £850; debit drawings £16,300; debit stock £3,240. Accounts are closed:

Returns outwards

Trading a/c	210		80
			25
			105
	210		210

Rates

	625	P & L a/c	1,250
	625		
	1,250		1,250

Telephone

	212	P & L a/c	850
	216		
	248		
	174		
	850		850

Drawings

	4,075	Capital	16,300
	4,075		
	4,075		
	4,075		
	16,300		16,300

Stock

31 Mar 20*2	Trading a/c	3,240	31 Mar 20*3 Trading a/c	3,240
31 Mar 20*3	Trading a/c	3,970		

Tammy Mount

Trading and profit and loss account for the year ended 31 March 20*3

	£		
Purchases	41,903	Sales	102,786
Returns outwards	210	Returns inwards	460
	41,693		
Stock	3,240		
	38,453		
Cost of goods sold	63,873		
Gross profit			
	102,326		102,326

(Chapter 17 solutions — continued)

	£		£
Wages	25,600	Gross profit	63,873
Rates	1,250		
Telephone	850		
Net profit	36,173		
	63,873		63,873

Balance sheet as at 31 March 20*3

	£		£	£
Fixed assets		Capital		
Fixtures and fittings at cost	12,500	Add Profit		36,173
Vehicles at cost	17,300			50,093
	29,800	Less Drawings		16,300
				33,793
Current assets				
Stock	3,240			
Debtors	3,791	Current liabilities		
Bank	1,248	Creditors		4,286
	8,279			
	38,079			38,079

13. Trial balance totals £259,516 after inserting:
Debits – carriage outwards £1,642; rent £6,000; advertising £2,875; stock £7,621
Credit – capital £83,072.

Stock account

31 Aug 20*2 Trading a/c	7,621	31 Aug 20*3 Trading a/c	7,621
31 Aug 20*3 Trading a/c	8,470		

Rent payable

	£		£
	1,500	P & L a/c	6,000
	1,500		
	1,500		
	1,500		
	6,000		6,000

Carriage outwards

			£
	934	P & L a/c	1,642
	127		
	406		
	175		
	1,642		1,642

Capital account

			83,072

Advertising

			£
	76	P & L a/c	2,875
	211		
	99		
	2,489		
	2,875		2,875

Chetan Nath
Trading and profit and loss account for the year ended 31 August 20*3

	£	£		£
Stock		7,621	Sales	172,460
Purchases	81,236			
Carr. inwards	1,810			
	83,046			
		90,667		
Stock		8,470		
Cost of goods sold		82,197		
Gross profit		90,263		
		172,460		172,460

(Chapter 17 solutions — continued)

	£		£
Carriage outwards	1,642	Gross profit	90,263
Rent	6,000		
Rates	1,580		
Wages	32,460		
Advertising	2,875		
Net profit	45,706		
	90,263		90,263

Balance sheet as at 31 August 20*3

	£	£		£
Fixed assets			Capital	83,072
Premises at cost	60,000		Add Profit	45,706
Equipment at cost	24,000			128,778
		84,000	Less Drawings	23,100
				105,678
Current assets				
Stock	8,470			
Debtors	8,491		Current liabilities	
Bank	8,701		Creditors	3,984
		25,662		
		109,662		109,662

CHAPTER EIGHTEEN

1.
Delivery vehicles accounts

	£	
1 Jan *2 Bank	28,000	

Provision for depreciation of delivery van

		£
	31 Dec *2 P & L a/c	5,000
	31 Dec *3 P & L a/c	5,000

3.
Machinery account

	£		£
1 April *1 Bank	13,000		
1 April *2 Bank	16,000		
1 Oct *2 Bank	10,000		

Provision for depreciation of machinery

		£
	31 Mar *2 P & L a/c	1,300
	31 Mar *3 P & L a/c	3,400

Balance sheet extracts

As at 31 March 20*2

	£	£
Machinery at cost	13,000	
Less Depreciation	1,300	11,700

As at 31 March 20*3

	£	£
Machinery at cost	39,000	
Less Depreciation	4,700	34,300

5.
Vehicles account

	£		£
1 Oct *2 Balance b/d	120,000	Jul *3 Disposal account	21,000
1 Oct *3 Balance b/d	99,000	30 Sept *3 Balance b/d	99,000

Provision for depreciation of vehicles

	£		£
June *3 Disposal	19,000	1 Oct *2 Balance b/d	73,000
30 Sept *3 Bal c/d	54,000	30 Sept *3 Bal b/d	54,000
		30 Sept *3 P & L a/c	24,750

5.

Bad debts account

31 Jan *1	Debtor	700	31 Jan *1	P & L a/c	700
31 Jan *3	Debtor	200	31 Jan *3	P & L a/c	200

Provision for doubtful debts accounts

			31 Jan *1	P & L a/c	300.00
31 Jan *2	Bal c/d	362.50	31 Jan *2	P & L a/c	62.50
			1 Feb *2	Bal b/d	362.50
31 Jan *3	Bal c/d	395.00	31 Jan *3	P & L a/c	32.50
			1 Feb *3	Bal b/d	395.00

Profit and loss account extracts for year ended

	31 January 20*1	31 January 20*2	31 January 20*3
Bad debts	700		200
Provision for doubtful debts	300	62.50	32.50

Balance sheet extracts as at

31 January 20*1			31 January 20*2		
Debtors	12,000		Debtors	14,500	
Less Provision	300	11,700	Less Provision	362.50	14,137.50
31 January 20*3					
Debtors	15,800				
Less Provision	395	15,405			

7.

Provision	P & L a/c entry	Balance sheet detail		
	£		£	
230	50 expense	Drs	23,000	
		Less Prov	230	22,770
270	40 expense	Drs	27,000	
		Less Prov	270	26,730
250	20 income	Drs	25,000	
		Less Prov	250	24,750
260	10 expense	Drs	26,000	
		Less Prov	260	25,740

9.

Bad debts account

Defius	154			
Ralph	345			
Iain	620			
Gordon	87	P & L a/c	1,206	

11. Provision £1,000

Balance sheet extract

Debtors	40,000	
Provision for doubtful debts	1,000	39,000

13. £234 + £258 + £38.10 + £36.50 + £128 = £694.60

15.

Provision for doubtful Debts

			1 May *2	Bal b/d	850
30 April *2	Bal c/d	1,100	30 April *3	P & L a/c	250
			1 May 20*3	Bal B/d	1,100

Disposal of vehicles account

Vehicles	21,000	Depreciation	19,000
		Cash	800
		P & L a/c (loss)	1,200

Balance sheet extract as at 30 Sept 20*3

Vehicles at cost	99,000	
Less Dep'n	78,750	20,250

7. £1,900

9. £12,000; £7,200; £4,320.

11.

Provision for depreciation of equipment

		31 Dec *2	P & L a/c	6,000
		31 Dec *3	P & L a/c	6,000

13.

Provision for depreciation of lorry account

28 Feb *3	Bal c/d	117,600	28 Feb *2	P & L a/c	84,000
			28 Feb *3	P & L a/c	33,600
		117,600			117,600
			1 Mar *3	Bal b/d	117,600
			29 Feb *4	P & L a/c	13,440

15.

Disposal of machinery account

Machinery	45,000	Depreciation	9,000	Loss on disposal £5,000
		Cash	31,000	
		P & L a/c	5,000	
	45,000		45,000	

17.

Disposal of machinery account

Machinery	19,000	Depreciation	6,000	Profit on disposal £250
P & L a/c	250	Cash	13,250	
	19,250		19,250	

19.

Disposal of vehicle account

Vehicle	26,000	Depreciation	16,640	Profit on disposal £140
P & L a/c	140	Cash	9,500	
	26,140		26,140	

CHAPTER NINETEEN

1.

Bad debts account

Biff	451	31 Dec *3	P & L a/c	662
Treadus	159			
Victor	52			

3.

Provision for doubtful debts account

Yr 2	Bal c/d	420	Yr 1	P & L a/c	400
			Yr 2	P & L a/c	20
Yr 3	Bal c/d	500	Yr 3	P & L a/c	420
			Yr 3	P & L a/c	80
			Yr 4	Bal b/d	500

Bad debts account

P. Snow	45	
J. Gatewood	239	
F. Golightly	213	
D. Mark	651	P & L a/c 1,148

Profit and loss account extract

Bad debts 1,148
Provision for doubtful debts 250

Balance sheet extract

Debtors 44,000
Provision for doubtful debts 1,100   42,900

17.

Geot Ltd

Bad debt recovery 288	Cash	288

Bad debt recovery

	Geot	288

Cash

Geot	288	

19.

Provision for doubtful debts account

31 Oct *3 Bal c/d	2,050	1 Nov *2 Balance b/d 1,750
		31 Oct *3 P * L a/c 300
	2,050	2,050
		1 Nov *3 Bal b/d 2,050

Bad debts account

Thaker	216	
Simms	97	
Hurd	184	
Fletcher	109	P & L a/c 606

Broadbent

Bad debt recovery a/c 246	Cash	246

Bad debt recovery account

	Broadbent	246

Profit and loss account

Bad debts (606 – 246) 360
Provision for doubtful debts 300

CHAPTER TWENTY

1. **Sven Thomas**

Trading account for the year ended 30 September 20*3

	£	£
Sales		51,239
Less Cost of sales		
Stock as at 1 Oct 20*2	1,456	
Purchases	29,675	
Less Returns outwards	197	
	29,478	
	30,934	
Less Stock as at 30 Sept 20*3	1,503	
		29,431
Gross profit		21,808

3. **Greta Freer**

Trading account for the year ended 31 January 20*3

	£	£
Sales		56,999
Less Cost of sales		
Stock as at 1 Feb 20*2	456	
Purchases	24,761	
Less Returns outwards	642	
	24,119	
	24,575	
Less Stock as at 31 Jan 20*3	488	
		24,087
Gross Profit		32,912

5. **Alec McDuff**

Trading account for the year ended 31 December 20*3

	£	£	£
Sales			63,971
Less Returns inwards			773
			63,198
Less Cost of sales			
Stock 1 Jan 20*3		938	
Purchases	20,098		
Carriage inwards	438		
	20,536		
Less Returns outwards	629		
		19,907	
		20,845	
Stock as at 31 Dec 20*3		1,006	
			19,839
Gross profit			43,359

7. **Clyde Buno**

Trading and profit and loss account for the year ended 31 December 20*3

	£	£
Sales		23,567
Less Cost of sales		
Stock as at 1 January 20*3	1,996	
Purchases	14,674	
	16,670	
Stock as at 31 December 20*3	2,352	
		14,318
Gross profit		9,249
Less Expenses		
Wages	2,391	
Motor expenses	1,743	
Rent	700	
Insurance	980	
General expenses	793	
		6,607
Net profit		2,642

9. **Raagi Hosah**

Trading and profit and loss account for the year ended 31 March 20*3

	£	£	£
Sales			80,705
Less Cost of sales			
Stock		1,342	
Purchases	45,773		
Less Returns outwards	1,189		
	44,584		
	45,926		
Stock		2,753	
			43,173
Gross profit			37,532
Less Expenses			
Rent	3,500		
Motor expenses	3,679		
Wages	16,875		
Insurance	2,050		
General expenses	4,992		
			31,096
Net profit			6,436

11. David Mark
Trading and profit and loss account for the year ended 31 January 20*3

	£	£	£
Sales			107,500
Less Returns inwards			491
			107,009
Less Cost of sales			
Stock		4,455	
Purchases	54,892		
Carriage inwards	277		
	55,169		
Less Returns outwards	1,309		
		53,860	
Stock		58,315	
		2,774	
		55,541	
Gross profit			51,468
Less Expenses			
Wages	36,783		
Rent and rates	3,784		
Heat and light	5,785		
Motor expenses	10,648		
General expenses	2,888		
		59,888	
Net loss			8,420

13. Ted Croft
Trading and profit and loss account for the year ended 30 September 20*3

	£	£
Sales		79,261
Less Cost of sales		
Stock	6,754	
Purchases	34,976	
	41,730	
Stock	5,872	
		35,858
Gross profit		43,403
Less Expenses		
Motor expenses	5,674	
Telephone	973	
Rent	4,500	
Wages	32,710	
Insurance	1,856	
General expenses	6,731	
	52,444	
Net loss		9,041

Balance sheet as at 30 September 20*3

	£	£
Fixed assets		
Delivery van	23,000	
Office equipment	13,700	
		36,700
Current assets		
Stock	5,872	
Debtors	6,523	
Bank	1,021	
Cash	75	
	13,491	
Less current liabilities		
Creditors	3,750	
		9,741
		46,441
Capital		70,482
Less loss		9,041
		61,441
Less drawings		15,000
		46,441

15. Rajan Rander
Trading and profit and loss account for the year ended 31 March 20*3

	£	£	£
Sales			141,809
Less Returns inwards			1,834
			139,975
Less Cost of sales			
Stock		2,570	
Purchases	67,813		
Carriage inwards	1,003		
	68,816		
Less Returns outwards	458		
		68,358	
		70,928	
Stock		3,339	
		67,589	
Gross profit			72,386
Less Expenses			
Carriage outwards	751		
Wages	34,671		
Rates and insurance	1,962		
Motor expenses	9,701		
Heat and light	3,559		
General expenses	7,682		
		58,326	
Net profit			14,060

Balance sheet as at 31 March 20*3

	£	£
Fixed assets		
Fixtures and fittings at cost	3,800	
Delivery vehicle at cost	8,450	
		12,250
Current assets		
Stock	3,339	
Debtors	4,634	
Bank	2,579	
Cash	89	
	10,641	
Less Current liabilities		
Creditors	8,463	
		2,178
		14,428
Capital		17,118
Add Net profit		14,060
		31,178
Less Drawings		16,750
		14,428

CHAPTER TWENTY-ONE

1. Hanif Mohammed
Trading and profit and loss account for the year ended 28 February 20*3

	£	£
Sales		123,601
Less Cost of sales		
Stock	8,963	
Purchases	56,817	
	65,780	
Stock	7,432	
		58,348

(continued)

	£	£
Gross profit		65,253
Less Expenses		
Wages	39,113	
Rent	2,200	
Light and heat	8,617	
General expenses	2,834	
Motor expenses	4,619	57,383
Net profit		7,870

Balance sheet as at 28 February 20*3

	£	£	£
Fixed assets			
Premises at cost		100,000	
Equipment at cost		16,000	
Delivery van at cost		8,000	124,000
Current assets			
Stock		7,432	
Debtors		8,607	
Bank		1,281	
Cash		45	
		17,365	
Less Current Liabilities			
Creditors	7,614		
Accrued expenses	200	7,814	
		9,551	133,551
Capital			139,181
Add Profit			7,870
			147,051
Less Drawings			13,500
			133,551

3. Hibo Ahmed
Trading and profit and loss account for the year ended 31 May 20*3

	£	£
Sales		206,981
Less Cost of sales		
Stock	12,461	
Purchases	132,778	
	145,239	
Stock	13,106	132,133
Gross profit		74,848
Less Expenses		
Wages	47,151	
Rent	6,000	
Insurance	1,759	
Motor expenses	8,123	
Advertising	2,164	
General expenses	8,837	74,034
Net profit		814

Balance sheet as at 31 May 20*3

	£	£	£
Fixed assets			
Office equipment at cost		32,716	
Delivery vehicle at cost		23,500	56,216
Current assets			
Stock		13,106	
Debtors		5,871	
Cash		236	
Pre-payment		628	
		19,841	
Less Current liabilities			
Bank overdraft	4,798		
Creditors	7,162		
Accrued expenses	814	12,774	
			7,067
			63,283
Capital			100,969
Add Profit			814
			101,783
Less Drawings			38,500
			63,283

5. Lynn Parker
Trading and profit and loss account for the year ended 31 October 20*3

	£	£	£
Sales		192,587	
Less Returns inwards		1,111	191,476
Less Cost of sales			
Stock		2,468	
Purchases	64,128		
Less Returns outwards	382	63,746	
		66,214	
Stock		3,199	63,015
Gross profit			128,461
Less Expenses			
Wages		67,491	
Rent and rates		5,400	
Advertising and insurance		3,780	
Light and heat		6,437	
Motor expenses		18,542	
Depreciation: Office equipt	1,706		
Vehicles	6,624	8,330	109,980
Net profit			18,481

Balance sheet as at 31 October 20*3

	£	£	£
Fixed assets			
Office equipment		17,400	
Less Depreciation		10,580	6,820
Delivery vehicles		46,000	
Less Depreciation		36,064	9,936
			16,756
Current assets			
Stock		3,199	
Debtors		14,673	
Cash		430	
		18,302	
Less Current liabilities			
Creditors		5,799	

	£	£	£
Bank overdraft	4,372	10,171	8,131
			24,887
Capital			27,706
Add Profit			18,481
			46,187
Less Drawings			21,300
			24,887

7. Gladys Jones

Trading and profit and loss account for the year ended 31 October 20*3

	£	£	£
Sales		296,431	
Less Returns inwards		816	
			295,615
Less Cost of sales			
Stock		18,461	
Purchases	115,268		
Carriage inwards	348		
	115,616		
Less Returns outwards	203		
		115,413	
		133,874	
		16,984	
			116,890
Gross profit			178,725
Less Expenses			
Insurance		2,220	
Wages		105,892	
Motor expenses		8,420	
Light and heat		2,436	
Telephone		1,699	
General expenses		7,421	
Provision for doubtful debts		24	
Discount allowed		436	
Depreciation: Premises	2,400		
Office equipt	1,500		
Vehicles	4,320		
		8,220	
			136,768
Net profit			41,957

Balance sheet as at 31 October 20*3

	£	£	£
Fixed assets			
Premises	120,000		
Less Depreciation	55,200		64,800
Office equipment	15,000		
Less Depreciation	7,500		7,500
Vehicles	50,000		
Less Depreciation	43,520		6,480
			78,780
Current assets			
Stock		16,984	
Debtors	15,200		
Less Provision	304	14,896	
Bank		6,132	
Cash		228	
Pre-payment		180	
		38,420	

Less Current liabilities	£	£	£
Creditors	12,684	13,035	
Accrued expenses	351		
			25,385
			104,165
Capital			104,958
Add Profit			41,957
			146,915
Less Drawings			42,750
			104,165

9. Isadorah Boom

Trading and profit and loss account for the year ended 30 April 20*3

	£	£	£
Sales		97,481	
Less Returns inwards		127	
			97,354
Less Cost of sales			
Stock		6,483	
Purchases	48,972		
Carriage inwards	348		
	49,320		
Less Returns outwards	197		
		49,123	
		55,606	
		6,543	
			49,063
Gross profit			48,291
Discount received			432
			48,723
Less Expenses			
Carriage outwards		812	
Bad debts		574	
Wages		18,841	
Rent		6,000	
Light and heat		3,481	
Telephone		1,856	
General expenses		15,860	
Provision for doubtful debts		44	
Provision for depreciation:			
Machinery	6,000		
Equipment	2,250	8,250	
			55,718
Net loss			6,995

Balance sheet as at 30 April 20*3

	£	£	£
Fixed assets			
Machinery	60,000		
Less Depreciation	42,000	18,000	
Equipment	36,000		
Less Depreciation	33,750	2,250	
			20,250
Current assets			
Stock		6,543	
Debtors	6,400		
Less Provision	320	6,080	
Cash		136	
Pre-payment		500	
		13,259	

Less Current liabilities

	£	£
Creditors	2,968	
Bank overdraft	2,487	
Accrued expenses	380	5,835
		7,424
		27,674
Capital		48,169
Less Loss		6,995
		41,174
Less Drawings		13,500
		27,674

11. Jack Simms

Trading and profit and loss account for the year ended 30 September 20*3

	£	£
Sales	313,461	
Less Returns inwards	813	
		312,648
Less Cost of sales		
Stock		26,381
Purchases	197,384	
Less Goods for own use	2,500	
	194,884	
Carriage inwards	277	
	195,161	
Less Returns outwards	212	194,949
		221,330
		27,492
		193,838
Gross profit		118,810
Discount received		1,346
Commission received		4,892
		125,048
Less Expenses		
Rates	3,510	
General expenses	8,274	
Wages	60,187	
Motor expenses	13,981	
Bad debts	2,643	
Provision for doubtful debts	78	
Loan interest	1,500	
Discount allowed	814	
Carriage outwards	1,732	
Depreciation: Premises	2,000	
Equipment	10,000	
Vehicles	12,096	24,096
Net profit		116,815
		8,233

Balance sheet as at 30 September 20*3

	£	£	£
Fixed assets			
Premises	200,000		
Less Depreciation	88,000	112,000	
Equipment	100,000		
Less Depreciation	60,000	40,000	
Vehicles	84,000		
Less Depreciation	65,856	18,144	170,144

	£	£	£
Current assets			
Stock			27,492
Debtors		28,000	
Less Provision		700	27,300
Bank			4,986
Cash			512
Pre-payments			1,270
Commission owed			180
			61,740
Less Current liabilities			
Creditors		16,497	
Accrued expenses		853	17,350
			44,390
			214,534
Capital			91,289
Add Profit			8,233
			99,522
Less Drawings			34,988
			64,534
Long-term liability			
Loan			150,000
			214,534

CHAPTER TWENTY-TWO

1. Prudence; materiality; consistency.
3. Should not be included – money measurement/objectivity.
5. £4,000; accruals
7. Reliable.

CHAPTER TWENTY-THREE

1. Moin Syyed

Manufacturing account extract for the year ended 28 February 20*3

	£
Stock of raw materials	23,658
Purchases of raw materials	156,364
	180,022
Stock of raw materials	18,439
Raw materials consumed	161,583
Direct wages	236,451
Royalties	35,000
Prime cost	433,034

3. Jane Doyle

Manufacturing and trading account for the year ended 31 July 20*3

	£	£
Stock of raw materials		17,650
Purchases of raw materials	203,510	
Carriage inwards	1,350	204,860
		222,510
Stock of raw materials		23,510
Raw materials consumed		199,000
Direct wages		123,930
Prime cost		322,930

	£	£
Factory overheads		
Indirect wages	58,900	
Rent and rates	37,800	
Power	38,900	
Light and heat	9,450	
Insurance	14,620	
Depreciation of machinery	87,000	246,670
		569,600
Work in progress 1 Aug 20*2	8,570	
Work in progress 31 Jul 20*3	(7,340)	1,230
Total production cost		570,830
Stock of finished goods		10,760
Total production cost		570,830
		581,590
Stock of finished goods		10,740
Cost of goods sold		570,850
Gross profit		342,996
Sales		913,846

5. **Harry Parker**
Manufacturing account extract for the year ended 31 October 20*3

	£
Total production cost	1,326,900
Gross profit on manufacturing	773,100
Transfer price	2,100,000

Trading account for the year ended 31 October 20*3

	£
Stock	186,000
Transfer price of manufactured goods	2,100,000
	2,286,000
Stock	191,450
	2,094,550
Cost of goods sold	1,116,050
Gross profit	
Sales	3,210,600

Profit and loss account extract for the year ended 31 October 20*3

	£
Gross profit on manufacturing	773,100
Gross profit on trading	1,116,050
Total gross profit	1,889,150

7. **Hilary Nike**
Manufacturing account extract for the year ended 31 March 20*3

	£
Total production cost	943,750
Gross profit on manufacturing	377,500
Transfer price	1,321,250

Trading account for the year ended 31 March 20*3

	£
Stock	85,820
Transfer price of manufactured goods	1,321,250

	£
	1,407,070
Stock	87,360
Cost of goods sold	1,319,710
Gross profit	128,850
Sales	1,448,560

Profit and loss account extract for the year ended 31 March 20*3

	£
Gross profit on manufacturing	377,500
Gross profit on trading	128,850
Total gross profit	506,350

9.

	£		
Cost Price	2,720	Profit element	1,360
	960		120
	750		150
	1,115 (rounded)		335
	6,000		4,500

11. **Provision for unrealised profit**

	£		£
Balance c/d	3,816	Balance b/d	3,444
		P & L a/c	372
			3,816
		Balance b/d	3,816

13. **Manufacturing account extract for the year ended 30 November 20*3**

	£
Stock of raw materials	7,968
Purchases of raw materials	102,177
	110,145
Stock of raw materials	8,429
Raw materials consumed	101,716
Direct labour	82,440
Royalties	1,200
Prime cost	185,356

15. **Trogle**
Manufacturing account for the year ended 30 June 20*3

	£	£
Stock of raw materials		17,480
Purchases of raw materials		234,772
		252,252
Stock of raw materials		18,597
Raw materials consumed		233,655
Direct labour		419,828
Royalties		12,500
Prime cost		665,983
Factory overheads		
Rent	9,500	
Insurance	8,030	
Power	18,400	
Indirect wages	21,720	
Depreciation of machinery	45,000	102,650
		768,633
Work in progress		8,977
		777,610

Work in progress   10,431
Total production cost   767,179

17. Dreght and Sons
Manufacturing account for the year ended 31 March 20*3

	£	£
Stock of raw materials		8,162
Purchases of raw materials	112,431	
Carriage inwards	798	
		113,229
		121,391
Stock of raw materials		7,466
Raw materials consumed		113,925
Direct wages		189,410
Prime cost		303,335
Factory overheads		
Indirect labour	64,822	
Power	17,461	
General overheads	20,973	
Depreciation of machinery	28,000	
		131,256
		434,591
Work in progress		6,183
		440,774
Work in progress		5,774
		435,000
Gross profit on manufacturing		130,500
Transfer price		565,500

Trading Account for the year ended 31 March 20*3

	£
Transfer price of manufactured goods	7,451
	565,500
	572,951
Stock	8,549
Cost of goods sold	564,402
Gross profit	309,040
Sales	873,442

19. Provision for unrealised profit

	£		£
Balance c/d	7,500	Balance b/d	6,300
		P & L a/c	1,200
	7,500	Balance b/d	7,500

21. Provision for unrealised profit

	£		£
Balance c/d	38,250	Balance b/d	34,500
		P & L a/c	3,750
	38,250	Balance b/d	38,250

23. (a) Sandra Gavington
Manufacturing account for the year ended 31 December 20*3

	£	£
Stock of raw materials		7,966
Purchases of raw materials		214,283
		222,249
Stock of raw materials		8,618
Raw materials consumed		213,631
Direct wages		128,250
Royalties		19,500
Prime cost		361,381
Factory overheads		
Indirect wages	63,489	
Power	18,240	
Insurance	7,220	
General overheads	23,470	
Depreciation of machinery	80,000	
		192,419
		553,800
Work in progress		6,200
		560,000
Work in progress		8,000
Total production costs		552,000
Gross profit on manufacturing		110,400
Transfer price		662,400

(b) Trading account for the year ended 31 December 20*3

	£
Stock	14,880
Transfer price of manufactured goods	662,400
	677,280
Stock	16,440
Cost of goods sold	660,840
Gross profit	239,160
Sales	900,000

(c) Provision for unrealised profit

	£		£
Bal c/d	2,740	Bal b/d	2,480
		P & L a/c	260
	2,740	Bal b/d	2,740

(d) Profit and loss account extract for the year ended 31 Dec 20*3

	£	£
GP on manufacturing	110,400	110,140
Less Prov. for unrealised profit	260	
Gross profit on trading	239,160	239,160
Total gross profit		349,300

(e) Balance sheet extract as at 31 December 20*3

	£	£	£
Stocks: Raw materials			8,618
Work in progress			8,000
Finished goods	16,440		
Less Provision	2,740	13,700	
			30,318

CHAPTER TWENTY-FOUR

1. Girazeb Ltd

	£
Net profit	347,230
Corporation tax	117,450
Profit after tax	229,780
Ordinary dividends:	
Paid	34,500
Proposed	112,600
	147,100
Retained profit for year	82,680

3. Arbres Ltd
Balance sheet as at 30 April 20*3

	£	£
Fixed assets		
Machinery at cost	80,000	
Vehicle at cost	40,000	
		120,000
Current assets		
Stock	25,000	
Trade debtors	15,000	
Bank	1,000	
	41,000	
Creditors: amounts due in less than one year		
Trade creditors	11,000	
		30,000
		150,000
Authorised share capital		
500,000 Ordinary Shares of 50p each		250,000
Issued share capital		
300,000 Ordinary shares of 50p each		150,000

5. Duvase
Balance sheet as at 30 November 20*3

	£	£
Fixed assets at cost		120,000
Current assets	22,000	
Bank	335,000	
	357,000	
Creditors: amounts due in less than one year		
Trade creditors	8,000	
		349,000
		469,000
Share capital and reserves		
Ordinary shares of £1 each		300,000
Share premium account		120,000
Profit and loss account		49,000
		469,000

7. Ousby Ltd
Balance sheet as at 1 November 20*3

	£	£
Fixed assets at valuation		400,000
Current assets	40,000	
Bank	8,000	
	48,000	
Creditors: amounts falling due in less than one year	36,000	
		12,000
		412,000
Share capital and reserves		
Ordinary shares of 10p each		200,000
Revaluation reserve		150,000
Profit and loss account		62,000
		412,000

9. Douglas Ltd
Profit and loss appropriation account for the year ended 28 February 20*3

	£	£
Net profit		312,000
Corporation tax		82,000
Profit after tax		230,000
Transfer to general reserves		50,000
		180,000
Dividends: paid	40,000	
proposed	60,000	
	100,000	
Retained profit for year		80,000

Balance sheet as at 28 February 20*3

	£	£
Fixed assets at cost		300,000
Current assets	150,000	
Creditors: amounts due in less than one year		
Corporation tax	82,000	
Proposed dividend	60,000	
	142,000	
		8,000
		308,000
Share capital and reserves		
Ordinary shares of £1 each		178,000
General reserve		50,000
Profit and loss account		80,000
		308,000

11. Hox Ltd
Balance sheet as at 1 June 20*3

	£	£
Fixed assets at valuation		300,000
Current assets	23,000	
Bank	18,000	
	41,000	
Creditors: amounts falling due in less than one year	40,000	
		1,000
		301,000
Share capital and reserves		
Ordinary shares of 25p each		70,000
Revaluation reserve		120,000
General reserve		30,000
Profit and loss account		81,000
		301,000

13. Norest Ltd
Balance sheet as at 1 February 20*3

	£	£
Fixed assets at cost		60,000
Current asset	15,000	
Bank	31,000	
	46,000	
Creditors: amounts falling due in less than one year	9,000	
		37,000
		97,000
Share capital and reserves		
Ordinary shares of 25p each		55,000
Share premium account		25,000
Profit and loss account		17,000
		97,000

15. Smith-Patel Ltd
Balance sheet as at 1 April 20*3

	£	£
Fixed assets at valuation		750,000
Current assets	100,000	
Bank	320,000	
	420,000	
Creditors: amounts falling due in less than one year	70,000	
		350,000
		1,100,000
Share capital and reserves		
Ordinary shares of £1 each		600,000
Share premium account		100,000
Revaluation reserve		250,000
Profit and loss account		150,000
		1,100,000

17. Stephanie Hood Ltd
Profit and loss appropriation account for the year ended 30 April 20*3

	£	£
Net profit		267,432
Corporation tax		58,196
Profit after tax		209,236
Less Transfer to general reserve		50,000
		159,236
Preference dividends:		
Paid	3,000	
Proposed	3,000	
Ordinary dividends:		
Paid	12,000	
Proposed	26,000	44,000
Retained profit for year		115,236

Balance sheet as at 30 April 20*3

	£	£
Fixed assets at cost		950,000
Less Depreciation		230,000
		720,000

	£	£
Current assets		
Stock	143,461	
Trade debtors	21,380	
Bank balance	34,802	
	199,643	
Creditors: amounts falling due in less than one year		
Trade creditors	17,211	
Corporation tax	58,196	
Dividends	29,000	
	104,407	
		95,236
		815,236
Share capital and reserves		
Ordinary shares		400,000
6% preference shares		100,000
General reserve		120,000
Profit and loss account		195,236
		815,236

CHAPTER TWENTY-FIVE

1. Waystrell Ltd
Reconciliation of operating profit to net cash flow from operating activites

	£
Operating profit	167,549
Depreciation	26,000
Loss on sale of fixed asset	2,350
Increase in stock	(280)
Decrease in debtors	760
Increase in creditors	180
Net cash inflow from operation activities	196,559

3. Increase in creditors; decrease in stock.
5. All items except receipts from sale of stock.

CHAPTER TWENTY-SIX

1. Gross profit margin $\dfrac{GP}{Sales} \times 100 = \dfrac{57,000}{213,000} = 26.76\%$

   Net profit margin $\dfrac{GP}{Sales} \times 100 = \dfrac{18,000}{213,000} = 8.45\%$

   Overheads in relation to turnover $\dfrac{Expenses}{Sales} \times 100 = \dfrac{39,000}{213,000} = 18.31\%$

   Rate of stock turnover $\dfrac{COGS}{Ave.\ stock} = \dfrac{146,000}{20,000} = 7.3$ times

3. (a) $\dfrac{Sales}{Fixed\ assets} = \dfrac{350,000}{170,000} = 2.06$ times

   (b) $\dfrac{Current\ assets}{Current\ liabilities} = \dfrac{50,000}{10,000} = 5:1$

   (c) $\dfrac{Current\ assets - stock}{} = \dfrac{26,500}{10,000} = 2.65:1$

(d)
$$\frac{\text{Drs} \times 365}{} = \frac{13,500 \times 365}{} = 15 \text{ days}$$

(e)
$$\frac{\text{Crs} \times 365}{} = \frac{10,000 \times 365}{} = 23 \text{ days}$$

5. (a) 26.9% (b) 9.66% (c) 17.24% (d) 10.11% (e) 4.24 times (f) 1.58 times (g) 4:1
(h) 1.84:1 (i) 46 days (j) 42 days

7. (a) 58.97% (b) 36.75% (c) 22.22% (d) 32.58% (e) 6.4 times (f) 0.78 times
(g) 2.53:1 (h) 1.47:1 (i) 30 days (j) 56 days
Net profit margin has improved. It has increased by 7.27%. This means that Zena now earns £7.27 more net profit per £100 sales than she did last year. This could be because of an increased gross profit percentage or a reduction in the proportion of expenses paid in relation to sales revenue.
Net current asset ratio has deteriorated by 0.25%. Last year each £1 of current liabilities was covered by £2.78 current assets. Now each £1 is covered by £2.53. Although there has been a reduction, current liabilities are adequately covered.

9. (a) 40.26% (b) 13.59% (c) 26.67% (d) 22.84% (e) 6.97 times (f) 1.68 times
(g) 1.89:1 (h) 0.74:1 (i) 23 days (j) 61 days
Gross margin has deteriorated from 48.3% to 40.26%. This could be because of selling more cheaply while cost of sales remains static or has increased or prices of purchases have increased while selling price has remained the same or has been reduced. Net margin has fallen too, but only by 1.18%. The fall may be because of the fall in gross margin. However, the proportion of sales revenue taken up by expenses has fallen significantly and this is a good point. Debtors are taking one day more to settle their debts but the figure is still highly acceptable. Selena is paying her creditors 16 days slower than in the previous year. Care must be taken not to alienate suppliers.

CHAPTER TWENTY-SEVEN

1. Selling and distribution; direct production; direct production; factory overheads; administrative overheads; direct production; direct production; factory overheads; selling and distribution; administrative overheads.

3.

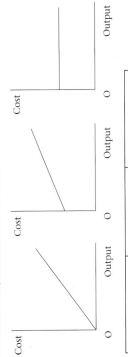

5.

2,040	230	2,100
2,210	230	2,270
2,380	230	2,440
	230	2,610

7. (a) £4,870 (b) 28.3 pence per mile (c) 4.1 pence per mile (d) 32.5 pence per mile

9. (a) Direct material cost | Variable | Direct labour costs | Variable | Production overhead
Semi-variable | Other overheads | Fixed
(b) £75,000

CHAPTER TWENTY-EIGHT

1. Akhtar Ltd
Marginal cost statement for the year ended 30 June 20*3

	£	£
Sales revenue		600,000
Direct materials	130,000	
Direct wages	120,000	
		250,000
Total contribution		350,000
Less Fixed costs		
Factory overheads	60,000	
Selling and distribution costs	70,000	
Administration overheads	80,000	
		210,000
Net profit		140,000

3. Guillaume
Marginal cost statement for the year ended 31 August 20*3

	£
Sales	630,000
Direct costs	301,000
Total contribution	329,000
Less Fixed costs	16,000
Net profit	313,000

5. 1,852 units Sales revenue £92,600
7. (a) 1,459 relurs Sales revenue £116,720
(b) 541 relurs
9. (a) 887 kuilps Sales revenue £42,576
(b) 2,513 kuilps
11. Sales of 1,830 tunfos would yield a profit of £35,000.
13. £622,084
15. Break-even 667 units. Margin of safety 333 units.
17. Break-even 6000 frootos. No margin of safety. At this level of production a loss of £5800 occurs.

CHAPTER TWENTY-NINE

1.

	May	June	July
Closing stock	36	43	52
Sales	300	360	432
	336	403	484
Opening stock	–	36	43
Purchases	336	367	441

3.

	March	April	May
Balance b/fwd	48,000	56,000	64,000
Sales	56,000	64,000	72,000
	104,000	120,000	136,000
Cash	48,000	56,000	64,000
Balance c/fwd	56,000	64,000	72,000

5.

	June	July	August
Balance b/fwd	14,250	19,000	23,750
Purchases	19,000	23,750	28,500
	33,250	42,750	52,250
Cash	14,250	19,000	23,750
Balance c/fwd	19,000	23,750	28,500

	October	November	December
Balance b/fwd	(350)	(4,550)	1,700
Receipts	61,900	60,250	64,950
	61,550	55,700	66,650
Payments	66,100	54,000	59,100
Balance c/fwd	(4,550)	1,700	7,550

7.

	August	September	October
Receipts – Cash sales	90,963	106,125	116,230
Payments – Creditors	29,650	35,050	38,400
Wages	19,100	28,000	21,500
Rent and rates	2,800	2,800	2,800
Other expenses	5,700	5,500	5,300
Machine purchase		84,000	
	57,250	155,350	68,000
Balance b/fwd	2,100	35,813	(13,412)
Receipts	90,963	106,125	116,230
	93,063	141,938	102,818
Payments	57,250	155,350	68,000
Balance c/fwd	35,813	(13,412)	34,818

9.

	February	March	April
Receipts – Debtors	21,000	28,000	30,000
Payments – Purchases	12,000	9,000	10,000
Expenses	20,000	22,000	18,000
Purchase of office machinery	24,000		
	56,000	31,000	28,000
Balance b/fwd	3,200	(31,800)	(34,800)
Receipts	21,000	28,000	30,000
	24,200	(3,800)	(4,800)
Payments	56,000	31,000	28,000
Balance c/fwd	(31,800)	(34,800)	(32,800)

11.

	April	May	June
Receipts – Cash sales	40,000	50,000	56,000
Payments – Cash purchases	1,500	1,250	1,750
Creditors	19,000	28,500	23,750
Expenses	16,000	24,000	20,000
	36,500	53,750	45,500
Balance b/fwd	(1,500)	2,000	(1,750)
Receipts	40,000	50,000	56,000
	38,500	52,000	54,250
Payments	36,500	53,750	45,500
Balance c/fwd	2,000	(1,750)	8,750

13.

	July	August	September
Receipts – Cash sales	3,000	3,250	3,200
Debtors	58,900	57,000	61,750
	61,900	60,250	64,950
Payments – Cash purchases	3,800	4,200	3,900
Creditors	27,000	28,800	34,200
Wages	13,000	12,500	12,500
Other expenses	8,300	8,500	8,500
Shop fittings	14,000		

15.

	October	November	December
Receipts – Cash sales	26,100	30,600	38,700
Debtors	2,400	2,900	3,400
	28,500	33,500	42,100
Payments – Purchases	1,500	2,400	3,500
Creditors	10,800	11,700	13,500
Wages	4,500	6,000	6,500
Rent	400	1,600	450
Other expenses	3,400		980
Balance b/fwd	670	8,570	20,370
Receipts	28,500	33,500	42,100
	29,170	42,070	62,470
Payments	20,600	21,700	24,930
Balance c/fwd	8,570	20,370	37,540

Tommy Chan
Budgeted trading and profit and loss account for the three months ending 31 December

	£	£
Sales		106,000
Less Cost of sales		
Stock	7,000	
Purchases	74,000	
	81,000	
Stock	8,000	
		73,000
Gross profit		33,000
Less Expenses		
Wages	17,000	
Rent	625	
Other expenses	5,980	
Depreciation of office equip't	1,350	
		24,955
Net profit		8,045

CHAPTER THIRTY

1. Benefits:
   • Increased skill levels
   • Staff development
   • Time to spend on other activities.
   Problems:
   • Stress – fear of technology
   • Redundancies

3. • No action
   • Meet anglers – discuss problem
   • Investigate claim – if true, investigate any pollution
   • Investigate other cooling methods.

Index

Page numbers in *italics* refer to diagrams.